5th EDITION

D0567797

Instructor's Resource Manual

The
St. Martin's
Guide to Writing

5th EDITION

Instructor's Resource Manual

The
St. Martin's
Guide to Writing

Rise B. Axelrod
California State University, San Bernardino

Charles R. Cooper
University of California, San Diego

Lenora Penna Smith
University of Houston

Alison M. Warriner
Sacred Heart University

ST. MARTIN'S PRESS
New York

Manufactured in the United States of America.
1 0 9 8 7
f e d c b a

For information, write:
St. Martin's Press
175 Fifth Avenue
New York, NY 10010

ISBN: 0-312-11640-3

CONTENTS

PART THREE: TEACHING RESOURCES

7 A SELECTED BIBLIOGRAPHY IN RHETORIC AND COMPOSITION 256

8 A SELECTION OF BACKGROUND READINGS 263

5th EDITION

Instructor's Resource Manual

The
St. Martin's
Guide to Writing

CHAPTER 1

Helpful Advice for New Instructors

This chapter is designed for instructors who have never taught a writing class before and who may not have taught any college-level class. The suggestions are intended to be helpful but not prescriptive and to anticipate problems and difficulties that can be averted. Instructors who have taught in other fields but who are teaching writing for the first time may also find this material useful. We have decided on a temporal organization, since new instructors have told us that a timeline of tasks helps them get organized. This chapter is designed to be used for quick reference as well, with many headings that we hope will make information easy to find.

SEVERAL MONTHS BEFORE THE CLASS

Many new instructors are not lucky enough to know five or six months in advance that they will even be teaching, much less which sections and what schedule. Following are some things you should do as soon as you can.

Reading the Writing Program Literature

As soon as you know that you will be teaching a writing course, it's a good idea to read the course description in the school catalogue and to read any literature published by the department for their instructors. Many schools have particular philosophies that guide their writing programs, and many have particular requirements and policies that all instructors must follow. You might learn which texts (in addition to *The St. Martin's Guide*) are required or recommended, how many pages students must write, how many revisions are suggested, whether or not students have a writing center or workshop attached to the course, the department plagiarism policy, etc. You will need to know how many weeks the term runs (make a copy of the year's calendar to carry with you) and whether or not the *Guide* is closely or loosely followed (see Chapter 5 in this manual for suggested course plans for a quarter, a semester, and a year, and for particular focuses). If there is a faculty handbook, read that too. As you're reading the literature, write down any questions you have.

Meeting with the Program Director

Armed with your questions, meet with the director of the writing program or the department chair. Tidbits of information that escape written literature are often passed on in these short interviews. At this time you can request book order and schedule forms, and you can let the director or chair know what kind of schedule fits your needs best (although you should realize that, as a newcomer, you very well may be assigned an 8:00 A.M. class five days a week).

Either during this meeting or from other sources, try to find out as much as you can about the makeup of the student body: average SAT or ACT scores, ethnic breakdown, gender breakdown, commuters, residents, part-timers, full-timers, etc. The more you know in advance about your students, the more appropriately you can plan course material and strategies. Get copies of sample essays or placement exams to get a sense of the writing competence expected of students. You also need to know if there are any prerequisites for your course. If you can, obtain a copy of the evaluation form used in your department. It's useful to see in advance the qualities that are valued by your institution.

Ordering Books

Usually books for the course need to be ordered several months in advance. Your department will find a way to get the book forms to you, but you should check. To fill the form out properly, you need to know the author, title, publisher, edition, and ISBN number (on the inside of the front cover or front page, down below the publication date). The book form will also have a box you should check if you need a desk copy for yourself (free of charge). Sometimes your department will order a batch of instructors' copies.

In addition to *The St. Martin's Guide to Writing,* you may need to order supplementary books. Some institutions require trade books such as an autobiography or a book on current social issues—trade books in the same genres as some of the *Guide's* assignments. You may have to choose among several recommended books. If your choice is not limited, call up several publishers and order review copies for yourself (the department secretary probably has the numbers). Review these books carefully because not only do you have to live with your decision over the course of the term, but you also have to read many students' papers that result from the book you choose. Think carefully how these books would fit the writing assignments you've decided to use from *The St. Martin's Guide to Writing.*

You may want to consider the following books that were developed to complement the *Guide*:

- *Free Falling and Other Student Essays* (third edition)
- *Who Are We? Readings in Identity and Community and Work and Career*

Scheduling Classes

Department chairs and program directors usually arrange schedules a term in advance. You may be asked to indicate the most convenient time slot for your course. As a new instructor, you may not get your first choice, but there's no harm in trying. Be mindful of your other commitments—do you have children to get to school in the morning or pick up in the afternoon? If you are a graduate student instructor, are you taking a class? Most instructors prefer to teach between 10:00 and 2:00, two days a week; you might bear in mind your prospects for these prime hours when you put in your request.

A COUPLE OF MONTHS BEFORE THE CLASS

Reading the Textbooks

Read the books for your course with an eye toward how you can use them. Remember that textbooks are not made to be read straight through. They should be viewed as tools for teaching. Think about how you would choose the Part I chapters—all of which have the same basic structure. How would you integrate strategies from Part III chapters (noted in marginal cross-references)? This *Instructor's Resource Manual* is full of advice on these and other issues.

Many books can be taught in a variety of ways and arrangements (see the Sample Course Plans in this manual), and it helps considerably to have an overview before you start planning your course. If you have the time—and in the long run it is worth the time—do some of the assignments yourself so you know exactly what your students will be doing. Consider, for example, how you could introduce the general, all-purpose Invention Strategies in Part III of the *Guide* bit-by-bit as your students work through the more specific invention activities in the Guide to Writing of each Part I chapter.

A FEW WEEKS BEFORE THE CLASS

Finding Out Department Policies

- *Your Office and Office Hours.* You may share an office or have one to yourself. Find out where it is and whether you have a phone (with access to the outside world or just to internal networks). Get the key, if there is one. Also, ask what other amenities you can count on—such as office equipment and supplies.

    Find out department policy on office hours, and plan your week with them in mind. Some instructors like office hours just before and/or just after class, because students find those hours convenient. Other instructors, though, find office hours before class intrusive, either because they need the time to prepare or because they need quiet time before a class, and office hours after class bothersome, because students follow them back to the office with complaints. However you work it out, it's a good idea to schedule your office hours on at least one day different from your classes so that students who have blocks of classes around yours can find time to see you. It hardly needs to be said—but we'll say it anyway—that office hours are just as inviolable as classroom hours. They may not *feel* as important, but to a student who has taken time off from work and driven forty-five minutes to meet you during your office hour, they are. Obviously, if you're sharing the office with another instructor, you will need to coordinate your schedules.
- *Faculty Identification Card.* Most institutions require a picture for their ID card. Since it is usually needed to get a parking permit, you should find out where and when to get this card. You'll probably need your faculty ID to use the library.

- *Plagiarism Policy.* Find out your department's plagiarism policy. If the department does not provide you with clear-cut consequences or penalties, you should think through your own views on plagiarism before you put your syllabus together. (See the section on plagiarism at the end of this chapter in the manual.)

- *Grievance Procedures.* Students need to know what recourse they have if they are unhappy with a grade, with some perceived ill treatment, or if they have a serious complaint of any kind. If you familiarize yourself with your department's grievance procedure ahead of time, and if you have it at hand when you might need it, you will be able to deter unpleasant scenes. (See the discussion below on Responding to Complaints about Grades.)

- *Department Evaluation Policies.* Your department may have specific evaluation policies, such as a portfolio system of grading, minimum requirements for passing, diagnostic exams, and/or exit exams. Diagnostic exams may be given before school starts or on the first day of class (which could considerably change your plans for the first day!). Exit exams may be on the last day of class or sometime during the final exam period. There may be a set of written standards for evaluation that you will want to review before assembling your syllabus. A portfolio system might require you to commit time at the end of the term. For guidelines on evaluation (within the bounds of your institutional requirements) also see the section of the manual on Evaluation Practices.

- *Parking.* For some institutions, parking is no problem and you can simply park on campus wherever you find a space. For others, there's a monthly fee. If you can, get your parking sticker (and pay your fee) well in advance of orientation, since once students arrive on campus the parking office will be jammed.

- *Library Resources and Tours.* If you are new to the campus, take a walk around and explore the library. See how it's laid out, where the resources are for composition books and for research papers; introduce yourself to the library staff; and generally get a feel for what's offered. Use the computer system. Pick up a library card for yourself. Inquire about a tour for your students during their class time, and find out how far in advance you need to schedule it.

- *The Writing Center.* If your campus has a writing center separate from where you work, drop in there too, to see their facilities (some have computers and most have tutors) and to meet the staff. Find out how to refer students and monitor their attendance.

- *Facilities for the Disabled.* All educational institutions are legally required to follow certain guidelines in dealing with disabled students. Some campuses are fully equipped with facilities for physically disabled students. Some have instructors trained in diagnosing and helping students with learning disabilities. Find out what is required of you as an instructor, what accommodations you must provide to make it possible for students to complete the work in your course. Write down the names and numbers of people to contact. See p. 20 for suggestions on how to help disabled students in your class.

- *Computers.* During your campus tours, include the computer labs. Are there trained personnel to help students? Write down the lab hours and phone number, and pick up any materials that might help. Is e-mail available for you? Note the computer locations on campus (so that when a student complains that the printer in the main computer lab is broken, you can send him or her to another lab to print out the paper).

- *Media Support.* Some institutions have media support services, where you can arrange for an overhead, a VCR, a projector, a tapedeck, etc. Many instructors use a VCR to show a film for students to evaluate (Chapter 8 in the *Guide*).
- *Duplicating.* Institutions vary greatly in their attitudes toward duplication. You may have access to a copy machine at any time. You may have a code you need to obtain; usually the secretary will have it. You may have to go to a duplicating service somewhere else on campus. You may even be responsible for your own copying. If you are planning to assemble a course reader of your own to complement the *Guide,* allow at least a month for the duplicating service to obtain copyright permission. Every essay you include should have the full copyright information (author, title, where and when originally published and by whom); otherwise, the delay might be so long you won't be able to use your reader. Call ahead to find out other restrictions.
- *Sick or Absent Days.* If you're sick, you can cancel your class. Most instructors don't want to, no matter how awful they feel, but if you should be in bed or if you are contagious enough to endanger the students' health, you should cancel. (The same goes for office hours.) Usually if you cancel only one class you can simply call the secretary or the program director and arrange for someone to post the cancellation on the blackboard.

    If you must miss more than one class in a row, you might want to arrange for someone else to substitute teach. If you know you will miss a class because of a conference or other professional obligation, you can make up the lost time by holding student conferences or by arranging for a library tour, computer lab, or peer review on the day you are gone.

Constructing a Syllabus

The course syllabus is a contract between the student and the instructor and is viewed as such in a court of law, so it must be clear and inclusive. Your institution may have specific items that need to be in every syllabus; if you have not received any guidelines, you should ask. The suggestions we offer here will make for a long, detailed syllabus that will cover most eventualities. If you put all this information on a computer, you can usually reuse it with minor modifications. Before you assemble your syllabus, check the previous section on department policies to make sure you have all the information you need.

    Include in your syllabus:

Title of course: the number and the catalogue name.

Course credit hours and prerequisites: A first-semester course may not have prerequisites, although you might want to mention that the student will need to have taken the placement exam or passed whatever basic course might have preceded this one. A second-semester course usually requires that the student has either passed the first-semester course or has placed out of it.

Times, days, and location of class

Your name: If you want a particular title, include it, such as Dr., Ms., etc., so students will know.

Your office location: room number and building.

Your phone number: of your office. You will probably know instantly whether or not you want to give out your home phone number; it's a gut feeling. Arguments in favor: Students can reach you and can clear up problems without having to see you; if a student is having a problem with a paper, sometimes a quick conference on the phone can yield much better work and save you time in the long run. Arguments opposed: Students will call you at home, and you might be exhausted, or asleep, or in the midst of a very intense conversation. You can, of course, limit the times when students can call you, and you can use an answering machine to screen your calls, but you have every right not to give out your home phone number unless you want to. If you have an E-mail address, you may want to include it. Electronic communication may work as a substitute for a phone call.

Your office hours: You might want to add "and by appointment" to the hours you list. Most institutions require regularly scheduled office hours in addition to those made by appointment.

Required texts: List all the texts students *must* buy, and it helps if you list them according to MLA style so you have at least one ready example for them if they need it:

Axelrod, Rise B., and Charles R. Cooper. *The St. Martin's Guide to Writing.* 4th ed. New York: St. Martin's, 1994.

Free Falling and Other Student Essays. 3rd ed. Ed. Paul Sladky. New York: St. Martin's, 1994.

Additional required material: such as floppy disks, a three-ring notebook for journals, a portfolio, the duplicating fee, etc.

Recommended texts: such as a college dictionary or a handbook.

Course description: Some institutions provide you with the description they want in your syllabus or you can write your own. Convey the goals of the course and how they will be achieved. If you're at a complete loss, you could place the catalogue description here, although this is a fine place to assert your own style.

Required papers and revision policy: Let students know how many papers they will need to write to reach the requirement. Explain your revision policy: If a student wants to revise a paper that has been graded, how will you evaluate that paper—count the grade on the revision only? average the two papers together? And when must all revised papers be turned in?

Late paper policy: Usually it is up to you to decide whether or not to accept late papers. You could allow one paper to be one week late, while requiring all the other papers to be promptly submitted. Such a policy requires careful record-keeping. Many instructors find it easier simply to allow no late papers, and then if a student does have a serious problem, to judge the case as it occurs. If your department requires submission of a minimum number of papers, you may have to accept them late. You might consider imposing a penalty for late papers.

Journals: Refer to Assigning Journals in the Teaching Practices section of this manual for advice on handling journals. Be sure your syllabus is clear about the requirements for journals (how many entries per week, what kind of entries, etc.) because otherwise students might not take them as seriously as the more "formal" papers. Departments using a portfolio system may have particular guidelines for journals.

Oral reports or other responsibilities: If you require an oral report or a group presentation, include it here.

Conferences: If you require individual or small-group conferences with students, let them know that they are required and when they will be held. (See Holding Conferences in the Teaching Practices section of this manual for advice.)

Class attendance and participation: Some institutions have guidelines or strict policies on how many classes students are allowed to miss without penalty and what the penalties are when students miss a certain number. If your institution doesn't have a policy, decide on what you think is fair. Indicate whether you require a note from the doctor or school clinic, especially for an extended absence. Here also include what you expect for class participation and whether you give credit for it. Remember that students from other cultures may find it more difficult to speak up in class, so your policy should allow for these differences.

Academic honesty: Be as clear as you can in your definition of plagiarism, in your expectations of students, and in your penalties. See the section in this manual on how to prevent and handle plagiarism. Some institutions have policies on plagiarism, and of course you will want to follow them.

Grades: Let students know what weight each component of the course bears: each paper, journals, class participation and attendance, revisions, presentations. If you are on a portfolio system, let them know how it works. Grades create enormous anxiety in students, and it helps them considerably if they know ahead of time exactly how they are being evaluated.

Resources: Include here the information about the library, the computer lab, learning disabled facilities, the writing center or tutoring facilities if you have them, their hours, their phone numbers, their locations, etc.

Schedule: As part of your syllabus, make a calendar with due dates for papers and daily assignments clearly marked.

Composing a Student Questionnaire

A student questionnaire gives you information that can be useful throughout the term, and that can be used as a starting point for a personal, get-to-know-you conference at the beginning of the term (see Holding Office Hours and Conferencing). You can provide them with 4 × 6 cards and tell them what information you'd like, or you can ask questions on a regular sheet of paper, allowing space for their responses. Examples of information you might need:

- name and phone number (home and work)
- high school attended
- writing courses taken
- what kind of reading and writing they prefer
- what they think are their writing strengths and weaknesses
- their academic interests
- their "outside" interests—hobbies, athletics, etc.
- whether they work and, if they do, where and their hours

You might also ask if they have any particular expectations of the course or if they have any questions for you. If you duplicate the questionnaire when you duplicate your syllabus, you will have both ready for the first class.

Making a Phone List

List numbers that you and/or your students will need often, such as those you collected for the library, writing center, computer center, etc. At the top of the list, put the number for security and for emergencies. You should memorize the security phone number. You can either append this list to your syllabus or duplicate it separately.

A FEW DAYS BEFORE CLASS

- Check your mailbox regularly. There is usually a flood of correspondence, much of it directive, at this time; you'll get information about student services, department or program meetings, your responsibilities on the first day of class, etc. Your class list(s) should appear on or before the first day.
- Submit your syllabus, assignment sheet, and questionnaire for duplication (or duplicate them yourself, depending on how it works). Make a few extra copies of everything for students who inevitably lose them or for latecomers.
- Post your name and office hours on your door and give them to the department secretary; even before classes, some students will need to see you.
- Check the bookstore to see whether the books for your course have arrived and where they're located. Don't wait until the first day of class for this or for any other bookstore errands, since the bookstore is usually very crowded the first week of classes.
- Check your classrooms to see that they're all set up: enough chairs, chalk, access for the disabled, etc. If there are not enough chairs (you should know the number you need from your preliminary class list), call the plant or maintenance department. For chalk and other supplies, check with the department secretary. If you don't know whether or not the room is accessible, try to get to your room without taking any stairs at all. See if there's a ramp from outside, if there's an elevator inside, and trace the entire route yourself. If there is even one single step, someone in a wheelchair could not get in.

THE FIRST DAY OF CLASS

Following School Policies

If your department has a diagnostic exam or any other exercises planned for your first class, know where to pick up the necessary exams or forms and how much time you need to allow. If you are responsible for duplication, make enough copies for two or three extra students. Who reads them—you? By when? If you know that many more people will show up at the first class than can possibly be admitted, make lots of extra copies, not only of any exams, but of syllabi as well.

Controlling Jitters

Everybody has them, even instructors who have been teaching for years. The best way to control them (there's no way to prevent them!) is to be completely prepared. Know where your parking lot is (and how likely it is you'll be able to find a spot), know where your classroom is, locate the restroom in advance so you have a private place to calm down before you walk in (or to collect yourself after a dash through the rain— sometimes weather can change your whole notion of the first day)—do whatever it takes to help you feel you are in control. Assemble everything you will need to distribute the night before: your duplicated syllabi and accompanying assignment sheets, questionnaires, calendar, etc. (you'll sleep better). Most manuals for teachers recommend that you arrive at your classroom a few minutes early; this sets a good example for your students and allows them time to approach you with any problems they might have. Remember, though, that your classroom may be occupied by the class before yours, so there's no sense in arriving much earlier.

Arranging the Classroom

Many instructors prefer students to sit in a circle. Writing classes are usually small enough. Circles are not possible in rooms where the chairs are bolted to the floor, of course, or in a computer lab. They are, though, conducive to large-group discussion and to a more engaged class. If you do want the class in a circle, you will probably have to be insistent; once students settle in, they don't want to move. Make them move the chairs. You'll probably have to insist on this for a few classes, but it will be worth it, and eventually they'll automatically rearrange the room as soon as they walk in—and put chairs back before leaving.

Write course information on the board. Include the number, name, and times of your course, and your own name. (Some students may leave when they realize they're in the wrong class.)

Taking Attendance

Near the beginning of class you should take attendance from the sheet sent by the registrar. Some students who are not on your registration sheet will think they are in your class, and, conversely, some on your sheet will not be there. Your institution will let you know what to do about these students. If you are in doubt, allow students to stay and see if you can untangle things after class. A call to the registrar or the program director can usually solve these problems.

Reviewing the Syllabus

Most instructors hand out a syllabus during the first class, and many go over it right away. If your syllabus is as lengthy as the one proposed above, reviewing might take the whole class time, especially if the class is less than an hour. An alternative to spending the whole class on the syllabus (which can be pretty boring) is to tell students to take it home, read it through, and write down any questions they have. The one problem with this is that some of them might not read it, and this is one document you really want them to read. Some instructors highlight the disciplinary aspects—penalties for absences, lateness, plagiarism, incomplete work, etc.—and merely list the other categories so students know they're there. Be aware, though, that students with hidden learning disabilities may need to *hear* the syllabus read as well as to read it themselves.

Getting to Know Your Students

If you've decided not to go over the syllabus in detail, you might want to try a few games in class so students can get to know each other (and you—include yourself in these games). If you do go over the syllabus, save these games for the second class.

- *Circle Name-Game.* Put the students in a circle if they're not already in one. Starting with the student to your left, ask her to give her name and where she's from. The next student then says the first student's name and his own; then the third student says the names of the first two and her own, and it goes like this all the way around the room. You are the last one and must say them all. No one is allowed to write the names down. Sometimes instructors alter this game to include a mnemonic to help: Hip-hop Harry, Preppy Pauline, etc. (Let them make up the mnemonics.)
- *Introduction Game.* Have students break up into pairs and interview each other. They have ten or fifteen minutes to exchange information (this leads to lively conversations) and then they must introduce each other to the class. Sometimes students go up front to do this, or they can stand by their chairs. This activity will probably spill over to the second class.
- *Find-the-Person-Who Game.* Have students write down on a piece of paper five things about themselves, one of which only they could know. For instance, one young man wrote: tall, athletic, likes computers, wants to be a doctor, cat named Lestat; a young woman wrote: soccer player, vegetarian, plays the piano, member of Greenpeace, has a wetsuit. The first four categories could refer to any number of students, male or female, but no one else in the room has a cat named Lestat or a wetsuit. Once all students have written down five things, they hand in their papers to you, you shuffle and redistribute them, and their task is to walk around the room searching for the person who belongs to the sheet. This is a very active game, noisy and funny, and students like it (but the noise could bother the class next door). When you find your person, you interview him or her. Someone is also looking for you, and when they find you, they interview you. It's chaotic and social. After the interviewing is completed, everyone introduces his or her "found" person to the class. This activity could also spill over to the second class.
- *Exercise 1.3:* Ask students to write their similes or metaphors on the back of the information card or questionnaire. In small groups, they introduce themselves, share what they've written, and discuss what the similes and metaphors suggest about their individual writing experiences. Next, they discuss what the similes and metaphors suggest about them as a group and present their findings to the class. Some groups may decide to read aloud what each student has written; others may compose a new simile or metaphor that represents the group as a whole. The reporter for each group is also responsible for introducing the members of that group to the class and you.

Getting Students Working

Give them homework. It provides you with material for the second class and sets the right tone. Students have been told over and over that college is hard work, so you might as well take advantage of their expectations. You could also give them a writing assignment if you don't play any games and don't have a diagnostic exam. Or, you could allow at least fifteen minutes at the end of the class for students to fill out questionnaires. Keep them until the end of the class period. You are setting a standard. The first day is crucial for setting the tone for the term; you don't want to give students the impression that you have time to spare.

THE SECOND DAY OF CLASS

Because you've made it through the first class, you may think you're immune to the jitters, but the second class can surprise you. After all, now the syllabus is done and the games are over and the work has to start. The same attitude, though, will calm you down: Be prepared, and do everything you can to feel as though you're in control.

What you do on the second day depends a great deal on what you did the first day. If students took the syllabus home, you should give them time for questions. Even if you went over the syllabus in class, you still should ask if they have any questions. Keep in mind that you may see students on the second day of class who are attending for the first time.

Remember to take roll. Make a habit of it; some schools require a record of attendance because students' scholarships and financial aid depend on regular attendance. An alternative way of taking roll and helping students remember each others' names is to hand out blank 5 × 8 index cards. Have students fold them in half so the cards stand up and print their first names with a marker so they're legible from across the room. At the beginning of class, you pass the cards out, and at the end students return them to you. During the class, students stand them on the desks or suspend them from the edge of the desks.

You might try more get-to-know-you tactics. If you played the circle name-game in the first class, you could run through it again to cement the names. If you played either of the other two games, you probably didn't finish, so you can finish now.

Getting Students Writing

To set the tone for a writing course, it's a good idea for students to write as soon as possible. You could assign any of the early writing assignments in the Introduction to the *Guide* (see Exercises 1.1–1.5), or you could plunge right into the chapter you've assigned first. Some instructors feel guilty about having students write in class because they feel they should be instructing. But there are many advantages to writing in class: Writing is then elevated in students' eyes because the instructor takes class time for it; class discussions are stronger and more lively because students have something they believe in and can refer to; the invention strategies lead to new ideas that get the students excited. Furthermore, if you have any plagiarism problems later, you have several in-class writing samples for comparison. If you're worried that you're not using class time to teach, try writing yourself while they're writing; this will convince you better than anything we can say that learning is going on. The *Guide* offers a wide variety of in-class possibilities for writing, including the Analyzing Writing Strategies and Connecting to Culture and Experience sections following each reading in Part I. You also can turn to Chapter 2 for myriad suggestions for writing in class. You can let students include their in-class writing in their journals, if you assign journals (see the *Guide* and this manual on journals). After they finish writing, ask a few students to read what they've written. Usually a few will quickly speak up, but if they don't, let the silence stretch for a minute or two. If someone looks sort of eager, call on him or her. If they seem really uncomfortable, you might want to try small groups.

Trying Small Groups

Probably finishing up the games and in-class writing will take up most of the second class, but if it doesn't, or if you're having trouble getting volunteers to read their writing, try small groups. First-year students are especially fond of small groups because they feel far less threatened and they get to know their classmates. For starters, you can just arbitrarily go around the classroom, clumping together the four students closest to each other. Have them read to each other. You can circulate and listen. If there's time, they can choose one from the group to read to the class. For more on small-group work, as well as on collaborative work, see pp. 43–45.

Remembering Homework

If you plan to collect their homework, make sure you do so; it's easy to forget. If you're going to use their homework in class, try to connect what they did to an in-class writing assignment. For instance, if you assigned Exercise 1.4 from the *Guide* for homework, you could link it with Exercise 1.5 for in-class writing.

Remind them of their next homework assignment. Students straight out of high school sometimes find it astonishing that they have homework every night in college. There's no harm in reminding them.

ONCE CLASSES ARE UNDER WAY

Keeping a Teaching Journal

A teaching journal accomplishes a number of purposes: You create a record of what works and doesn't work in the classroom and in your preparation; you document your progress as a teacher; you remind yourself of what you did in the last class. Some instructors buy a calendar with pages large enough to accommodate their daily comments on classes; others use a looseleaf notebook for flexibility. Teaching journals can be particularly useful if you plan to teach the same or a similar course again, and/or if you hope to publish or report on pedagogical techniques or on how your department's philosophy works in practice. New instructors who keep a teaching journal report that it is heartening to read it throughout the term and see progress. Some of our instructors write after every class and then refer back to previous entries before planning the next class.

Budgeting Time

If you have assembled a detailed assignment sheet, you have already taken one step toward budgeting your time. Nevertheless, once the duties of the term kick in, you may find yourself panicking: How can you possibly respond to forty papers, read the assignment, prepare for class, and sleep before Monday? Almost anyone who has taught writing knows that weekends are for work, but you can and should comfort yourself with the knowledge that most terms are no longer than sixteen weeks, and several are shorter. Go ahead, count the weeks that are left; it might help. Try to prioritize; which task is making you most uncomfortable? If you do what is hurting you the most, you'll feel better.

Often, responding to student papers is the most difficult task for new instructors because it takes longer than you ever dreamed and it's *hard*. The more papers you do, the more are behind you, and the better you get. Papers near the end of a batch almost always go more quickly than those first few because you've learned what to look for. Realize your limits on papers, since your mood will affect how you respond, and try not to do more than you can respond to fairly and with good intentions. It's tempting to try to do them all at once and get them behind you, but usually it's better to space them out and fill the interstices with class preparation or other work (or play).

If you've reached a point where you can hardly breathe because you feel so pressured, it's time to rearrange the schedule. You may have assigned too many papers, or you may be working too hard on homework that needs only a comment or two, or you may not even know why you feel so buried. You are the instructor, though, and it's your course. You can change it. Your students will get a fairer shake from you if you respond well to one essay than if you try to squeeze in two. As teachers, most of us overextend ourselves, and only we can help.

Keeping Your Sanity and Your Temper

Writing in your teaching journal can help you keep your sanity; most writing instructors know the purging value of writing problems down. If you are having trouble keeping your temper outside the classroom (inside the classroom is discussed below), you don't want to wait until you explode in front of your director or chair. If you are aggrieved because of departmental policies, find out the grievance procedure and follow it; that's what it's there for. If you are overextended and you can't change it by changing your course, discuss options and alternatives with a trusted colleague. If you don't have a trusted colleague, try a friend; people outside academia can sometimes see us more clearly than we can see ourselves. There are, of course, other methods of dealing with stress, but they are outside the scope of this manual.

Evaluating Your Teaching

Your teaching journal will provide you with a forum for self-evaluation. It helps to review past entries periodically, since they can make you see how far you've come or perhaps see patterns emerging. New instructors are usually evaluated in the second half of their first term of teaching, although some departments wait until the second term. Back before the term started, you may have obtained colleague evaluation sheets, which you might want to review beforehand.

Some institutions give you notice that you will be observed, asking you when a good time would be and telling you who will observe you. Other institutions evaluate without warning, and you must just do the best you can. If you do know ahead of time, it's courteous to make copies of the assignment for that day, and, if you can, of the reading as well, and give them to your colleague. Ask your colleague whether or not he or she wants to be introduced to the class. Some institutions prefer that you not tell students ahead of time that you are being observed.

If you are given a choice of days, choose one that will show what you normally do and what you do well (this is no time to be modest). It's best not to choose a day when students are giving oral reports or are engaged in workshop activities, since these activities don't show the class in action (or you either, for that matter). As with first-day jitters, colleague evaluations can be nerve-wracking, but they are also extremely useful.

Ask if you can have a follow-up conference with your colleague for feedback. It's also useful to ask him or her to look for particular strategies or techniques that you want to improve or to showcase. If you feel as though you've had a successful class, ask if your colleague will write up an evaluation to be placed in your dossier.

Observing Other Classes

Observing might be built into your writing program, but if it isn't, it's a wonderful teaching tool. Some instructors will not welcome observers, but most will, and all you have to do is ask. If there are instructors in your department who have a reputation for good teaching, start with them. It's true that it takes time out of your busy schedule, but observing saves time in the long run because you often learn more efficient ways of teaching from experienced hands. In some institutions you can audit your colleagues' classes for the whole term.

Holding Office Hours and Conferencing

Although some students will quickly seek you out, most need to be encouraged to come to office hours. Remind them periodically of when you hold your hours, and use minor complaints in class to urge students to come to your office.

Requiring an early short individual conference will help considerably, simply because students have to find your office and they get to see you as a person. You can schedule them for ten-minute conferences by passing around a sign-up sheet for slots you've set aside in the first two or three weeks of school. Remember when mapping the schedule to allow time for yourself—at least ten minutes each hour—to take a break, have a drink, make a phone call, etc.

In these short conferences, you can work off the questionnaire you handed out the first day of class, asking students about their reading and writing activities and jobs. Some students will be taciturn during the conferences, but most respond well and will turn up in your office later on. If you have a hundred students and can't possibly give them all ten-minute conferences, schedule small-group conferences instead, where four or five students come in at the same time for about fifteen minutes. They still get to find your office, and although they may not get to know you as well, they associate your office with more individual attention.

At certain times in the term—before a paper or something else substantial is due—students suddenly discover your office hours and you can end up with a line of them waiting impatiently outside your door. If you can tell at a glance that you'll never be able to see all of them, see if you can make other arrangements. Try a triage system first. Ask who has just a quick question, who can't come at any other time, who has been waiting the longest. Ask if any have problems in common—you might be able to form a small group then and there. Let them know that you have other office hours (and you might mention that you've spent many a lonely hour in your office with no one coming in) and that you also make appointments. If they get the impression that you're doing the best you can under trying circumstances, they will usually work it out among themselves fairly well.

There is ample information on conferencing in Chapter 2 of this manual, Teaching Practices. New instructors should be aware that sometimes students simply don't show up. Some of them are apprehensive, some are unprepared, and some don't care. It's important to follow through on these students, giving them another chance if you're comfortable doing that, or threatening them with a lowered grade if that's more your style. It's infuriating to set aside a half-hour for a student who's a no-show, so bring some work with you to diffuse your anger.

Handling Problems

Emotions.   When you are in your office, whether during regular hours or at other times, students sometimes come to you with problems. Most of these problems are fairly minor: They will weep over a grade, or they'll be furious with another teacher, or they will have relationship struggles that they'll tell you about. These are emotional difficulties that most instructors deal with as they would with any human being, by offering sympathy, respect, judicious (restrained) advice. Know the number of your counseling service, and know your emergency numbers just in case an emotional situation escalates into a medical one.

Manipulators.   More serious (for you) are students who are manipulative. They usually are driven by desperation; nevertheless, they are trying to get away with something. Some will come to you with a rough draft and ask you to go over it with them, but what they really mean is that they want to make a polished copy out of it. You can direct them to the writing center, if you have one. Occasionally, just telling them that what they're asking for is unfair will be enough.

Some students will come to dispute a grade. There are various methods to deal with this problem. One of our instructors tells students they must wait twenty-four hours before coming to her with a returned paper, and then they can come only if they have written a response to her comments. At the very least, you should require that students have reread their essays and have read your comments before meeting with you. Occasionally, a student will have a grievance about a grade that has merit. If you think this might be the case, take the paper home to look it over in private. It may be that you misrecorded the grade, or it may be that you failed to see the beauty of this paper because you were in less than an objective state. These cases are rare, but they do occur. You can change your mind.

Harassment.   Both men and women are subject to harassment. We assume you understand that you should not harass your students. Most institutions have strict policies on sexual behavior between faculty and students, and if you don't know what they are, you should find out. This applies particularly to graduate student instructors, who may feel exempt but are not. What we are concerned with here is the reverse, harassing the instructor. Instructors usually leave their doors open during office hours; harassment is less likely to occur in public space. If at any time a student does anything that makes you uncomfortable, such as touching you or talking to you suggestively, it's your responsibility to let this student know that his or her behavior is inappropriate. Students get crushes on faculty, and it's easy for them to lose sight of the proprieties. The only one with enough authority to break through their miasma is you. You can try to be tender of their egos, but you also must be clear and emphatic. Sometimes it helps to rehearse what you will say in an anticipated situation ahead of time. It may also help to have another instructor present whenever you meet with this student in your office, and be sure to keep the door open at all times.

Students Who Sleep in Class, despite Your Riveting Presentation.   Before you embarrass a student in class, try talking to her in private. It may be that she has physical problems or has other difficulties that call for understanding instead of impatience. Explain to her that it's distracting for *you* to have to look at a sleeping student, not to mention the bad example it sets for the class. Remind her that it's not easy to form a good opinion of a student's engagement with the class if she's sleeping through it. If the student continues to sleep, you can try a small amount of embarrassment to see if that will help; you might walk over and tap her shoulder, or call out to her, or otherwise call attention to her. If students know you will not just ignore them, they might make more of an effort. Designing every class so that students have something active to do—in pairs, small groups, or individually—might also help. If everything else fails, you can tell the student that if she's sleeping in class you will count it as an absence and then proceed with your class guidelines on absences.

Students Who Are Talking among Themselves.   Again, taking students aside privately is the first step; ask them what they were talking about first, to see if you were right that they were not paying attention (sometimes you will be alerted to a problem you didn't know existed, such as that they don't understand something that was said). If they are just chatting about something unrelated to the class, tell them the same things you tell the sleeping student—that they distract the class, they distract you, and it's hard not to form a bad opinion of their performance. If they persist, separate them. Yes, it feels like high school, but it works. If they behave like high schoolers, they will get treated like high schoolers.

Aggressive or Belligerent Students.   These can be extremely difficult for a new instructor to handle, since they aren't willing to follow the rules and they usually make you either intimidated or angry (or both). We've found that young female instructors are more vulnerable to bullying than older instructors, particularly males. It may have nothing to do with how you're handling the class, though being impersonal and emphatic might help. What aggressive students are doing requires instant response. If a student has lost his temper with another student, you need to be an arbiter, even if you'd rather just leave. Instead of characterizing the student, describe his behavior: "Insulting and swearing at another student is inappropriate behavior in the college classroom, and you either have to stop now or leave the room." Unless you feel the upsetting issue is worth discussion right then, it's best to move on to another topic and to talk to the student after class. Remember that students who lose their tempers are not always simply being rude. They may have complicated reasons for some of their reactions that you are unable to understand; they may even need counseling. If a student is really out of control or threatening, you should ask him to step outside the classroom with you and see if he can get hold of himself. But remember that if a student refuses to leave the room, there is little you can do to make him or her do so, so be careful not to back yourself into a corner. You might need to call security or send another student to make the call. For persistent problem students, speak to the composition program director or department chair. You might also consult the counseling center or ombudsperson.

Racism, Sexism, Homophobia, etc.   These are all thorny and difficult to handle. How you handle them depends in part on your own views. The issue, of course, is freedom of speech versus hate speech, and some campuses have laws that you would be expected to follow. Some instructors announce early in the term—the first or second class—that remarks that are racist, sexist, or homophobic will not be tolerated in their classrooms. If you are going to make such an announcement, you should be prepared for resistance from some students and for questions about how one defines these terms. It might be useful to devote class time to such definitions, perhaps when you are covering the chapters on defining, explaining a concept, arguing, or evaluating. Some essays in the *Guide* treat this issue, specifically "Street Hassle" (Chapter 7). The *Guide* also refers in every chapter to audience and how important it is to writing, and you could help students understand this concept more clearly by talking about the effect on an audience—including the audience in the classroom—of language that harms. Students fresh from home will share the prejudices of their cultures; usually the classroom is diverse enough these days that you will get a cross-section of views from your students that will bring these difficult issues into the open from many perspectives. If one of these "isms" seems particularly prevalent in your class, you might want students to write on it.

Students on Alcohol and Drugs.   You should know what facilities are offered at your institution to help students who have drug and alcohol problems. Usually your health clinic or hospital will have literature on how to spot substance abuse in your students; ask them to put you on their mailing list. Students who are behaving unusually are those to watch—those who seem exaggeratedly sleepy, wired, silly, talkative, disjointed, erratic, or depressed. Also watch for students who stop showing up at class or whose attendance is erratic. If you suspect abuse, your clinic may have advice for you about steps you should take. Problems like these are usually out of your range, although the one thing you probably shouldn't do is ignore them. If you have substantial reason to believe a student is in serious trouble, you should consult with your director or chair about school policy and procedures.

Learning How to Listen

Probably the best piece of advice we can give a new instructor is to listen to the students. New instructors are often so concerned with what they themselves are going to say that they don't pay attention to the student. You have good reasons to worry about what you're saying, since it's your responsibility to be teaching, keeping order, and keeping the class focused. But especially, in writing courses students often can help each other as much as you can help them. The best part about listening, though, is that the students will give you material with which to work. Remember that you know more about writing than they probably ever will and that when they talk to you, your mind will grasp what they say and make a natural lesson out of it. Trust yourself. Listening means you have to be actively hearing your students and allowing some give-and-take. It means that you won't always have complete control over the material or what gets learned, but it also means that you will never run out of material or ideas, because you can always respond. In addition, students who are heard respect you and themselves—an atmosphere very conducive to learning.

Lecturing

Writing instructors usually don't need to lecture the way faculty do in some other disciplines, but if you have about fifteen minutes' worth of information you want to pass on, you may want some tips on lecturing. Practice your rhetorical skills: Do the best you can to make your material interesting to your audience. Use examples that will appeal to first-year students. Move around, vary your voice, use the blackboard or other visual aids. Stop to ask questions or get feedback. Remember that even the best listeners tune out parts of a lecture, so repeat key points. Tell them *why* this material is important for them to learn. Follow a lecture with an activity—have them move into small groups or write in their journals something you said.

Conducting Small-Group Work

For information on how to conduct successful small-group work, see the Teaching Practices sections on Organizing Workshops and Setting Up Collaborative Learning Groups in this manual. The *Guide* proposes several small-group activities that have been classroom-tested; the collaborative activities in each Part I chapter can be particularly helpful, either in small or large groups. New instructors often have the same anxieties about small groups that they have about students writing in class; they think they should be teaching, and they worry that the students will drift off task and end up talking about parties or their families or jobs. It's true that small groups are vulnerable to such discussions, but this manual offers many suggestions in Chapter 6 on teaching each text chapter to keep students engaged with class material.

The key is to help the groups by keeping the material manageable and by appointing one or two students to responsible roles so *they* will keep everyone focused. We find that small groups are particularly fruitful when each one has a different task that is later shared with the class as a whole; sometimes they even deal with different texts (that everyone has read). In these conditions, they fulfill multiple roles, first as discussers focused on a text, then as presenters to the larger group and facilitators of that discussion. If you move among the groups, joining in now and then, you can usually ensure that they will limit their social conversations.

Facilitating Class Discussion

If you want the whole class to participate in an activity, you will be more successful if you make it something about which they are all likely to make a contribution. If a large group focuses on one text, all together, very often only the students who are good at textual interpretation will have something to say. But if you are, say, brainstorming for an essay topic, almost everyone could have ideas, and if you write them on the board, more ideas will occur to them as you go along. The best large-group activities are those that call into play a range of talents, where students aren't simply responding to a text but are trying to solve a problem with several different strategies. For instance, if you are teaching the Defining chapter, and if students have defined a concept for their homework, you can ask them to read these to the class and let the large group figure out together how these definitions could lead to a paper. In fact, whenever you are trying to conduct a large-group discussion and you want to prevent the same few quick students from taking over, asking students to write on the topic ahead of time gives those who like to think things over a chance to do so; then they will be much more likely to contribute. Remember, too, that if you listen to students, they will be more likely to speak up because they think they're being heard. See Presenting and Discussing Readings under Teaching Practices for more about large-group discussion, and remember the Connecting to Culture and Experience activities following each reading in the *Guide*.

Teaching about Plagiarism

In recent years, especially since the computer has become commonly used in writing classes (students can download from myriad sources that you may never have seen), plagiarism has become a more complex issue. Students fresh out of high school may have very little—or even no—notion of what plagiarism is. They may have been taught to summarize out of encyclopedias or other sources for research papers in high school, but may not have been given instruction on how to cite. We believe that devoting class time to this topic is the best way to teach students what plagiarism is and how to avoid it. To help students understand the different forms plagiarism takes, we use an exercise based on an excerpt from *Habits of the Heart: Individualism and Commitment in American Life,* by Robert Bellah et al. You can distribute copies of this exercise, which appears at the end of this chapter of the manual, and ask students to determine which passages they think are plagiarized. We also include an instructor's key that you can distribute after class discussion.

Most students have no intention of plagiarizing; they really just don't understand what it is. Once they understand how their writing gains credibility when it integrates authoritative sources and how simple it is to acknowledge sources, they will willingly do so. However, if you do suspect a student of plagiarism, follow the procedures outlined in your institution's policy statement. One way of dealing with suspected plagiarism is to try to locate the source—rarely an easy task. If you can find the source, then ask the student to come for an appointment and tell him or her what you have found. Most students quickly confess, are remorseful, and often they will tell you the pressures they feel that made them plagiarize. You then follow the policy you have established for plagiarism, such as an F on the paper and perhaps an opportunity to rewrite. If a student denies plagiarizing and you have not been able to locate the source, you can show him or her the differences between the style of the plagiarized paper and his or her own typical style. If the student still denies plagiarism and you are fairly certain it has occurred, you can take the paper to your chair or to the board that mediates these issues.

Since plagiarism is such a problem on college campuses and since it is such an uncomfortable experience for new instructors, here are some hints on how to prevent it:

- Emphasize the professional ethics involved; make sure students know how egregious a transgression it is, and give them examples to help them understand why (for example, they wouldn't want to be taking medicine formulated from research that was stolen and perhaps taken out of context).
- Have students submit copies of their sources with their papers; such a policy is tough on trees but is effective for preventing plagiarism and can also be used in commenting on their process.
- Provide students with some of the material for their research (such as passages from a trade book) and require them to use it along with their own sources; this will prevent wholesale lifting of, say, fraternity-file papers, since your sources must be included.
- Require students to turn in all stages of their invention or research work and, of course, all drafts.
- Be mindful of a student who seems extraordinarily pressured or behind; even students who are honest can sometimes feel tempted when they see no alternatives.

In our culture, we still believe in the ownership of the expression of ideas in our scholarship, and unless that notion changes, we must ensure that our students know what plagiarism entails and how to prevent it.

Helping Students Who Are Physically or Learning Disabled

By now you know what facilities your institution offers for physically or learning disabled students. Some institutions will alert you ahead of time that you will have such a student in your class. Basic good sense dictates that you do the best you can to treat these students normally, while quietly making any arrangements necessary for their comfort and ease. For anyone in a wheelchair, a position close to the door is helpful, and you should create enough space around the wheelchair so it can be turned around easily. If the student has a scribe or assistant, find out that person's name and try to include him or her in the class (they do a lot of the work). If the student is blind or hearing impaired, ask which position in the classroom is best. Go ahead and ask all the questions you can think of; the student knows better than you can guess what will help most. During class discussion, make a conscious attempt to include these students. For in-class writing, quizzes, and exams, disabled students will need special arrangements, so ask ahead of time what you can do.

Learning disabled students are sometimes aware of their disability, but sometimes they are not. So many learning disabilities are related to reading and writing that writing instructors are frequently in a good position to spot them. Students who have these disabilities may display the following symptoms: very slow reading pace; inability to focus; difficulty in comprehending texts; unusual and strange (to us) sentence structure; very slow writing pace; inability to produce hierarchies (outlines, maps, etc.). Put the student in touch with any specialist your campus offers, and check on his or her progress regularly. If you know that a student is learning disabled, you can, and in some cases must, make arrangements for more time for reading and writing or perhaps for shorter assignments. Also, you might want to arrange regular conferences, either with yourself or with a tutor.

Livening Up Dead Days

Most classes go very well, even for neophytes. Students want to be there, and most of them have done the homework. They're often eager first-year students excited about college or returning students paying their own way. On occasion, though, even the most scintillating teachers suffer through dead days. New instructors don't know about dead days until they're in the middle of one. They're the days when you are trying to conduct a class and everyone is somewhere else. The students are still physically in the classroom, but they are beyond your communicating abilities. Most of them don't even care. They will sit like lumps, and you will try harder and harder to reach them or to be entertaining, until you suddenly realize what you're doing and get mad at everybody, including yourself.

If you run into a dead day, forgive yourself immediately. We don't know a professor on earth who hasn't suffered from them at one time or another. The best thing to do about them is to anticipate them—they are preventable. Dead days usually occur when students have either worked or played very hard—for example, every day a major paper is due, the first day of class after a big weekend such as parents' or homecoming, classes during midterms, and classes after a national or local crisis that has wrenched them (we recall dead days after the Oakland fire, the L.A. earthquakes, the Gulf War declaration, the Thomas/Hill hearings).

We are not suggesting you jump through hoops to pull your students out of their lethargy, but we are suggesting you break from the normal class pattern to provide a change. In the *Guide* there are several suggestions that will help with these days; you can open to almost any page and focus on an exercise or two, or you can perform a "close reading" on one of the shorter texts. On one dead day, we asked students to read the first three examples in the Narrating chapter, choose the one they preferred, and imitate the author's style with a story or narration of their own. Almost every student chose that entry to place in his or her portfolio.

Here are some additional suggestions: On dead days you can anticipate in advance, schedule a library tour, a film, a computer lesson, a field trip (that has something to do with writing or research), or just a class in another locale. Or, bring activities that will force students to become engaged; for instance, on one day when a paper was due, we brought in torn-out magazine pages that depicted complex scenes. We asked students to break into small groups and construct a story about the scene, using the descriptive and narrative talents that they had acquired from reading the corresponding chapters in the *Guide*. The collaborative stories turned a potential dead day into a creative day, and we had five proud readings of stories in the class. The activity started students on their next assignment (the Profile paper) without their really knowing it. Another day, just before midterms, we assigned the chapter in the *Guide* that covers written essay exams. Almost all classes can be rescued by engaging the students in informal writing tasks: freewriting, collages, "found poems," dialectical notebooks, oral text rendering, storytelling, pro/con arguing, collaborative writing. Debates can enliven classes that are reading the argument chapters.

Missing Class or Losing Your Books

Sometimes new instructors miss a class, or assume there is a holiday when there isn't, or somehow or other just don't show up. The best way to prevent this, of course, is to write in your personal calendar all the posted school holidays and your own schedule (with room numbers). If you miss a class, you can try to schedule a make-up on another day, but it's not easy to find a common time for all students to come. Usually you just have to accept your mistake. You can apologize to your students and anyone else you feel needs to know, and go on from there.

If you left your books at home or didn't have time to prepare, you will have to wing it. You can usually find another book, either from a colleague, the secretary, or the library. But if you're there in the classroom with no material, turn the tables: Have the students teach you. Tell them what happened, and put yourself in the student role and them in the teacher role. They can present the lesson of the day to you. This can turn into such a wonderful exercise that you might even find yourself faking it.

If none of these solutions appeals to you, here's one more: Tell the students that you want a sense of how much they've learned so far. Give them this assignment: "Write a clear, well-developed, organized letter-essay to your high school English teacher that explains at least three important features of writing that you have learned so far this term. To illustrate these features, use material from the *Guide*. Be sure to include the *reasons* we use these features (in other words, the *why* as well as the *what*). You are free to refer to *The St. Martin's Guide to Writing* and to your journal (your written responses to the Thinking Critically about What You Have Learned at the end of each Part I chapter might be very helpful). You have —— minutes." This exercise will take the full class time and will provide you with some valuable insight on what and how much your students are learning, and you can fall back on this exercise any time in the term (except, of course, the first few days). It can also be used by students as a journal entry or draft toward their Portfolio Self-Evaluation Essay.

Handling a Wide Disparity in Level

The exercises in the *Guide* are geared for a full range of student skills and abilities, so you can be confident that most students will be challenged at the appropriate level. However, sometimes in class you may find that one or two students need more instruction and help than the other students, and you might be spending more time on their questions than you think is appropriate. Conversely, one or two "overprepared" students might dominate discussion or question sessions, and they may move the class more quickly than is comfortable for the other students.

First you should try to determine whether or not you are right: Is the class slowed down by those questions? Are the students left behind by the quick pace? Find out by asking some students who do average work. Ask them after class or during office hours, but don't explain why you're asking—just pose your question (you could ask them to write an answer).

If there *is* a disparity in learning pace and level, try to judge how many students are affected. If half the class is having trouble with a new writing activity or strategy, then you probably should spend more class time on it. But if only two students are, have them see you during office hours together, or send them to the writing center.

You can form small groups during your office hours, so they can struggle with the new material together. You could form study groups to meet outside of class—though this can be difficult for commuters and students who work. You could give extra assignments from the *Guide* from the supplementary sections referred to throughout the chapters. It's important for less adept students to feel comfortable about asking questions in class, so it's best not to discourage them from speaking up. Instead, give them every opportunity to keep up with the work by providing extra time yourself and by encouraging (or requiring) them to use your institution's facilities.

You might want to approach the more adept students from a different angle. If they are dominating the discussion to the point where other students are shut out, you probably should talk to them privately. Again, you don't want to discourage students from being curious and engaged, but you don't want them taking over the classroom either.

If they are bored in your class because of the pace, see what you can do to challenge them. If it's early in the term, check their placement scores; it may be that they shouldn't even be in your class. Sometimes students can waiver or CLEP (CLEP is a test that determines whether a student has college-level knowledge) a class and move immediately into a higher level. If they are correctly placed, see whether they are willing to do extra work to keep themselves engaged. You could offer them extra credit, or you might be able just to appeal to their need to be challenged. Usually students who are accelerated can themselves recommend assignments that would challenge them, but if they don't, you can suggest that they do research, either field or library, or that they do extra writing. If they're very good writers, look into the possibility of their working in the writing center as peer tutors.

Assigning Journals

Elsewhere in this manual are several pages on student journals. (See Chapter 2: Teaching Practices.) The only additional information new instructors might need is that students won't take these journals seriously unless you do. Journals are extremely useful for students and for you. If you assign Analyzing Writing Strategies following each reading or Thinking Critically about What You Have Learned at the end of each Part I chapter, these writings can become part of a student's journal. Students can write substantial sections of their papers—especially the invention work—in their journals (guaranteeing revision). They can write about what's bothering them, exercise all their new skills, find out what they know (which is often something they didn't know they knew), tally up what they've learned, and best of all for some students, do all this writing without having to worry about strict evaluation. For many students, it's an enormous relief to be able to write without having to worry about comma placement, the perfect word, or whether every paragraph flows logically from the last. Journals can help students discover that writing is cognitive, epistemic, and heuristic—though they are not likely to use those words.

Even though journals are common in college, few students will have written journals in high school, and they are unaccustomed to taking seriously work that is generally unevaluated. They may know in the abstract that their journals count for, say, 20 to 30 percent of their grades, but it's hard for them to believe it when they do not get back grades with each entry. One way to help them believe it is to collect their journals often. Another way to emphasize their importance is to connect journal homework with class work. When students answer questions about the readings in their journals, they take their journals more seriously, and class discussion benefits.

Because journals are a form of communication between student and instructor, you may discover information about your course that otherwise would have gone unnoticed. You may read that the load is too heavy, that a concept is ungrasped, or that some student had his feelings hurt in class or by you. You can respond accordingly.

If you worry that journals seem like a lot of work, remember that students who write often are usually more engaged in class and write better papers because they've done the preparatory work. Journals do take some time and effort, but they pay off over the course of the term.

Assigning Papers

With the syllabus, give students a sheet that outlines your format requirements. This format should state name, course and instructor, date, title, preferred margins; spacing, typing, and proofreading requirements; and your policies on other matters, such as whether or not they should include a cover sheet, a binder, rough drafts, etc. The more written information you provide, the more likely you'll get what you want. Remind students that you would prefer handwritten corrections to uncorrected mistakes (they tend not to believe this, so it's smart to emphasize it).

When you comment on papers, consider your students. Try to *describe* what you see rather than just *evaluate*. Our experience is that students usually take criticism very well, if it's clear and seems fair. They do *not* respond well to irony. Final comments that sum up your marginal responses are important. You might type end comments on the word processor. Such a practice makes the students feel as though they are in a written dialogue with the instructor, and they usually seem to feel even more weightily the importance of writing. In addition, you will have your previous comments in your computer and can refer to them as you evaluate the student's next paper. You can see if a student is repeating problems or has improved. See Chapter 3, "Evaluating Practices," for more detailed advice.

Having Students Comment on Each Other's Drafts

Peer response is also discussed elsewhere in this manual under Organizing Workshops in Chapter 2: Teaching Practices. Be aware that some students won't show up for class on a day set aside for workshops unless they have a completed, polished draft. You might want to establish a firm policy about coming to class on peer review days (that day could count double). Others will come to class with nothing or just sketchy notes, and hope the peer reviewer will come up with material for them. This, of course, is irritating to the peer reviewer. In addition, many students will feel incapable of evaluating papers.

It's valuable to remind them of two things: one, they are members of the audience for this paper and are bound to have some reaction, even if they know very little about the subject. They all are capable of knowing how many times they had to read a sentence before they could understand it or how difficult it is to follow a train of thought when there is no discernible organization. All they have to be are *readers*, who then write down their responses. The second thing they need to realize is that responding to other writers' drafts will help them review their own drafts with a critical eye. In other words, the critical reading skills they are developing are transferable to their own writing. In the first few workshop sessions, students may feel discouraged about their abilities, but they will learn.

Some instructors make the first workshop a surprise. The students come in with their first completed college paper, ready to hand in the most perfect work they can turn out. Many of them have been up all night. You collect all the papers, making the point that these are "final" copies, the best conceivable work, etc., and then shuffle them up and hand them back out, making sure no student gets his or her own. They then respond to each other's papers in class and take them home again to revise for the next class. Even if the peer review isn't all that helpful—though usually it is—students get to reread with a critical eye their own work after they had thought they were finished. There is no quicker or more effective way to convince a student of the value of revision.

Writing Some of the Assignments Yourself

Most instructors will cringe at this advice—but we really mean it, especially for new instructors. All of the assignments in the *Guide* have been student-tested, but it still doesn't hurt to know yourself, firsthand, which of the many options offered are most valuable for your style of teaching and your approach to writing. Even if you write only shortened versions of assignments, you will be getting a feel for what one learns (and doesn't learn) from particular tasks. Another great advantage is that you can share your work-in-progress with your students. Students absolutely love it when their teacher writes with them. You are not only showing them that their student writing assignments are worth your time and effort, but you also will be showing them how you yourself can have difficulty or success with the same tasks they are performing. New instructors benefit immensely from this exercise.

Responding to Complaints about Grades

Now and then a student may disagree with a grade you give. Offer to take the paper home for review. (Resist the temptation to get this over with by doing it in front of the student—you may end up arguing over minor matters.) Make sure you have given the paper the grade you think it deserves. As a beginning instructor, you may be uncertain your evaluation is appropriate. If so, show it to a more experienced instructor or the director of the composition program. Jot down notes that support your opinion. Write or talk to the student about your decision. Try to connect the problems you see with the requirements of the assignment, so the student understands that the paper is not meeting the standards for this section. For instance, a student may take a strong position in an explanation paper, without developing a detailed definition of the concept to be explained. Or a student might present a very sound argument with strong support but not anticipate opposing views. If the problem is not with the nature of the assignment but with the expression or style, you might want to show the student a sample of prose on a similar topic that is clearly written. If the student is still resistant, offer him or her a copy of the grievance procedure (that you got from the secretary before the term started). There is no need to prolong the discussion, since you have explained your reasons and the student still disagrees. Send the student off with the next step to take, and see what happens. Make sure you have a copy of the original paper that you graded (so the student can't change it), a copy of your original remarks, and a copy of the additional remarks you made when you reread the paper. This paper trail may be necessary if the student follows through. You might want, at this point, to alert the people who would receive the grievance that it might be coming their way.

HALFWAY THROUGH THE TERM

Soliciting Student Evaluations

Even if you think things are going swimmingly, you should solicit a mid-course written evaluation to make sure you are on target. New instructors might miss some of the more subtle signals students send out, or they might even think the term is going horribly when really the students are very happy. Why not find out? Far enough into the term for students to have formed an opinion, but not so far that it will be too late to do anything about a problem, hand out a questionnaire. We recommend a written questionnaire rather than a class discussion because students will sometimes be more honest on an anonymous piece of paper than in class. Allow about twenty minutes, and ask questions like these:

1. What are you learning from the textbook?
2. Do you find the readings useful?

3. What do you think of the comments on your papers?
4. Would you like more lecture? class discussion? small-group work? If so, what would you sacrifice that we do now?
5. Have you come to office hours? Why, or why not?
6. Do you think the work load is fair? If you think it's unfair, how would you change it?
7. How can you improve your workshop responses, and how could your reviewers help you more?

Responding to Student Comments

Respond to these questionnaires. You will see patterns as soon as you read them. If students seem perfectly happy, then great—tell them so in the next class period. If they have a few complaints that thread through the questionnaires, see if there are ways you can address them. If the reading load is too heavy, consider lightening it. Same for the writing load. If one student complains bitterly about something ("you never say anything good about my papers, you never call on me in class, you're always too busy to talk to me, other instructors grade completely differently"), name the problem and ask the student who complained about that problem to come to you after class. Make clear that the student won't be penalized; you just want to remedy the problem.

Don't be discouraged by a few complaints that seem unfair to you. Even in the best classes, a few students will find something that bothers them. Concentrate on the sense you get from the batch of questionnaires as a whole, not on the few complaints embedded in the batch. New instructors are especially vulnerable to a few cranks, so reread the good ones to set yourself straight. (If you're really worried, show them to a colleague and ask for a frank opinion.)

Do take steps to correct problems that you see. After all, how can you be expected to do everything right the first time? If you make changes in the assignments or in the schedule (you might even have to drop a paper), rewrite the rest of the term in a new schedule; don't trust the students to write down your emendations to the assignment sheet. Give them a new one.

Assigning Midterm Grades

Some institutions have systems to let students know their status toward the middle of the term. These are especially important for first-year students, who may have little notion of how they're doing in college. Even if you aren't giving formal grades to students in their first few assignments, or if you're on a portfolio system, you may have to assign a grade at midterm. So keep a record of your opinion of each student's work, even if you aren't giving grades yet. See Chapter 3: Evaluating Practices, for advice on midterm grading.

Helping Students Who Are Slipping through the Cracks

Every term you will have one or two students who just may not make it through your course. This is especially true of first-term, first-year students. These students may be adjusting to being away from home, to new freedoms, and to (sometimes) noisy residence halls. They are learning how to prioritize and how to live on their own. We often need to help students develop these new skills. If a student is not performing well in your course, you might want to ask for a conference. Or you might write a note, pointing out that assignments X and Y are missing and when they must be made up. If students know that you are keeping track of them, they might respond immediately. If you make an effort and nothing happens, you could try phoning or contacting the student's advisor.

Express your concern, and ask why the work remains undone. Ask why first, before you indicate the danger the student is in, since the student may have some truly wrenching reason. Once you know the reason, you can then make it clear that the student might not pass your class if the work is not made up and changes are not made. Try to remember that many first-term students are frightened of professors and don't understand the function of office hours. If you are considerate and gentle, at least at first, you could be quite helpful and avoid tears, or worse, anger and defensiveness. If the student has good reasons, you might want to draw up a make-up schedule for the rest of the term. The student can help you with this. Put the schedule in writing, with one copy for the student and one for you, so you can keep track.

Recognizing Your Limitations

Some students attend college for unfathomable reasons. And some leave for the same. Some didn't want to come in the first place, but were pressured by parents. Some can't afford it. Some have other priorities or problems that must take precedence for a while: children, marriage, a job, travel, illness, drug addiction, psychological difficulties. Students who decide to leave may do so without ever letting you know; they just disappear. Others may spend hours in your office working through their decisions. Some students may talk to you in all earnestness about reasons for staying or leaving that might in the long run have nothing to do with their *real* reasons. You can do your best to help; you can recommend talking to their academic advisor, seeking counseling, talking to a religious advisor, their parents, etc. But when push comes to shove, you may not be able to "save" them, at least for this year. They may return to college or they may not, but after you've done everything you can think of, you may just have to let go. You may finally have to say: "I've done everything I can to help you, but I can't make up your mind for you or do your work for you. If you don't complete the work on time in our schedule, you will not pass the course." These things are hard to say to students, but you must realize that you yourself are not responsible for forcing them out of college—you are simply setting reasonable, justifiable limits. That's your responsibility. The students are better off if you are clear with them than if you let them continue to eat up your time and your emotions—they themselves don't feel good about such behavior.

NEAR THE END OF THE TERM

Make a point of reviewing policies about exit exams, final exams, final papers, etc. Even if you made such policies clear in your syllabus, it helps to reiterate the requirements for their final papers or their portfolio reviews. First-year students especially get a little boggled by finals and the end-of-term pace, so any way you can help them keep track of everything is useful.

Giving Students Incompletes

There are many varieties of incompletes, some legitimate, some not. If your department has a policy of no incompletes, then you have no choice. But some institutions are fairly liberal with incompletes. In the absence of departmental policy, you should decide what your policy is. Only in extreme emergency? (and what is that—death or serious illness?) Only if three-quarters of the work is already done? Only for the last paper? Once you have decided on your policy, you will have fewer problems, especially if you have written it on your syllabus. The student to be wary of is the one who comes to you the last week of school but who has only attended sporadically, if at all, since the first two or three weeks. The student will explain why he did not come to class. He may say he has several of the papers finished and ask when he can submit them. Unless your policy is extraordinarily liberal, you should give this student a firm "no." If he says other teachers are letting him make up the work, you can calmly but emphatically explain that yours is a course in the process of writing and that therefore handing in final papers is insufficient.

Extending Office Hours

Many instructors offer extra office hours during the last two weeks of class. Students then have the opportunity to clear up any issues that have been puzzling them; they have a chance to get extra help on their final papers or on revising selected papers for their portfolios.

Scheduling Student Evaluations

Most institutions ask you to schedule approximately twenty minutes of class time near the end of your course for students to fill out their evaluations of you. If you tell students ahead of time which day you will hand out these evaluations, you might get a better turnout. If there isn't a policy about whether or not you should stay in the classroom, everyone might be more comfortable if you leave. Ask for a student volunteer to collect the evaluations and take them down to the program coordinator or department chair (or wherever they're supposed to go). Be sure to allow plenty of time for these since you don't want your students to rush over them (and you want them at least to be well written!).

Helping Students End Well

Students appreciate an instructor who takes care of needs they didn't know they had. Invite students to give you a prestamped grade card or a large envelope if they want their last papers or their portfolios mailed back. If you will be on campus after classes are over, tell students the day and time they can pick up their papers or portfolios. Some instructors post grades on their office doors; if you post grades, be sure to protect the identity of the students. (The Family Educational Rights and Privacy Act of 1974 prohibits the release of a student's grades to anyone but the student.) Use a code designated by the student—something other than the student number or Social Security number—and an order other than alphabetical to protect the students' anonymity.

Leaving a Paper Trail

You should keep records of the work you and your students do. Such a record will help you if there is a grade dispute or if a student complains of discrimination. The rule of thumb is that whenever there is a problem, record it in writing. If you find that a student is plagiarizing, keep a copy of the paper, the material plagiarized (if you have it), other work written by the student (especially in-class work), and your note to the student about the plagiarized paper. This last is important because you'll need to show the warning that was issued and the penalty imposed. If a student has been warned repeatedly through the term that she will fail unless she completes certain work, you will have strong evidence to win a grade dispute. Keep these records, along with your syllabus, assignment sheets, any revisions, and other correspondences with your students, for six years.

THE LAST CLASS

Some instructors want to go out in a blaze of glory; others prefer to go quietly into the night. If you are among the latter, just make the last class a final acceptance of papers and let the students go. Or, if papers are handed in at the end of finals week, make the last class a final review session. But if you do feel like closure, there are many approaches.

Many instructors throw a party. Students themselves can bring everything—a potluck—and then all you have to do is allow it to happen. If you like an even stronger sense of closure, have everyone read aloud from something they wrote for class, or recall something they learned from one another. You will be able to think of a ceremony that will please you and your students.

AFTER THE LAST CLASS

The registrar will let you know when you should turn in your grades; make a note of the date. Some students may turn in their papers late, so be prepared with your policy. Often students will include cards or notes with their final papers or their portfolios. *Don't open the cards until you have given them their grades.* Even the most stalwart and just of us can hardly help but be influenced by an outpouring of affection and gratitude.

If a student gives you a present, you should probably refuse it, especially if it's valuable, unless you know the student well and are certain in your heart that it is not a bribe. In some cultures, it is proper to give the instructor a gift (and it's considered an insult not to). You may have to explain that in our culture things are different. If the class gives you a present, pat yourself on the back.

Keep a record of the grades you give your students. Keep a record of your course material in case you use it again.

Great good luck with your first year of teaching; we hope that it is only the first of many years in this most gratifying and rewarding profession.

FOR STUDENTS

PLAGIARISM: IN-CLASS EXERCISE

Read this passage from Robert Bellah, taken from *Habits of the Heart: Individualism and Commitment in American Life* (pp. 144–47). Then read the following paragraphs excerpted from student essays. Determine which excerpts contain plagiarism and what's plagiarized.

> Both the cowboy and the hard-boiled detective tell us something important about American individualism. The cowboy, like the detective, can be valuable to society only because he is a completely autonomous individual who stands outside it. To serve society, one must be able to stand alone, not needing others, not depending on their judgment, and not submitting to their wishes. Yet this individualism is not selfishness. Indeed, it is a kind of heroic selflessness. One accepts the necessity of remaining alone in order to serve the values of the group. And this obligation to aloneness is an important key to the American moral imagination. Yet it is part of the profound ambiguity of the mythology of American individualism that its moral heroism is always just a step away from despair. For an Ahab, and occasionally for a cowboy or detective, there is no return to society, no moral redemption. The hero's lonely quest for moral excellence ends in absolute nihilism.

Excerpts from Essays Written by Students

1. Our modern urban hero is like the cowboy or the detective in his isolation from his own community. He selflessly stands outside his community in order to help it; he resists any desire to join its members because his mission depends on his resistance to conformity. He must rely on his own moral vision and on his ability to transcend community values to see and implement the larger picture that only he can imagine.

2. The heroes in our modern large cities are the natural legatees of the heroes of America since it was founded. Who hasn't read about the pioneer setting out across the plains to conquer the new land, or of the lonely cowboy protecting his ranch from marauders? Our modern urban hero must also stand tough and alone, not succumbing to gang mentality or to political pressures or to any kind of community pressure; he must stay true to his values no matter what the consequences.

3. The modern urban hero is different from the men who have served as the trademarks of American individualism, like Shane and Sam Spade. Those heroes were on a lonely quest for moral excellence that ended in absolute nihilism, with no role in the community except as an outsider. The modern urban hero, on the other hand, must be tightly integrated into the community. He must be adept at garnering community approval and commitment, and if the community suspects that the hero might become too individualistic, or might impose his own distinctive morality upon the group, the members will remind the hero that he is one of them. The hero will quickly respond and will consult with his community before taking any action.

4. The modern urban hero is similar to the frontier heroes of America's past. He must be able to stand tall, to reject others, to withstand their judgment, and to not submit to other desires. According to Robert Bellah, "this individualism is

not selfishness; . . . it is a kind of heroic selflessness" (146) that allows one to serve the values of the group. These leaders find their satisfaction in personal fulfillment and achieving their ideals; they don't need connection to the community.

5. Even though modern urban heroes are deeply involved with the members of their community, they do share some of the characteristics of the American individualist explored by Robert Bellah in *Habits of the Heart*. Bellah points out that a traditional individualist "is always just a step away from despair [because] . . . there is no return to society, no moral redemption. The hero's lonely quest for moral excellence ends in absolute nihilism" (146). Bellah bases his conclusion on his belief that an individualist, such as a cowboy or a detective, "can be valuable to society only because he is a completely autonomous individual who stands outside it. To serve society, one must be able to stand alone, not needing others, not depending on their judgment, and not submitting to their wishes" (146). Like Bellah's individualists, modern urban heroes are often subject to despair, but their despair is based more on their hopelessness about their cause than on their isolation from their community. They are more likely to do the opposite of Bellah's individualist, in that they depend on their community's judgment and wishes, even as they assume positions of leadership: They are individualists within a community.

INSTRUCTOR'S KEY

PLAGIARISM: IN-CLASS EXERCISE

Read this passage from Robert Bellah, taken from *Habits of the Heart: Individualism and Commitment in American Life* (pp. 144–47). Then read the following paragraphs excerpted from student essays. Determine which excerpts contain plagiarism and what's plagiarized.

> Both the cowboy and the hard-boiled detective tell us something important about American individualism. The cowboy, like the detective, can be valuable to society only because he is a completely autonomous individual who stands outside it. To serve society, one must be able to stand alone, not needing others, not depending on their judgment, and not submitting to their wishes. Yet this individualism is not selfishness. Indeed, it is a kind of heroic selflessness. One accepts the necessity of remaining alone in order to serve the values of the group. And this obligation to aloneness is an important key to the American moral imagination. Yet it is part of the profound ambiguity of the mythology of American individualism that its moral heroism is always just a step away from despair. For an Ahab, and occasionally for a cowboy or detective, there is no return to society, no moral redemption. The hero's lonely quest for moral excellence ends in absolute nihilism.

Excerpts from Essays Written by Students

1. Our modern urban hero is like the cowboy or the detective in his isolation from his own community. *He selflessly stands outside his community in order to help it;* he resists any desire to join its members because his mission depends on his resistance

to conformity. He must rely on his own moral vision and on his ability to transcend community values to see and implement the larger picture that only he can imagine.

Commentary: Compare the italicized language to Bellah's: "can be valuable to society only because he is a completely autonomous individual who stands outside it. To serve society, one must be able to stand alone." Even though it is greatly condensed and in simpler language, the *idea* is Bellah's, not the student's.

2. The heroes in our modern large cities are the natural legatees of the heroes of America since it was founded. Who hasn't read about the pioneer setting out across the plains to conquer the new land, or of the lonely cowboy protecting his ranch from marauders? Our modern urban hero must also stand tough and alone, not succumbing to gang mentality or to political pressures or to any kind of community pressure; he must stay true to his values no matter what the consequences.

Commentary: No plagiarism; all these ideas are either common knowledge or are original with the writer.

3. The modern urban hero is different from the men who have served as the trademarks of American individualism, like *Shane and Sam Spade. Those heroes were on a lonely quest for moral excellence that ended in absolute nihilism, with no role in the community except as an outsider.* The modern urban hero, on the other hand, must be tightly integrated into the community. He must be adept at garnering community approval and commitment, and if the community suspects that the hero might become too individualistic, or might impose his own distinctive morality upon the group, the members will remind the hero that he is one of them. The hero will quickly respond and will consult with his community before taking any action.

Commentary: This example is a close call because so much of the paragraph is original thinking. But the examples of Shane and Sam Spade together imitate Bellah, and the italicized sentence is clearly plagiarized. This would be a good place to point out how simple it would be to acknowledge Bellah, especially since so much of the paragraph is the student's own ideas. You could tell the student to come up with her own individualists, instead of Shane and Sam Spade, or that she could introduce Bellah before she mentions them: . . . who have served as the trademarks of American individualism, like, as Robert Bellah suggests, Shane and Sam Spade. However, according to Bellah, "the hero's lonely quest for moral excellence ends in absolute nihilism" (146), while the urban hero must be tightly integrated into the community. This is also a good time to point out how you can use a source both for support for your own point—or as a starting place for disagreement (since this urban hero is different from the typical American individualist).

4. The modern urban hero is similar to the frontier heroes of America's past. He must be able *to stand tall, to reject others, to withstand their judgment, and to not submit to other desires.* According to Robert Bellah, "this individualism is not selfishness; . . . it is a kind of heroic selflessness" (146) *that allows one to serve the values of the group.* These leaders find their satisfaction in personal fulfillment and achieving their ideals; they don't need connection to the community.

Commentary: The italicized passages are clearly plagiarized, but students may not realize it because the first is paraphrased and because Bellah is mentioned and quoted. Point out that whenever you paraphrase, you must give the source, and whenever you lift sentences or ideas directly, they must *all* be in quotes. Furthermore, there is a much more subtle form of shaky scholarship here that you can note. This student implies that Bellah's passage condones individualism as selfless behavior that allows one to serve the group; he juxtaposes passages to serve his own purposes, and he goes on to say that these qualities of individualism are satisfying and fulfilling. Since this interpretation does not coincide with Bellah's purposes (this is not a vision that "ends in absolute nihilism"), the student is not being fair to Bellah. He could fix it by inserting what he left out and by distinguishing Bellah's opinion from his own: "this individualism is not selfishness. Indeed, it is a kind of heroic selflessness. One accepts the necessity of remaining alone in order to serve the values of the group" (146). Although Bellah's individualists are close to despair and feel painfully isolated (146), our modern leaders find their satisfaction in personal fulfillment, etc. If you choose to show this last alteration, point out again how you must cite a page number when you paraphrase.

5. Even though modern urban heroes are deeply involved with the members of their community, they do share some of the characteristics of the American individualist explored by Robert Bellah in *Habits of the Heart*. Bellah points out that a traditional individualist "is always just a step away from despair [because] . . . there is no return to society, no moral redemption. The hero's lonely quest for moral excellence ends in absolute nihilism" (146). Bellah bases his conclusion on his belief that an individualist, such as a cowboy or a detective, "can be valuable to society only because he is a completely autonomous individual who stands outside it. To serve society, one must be able to stand alone, not needing others, not depending on their judgment, and not submitting to their wishes" (146). Like Bellah's individualists, modern urban heroes are often subject to despair, but their despair is based more on their hopelessness about their cause than on their isolation from their community. They are more likely to do the opposite of Bellah's individualist, in that they depend on their community's judgment and wishes, even as they assume positions of leadership: They are individualists within a community.

Commentary: This passage is not plagiarized. Note that Bellah is quoted in support of a larger topic the student is exploring, and the student's points are salient. In fact, the student is showing that she is aware of a common view of individualism—she enhances her ethos with her knowledge of the context of her assertions—yet she shows how her individualists are different from the standard ones. You can emphasize in the first quote that when you insert any words into a quoted passage those words must be in brackets, and whenever you leave anything out, you must insert an ellipsis.

CHAPTER 2

Teaching Practices

In this chapter, we discuss ways you can conduct conferences with students, organize in-class workshops, have students keep journals, present and discuss readings, set up collaborative learning groups, and conduct community service learning projects. The methods we suggest here are ones we have borrowed from others or developed on our own while teaching the assignments in this book.

HOLDING CONFERENCES

Conferences with students are time-consuming and difficult to schedule when classes are large, but we recommend them highly as a teaching practice even if you can see students individually only once or twice during the course. Conferences may replace class meetings altogether as the forum in which instructor and students meet, and we have successfully used this format for writing courses. Usually, however, we use conferences in addition to class meetings, because the combination allows us the benefits of group discussion of assignments, drafts, and readings, as well as the chance to work closely with each student and attend to his or her individual needs. Conferences allow the instructor to develop a rapport with students, thus building the trust and self-confidence that many students need before they will take the risks in their writing that lead to real progress. For many students, these conferences are their only opportunities to work individually with a college instructor.

A conference may be scheduled at any time during the composing process. We find it most useful after the first or second draft of an essay has been written, at a point when the student has spent some time thinking about the assignment, generating invention notes, and making at least one attempt to put the ideas into draft form but before the student has finished work on the essay. Ideally, the first draft is discussed in a conference and the second draft in a workshop with other students, or vice versa, before the student writes the final revision of the essay. We do not discuss finished essays in conferences: The time is just too valuable to spend it justifying our remarks on the revision of the previous paper.

In the one-term (ten-week) courses we have taught, we like to see students in conference three times. The second of these, the midterm conference, allows us to review the student's progress and discuss the goals for the remainder of the course.

Individual Conferences

We find that the best length for individual conferences is half an hour, although it is possible to make some progress in twenty minutes if the time is spent carefully.

The student comes to the conference with a draft in hand and may at first expect you to play the role of mechanic, making the necessary repairs on it while he or she waits in anxious silence. It is often tempting to take the draft from the student and go to work on it, but this defeats the object of conferencing, which is to help students to learn to work on their own drafts. To this end, we leave the draft in the student's hands for most of the conference and usually begin by asking the student either to read it aloud or talk about it. In the most successful conferences, the students do at least half the talking; our comments merely draw them out and let them make discoveries for themselves.

Students can come to conferences well prepared to talk about their drafts and to take responsibility for solving problems—if they have specific guidelines for preparing themselves. At the end of each of the Detailed Chapter Plans sections in Chapter 6 of this manual, we provide conference-planning forms for students to fill out, a form for each assignment in Part I of the text.

Small-Group Conferences

An alternative to the individual conference is the small-group conference. Instead of meeting with each student for half an hour, the instructor might meet with three students for an hour, spending twenty minutes on each student's draft. In a typical group conference, each student brings copies of the draft for the other two students and the instructor. They each read their drafts aloud while the listeners make notes on their copies. At the end of each reading, the instructor leads a discussion about the draft, with the other two students contributing their views and suggestions. After twenty minutes, the writer collects the annotated copies, and attention turns to the next student's draft.

The group conference lacks the privacy of an individual conference, an important consideration for shy students. On the other hand, the group may generate ideas that would not emerge in a one-on-one conference. Some of the comments we make about the first student's draft usually apply to the other two as well, and students often decide to change their own drafts after the discussion of another student's draft. Neither conference format is inherently better than the other; we recommend that you try both to decide which you prefer.

ORGANIZING WORKSHOPS

The workshop brings class members together to read and respond to work in progress—usually the first or second draft. There are many possible variations in the format of a workshop, including the following ones that have worked for us. For more general advice to new instructors, see Chapter 1.

Written Response

Because students don't hear or remember everything a critical reader says about a draft, we find it helps when students write up their responses so that the writers can refer to them later when they actually revise. We also find that when students are given guidance and time, they can give a very thoughtful, useful response—one that helps them as writers as well as helping their workshop partner.

We typically begin by asking students to exchange their drafts with another class member. As students first exchange drafts, they could brief their partners on particular points they would like the partners to look at. Each student then spends ten to twenty minutes reading the partner's draft silently and writing a critical response to it. Activities and questions found under Critical Reading Guide in each of the chapters in Part I lead students through this process. They write their responses on separate sheets of paper, labeled at the top to look like this:

Proposal Essay Draft 2

Workshop Response for John Smith by Mary Jones

While students are working silently on each other's drafts, you may choose to move among them to offer advice. Alternatively, you can arrange in advance for one or two students to bring copies of their drafts for you to review during this time. When students have finished writing, they return the draft with their written comments, taking a few minutes to look over the response and ask the partner about anything confusing. To facilitate this critical exchange, you may want to pair students according to their writing abilities, changing the pairs so that each student receives comments from several others during the course. Another option is to organize students into small groups instead of pairs, each group including some stronger and weaker writers.

Novice writers tend to write their first workshop responses with some anxiety. A few will launch into devastatingly honest evaluations of a partner's draft, but most err on the side of conciliation. Influenced perhaps by the knowledge that their own drafts are undergoing similar scrutiny, they are usually eager to praise and offer little substantial criticism. At the beginning of the course, they also lack the experience to make recommendations to the writer.

One way to address this problem in the first workshop is to take students through the activities and questions in the Critical Reading Guide, modeling for them the kind of critique that would let the writer know what works, what needs work, and what might be done to revise the essay. A good response points to specific things in the draft, describing their effect on the reader tactfully but honestly, and suggests options the writer might consider. Questions to the writer beginning "How about . . . ?" are often useful. To model such a critique, you can use copies of a class member's draft or copies of an anonymous draft written for a similar assignment in a previous course. You can also review with students the sample critical reading in the Writer at Work section at the end of Chapter 3 of the *Guide*.

Discussion

Another way to organize the workshop is around oral reading and response. One possibility is to arrange in advance for one or two students to bring enough copies of their drafts for the other class members to share—a copy for every two students. The writer tells the class about any particular problems he or she has had in the draft and then reads it aloud while the rest of the class follows along on the copies, making marginal notes where appropriate. The class will respond better if they hear and see the draft simultaneously. At the end of the oral reading, the instructor chairs a discussion of the draft, appointing a scribe to record the comments for the writer. The activities and questions in the Critical Reading Guide can form the basis of this discussion. At the end of the discussion, the scribe gives the writer the discussion notes and other students pass along their copies with marginal notes.

This whole-class discussion of one draft at a time simulates the traditional writers' workshop widely used in MFA programs. Many instructors using this workshop format ask that the writer not participate in the discussion. There are good reasons for this rule. At the draft stage, writers need to know the immediate personal responses and evaluative reflections of readers. They need to listen to the discussion, reflect thoughtfully on what readers say, why they misunderstand, what they have questions about. The writer needs to watch postures and facial expressions. Were the readers really interested in this draft, or is the discussion lifeless and perfunctory? What things do readers point to? What do they ignore? What seems to confuse them? What do they understand best and seem most pleased about? Is the discussion desultory, moving from one point to the next with little connection or sequence? Or does the discussion have a direction, with many people involved making their contributions? From watching this sort of discussion of one's draft, a writer can know whether it struck readers as boring or engaging, pointless or informative, unsupported or convincing. The writer benefits especially if readers are specific and provide written reactions at the end of the workshop.

You may choose to begin a workshop with class discussion and then allow some time for students to exchange drafts and written analyses, so that you can review basic features and requirements of the assignment. Even with the Guide to Writing, there will still be students who have not yet brought the assignment into focus. By concentrating initially on one or two papers with the whole class, you can remind students of the basic features of that kind of writing. At the end of the discussion, you can summarize these basic features on the chalkboard and relate them to points in the Critical Reading Guide. This should give students more confidence in helping each other and keep them focused on the central issues of the assignment rather than the peripheral ones.

Working with the whole class on one draft also allows you to make observations that are relevant to the assignment and not just to the draft in hand. An alternative is to divide the class into small groups of four or five, with one member of each group bringing copies of his or her draft for the others in the group and reading it aloud to them. If there is time, a group could respond to several students' drafts—at least superficially. In a large class, this allows more students to receive group responses to their drafts and encourages the more reticent students to participate in the discussion. You can join one group or move among the groups. This format works best when students know what is expected and can work productively without your guidance.

Practical Considerations

1. When a student comes to class late or without a draft, you have several options, depending on which workshop format the class is using:
   - conduct a conference with the student
   - have the student join a pair and read a draft page by page as one partner finishes
   - have the student respond to a copy of a draft that has been duplicated for the whole class

   In all these cases, the student must be reminded that he or she is responsible for obtaining another student's response to his or her own draft. You could require the student to get a written comment from a writing center tutor. Specify that the tutor should follow the guidelines for the Critical Reading Guide.
2. You can choose whether to have students work in pairs or small groups or whether to lead a discussion in which the entire class participates.
3. When the first and second drafts of the same assignment are read in subsequent workshops, some instructors ask students to choose a different partner to respond to the second draft. Other instructors allow students to choose the same partner to read the second draft, so that the partner can comment on the progress the writer has made since the first draft.
4. Some instructors find it useful to have students put their phone numbers on their workshop responses, so that writers can call their workshop partners if they find they have questions as they revise their drafts.
5. Some instructors ask all students to bring an extra copy of their drafts. During the workshop, while pairs are quietly writing their critiques of each other's drafts, the instructor quickly reviews all drafts, noting the most glaring problems.

ASSIGNING JOURNALS

Many writing teachers appreciate the value of journals in a writing course. The brevity, frequency, and informality of entries in a journal allow students to use writing in many more ways than they do in formal essays. In our courses, students keep a journal in which they respond to Analyzing Writing Strategies and Connecting to Culture and Experience following every reading in *The St. Martin's Guide* or to further questions and assignments provided by their instructors. Journal assignments can be used to challenge students to engage in a wide range of critical thinking activities, including responding to readings and practicing various thinking and writing strategies. Although journal entries may be written outside of class, they can be written in class—for example, to begin discussion of the reading, to summarize a discussion, or to reflect on what they have learned, perhaps using the set of metacognitive activities at the end of each Part I chapter.

Practical Considerations: Assigning, Monitoring, and Responding to Journal Questions

Some instructors hand out a weekly set of three to five journal tasks, which may include *Guide* tasks and activities, while others provide students at the beginning of the quarter with a list of tasks for the entire course, specifying weekly due dates. A few instructors collect journal entries only every few weeks; most, however, find it worthwhile to collect and respond to them on a weekly basis. Although some instructors ask students to keep their journals in spiral-bound notebooks, you may want to have your students write each journal entry on a separate sheet of looseleaf notebook paper, labeled with their names, the week number, and the number of the entry (or whatever information best facilitates your record-keeping system). This makes collecting their completed journal entries for each week somewhat easier and enables them to use a computer if they like.

Responding to journal entries need not be time-consuming. A few suggestions or words of encouragement in the margins are generally sufficient to let students see that you've read their entries. Although some instructors use informal marking systems such as plusses, checks, and minuses, journal entries really should not be graded or judged for mechanical correctness. Instead, they should be evaluated for quantity and for quality of thought. It is important that students understand from the very beginning that the journal, although informal, is neither a private diary nor busy-work but a serious component of the course, and that you will expect their journal entries to be thorough, thoughtful, even provocative.

Planning a Sequence of Journal Questions

It takes careful planning to coordinate your own journal tasks with the reading selections for the course. A planned sequence of journal questions allows students to reflect on what they have learned and to see connections between the various components of your course. In particular, journal questions can help them make connections between the assigned readings and their own writing.

Sample Journal Questions

In general, journal assignments help students to improve their writing skills by exercising their critical reading and thinking skills. Journal questions can guide students to identify certain strategies in the texts they're reading and then practice these writing strategies on their own. The following list of kinds of questions, which is by no means exhaustive, suggests a range of possibilities for the journal.

Analyzing and Responding to Readings.   Some instructors use the journal exclusively for this purpose, calling it a Reader's Journal instead of a Writer's Journal. They ask their students to answer questions following the readings in Part I chapters, as well as questions they pose about trade books they assign. You could also assign critical reading strategies from Chapter 12 or invite students to select the ones they find most useful.

See the discussion in the next section, Presenting and Discussing Readings, for ideas about using journal writing to encourage critical reading and to prepare for class discussions of assigned readings.

Applying Rhetorical Strategies.   Other questions help students apply strategies they see in their reading to their own essays:

In Chapter 13: Cueing the Reader, you learned about various strategies to make your writing more readable. Discuss one cueing strategy that would remedy a particular weakness that you have or someone else has noticed in your writing. Give an example of the problem in your writing, showing how you would use this cueing device to solve it.

Experimenting and Adapting.   Many questions of this type encourage students to experiment with general rhetorical strategies and to adapt these strategies to different types of discourse. These questions, some of which refer to reading passages provided by the instructor, help students develop an awareness of the many choices—voice, style, tone—involved in taking a particular rhetorical stance:

Take an issue which you know a lot about and argue for or against it in the most *unauthoritative* voice you can.

"Translate" some fine writing into bureaucratese, as George Orwell does with the following biblical passage. Then reflect on what makes the writing good in one passage and bad in the other.

I returned and saw under the sun, that the race is not to the swift, nor the battle to the strong, neither yet bread to the wise, nor yet riches to men of understanding, nor yet favor to men of skill; but time and chance happen to them all.

Objective consideration of contemporary phenomena compels the conclusion that success or failure in competitive activities exhibits no tendency to be commensurate with innate capacity, but that a considerable element of the unpredictable must invariably be taken into account.

Preparing to Write Formal Essays.   Some journal assignments help students prepare to write their own essays by testing ideas, practicing parts of essays, or writing mini-essays developing one basic feature of the genre. This type of journal question can be used as a supplement to the invention sequence for each Part I assignment:

Write a mini-evaluation of one of your former teachers, developing *one* reason for your evaluation. One full page should be adequate. Be sure to follow the guidelines discussed in class and outlined in Chapter 8: Justifying an Evaluation.

Write two different thesis paragraphs for the essay interpreting a story. You may want to try casting the same idea in two different ways, or you may make very different claims in each. State both of these and indicate how you are going to support each one.

Practicing Editing Skills.   Some journal questions may ask students to practice editing skills, ranging from punctuation to the use and acknowledgment of sources. You could use the Editing and Proofreading guides in each chapter applied to the students' own writing or to passages you distribute.

Make a works cited list for books used in this class, a short story in an anthology, a magazine article, and a newspaper article.

Photocopy a page from your evaluation essay and staple it to your journal entry. Then do some close editing as we did in class today. Use the Editing and Proof-reading guide to look for any problems.

Reflecting on Your Learning.   Finally, you could use the journal as a place for students to reflect on what they are learning in the course as well as in other courses. The metacognitive activities in Thinking Critically about What You Have Learned at the end of each Part I chapter could be used here or you could devise additional journal questions.

Now that midterms are over, describe how you analyzed one essay exam question you encountered. How did our review of the essay exam chapter in *The St. Martin's Guide* help?

Looking back over your other courses this term, list the kinds of writing you had to do. Then choose one kind of writing and describe its basic features.

You will no doubt think of still other ways of using a journal to complement *The St. Martin's Guide.*

PRESENTING AND DISCUSSING READINGS

Reading plays a very important role in a writing course. We encourage students to read *as writers*—to examine not only the content of a text but also various features and strategies they can adapt for use in their own writing. We also want them to learn to read *with a critical eye*—to question rather than accept unsupported assertions, to differentiate between fact and opinion, to evaluate arguments, and to examine assumptions. Chapter 12 presents an array of critical reading strategies, and each Part I chapter follows readings with questions on Connecting to Culture and Experience and Analyzing Writing Strategies. These could be used as the basis for small-group or whole-class discussion. We emphasize that our courses are discussion seminars and that we expect every student to participate in the discussions.

Helping Students Prepare for Successful Discussions

In order for discussions of the readings to succeed, we try to ensure not only that students have done the reading carefully but also that they are prepared to discuss it, with us and with each other. Instructors can use many different strategies both for ensuring that students do the reading in the first place and for guiding them to get the most out of class discussions.

Encouraging Students to Do the Reading.   Simply letting students know on the syllabus that they will be expected to answer journal questions and participate in discussions (and that they will be evaluated on their journals and class participation) is enough to motivate most students, most of the time. However, many instructors find it worthwhile to take further measures to ensure that all of the students do all of the reading.

Nearly all instructors assign journal questions on the readings as homework, and then call on several students at random to read their journal entries aloud at the beginning of the class. Some instructors use *in-class* journal questions on the readings as quizzes. Since the topics of these questions are not announced in advance, students know that they must complete the assigned reading in order to be prepared. You could use an informal grading system to arrive at a "preparation grade" for the course.

Helping Students Get the Most out of the Reading.   Experienced writing teachers know that asking the right questions about reading can encourage close reading. Carefully planned journal questions—questions that do not merely test students' comprehension but ask students to read critically and to examine the text's rhetorical features and strategies—help students to read carefully and allow them to make thoughtful contributions to classroom discussion. The discussion and analysis questions which follow each reading in Part I of *The St. Martin's Guide* are questions of this type.

Although annotation is required in only one of our assignments (Chapter 10: Interpreting Stories), students find it an indispensable technique for critical reading. Annotating is particularly useful in preparing students for discussions of the readings, as their annotations serve to remind them in the classroom of the features and patterns they note as they read each piece. Annotating is illustrated in Chapter 12: A Catalog of Reading Strategies and in the Writer at Work section at the end of Chapter 10.

Many instructors ask students to read some texts not once but several times, annotating for different features each time. They prepare students to annotate by listing and discussing these features. For instance, students might annotate first for structure and organization, then for the basic features of the genre, and finally to note the writer's particular rhetorical strategies.

Because the idea of annotation is likely to be new to most students, many instructors find it helpful to prepare students for making their own annotations by providing a sample of a thoroughly annotated text or by talking students through a page of text as they annotate it. It is also a good idea to collect students' earliest tries at annotation in order to monitor and encourage their attempts.

Chapter 12 also offers many other strategies for critical reading you can use as the basis for class discussion, such as looking for oppositions, reflecting on challenges to your beliefs, and evaluating the reasoning or credibility.

Facilitating Successful Classroom Discussions

Remind students of the connection between the reading and their own writing. To begin, you could call on several students to read their answers to journal questions, or you can pair students up to work on different parts of the reading and then report their findings to the class. The aim is to involve them from the start in an active examination of the text and also to engage them in collaboration of some kind. We find the best way to do this is to ask "real" questions that require close analysis, for example, of how a particular strategy works or falls short. (Here you can rely on Analyzing Writing Strategies following each reading.)

To complete the discussion, ask students to summarize the main things they have learned. Some instructors go around the room, asking students to make a brief comment, pointing to a strategy they could imagine trying in their own writing or, adversely, something they will try to avoid doing. They might also compare and contrast different readings in the chapter. A principal aim of discussion of reading in a writing course, we think, is to show students that they can write as effectively as—or even more effectively than—the professional and student writers they're reading.

Some Practical Considerations

Give up on discussions that don't seem to be going anywhere or that aren't engaging most of the students. Do not stay on a single point (or a single essay) for too long. Instead, keep the pace up so that students stay attentive.

Try to involve every student in every discussion so that a few students are not doing all the talking. Many students are somewhat shy about speaking in class, so involving them may take some special effort on your part. One way to elicit a spoken response from even the shyest of students is to ask a simple, low-key question such as "What is memorable about the piece?" Most students should be able to answer this question on the spot, and they can be encouraged to speculate about what makes the piece memorable.

Many instructors find that group activities are a good way of getting students involved in discussions. Some instructors assign each essay in a chapter to a group of three or four students and ask each group to annotate the essay, either for a set of features or for a single feature. Each group then leads the discussion of its essay, beginning by reporting its observations to the rest of the class. This type of activity is particularly useful for involving students in discussion: The students in the audience are aware that they, too, will have to lead the class discussion, and this awareness makes them more likely to contribute.

SETTING UP COLLABORATIVE LEARNING GROUPS

There is a growing interest—and an expanding literature—in collaborative writing and learning. For twenty years or more in the schools there has been serious experimentation with collaborative learning indicating that students learn more through carefully planned small-group activities.

Collaborative learning has always been central, of course, to writing-workshop courses and to any composition course where students discuss work in progress. For quite a while now, experienced, informed writing instructors have seen themselves as collaborators with students to improve their composing, rather than as error sleuths or test givers or even as evaluators.

And there is new interest within composition studies in collaborative *writing*—those occasions in academia, business, and the professions when two or more writers collaborate to produce a single piece of writing. Several of the writing assignments in Part I lend themselves very well to collaboration. Explaining concepts (Chapter 5), especially if based on research, works well, but writing profiles (Chapter 4) seems to require such a strong vision to put together all the information and impressions that it is harder to bring off effectively. Any of the argument chapters—6 through 10—could be used. Collaborating on the position paper would be especially challenging if students' views on the issue were opposed. The proposal is the most obvious choice and the one written collaboratively most often outside the classroom.

Collaborative Learning Assignments

We sometimes ask students to meet in small groups *outside of class* to discuss *readings* and either plan an oral report or complete tasks we pose. These meetings are occasions primarily for rereading and talking, though some writing usually results as well. We sometimes talk about these groups as collaborative *reading* groups.

Here are our two basic activities you might try:

Group Report on a Reading

Carefully read the essay assigned to your group and then meet with your group to prepare a presentation for the class. You may be asked to respond to the Connecting to Culture and Experience or Analyzing Writing Strategies tasks following the reading, or to a question posed in class.

You should expect other members of the class to be familiar with the essay you will present. Needless to say, be sure that you are familiar with the essays assigned to the other groups and prepared to participate in the discussions about these essays.

Group Evaluation of Two Readings

Your group has been assigned two readings. Carefully read the two essays before you meet with your group. Before you read, though, review the Summary of Basic Features section. Then, as you read both readings, take notes on how they fulfill the basic features of the genre. Decide on your own which reading you think is more effective and why.

Then meet with your group and discuss each person's choice. Try to arrive at a consensus. If you cannot agree, feel free to file minority and majority reports. In your report (or reports) you should explain your group's judgment and the reasons for making it.

You should expect other members of the class to be familiar with these essays. Needless to say, be sure that you are familiar with the essays assigned to the other groups and prepared to participate in the other groups' presentations of their evaluations.

You will see many possible variations on these basic activities. For example, for the evaluate-two-readings activity, you could ask groups to report on similarities and differences between the two readings rather than to argue that one is more effective than the other.

How do you arrange collaborative reading groups? As soon as possible, assign each student to a group of four. You may have one group of three or five; but five have greater difficulty in finding a common meeting time than four, and three are sometimes reduced to two and then are not really a group. If students drop out during the term, you may need to combine reduced groups. On what basis do you form these groups? Try to avoid homogeneous groupings. We recommend a mix of different genders, cultural backgrounds, age, or other factors that will ensure a heterogeneous group. You may also want to ensure a range of abilities in each group.

Give students an opportunity to meet in class to schedule a regular time to meet outside of class.

Explain to them that the collaborative discussion of readings will contribute to their success in your course and offer them general guidelines for collaboration. Their goal—at least in these two basic activities—is to prepare a brief report (five to eight minutes, depending on how many groups you have and how long your class meets) on what they learn about the readings. Tell them they must report as a *panel,* with each person contributing. Since the reports tend to sprawl, you will have to enforce time limits so all groups may report and you will have time for other activities.

CONDUCTING COMMUNITY SERVICE LEARNING PROJECTS

Another area gaining increasing interest and scholarly attention is community service learning, which involves engaging in volunteer activities outside the classroom, within a particular community, and writing with a specific public audience in mind. The advantages of involving students in community service while enrolled in composition courses are obvious. Students become involved in projects that increase their civic awareness and prepare them for future roles as engaged citizens. In addition, they gain an understanding of writing as a social act and an increased recognition of the importance of the rhetorical dimensions of specific kinds of writing.

Several of the writing assignments in Part I reflect the kind of writing that might actually engage individuals outside of the academy. These assignments are also well suited to community service, which involves students in working through real issues that affect their communities. The following assignments might include a community service component:

- Arguing a Position
- Proposing a Solution
- Justifying an Evaluation
- Speculating about Causes

Students might submit an editorial to the Op Ed page of the local newspaper or send a proposal in the form of a letter to a local official or government body. These assignments might be completed by individual students or in collaboration with other students. Students might also collaborate with individuals outside the academic setting—members of specific community groups or organizations, for example.

You might allow students to choose their own community service projects in their own neighborhoods, or you might limit your students to a specific location or arrange for your class to become involved in a specific project. For example, in a course at the University of Houston, students were limited to projects connected with a city park, which includes several museums, an outdoor theater, a public golf course, gardens, and a zoo. The writing that resulted from these projects included proposals to the director of exhibits at a children's museum and the curator of the energy wing of a science museum.

In order to make community service learning projects work, you should be sensitive to the kinds of problems students may face. Some students may have difficulty getting to a project site far from campus. Asking students to collaborate and share transportation or limiting projects to the campus community might solve this problem.

For additional information on conducting community service learning projects, see the bibliography in Part III of this manual.

CHAPTER 3

Evaluation Practices

This chapter includes some general advice about responding to student writing; assigning portfolios; responding to error; managing the paper flow and keeping records; and getting course evaluations.

GENERAL GUIDELINES FOR RESPONDING TO STUDENT WRITING

This section offers general guidelines for responding to invention work, drafts, and revisions. It opens with a discussion of the basis for response, pointing to the sources of criteria and standards within each of the writing assignment chapters (2–10) in *The St. Martin's Guide to Writing*.

The Criteria for Response

We need to consider first the basis for response. This basis comes from the writer's purpose and intended audience and from the genre constraints and possibilities of the particular writing situation. Possible purposes and stances toward readers are addressed in the Purpose and Audience discussion of each of the writing assignment chapters (2–10) in *The St. Martin's Guide to Writing*. Genre possibilities are discussed and illustrated in the Summary of Basic Features section of the same chapters. These features and their characteristic—though varied—patterning define each genre, having evolved from writers' practices over many years in particular writing situations.

Students find themselves—thanks to you and the text—in the situation, let's say, of writing about a remembered event. There are many possibilities open to them for translating this remembered experience into a vivid, memorable, coherent story. Which possibilities they grasp—that is, which features they select and the way they pattern them—depends on how they want to present themselves to particular readers.

The Summary of Basic Features in each of the writing assignment chapters provides the basis for evaluating students' work. These become criteria for responding to a draft or revision when, with the student's purpose and readers in mind, you (or other students) ask: Given his or her purpose and readers, has the writer finally realized the possibilities of this genre? Has the writer overlooked any features? How well has the writer used the features he or she has chosen? These general questions are treated in several places in each writing assignment chapter:

- *Analyzing Writing Strategies* questions following each reading
- *Testing Your Choice: A Collaborative Activity* in the Invention section
- *Setting Goals* in the Planning and Drafting section
- *Critical Reading Guide*
- *Solving the Problems* in the Revising section

They are illustrated, discussed, or experienced directly in various other places in Chapters 2–10, including the writing scenarios that open each chapter, the collaborative activities, the readings and their commentaries, and the A Writer At Work discussion that concludes each chapter.

It can be safely said that *The St. Martin's Guide to Writing* doesn't conceal its expectations of students. By the time they've worked their way through a chapter—analyzing readings, studying commentaries, reviewing basic features, completing invention—they should, if they've been at all alert, be ready to draft an essay which reflects a good understanding of the writing situation. With the help of the Critical Reading Guide, they should then be prepared to respond confidently to a draft and to comprehend any suggestions that you might offer. When they revise, the suggestions for Solving the Problems should seem almost predictable. They should, in other words, know the criteria for evaluating writing of the type they are attempting. And having come this far with them, you should be confident about responding appropriately and helpfully to their final drafts.

Principles of Response

To complement your own insights about responding to student writing from your experience as a teacher and writer, *The St. Martin's Guide* provides a clear basis for responding to student work in each of several diverse genres. This basis for response might be thought of as essential knowledge for fostering students' writing development. With this as a starting point, what principles, then, might guide an instructor's response to student writing? From long experience in the classroom and from devotion to the growing literature in composition studies, we've settled on the following principles.

- Students need response to their work at every stage of composition, not just at the revision stage. Response to a topic choice, to initial invention work, or to a first draft may be decisive in enabling the student to produce a revised essay that invites and justifies your thoughtful evaluation.
- Response at the draft stage should anticipate immediate revision and specifically encourage a student to persist through one or more revisions.
- Response to errors in grammar and usage, punctuation, and spelling should be reserved for later drafts.
- For response to lead to motivated, productive revision, it must take account of the student's purpose and audience, the particular ideas in the essay, and the constraints and possibilities of the genre or writing situation. General advice, interchangeable from one essay to the next, is usually fruitless.

- Students most of all need their teachers to be genuine *readers* of their work, not merely judges and error hunters. A readerly response helps students understand that writing is an important and irreplaceable form of interaction with others. It also helps them to imagine readers' response as they write.
- Response to drafts and revisions should be selective. Novice writers, like beginners at any complex human performance, can be overwhelmed and discouraged by too much advice.
- Students should share the responsibilities for response in a writing course. They should read and respond to one another's writing and solve problems in their own writing. The goal is for students to be able on their own to write purposefully, to imagine readers' questions or objections, to revise in order to say what they want to say as well as it can be said, and to correct errors and stylistic infelicities.

Responding at the Invention Stage

If you require students to complete all of the invention work—as we do in our programs—you may want to devote some class time to it, for coaching and response. We usually complete the first two steps in class, first listing topics and then choosing one. A whole-class effort always produces many more promising topics than students come up with on their own. Students first list some topics alone, but we then make one big list on the chalkboard from everyone. Some instructors begin evaluating topics here, pointing out both those that are problematic and those that are promising. Students also comment on the proposed topics.

Once students have chosen a topic, even a tentative one, they can always use some response. We evaluate each topic carefully at this point, helping them see the implications of a topic choice. Students will learn a great deal about the assignment from this kind of response to their topics.

For the first assignment of the term, you may also wish to schedule time for students to start exploring their topics in class. In our programs, we ask three or four students to read these invention notes aloud and then we draw them out about what they seem to be learning. Our purpose is to overcome the strangeness of systematic invention work—few students, if any, have ever done it—and to help them see what productive invention writing might look like.

Many instructors find it best to set due dates over the next week or so for the remaining stages of invention work. We may again ask a few students to read aloud certain parts or allow some class time for them to work in small groups, to talk to each other about what they are learning about their topics through their invention work. This can also be a good time for students to be analyzing chapter readings or, if that is behind them, discussing essays in *Free Falling*, the collection of student essays that accompanies *The St. Martin's Guide*. Because these essays were all written for the writing assignments in the *Guide*, they serve as trustworthy examples of the kind of writing students using our text are working to produce.

When the invention work has been completed, we think it's wise to collect it—if only for the first assignment—in order to find out whether students are getting something from it. We don't try to predict how useful a particular student's invention will turn out to be, but we know from many years of coaching and observation that the most productive invention work has an exploratory, even playful, quality. It is specific, or concrete, rather than general. It follows up on images, pushes ideas rather than letting them drop. It is sometimes digressive and fragmentary, and it is relatively lengthy. It is rarely brief or cautious, and never perfunctory. In our program, we comment briefly on students' work in these terms; and, most important, we photocopy four or five pieces that meet these criteria and discuss them with the class.

Responding at the Draft Stage

Responses at the draft stage can come in peer workshops (meeting in class or out), conferences with you, or from you in writing.

In Workshops.   The key workshop resource in *The St. Martin's Guide* is the Critical Reading Guide section in each of the writing assignment chapters (2–10). These guidelines begin by helping students prepare their drafts for a critical reader by stating their purposes and readers in writing. Then, after exchanging drafts, they can follow the guidelines in order to analyze a draft and advise the writer about possible revisions. We ask students to write out their analyses, to deepen their understanding of the draft and also to provide the writer with a record of suggestions for revision. Peer discussion tends to be especially productive after students have spent a half-hour or so doing this kind of thoughtful, written analysis, in or out of class. We generally allow fifteen or twenty minutes for student pairs to discuss what they have learned from each other.

We find that we need to prepare students to respond to one another's work. To do so, we review the Critical Reading Guide and carefully explain that writers need to know *what the reader sees* and to garner *specific suggestions for revising.*

There are countless variations on this workshop scheme, all of them with merit. Advantages we claim for our scheme are that students follow assignment-specific guidelines and write before they talk.

Our instructors usually join in a group's discussion, instead of just looking on or listening in.

In Conferences.   The key to successful conferences is to get students to prepare carefully so that when they come to see you, they can do most of the talking and take much of the responsibility for improving their drafts.

We give students a form to fill in before coming to the conference, a different form for each writing assignment. You will find specially designed forms for each of the writing assignments in *The St. Martin's Guide,* ready for you to reproduce, in Chapter 6 of this manual.

Responding at the Revision Stage

By the time students complete an essay assignment, they will have generated a good deal of writing. For instructors, the goal is to have a system of reading and responding to it that allows us to give students helpful feedback while processing the pile of student work in a reasonable amount of time.

Helping Students Organize an Assignment Package.   You need to tell students exactly what materials are to be turned in with the final, revised essay. At the beginning of the course, we give students a handout that specifies what they are to turn in for each writing assignment. We ask for the following materials:

1. *Revision:* The final, revised version of the essay, typed and proofread, with any errors neatly corrected. It should be double-spaced, typed on one side of the page only, and numbered.
2. *Thinking Critically about What You Have Learned:* Written reflections (a page each) on writing, reading, and the social dimensions of the genre; one or more of these metacognitive tasks may be assigned. In *Reflecting on Your Writing,* the students analyze their problem-solving processes in writing and revising the paper. In *Reviewing What You Learned from Reading,* the students connect what they did in the paper with what they see other writers do in their essays in that genre. In *Considering the Social Dimensions,* the students respond to one of the For Discussion questions.
3. *A List of Problems in the Draft:* From the analysis completed in the Revising section of the *Guide.*
4. *Critical Comments:* Written comments about one draft, done by a classmate. The classmate's name should be on the response.
5. *Drafts:* One or more drafts, legible and labeled with the student's name, the assignment title, and the draft number. The pages should be numbered.
6. *Invention and Planning Notes*

We also ask students to put this work together with a large paper clip rather than in a bulky file folder. We find this assignment package reduces confusion, eases our management of the large amounts of writing, and speeds the reading and response process.

Before reading the packet, you might read the student's written reflections in response to the first two metacognitive tasks: Reflecting on Your Writing and Reviewing What You Learned from Reading. The reflections on writing, with its focus on how the student identified and solved a problem in the essay, presents a self-portrait of the student as a writer. We try to applaud the student's problem-solving efforts in order to bolster the student's confidence and encourage revising. We might draw the student's attention to another problem that needs solving and invite another revision focusing on this problem.

The reflections on what was learned from reading also can be used to consolidate and reinforce what the student has learned. We usually try to acknowledge strategies the student has successfully adapted to his or her own purposes and might point to one or two other strategies in the readings that the writer could use to help solve particular problems in the essay.

Surveying the Package and Completing Records. We start by skimming to see that all the assigned writing is there and to see what the student has accomplished in the invention and drafts. The invention tends to be a good indicator of the depth and thoroughness of the revised essay, and problems in the revision can often be traced to deficiencies in invention. We try to make this connection clear to students early in the course.

We keep track of each student's performance in all the various stages of the composing process for each assignment. (You will find the record sheet later in this chapter, ready for you to reproduce.) This sheet is for our own records, and students do not see it.

The students' self-evaluation (Thinking Critically about What You Have Learned in Chapters 2–10) prompts them to reflect critically on their composing process, to think about what they have written, and to take responsibility for the decisions they have made. At its worst, such a self-evaluation will say no more than "here-it-is-I-like-it-hope-you-do-too," as the student declines the invitation to take responsibility. At its best, however, it provides the student with an account of his or her composing process, and it provides you with a critical introduction to the essay. It can also reveal the student's level of involvement with the assignment. We usually read the self-evaluation carefully.

Responding to the Revised Essay.   Plan to spend several minutes responding to the revision. We make a few comments in the margins, noting both strong and weak points in the writing, and then we add a few sentences of comments at the end, on a separate sheet of paper. You may want to keep a copy of these comments for your own records. We try to find something in the essay to praise, and we find that critical comments work best when phrased in terms of what the student might have done in the essay or should try to do in the next one. Questions are useful, too, when they lead students to think about other ways they might have addressed the problems in the paper. This approach casts the instructor in the role of adviser rather than of judge.

Rise Axelrod responds to her students' final drafts by following the Critical Reading Guide in *The St. Martin's Guide*. In doing so, she models for students the kind of written responses she expects of them in workshops.

When time is limited, you need to respond to features in the essay in order of priority. In an autobiographical essay, we begin by considering the larger rhetorical issues: what the writer has tried to accomplish in telling the story, its structure, the beginning and ending, and the pacing of the narrative. Next, we look at some particular features of the genre: the quantity and vividness of descriptive details, the writer's recollection of feelings at the time of the event or toward the person, the use of dialogue, and the proportion of narration, description, and commentary in the story. (In Chapter 6, you will find brief guidelines for responding to each of the assignments in *The St. Martin's Guide,* listing the criteria for response and some typical problems.) Finally, we comment on the writer's style, diction, and sentence structure.

We advise against commenting on everything that could be improved in a paper. An inexperienced writer can be easily overwhelmed by too much criticism and become too discouraged to work on any of the problems. Rather, we try to focus on a few of the most important things that need attention, thereby giving the student achievable goals. We follow the same policy with mechanical errors and stylistic infelicities, assuming that if we mark every transgression in a weak writer's paper, the student may be overwhelmed. Later in this chapter is a plan for dealing with students' errors.

Finally, we do not hesitate to ask a student to revise still again an essay which fails to meet minimal requirements established by the readings, commentary, and Guide to Writing in each chapter. We find that this request sets standards more effectively than a low grade.

Some General Guidelines for Responding to Revised Essays

1. Check the package to be sure that all of the required parts are there. Note missing parts and comment on parts (the invention, for example) that please or disappoint you.
2. Read the revision through quickly to get the sense of it. Is it what you assigned? Does it look approximately right?

3. Decide first whether the package needs to be returned for further work before you can evaluate it. There are several reasons why you might want the student to do some additional work before you evaluate the package:
   - The package is substantially incomplete; the invention, workshop responses, self-evaluation, or one or more drafts are missing, or perhaps only the final revision is there.
   - The final revision is not typed, or is otherwise unreadable because of printer problems, worn-out ribbons, etc.
   - The revision does not meet the rhetorical situation: It is a problem solution essay rather than a cause essay, a person essay rather than an event essay, an evaluation essay without adequate evidence from the thing being evaluated, and so on.
   - The topic does not fall within the constraints of your assignment. (For example, you might have declared dormitory problems off-limits for the problem solution essay, and yet the student wrote about a dormitory problem.)
   - The revision is seriously disorganized.
   - The revision has major problems with style, mechanics, or English usage which seriously impair a reader's comprehension.

   If you return an essay package for further work, outline your reasons briefly, and ask the student to make an appointment for a conference to discuss his or her plan for revising. You might ask the student to review the readings and the Summary of Basic Features for this essay in *The St. Martin's Guide*. Set a deadline (from one to two weeks) for resubmitting the package. You want to make it clear that although the package does not yet meet your standards, you are convinced that the student is capable of succeeding with this writing assignment. You might ask the writer to (a) start over with a new topic, (b) substantially revise an entire draft, or (c) revise only one part of a draft.

4. If the revision is ready to be evaluated, look first for the strengths in the paper. What did the student do well or at least satisfactorily? Try to comment on some aspects of the paper of which you approve.

5. Does the revision show a grasp of the specific features of its type of writing? Usually, some features are represented more successfully than others. Which ones are handled well? Which ones could have been developed more successfully?

6. Does the revision seem coherent and organized? Are the transitions from one part to the next handled smoothly? Comment on structural elements that work well or that might be improved.

7. Consider writing style. College writers struggle to develop a natural, yet authoritative style. They may write in a style that is too casual or childlike, or they may try to write a ponderous "academic" prose. Some will have a wonderful, natural voice, with appropriate modulations for different readers. You may want to comment on the essay's style, pointing to one or two specific examples from the revision if you can.

8. What about errors? We expect revised essays to have been carefully edited and proofread, but most students are just learning to identify and edit their own writing. Since even the best essays often have some sentence-level problems, we like the "minimal marking" scheme described later in this section. This scheme allows us to respond first to substantive issues and then to return the paper to the student for another round of editing. This procedure reinforces the importance of editing but puts it in its proper place at the end of the writing process.

Grading.   Some instructors do not grade individual essays, though you may wish to. One argument against grading individual essays is that a letter grade is at best a cryptic indication of performance, and that grades on individual essays can involve instructor and students in unproductive appeals and justifications. Furthermore, the risk of a low grade can discourage an inexperienced writer from taking creative chances. Of course, students need some indication of their progress before the obligatory letter grades at the end of the course, so some instructors fill out midterm progress reports for all students indicating what grades they can expect at the end of the course if they continue at their present levels of performance. This form shows students where they need to focus their attention in the remainder of the course.

At the end of the course, these instructors use a final course report form to write a response to the final essay submitted and an evaluative summary of the student's performance in the whole course. (You will find these forms, ready to reproduce, later in this chapter.) This summary, and the course grade, are based on a quick review of a student's revised essays turned in along with the revision of the final essay. Considered also are records of a student's attendance, reading journal entries, quizzes, workshop responses, and any other assigned work. The final grade is based on three criteria:

1. Whether all the assigned work has been completed in a timely fashion.
2. Whether the work has improved during the course.
3. Whether revised essays are fully realized rhetorically; that is, whether the student's revisions reveal substantial learning about the rhetorical and composing possibilities of the various genres assigned in the course.

A Computer-Based Scheme for Responding to Student Writing

The widespread use of computers has had a significant effect on writing instruction. Many students type journal responses and final drafts of their essays on computers, and increasing numbers of students use computers for all stages of their composing process. Instructors use computers for a wide variety of teaching applications, from keeping student records to preparing daily lesson plans.

There are many useful commercial software programs available, including spreadsheet programs, database programs, and even specialized educational recordkeeping packages. Unless you have several hundred students or the need for sophisticated statistical breakdowns or test-score reports, however, a basic word-processing program is all you need to keep track of student progress in a course using *The St. Martin's Guide to Writing*.

One program, Microsoft Word, has a text-formatting feature called "hidden text." This text appears on the screen, but it does not print unless you use a special "print hidden text" command. This feature can be used to screen out your personal notes from your response to the student essay. You simply format any personal notes as hidden text. These notes can then be viewed on the screen or printed out for filing. The same document can be printed out for the student, with your personal notes hidden.

Your personal notes can be used for a wide range of purposes. Here you can comment, for example, on the student's need for campus support services, or on his or her class participation or helpfulness in collaborative groups. Later, you can work these observations about the student into responses to essays or into the midterm or final evaluation: "Your usage and style are much improved in this essay. Your sessions with the peer tutors seem to have paid off." "I notice you are always prepared for this class. This should give you confidence in contributing more often to class discussions."

If your word-processing program does not have a "hidden text" feature, you can easily create two files, pasting text from one file into the other. One file would contain your response to a student's essay, and the other file would contain both your response and your private comments under "Notes to the Instructor."

When you print out the response for the student, at the same time you can print out another copy with the hidden text printed to put into the student file for later evaluation at the midterm and at the end of the course. Then when it is time to evaluate the student you will have an up-to-date file with one set of comments for each assignment. Having this hard copy is also good security against data loss in case you experience problems with your computer or the disk.

RESPONDING TO ERROR

Responding to students' errors in mechanics, usage, and punctuation is no small matter in a writing course. First, it is not easy to reduce students' errors; second, it is all too easy for efforts at reducing errors to dominate a writing course, crowding out time for reading, thinking, and composing. For some time we searched for a sensible approach to responding to error and finally, in 1984, we found one we were willing to try: a scheme for "minimal marking" developed by Richard Haswell of Washington State University. Before looking at this scheme, however, we want to outline the principles supported by the current literature on error that guided our search.

Principles

Following are some widely accepted principles for dealing with error in a first-year college writing course.

- Attention to error must not prevent students from spending most of their time reading, discussing, inventing, researching, planning, drafting, and revising extended, multiparagraph discourse. This principle holds for all students, no matter how high their initial error rate.
- Too much emphasis on error limits students' focus to local sentence problems, when they should instead be focusing most of the time on global rhetorical problems. Overattention to error makes students cautious when they need to be taking chances, both to discover something to say and to find the sentences to say it.
- Correct style and usage are more likely to be acquired through reading, writing, and revising than learned through grammar study, rules and maxims, and exercises.
- If grammatical and stylistic concepts are taught directly, they should be taught thoroughly by providing students background information, adequate definitions, diverse examples and nonexamples carefully discussed, and practice with feedback. Too often, textbook explanations of grammatical concepts are clear to students only if they already know the concepts.

- Error merits close attention only when students are editing and proofreading final drafts.
- Instruction and response to student work must ensure that students take responsibility for finding, diagnosing, and correcting their own errors. The instructor must follow up by checking these corrections and requiring still further work on unacceptable corrections. If the instructor indicates which lines or sentences contain errors and refers them to the relevant section in a handbook, students can correct most of their errors in punctuation, mechanics, and usage.
- If students analyze their errors, they will find patterns that can focus and simplify their efforts at overcoming those errors. If, for example, a student had problems with internal sentence punctuation, he or she might review appropriate handbook explanations of comma usage.
- Instruction in error-correction must be individualized. Whole-class instruction in grammar, usage, or style should occur only occasionally if at all. Students can also get help at campus writing centers and from peer-editing and tutoring teams.

These principles can guide your dealings with error even for students whose error rate is high, who speak a nonstandard dialect, or who still struggle with English as a second language. Only those students who are still in the earliest stages of learning English as a second language should require special instruction, which should be offered by ESL specialists. These principles justify heterogeneous classes for first-year college writing programs and call into question programs that track students. Where students are tracked, these principles indicate a similar pedagogy for students on different tracks.

Minimal Marking

How, in a writing class, can you observe the principles outlined above? Haswell's "minimal marking" scheme provides one defensible, workable answer. The journal article in which Haswell first reported his scheme is reprinted in the selection of readings at the end of this manual. You might want to pause now to read it.

Using Haswell's scheme to mark a student's final draft, you indicate each obvious sentence-level error (spelling, punctuation, capitalization, and usage) with a check in the margin next to the line where the error occurs. No marks are made within the text itself. Put two checks next to ones with two surface errors. (In addition to checking lines with errors, you would, of course, respond as you usually do to content, structure, and style.) Students then are responsible to find, circle, and correct the surface errors you have checked. They can do this work right on their texts or on a separate page. They then return the essays to you so that you can review the corrections and either explain errors students were unable to correct or refer them to the appropriate section of the Handbook in *The St. Martin's Guide to Writing*. Students can also work in small groups, helping one another find and correct their errors.

Not only will this system reduce the time you must spend on error, but it also enables students to do the actual work. With Haswell's scheme, students are encouraged to be responsible for their own editing, rather than relying on the instructor to "correct" their essays. Also, this kind of marking can be done quite rapidly, even on first reading. It provides an outlet for the part of our teaching brain that is dedicated to reducing error without bludgeoning students with criticism. On the other hand, it satisfies the part of the student brain which expects us to point out errors. Yet the student must identify, diagnose, and correct the error.

Some further practical considerations: We strongly recommend that you check errors in one or two paragraphs only, or on one page only—especially on papers with many errors, for instance, or if your time is limited. Bracket the portion of the essay you marked. You can schedule class time for students to complete (or at least begin) their corrections, or you can ask them to complete the corrections outside of class and return the essay at the next class meeting. The success of this scheme depends on your evaluating students' corrections and then following up in some way on each remaining error. After indicating errors that still remain, you could follow up in a number of ways:

- confer with a student, explaining the errors and helping with the corrections
- indicate by page number or correction symbol the section of the text's Handbook where the student can find an explanation of the error
- ask students to meet with another student to work together on necessary revisions

At the end of this chapter, we've included the handout that Charles Cooper gives his students on correcting sentence-level errors. You may copy and revise it to use with your own students.

Extending the Minimal-Marking System

Haswell's scheme can be extended beyond "local" errors to deal with some errors of syntax, usage, style, and even discourse features; some instructors have done so. Consider the following system:

Marginal Symbol	*Type of Error*
✓	Local error
	spelling
	punctuation
	capitalization
	usage
	diction (redundancy, unnecessary intensifier or hedge, cliché)
s	Syntactic error
	fragment
	mixed construction
	faulty predication
	dangling or misplaced modifier
	faulty parallelism
St	Style problem
	strings of prepositional phrases
	overuse of *be*
	overnominalization
	compound-noun phrases
	overuse of passive voice

Marginal Symbol	*Type of Error*
	wordy phrase
	vague or obvious statements
c	Cueing problem
	thesis not explicitly stated
	forecast missing or incomplete
	transition faulty or missing
	paragraphing needed or unnecessary

You could limit your marking initially to local errors, or you might find your students ready at the beginning of the course to correct both local and syntactic errors. Depending on your students and the progress of the course, you might later want to mark style or cueing problems. All local, syntactic, and stylistic errors listed above are illustrated and explained in *The St. Martin's Guide*'s Handbook. There is even a specific correction symbol provided, in the Handbook section and on a correction chart on the inside back cover, that you could use for marking each of these errors. Students can find information about each cueing strategy in Chapter 13: Cueing the Reader; and, of course, these cueing strategies are illustrated in discourse-specific ways in each of the writing assignment chapters (2–10).

Other Ways of Involving Students

The minimal-marking scheme lends itself well to group work. Groups might meet before the final revision is due and read one another's essays, using Haswell's scheme to mark surface errors they find. They could then work individually to correct the errors, consulting with other students when they encounter difficulty detecting or correcting errors. If they are pressed for time, you might allow some class time for this activity on the day revisions are due, allowing students to correct surface errors neatly on their final revisions before turning them in. Groups might also discuss the error patterns typical of each group member and help one another see how to avoid these errors. Group work of this sort will not only encourage students to take more responsibility for their own writing, it will reduce the number of surface errors you ultimately have to deal with.

One caution: Students will miss many errors and be unable to categorize many errors they do identify. For this reason, at first we may do this work for them. (See Charles Cooper's plan at the end of this chapter.)

There are ways to bring discussion of error and style into the classroom, should you want to make time for it. Nancy Marks of Wright State University, for example, circulates transparencies in class and asks students to copy down any sentences from their essays where they suspect problems in conventions and style. Marks then projects the transparencies overhead and discusses the sentences with the whole class. Karen Hollis occasionally photocopies and hands out pages with stylistic problems from some of her students' revised essays, being careful that students' names not appear on the pages. Students then work in small groups to evaluate the style in one page of writing. Each group presents its findings to the class, pointing out stylistic problems and describing how revisions might be made.

MANAGING THE PAPER FLOW AND KEEPING RECORDS

In multistrand programs, instructors are often inundated with paper and become uncertain about which students have done what—and when. We have come to rely on two simple plans for managing the flow of paper and keeping a timely record of students' work. You can either record students' work after they have completed the entire assignment or record students' work as they move through the process.

Recording Work upon Completion of an Assignment

When students' final revisions are due, you can ask them to give you the revision as part of a package that includes all their work throughout the process on the assignment. Using the Student Record Form at the end of the chapter, you can easily record and evaluate briefly all stages of a student's work on one page.

Make one copy of the form for each student. With each student's name filled in on a form and the forms alphabetized in a folder, you are ready to keep exact records of a large stack of student work. The form is only for your records. Students need not see it.

You could also photocopy your written evaluation of each essay draft and revision and attach it to the form.

Recording Each Stage of the Process

The main advantage for students when you log each stage of their work as they complete it is that it helps to pace their work through the process and keeps them on schedule. Because you are seeing each stage of their work, they are more likely to remain engaged over several days instead of rushing to do it all at the end.

Here is advice from one instructor, M. A. Syverson, on keeping the paper traffic organized. For each of her classes, she sets up four file folders and keeps a checklist of work turned in (one for each essay assignment) and a checklist of journal entries turned in. (Both checklists are at the end of the chapter, ready to photocopy.) Here is Syverson's personal account.

Folder 1: Instructor's Lesson Plan. One file folder holds my lesson plans and notes. I use a colored folder to distinguish it from the other folders. I keep my lesson plan in reverse chronological order, with the current day's plan on top, and previous plans below it. On the inside front cover of this file folder, I staple two forms: the current essay's Checklist of Work Turned In on top, and under this, the Checklist of Journal Entries Turned In. When I assign the next essay, I simply staple the new Checklist of Work Turned In on top. In this way, I am always prepared to answer students' questions about which journals, drafts, or invention writings they are missing, to record late work as it is turned in, and to question late or missing work with students in class.

If you use a form for attendance, you might staple this form to the back cover of the lesson-plan folder.

Folder 2: Student Journal Entries to Be Checked. When students turn in their journal entries—I see them weekly—I put them alphabetically into this folder until I have a chance to check them off and respond to them.

Folder 3: Student Journal Entries to Be Returned. After I have checked journals off on the Checklist of Journal Entries Turned In and responded to them, I place them alphabetically in this folder until I can return them to students.

Folder 4: Student Work to Be Checked. It collects each stage of students' writing-process work for essay assignments. As each set of invention-writing or each draft is due for a conference or in-class workshop, I take it up, quickly alphabetize it, and place it in this folder until I can log it in on the Checklist of Work Turned In. I can sometimes find time to do this while students work in small groups. Once I have logged the work in, I return it to the students. If it is not possible to log the work in during class, I return it at the next class meeting or make arrangements for students to pick it up in the office the next day.

I must return each stage of work as quickly as possible. In fact, students need to have the work back to go on to the next stage. If you find it difficult to arrange quick returns, you could ask students to make you a photocopy of each stage of their work. You could then log completion of each stage and return only problematic work and recycle the rest since you will see it all again when the final package of work comes in on completion of the assignment.

I like to keep students on track by seeing each phase of the work as it is completed, even when I do not have time to review or respond to each stage of work. Where the invention work is missing or much too thin, for example, I can ask the student to complete it before beginning the first draft. This also gives me a chance to identify problem topics or students who might need extra campus support services.

Rationale.   Syverson's recordkeeping system may seem to involve a great deal of work, but it actually simplifies the task of keeping track of student work while allowing you to monitor and encourage it. It shows students that you are seriously interested in their progress and that you expect them to be responsible for keeping current with the work. It reduces the likelihood that students will fall behind, struggle halfheartedly to catch up, and become discouraged and finally overwhelmed. It will also reduce the number of student essays that are wide of the mark or based on an inappropriate topic choice, a major cause of instructor depression and burnout.

There are still other reasons for keeping such a comprehensive ongoing record of student work. Some students do not at first take seriously in-class workshops, knowing that their work will probably be seen only by the members of their workshop group. They may show up without a draft, or with a handful of notes in lieu of a draft, or with a page and a half of very skimpy writing. They may have little experience with the process of drafting, receiving feedback, and revising their essays several times, and it is most unlikely that they have ever done systematic invention work. Or they may not realize that drafts are a necessary part of the course work. Simply by taking up the invention and drafts, you give student writers the clear message that they are responsible for participating fully in *The St. Martin's Guide* writing assignments.

You can catch obvious problems by skimming the work or reading parts selectively. To get students off to a good start, you might briefly respond to all stages of the first assignment and then spend much less time with subsequent assignments. With a small student load or in a slow-moving course, you might, of course, respond more comprehensively to various stages of work.

Another reason for monitoring each stage of work is to identify students who need more intensive help with their writing—additional conferences, referral to the writing center or to language tutors, and so on. It is important to recognize any special problems students face as early as possible in the course and with each separate assignment.

Student writers in upper-division writing courses might not need or want this much attention to each phase of the writing process. First-year students, however, often need help sustaining work on unfamiliar and challenging writing tasks.

GETTING COURSE EVALUATIONS

Students' responses to your course may at first seem to have little to do with responses to their work. Certainly, getting their assessment of the course is a different order of assessment from responding to a draft. And yet, given the highly interactive, social nature of writing instruction, given the extent to which feelings and perceptions are involved, it is easy to make the case that getting students to assess the course must be part of a comprehensive evaluation scheme for a writing course. To pace a course appropriately, tap misperceptions, reduce confusion, clarify and justify certain activities (especially centrally important evaluation activities), you have to know what students are thinking. If students' expectations of conferences are different from yours, for instance, their surprise and disappointment will interfere with learning and revision. If workshops are going less well than you think, students will be frustrated and their eagerness to revise will be blunted. If students remain skeptical about systematic invention, they will treat it perfunctorily and their drafts will be thin. Finding out about any such perceptions, you can readily make explanations or adjustments. Analyzed judiciously, students' perceptions can improve your teaching and increase students' satisfaction and achievement.

End-of-course evaluation is quite common and may be part of some plan to evaluate instructors. Periodic mid-course evaluation is unfortunately less common, even though it can greatly improve a course-in-progress.

Collecting Mid-Course Evaluations

Collecting students' evaluations during the course can alert you to problems, questions, and confusion. There are various ways of getting their opinions: with brief index-card responses in class, with letters to you, and with journal entries.

Index-Card Responses.   Take a handful of index cards to class and give students two or three minutes to respond anonymously to a question you pose. You might simply ask them to write one question they have about the course or to identify one problem or concern they have. Or you can focus them on some specific aspect, asking them to write a question or identify a concern or problem related to the writing assignment they are working on; to the invention sequence, revision plan, or group inquiry activities found in their textbook; to writing workshops or conferences; to grading policy; and so on.

Try this strategy at least once or twice a month, and you can gain valuable information about both your students and your course. Most important, it ensures that you regularly assess all students' perceptions of your course, especially the perceptions of quiet and undemanding students. If you take responses at the beginning of a class meeting, you can respond during class (perhaps after reviewing the cards while students are engaged in small-group work). Most instructors get the responses at the end of class, however. They analyze and classify the responses later and then address selected concerns at the next class meeting. You might want to address easy-to-answer concerns first. You could respond humorously to trivial answers. You could also ask the *class* to propose solutions. All of this need not take more than ten or fifteen minutes. Your goal is to respond to concerns and answer questions and, most important, to do so in a way that shows your interest in students' perceptions and your respect for their concerns. You want to ensure that they will continue to take this evaluation opportunity seriously.

Letters.   Paul Hunter of North Lake College in Irving, Texas, asks students to write him letters, which he then reads from and comments on in class. Here is how he describes and justifies this requirement:

> From time to time during the semester, I'll ask my writing students to compose an informal, personal letter to me; each student's purpose is to explain how well he or she is progressing through the program and what parts of the program are especially daunting or vague.
>
> Though I never grade, correct, or return letters, I do circle parts of them, read them in class, and respond to whatever issues have been raised. Not only do these discussions help a student to see that other students share one of his or her concerns, the letters allow me an opportunity to point out to students that they and their classmates can—and do— write clearly and effectively. [Hunter, Paul. "What works for me." *Teaching English in the Two-Year College,* 9, 105]

Journal Entries.   When students write regularly in a course journal in which at least some of the entries are assigned by the instructor, one strand of work can inquire occasionally into students' perceptions of the course. Here is one classroom-tested set of such journal assignments:

1. What has most surprised you so far about this course? Account for your surprise. (This question and the next two are asked early in a course.)
2. What has most pleased you so far about this course? Most disappointed you? Account for your pleasure and disappointment.
3. How is this course different from your high school English courses, and how is it similar to them?
4. How is this course influencing your reading and writing in your other courses? Give specific examples.
5. How are your reading and writing changing as a result of this course? Give specific examples.
6. We are now at the halfway point in the course. What are you most pleased with about your development as a reader and writer? What are your goals for the second half of the course?
7. What one thing could I do to make the course more satisfying for you? What one thing could you do? Explain why these changes could be important for you.

Notice that these assignments deflect personal evaluations of other students and of you and invite frank assessments of progress, problems with assignments or materials, misunderstandings, special insights, frustrations.

Collecting and Analyzing End-of-Course Evaluations

Your program or department may give the same end-of-course questionnaire to students in all classes, and it may tell you everything you want to know about how students perceived your course. If not, you can easily devise your own end-of-course questionnaire.

Brief, written answers to questions you pose can tell you how students perceived your course and, most important, give you information that can help you improve the course the next time you teach it.

You can ask relatively open questions:

1. What were the most valuable components of the class to you? What were the least valuable? Why?
2. Has your writing improved? If so, how? Give me at least two or three *specific examples*. Do you feel more self-confidence as a writer because of this course? If so, exactly how?
3. In what way was I most helpful? Is there anything you would have liked me to do differently? What?
4. What one change would improve this course the most?
5. What should we have done more of? Less of?

Or you can ask questions about specific features of the course, perhaps new or problematic ones:

1. How would you evaluate the success of the in-class workshops in helping you improve your writing? Did you feel that you got and gave valuable responses?
2. Tell me about the most and least satisfying aspects of your conference with me.
3. How did your participation in the outside-of-class collaborative groups improve your work in this course? *Give specific examples*. Did you learn anything in the group that you could not have learned on your own? Tell me what, specifically. What problems did you encounter in your group? What might I have done to enable the groups to be more productive?

You can learn most from students' answers to questions like these—after you have basked in the flattery and praise, of course—if you carefully analyze all of the answers to one question at a time. Read with pencil in hand, making lists and notes, and perhaps tallying the frequency with which certain items are mentioned or opinions expressed on certain issues. You want to get beyond your general impressions in order to dig out specific information that may be useful to you next time you teach the course.

Use students' comments judiciously. Your goal is not to be the best-loved or most popular writing instructor in your program. Students are not experts in discourse theory and writing pedagogy. They lack your experience as a writer. They sometimes misperceive. Nevertheless, students' comments should be taken very seriously, as one essential piece of information about your teaching. Even their misperceptions are worth pondering.

MIDTERM PROGRESS REPORT

Student _____ Course _____

Instructor _____ Section _____

Date _____ Term _____

QUANTITY OF WORK Has the student completed all assignments?

Invention _____ Journal Entries _____

Drafts & Revisions _____ Quizzes _____

Workshop Responses _____ Revision Plans _____

Self-Evaluations _____ Attendance _____

QUALITY OF WORK To what extent has the student:

Used the Guide to Writing creatively? _____

Revised drafts substantially? _____

Given helpful workshop responses? _____

Written perceptive self-evaluations? _____

Edited and proofread carefully? _____

Used the journal productively? _____

Participated in class discussions? _____

These areas need special attention in the remainder of the course:

MIDTERM GRADE: _____

FINAL COURSE REPORT

Student _____   Course _____

Instructor _____   Section _____

Date _____   Term _____

Remarks on FINAL ESSAY _____

_____

_____

_____

_____

_____

_____

_____

Remarks on WHOLE COURSE _____

_____

_____

_____

_____

_____

_____

_____

_____

_____

FINAL GRADE: _____

CORRECTING SENTENCE-LEVEL ERRORS IN REVISIONS

When I read your revised essay, I will first read for your ideas, logic, and use of sources, and I will evaluate in writing what you have accomplished. Then, I will mark off a section of your essay—a paragraph, a page, sometimes more—and analyze it closely for sentence-level errors. Like a newspaper or book editor, I will look for all the places where you have not observed the conventions of standard edited English.

I will indicate any line in which there is a sentence-level error by putting a check in the margin. Two checks indicate two errors. I will also underline the error itself, and I may code one or more errors so that you can find information about them in the Handbook at the back of *The St. Martin's Guide to Writing.* The code will lead you to the page that will give you information about how to correct the error you have made.

After you have corrected all of your errors, I will check them.

Here is what you do:

1. Number each error.
2. With the help of the Handbook, identify each error and decide how to correct it.
3. On a separate piece of paper, rewrite every sentence in which there is an error. Do not write out just part of the sentence. *Write out the entire sentence,* unless you are correcting a misspelling.
4. Number your new sentences so that they correspond to the numbered errors.

If you cannot identify an error or figure out how to correct it, catch me after class or come to see me during my office hours.

This approach to error provides a highly efficient way for you to reduce errors in your writing. It is efficient for you and for me: I mark every error in just a small part of your writing instead of unsystematically marking an occasional error in all of your writing, and you work only on your own errors and learn quickly how to use a writer's handbook. Also, we do not waste time going over errors some of your classmates made but you did not make. You come to recognize the kinds of errors you make and learn ways to correct them. Most important, by correcting your own errors you learn how to avoid them.

As a college student, you must learn as quickly as possible how to observe the conventions of standard edited English. When you are inventing and drafting, you need not be overly concerned with conventions. However, when you have revised an essay and are ready to present it as your best work, you must attend carefully to conventions.

STUDENT RECORD FORM

Course _____

Section _____

Student _____

Midterm grade _____   Final grade _____

Assignment	Topic	Invention	Drafts	Critical Comments by	Revision Plan	Revision	Self-Evaluation

CHECKLIST OF WORK TURNED IN

	Invention	First Draft	Second Draft	Third Draft	Revision Plan	Final	Self-Evaluation	Further Revision	Workshop Response
Due date →									
Students' names:									

CHECKLIST OF JOURNAL ENTRIES TURNED IN

WEEK:	1	2	3	4	5	6	7	8	9	10	11	12	13	14
Students' names:														

CHAPTER 4

Assessment Practices

EVALUATING ACHIEVEMENT WITH PORTFOLIOS

Portfolio assessment deserves serious consideration in any writing program. More and more instructors and programs are assigning portfolios because they involve students in evaluating their own work and reflecting on their learning. Portfolios invite continuing collaboration among students and instructors with the goal of enabling each student to do his or her own best work. Instead of grading separate exercises or essays, the instructor focuses on helping students revise their work. The student then selects the best of this work for inclusion in a portfolio, usually at the end of the course. The student must justify the selections and also use the portfolio as an occasion to reflect on his or her learning and achievement during the course. Often the course grade is based on the entire portfolio.

In many sections of freshman composition at the University of Houston, where individual essays are graded, portfolios make up a large percentage of the students' final grades. Students are required to choose two essays to revise a second time. These revisions, along with a reflective essay (outlined in Chapter 24: Assembling a Writing Portfolio) are submitted at the end of the term. Instructors evaluate the entire portfolio holistically, reading the reflective essay first. This limited use of the portfolio system reveals to the students the importance of revising and critiquing their own work and gives students an opportunity to participate in their evaluation.

Some programs use portfolios in a more limited way as a basis for cooperative grading among instructors to ensure common course standards. In these programs, the portfolio may contain only revisions of two or three essays.

In *The St. Martin's Guide to Writing,* Chapter 24: Assembling a Writing Portfolio provides students with information and guidance on preparing a portfolio. It proposes a portfolio which presents several kinds of work from across the term, work including invention, drafts, revisions, critical responses, and a further revision of at least one essay. The chapter also prompts students to justify these choices and account for problems identified and solved in the further revisions. Most important, the student is guided in reflecting on learning and achievement for the entire course.

This plan gives the portfolio far more importance than any one essay assignment.

It provides a unique learning experience which enables students to review and consolidate all that they've learned and to be evaluated on what they themselves consider their best work. They participate in the evaluation by making choices, explaining and justifying those choices, and reflecting on their own personal achievement.

For this challenging assignment to work well, students need support and time. It cannot be done hastily over the final weekend of the course. Many instructors give it a full week at least. You might wish to schedule a conference with each student to discuss choices of work to include and the plan for a further revision of one essay. Encourage students to help each other.

EVALUATING WRITING ACHIEVEMENT WITH EXAMINATIONS

Many programs use essay examinations to measure a student's level of writing competency at the college level. Often, students must pass these exit exams in order to successfully complete a first-year composition class or, in some schools, to graduate. Many schools require students to take the test during the last two weeks of the course; others recommend that they take it after a certain number of credits have been earned. Some states require that students pass a writing test; for example, the Texas Academic Skills Program, or TASP, includes a writing assessment component. Students are generally given one to three hours to complete the writing assignment.

During the exam period, students typically are required to choose one topic from a list of two to six prompts. These writing prompts range in genre and subject matter, and cover a variety of social, educational, and personal issues. Sometimes the topics are drawn from student readings assigned over the course of the term. Essays are expected to be coherent and well-developed, and to demonstrate a sound understanding of rhetorical strategies and sentence-level conventions. Students should be able to work within the time allotted for planning, drafting, and revising their essays. They should be able to proofread and correct their essays, paying special attention to errors in usage, mechanics, and spelling.

Writing tests are usually graded by two faculty members who each evaluate the exams according to a number scale—for example, 1–5 points. Each reader grades the papers according to the same standard. Those who receive a high enough combined score, for example 6 or higher (3 points from each reader), automatically pass. Those who receive a score lower than a predetermined number (for example, 4) automatically fail.

A third faculty member may be needed to determine a pass or fail if a student's grade falls in the "neutral" range. In the above example, a score of 5 is neutral and therefore must be reevaluated by the third reader. The third reader is also necessary when the two primary evaluators are split in their opinions and cannot determine a closer score. When the two scores vary too greatly (for example, a 2 and a 4), the third person makes the decision.

PREPARING YOUR STUDENTS FOR A WRITING EXAMINATION

If your students are required to pass a writing test, *The St. Martin's Guide to Writing* offers many resources that you can use to help them prepare. Typically, essay examinations allow students to choose from as few as two and as many as six writing prompts, or essay questions. Almost any writing prompt a student might encounter will call for an essay in one of the nine genres covered in Part I of *The St. Martin's Guide to Writing*. Below is a sample of representative prompts found in writing assessment tests, classified according to the assignments in Part I.

Chapter 2: Remembering Events

- Most of us have had to deal with a family crisis (the death of a loved one, a serious illness, a sudden job loss, a legal entanglement, etc.) at some time. Discuss how you helped a friend or family member to cope with a specific family crisis.
- Many families have traditional celebrations of holidays each year. Recount for your friends the most memorable of your favorite events.

Chapter 3: Remembering People

- Describe the most influential academic role model in your life.
- Describe your brother or sister to a friend or relative, explaining how important he or she has been in your development.

Chapter 4: Writing Profiles

- Write a profile of a historic landmark in your neighborhood or in a nearby city.
- Profile a person you know or with whom you are familiar, and profile him or her according to the attributes you believe make him or her a true hero.

Chapter 5: Explaining a Concept

- Unity, coherence, and support are three concepts that essays cannot do without. Write an essay explaining these three concepts and why they are important.

Chapter 6: Arguing a Position

- Defend neat people from Suzanne Britt's attack in "Neat People vs. Sloppy People."
- Would a shortened workweek help relieve joblessness in this country? Write an essay that either supports or opposes the shortened workweek. Back up your argument with relevant points and illustrations, and keep in mind that your audience is an instructor.

Chapter 7: Proposing a Solution

- Inform a representative of the transit authority about ways to improve the transportation in your city.
- Inform your counselor about how you could improve your study habits.

Chapter 8: Justifying an Evaluation

- Compare and analyze the differences between your high school teachers and your college instructors.

Chapter 9: Speculating about Causes

- Consider a current trend in today's society, such as the decline in voting or the growing popularity of "exotic" foods, and discuss its likely causes.
- As the popularity of nighttime soaps such as *Melrose Place* continues to grow, with cultlike followings, speculate on some reasons why you think daytime soap operas continue to earn a bad reputation.

The best way to use *The St. Martin's Guide* to prepare your students for a writing test is of course to make full use of all its resources as you teach each assignment. In this way, you will cover a broad range of the activities—such as writing the thesis, forecasting in the introduction, concluding the essay, adopting appropriate writing strategies, using a sufficient amount of support, and refining usage and mechanics—that students will be required to demonstrate mastery of on a typical essay exam.

In addition to the assignments in Part I, several other sections of the *Guide* teach students strategies they may need to utilize in an exam. Each chapter in Part I focuses strongly on invention and research, as well as on planning and drafting and on revising and editing. Chapters 13 through 19 and Chapter 23 focus on strategies students may find useful in writing essay examinations. For example, for questions that ask students to remember events or people, students will probably need to narrate, discussed in Chapter 14: Narrating, or describe, covered in Chapter 15: Describing. Strategies presented in Chapter 18, which focuses on Comparing and Contrasting, are particularly useful when students are asked to make an evaluation. Chapter 19: Arguing, provides help for students who are required to take a position.

Instructors should also consider incorporating Chapter 11: A Catalog of Invention Strategies, into their preparation for the exam. In Chapter 11, students have an opportunity to practice mapping, brainstorming, and outlining procedures that will help them to narrow and focus a topic for an essay. Of course, some of the strategies in the chapter may be too time-consuming to use in a short exam period; nevertheless, students will find it useful to practice them in order to refine their mental planning strategies. Chapter 13: Cueing the Reader, covers many of the skills that students will need to demonstrate on a typical essay exam, including thesis statements, well-developed paragraphs, cohesive devices, and transitions. Although it concentrates on taking essay examinations in specific disciplines, Chapter 23 also provides useful general advice on test-taking strategies.

Locating Help in the Text

The chart below lists each of the genres students might encounter on an essay exam, as well as the other chapters in the text that can help students write an essay in that genre. If your school requires an essay exam, find out the kinds of questions your students will be responding to, and then use this chart when planning your syllabus to be sure that you will cover the information your students need to succeed.

Genre	Resource
Remembering Events	Chapters 2, 11, 13, 14, 15, 23
Remembering People	Chapters 3, 11, 13, 14, 15, 23
Writing Profiles	Chapters 4, 11, 13, 15, 23
Explaining a Concept	Chapters 5, 11, 13, 16, 17, 23
Arguing a Position	Chapters 6, 11, 13, 19, 23
Proposing a Solution	Chapters 7, 11, 13, 19, 23
Justifying an Evaluation	Chapters 8, 11, 13, 18, 23
Speculating about Causes	Chapters 9, 11, 13, 19, 23
Interpreting Stories	Chapters 10, 11, 23

CHAPTER 5

Suggested Course Plans

The *St. Martin's Guide to Writing,* Fifth Edition, offers an integrated first-year writing program adaptable to the needs of students and the special interests of instructors. It combines three books in one:

- a *rhetoric* with instruction in the major forms of nonfiction prose and in the basic strategies of writing, critical thinking, and researching
- a *reader* with thirty-five selections of contemporary prose by published and student writers, each accompanied by questions to develop analytical and critical reading skills
- a *handbook* with exercises and explanations of common errors in usage, style, punctuation, and mechanics

With its comprehensive coverage, *The St. Martin's Guide* can easily serve as the sole text for a quarter or a semester or as the main text for a year.

The Short Fifth Edition of *The St. Martin's Guide* is identical in content to the complete hardcover edition, except that the Handbook section has been dropped.

OVERVIEW OF THE TEXT

The St. Martin's Guide opens with a chapter that addresses the central concerns of this book: why and how we write. This introductory chapter focuses on the writing process, describing it through writers' testimony and offering practical advice on how to manage the process. The rest of the book divides into the following parts:

Part I: Writing Activities (Chapters 2–10)

These chapters cover nine kinds of nonfiction prose—autobiography, firsthand biography, profile, explanatory paper, position paper, proposal, evaluation, causal analysis, and literary interpretation. The writing assignments are versatile, producing short or long essays, based on personal experience and observation or on library research. New to this edition are suggestions for writing essays on two thematic strands, "identity and community" and "work and career." Students focusing on one of these strands throughout the course will gain in-depth knowledge in a specific area and will likely be more intellectually engaged with their topics. Each chapter includes the following components:

- writing scenarios and illustrative academic assignments
- collaborative activities
- reading selections, each followed by questions for discussion and analysis and by a commentary
- a summary of the basic features of the kind of writing illustrated by the readings
- a writing assignment based on the kind of writing treated in the chapter
- a Guide to Writing that includes strategies for invention and research, planning and drafting, getting critical comments, and revising and editing
- a Writer at Work profile of one student's writing process
- a set of three activities to help students think about what they've learned about the writing process, about the role of reading in writing, and about the social dimensions of the kind of writing they've studied in the chapter

Part II: Critical Thinking Strategies (Chapters 11–12)

This section provides two catalogs of heuristics to complement the Guides to Writing in Part I. Under Invention, you will find visually oriented heuristics such as cubing and treeing, in addition to writing activities such as looping, dramatizing, and questioning. The critical reading strategies include annotating, summarizing, exploring the significance of figurative language, looking for patterns of opposition, evaluating the logic of an argument, and recognizing emotional manipulation.

Part III: Writing Strategies (Chapters 13–19)

This section offers methods of cueing readers (thesis statements, paragraphing, cohesive devices, and transitions) as well as strategies for narrating, describing, defining, classifying, comparing and contrasting, and arguing. These chapters include extensive illustration from professional writers. Writing exercises, ranging from a sentence to a paragraph to a whole essay, ask students either to identify and analyze these writing strategies in reading selections in Part I or to practice using a particular strategy.

Part IV: Research Strategies (Chapters 20–22)

This section presents techniques for field and library research and research on the Internet, guidance on using and acknowledging sources following both the Modern Language Association (MLA) and the American Psychological Association (APA) styles, and a sample research paper.

Part V: Writing for Assessment (Chapters 23–24)

These chapters demonstrate strategies for writing essay examinations in courses throughout the college curriculum and for assembling a portfolio of work for evaluation in a course.

Handbook (complete edition only)

This section includes explanations, examples, and exercises. The Handbook opens with the Guide to Editing and Proofreading, briefly reviews sentence structure and the parts of speech, and presents strategies for correcting usage errors, improving style, and using punctuation correctly and effectively.

TEACHING MATERIALS THAT ACCOMPANY
THE ST. MARTIN'S GUIDE

The Fifth Edition of the *Guide* is accompanied by the following ancillary materials, which we hope you'll find useful.

Free Falling and Other Student Essays, Third Edition, edited by Paul Sladky (Augusta College), a collection of essays written by students across the nation using *The St. Martin's Guide.* The ten chapters in the book correspond with those in Part I of the *Guide.* The book includes forms for you or your students to submit their writing for publication in future editions.

The St. Martin's Manual for Writing in the Disciplines, by Richard Bullock (Wright State University), is a handy reference for faculty with ideas for using writing in courses across the curriculum. Among the topics covered are designing assignments that get students writing, using informal writing activities to help students learn, assigning portfolios, and responding to student writing.

Instructor's Resource Manual. Greatly expanded from earlier editions, this book now includes a catalog of helpful advice for new instructors (by Alison M. Warriner, Sacred Heart University); guidelines on common teaching practices such as assigning journals and setting up group activities; guidelines on responding to and evaluating student writing; suggested course plans; detailed chapter plans; an annotated bibliography in composition and rhetoric; and a selection of background readings.

Who Are We? Readings in Identity and Community and Work and Career. This brief collection of thought-provoking readings on "identity," "community," "work," and "career" complements the essays in the fifth edition and gives students additional perspectives on the new thematic strands.

Grammar Exercises for The St. Martin's Guide to Writing, by Charlotte Smith of Adirondack Community College, provides opportunities for practice and review. Designed to accompany the revised handbook, the exercise booklet includes more than forty exercises and an answer key.

MicroGrade: A Teacher's Gradebook is an easy-to-use new program for tracking grades and producing progress reports. It can be used on any computer system.

SUGGESTED COURSE PLANS

The St. Martin's Guide is a versatile textbook. It enables you to organize a writing course in many different ways and with quite diverse emphases. With it, you can design a course in which students base their writing solely on personal experience or knowledge or one in which they regularly use library resources. You can emphasize critical thinking and reading skills by focusing on the reading selections and their analysis questions along with the guides for critically reading a draft. You can develop a case study course around a problem of general interest by asking students to write reflective, explanatory, and argumentative essays about the same subject. You can help novice writers to grasp the fundamentals of written English or challenge experienced writers to stretch their abilities by focusing on stylistic options. You can structure your class around lectures, discussions, workshops, or conferencing.

Here we outline a variety of course plans suitable for different students' needs and instructors' preferences. These plans are constructed around the major writing assignments in Part I. We assume instructors would integrate material in Parts II–V and the Handbook into their course plans through reading assignments, classroom activities, and exercise assignments.

Course Plans That Include the Major Types of Writing in Part I

Following are four course plans (for a single semester, a two-semester sequence, a quarter, and a two-quarter sequence). For your convenience in reviewing the course plans, here is an outline of Part I that briefly defines each chapter's assignment:

Chapter 2: Remembering Events. Students write a narrative that conveys the significance of a past event.

Chapter 3: Remembering People. Students write a portrait that shows the person's importance in their life.

Chapter 4: Writing Profiles. Students observe and then present people or activities in their community.

Chapter 5: Explaining a Concept. Students investigate a concept and explain it to their readers.

Chapter 6: Arguing a Position. Students examine an issue and present an argument to support their position.

Chapter 7: Proposing a Solution. Students analyze a problem and develop a case for their own solution.

Chapter 8: Justifying an Evaluation. Students establish criteria on which they base an evaluation of something.

Chapter 9: Speculating about Causes. Students analyze a trend or phenomenon and propose possible causes for it.

Chapter 10: Interpreting Stories. Students analyze a short story and provide evidence supporting their interpretation.

The assignments in Part I move from reflective to informative to argumentative forms of writing. The reflective essays—Chapters 2 and 3 on remembered events and people—stress the exploration of memory and feeling. Students learn to find meaning in personal experience. They also learn to present their experience so that their readers can understand its significance and possibly relate it to their own lives as well as to human experience in general.

The informative essays—Chapters 4 and 5 on the profile and the explanatory paper—shift the focus from the personal and subjective to the public and objective. Students learn to gather, analyze, and synthesize information acquired either first- or secondhand by using invention heuristics as well as field and library research strategies (Chapters 20–22). In presenting what they have learned to their readers, students learn to organize and pace the flow of information and ideas so that readers' interest is aroused and sustained.

The argumentative essays—Chapters 6–10—require students not only to gather and analyze information and ideas but to deliberate upon them and to present the results of their deliberation in a carefully reasoned, well-supported argument. The position paper (Chapter 6) introduces students to the special rhetorical demands of argumentation. The proposal (Chapter 7) develops the idea that arguing can be a constructive activity, one that enables groups of people to take action together to solve common problems.

Evaluation, speculation about causes, and literary interpretation expand students' reasoning skills and audience awareness. Evaluation (Chapter 8) establishes in students' minds the need to build a case on shared assumptions and principles. Speculating about possible causes (Chapter 9) involves students in the special logical problems of determining causality. Literary interpretation (Chapter 10) engages students in the challenging task of interpreting stories and finding textual evidence to support their theses.

Any of the informative and argumentative essays in Part I can be used as the basis of a library-research paper project, large or small. Several documented essays are presented and discussed.

Single-Semester Course Plan

This plan is designed for a fifteen-week semester and features eight different essay assignments, including a final research paper project. The following materials are also covered: thesis statement and paragraphing strategies (Chapter 13), arguing strategies (Chapter 19), information on writing essay exams (Chapter 23), and chapters on library research (Chapters 21 and 22).

Wk. 1:   Ch. 1 (Introduction) and Ch. 2 (Remembering Events)

Wk. 2:   Ch. 2 (continued)

Wk. 3:   Ch. 4 (Writing Profiles)

Wk. 4:   Ch. 4 (continued)

Wk. 5:   Ch. 5 (Explaining a Concept) and Ch. 13 (Cueing the Reader)

Wk. 6:   Ch. 5 (continued)

Wk. 7:   Ch. 23 (Essay Examinations)

Wk. 8:   Ch. 19 (Arguing)

Wk. 9:   Ch. 6 (Arguing a Position)

Wk. 10: Ch. 6 (continued)

Wk. 11: Ch. 7 (Proposing a Solution)

Wk. 12: Ch. 7 (continued)

Wk. 13: Ch. 21 (Library and Internet Research), Ch. 22 (Using and Acknowledging Sources), and Ch. 9 (Speculating about Causes)

Wk. 14: Ch. 9 (continued)

Wk. 15: Ch. 9 (continued)

Two-Semester Course Plan

This two-semester plan allows you to supplement the Part I essays with writing assignments (the exercises specified) from Part III. The first semester introduces a range of writing strategies, moving from reflective to informative writing and concluding with a research paper project. The second semester opens with the strategy of arguing (Chapter 19) and covers the five argumentative chapters, ending with a six-week unit on interpreting literature.

First Semester

Wk. 1:	Ch. 1 (Introduction)
Wk. 2:	Ch. 14 (Narrating)
Wk. 3:	Ch. 2 (Remembering Events)
Wk. 4:	Ch. 2 (continued)
Wk. 5:	Ch. 15 (Describing)
Wk. 6:	Ch. 4 (Writing Profiles) and Ch. 20 (Field Research)
Wk. 7:	Ch. 4 (continued)
Wk. 8:	Ch. 4 (continued)
Wk. 9:	Ch. 13 (Cueing the Reader: selected exercises)
Wk. 10:	Ch. 16 (Defining: selected exercises)
Wk. 11:	Ch. 17 (Classifying: selected exercises)
Wk. 12:	Ch. 18 (Comparing and Contrasting: selected exercises)
Wk. 13:	Ch. 5 (Explaining a Concept) plus Ch. 21 (Library and Internet Research) and 22 (Using and Acknowledging Sources)
Wk. 14:	Ch. 5 (continued)
Wk. 15:	Ch. 5 (continued)

Second Semester

Wk. 1:	Ch. 19 (Arguing)
Wk. 2:	Ch. 6 (Arguing a Position)
Wk. 3:	Ch. 6 (continued)
Wk. 4:	Ch. 6 (continued)
Wk. 5:	Ch. 7 (Proposing a Solution)
Wk. 6:	Ch. 7 (continued)
Wk. 7:	Ch. 8 (Justifying an Evaluation)
Wk. 8:	Ch. 8 (continued)
Wk. 9:	Ch. 9 (Speculating about Causes)
Wk. 10:	Ch. 9 (continued)
Wk. 11:	Ch. 9 (continued)
Wk. 12:	Ch. 10 (Interpreting Stories)
Wk. 13:	Ch. 10 (continued)
Wk. 14:	Ch. 10 (continued)
Wk. 15:	Ch. 10 (continued)

Single-Quarter Course Plan

This plan, designed for a ten-week quarter, includes five assignments—one reflective, one informational, and three argumentative essays. Other chapters can, of course, be substituted and a particular kind of writing (reflective, for example) could be eliminated altogether.

Wk. 1:   Ch. 1 (Introduction) and Ch. 2 (Remembering Events)
Wk. 2:   Ch. 2 (continued)
Wk. 3:   Ch. 5 (Explaining a Concept) and Ch. 13 (Cueing the Reader)
Wk. 4:   Ch. 5 (continued)
Wk. 5:   Ch. 6 (Arguing a Position)
Wk. 6:   Ch. 6 (continued)
Wk. 7:   Ch. 8 (Justifying an Evaluation)
Wk. 8:   Ch. 8 (continued)
Wk. 9:   Ch. 10 (Interpreting Stories)
Wk. 10:   Ch. 10 (continued)

Two-Quarter Course Plan

In this plan, the first quarter covers reflective and informational writing concluding with a research paper project, and the second quarter treats argumentation.

First Quarter

Wk. 1:   Ch. 1 (Introduction)
Wk. 2:   Ch. 14 (Narrating) and Ch. 2 (Remembering Events)
Wk. 3:   Ch. 14 and 2 (continued)
Wk. 4:   Ch. 15 (Describing) and Ch. 4 (Writing Profiles)
Wk. 5:   Ch. 15 and 4 (continued)
Wk. 6:   Ch. 13 (Cueing the Reader)
Wk. 7:   Ch. 16 (Defining) and Ch. 5 (Explaining a Concept)
Wk. 8:   Ch. 5 (continued) plus Ch. 21 (Library and Internet Research) and Ch. 22 (Using and Acknowledging Sources)
Wk. 9:   Ch. 5 (continued) plus Ch. 17 (Classifying) and Ch. 18 (Comparing and Contrasting)
Wk. 10:   Ch. 5 (continued)

Second Quarter

Wk. 1:   Ch. 19 (Arguing) and Ch. 6 (Arguing a Position)
Wk. 2:   Ch. 6 (continued)
Wk. 3:   Ch. 7 (Proposing a Solution)
Wk. 4:   Ch. 7 (continued)

Wk. 5:   Ch. 8 (Justifying an Evaluation)

Wk. 6:   Ch. 8 (continued)

Wk. 7:   Ch. 9 (Speculating about Causes)

Wk. 8:   Ch. 9 (continued)

Wk. 9:   Ch. 10 (Interpreting Stories)

Wk. 10: Ch. 10 (continued)

Course Plan Based on Personal Experience Writing

This plan calls for writing based solely on memory and firsthand observation. Students begin by writing about past experience together with practice narrating and describing. The explanatory paper draws on information students are currently learning in their other classes, and the proposal invites them to solve problems facing groups to which they belong. The course concludes with the profile and a research paper based on field research techniques.

Wk. 1:   Ch. 1 (Introduction)

Wk. 2:   Ch. 14 (Narrating)

Wk. 3:   Ch. 2 (Remembering Events)

Wk. 4:   Ch. 2 (continued)

Wk. 5:   Ch. 15 (Describing)

Wk. 6:   Ch. 3 (Remembering People)

Wk. 7:   Ch. 3 (continued)

Wk. 8:   Ch. 13 (Cueing the Reader)

Wk. 9:   Ch. 16 (Defining)

Wk. 10: Ch. 5 (Explaining a Concept)

Wk. 11: Ch. 5 (continued)

Wk. 12: Ch. 7 (Proposing a Solution)

Wk. 13: Ch. 7 (continued)

Wk. 14: Ch. 4 (Writing Profiles) and Ch. 20 (Field Research)

Wk. 15: Ch. 4 (continued)

Course Plan Based on Research Writing

In this plan, students do field and library research, and write informational as well as argumentative essays. The first writing activity is a profile, a field-research paper. After completing defining exercises, students write an essay defining a concept. They then write a second essay explaining a concept related to a controversial issue. They then go on to write a position paper on the controversy. A proposal, a causal analysis, and a literary interpretation finish off the argumentative writing section of the course.

Wk. 1:   Ch. 1 (Introduction) and Ch. 4 (Writing Profiles)

Wk. 2:   Ch. 4 (continued) and Ch. 20 (Field Research)

Wk. 3:   Ch. 4 (continued)

Wk. 4:   Ch. 13 (Cueing the Reader) and Ch. 16 (Defining)

Wk. 5:   Ch. 5 (Explaining a Concept)

Wk. 6:   Ch. 5 (continued) plus Ch. 21 (Library and Internet Research) and Ch. 22 (Using and Acknowledging Sources)

Wk. 7:   Ch. 19 (Arguing)

Wk. 8:   Ch. 6 (Arguing a Position)

Wk. 9:   Ch. 6 (continued)

Wk. 10: Ch. 7 (Proposing a Solution)

Wk. 11: Ch. 7 (continued)

Wk. 12: Ch. 9 (Speculating about Causes)

Wk. 13: Ch. 9 (continued)

Wk. 14: Ch. 10 (Interpreting Stories)

Wk. 15: Ch. 10 (continued)

CHAPTER 6

• Detailed Chapter Plans

Each of the nine chapters in Part I focuses on a different kind of nonfiction prose that you may have your students write. The chapters all follow the same plan:

Chapter Introduction

- The Writing Situations introduce contexts and purposes for each kind of writing.
- Writing in Your Other Courses shows illustrative academic assignments from diverse disciplines, which help students recognize that they are likely to encounter the chapter's writing situation (or genre) again both as a parallel assignment in another college course and as a strategy that will play a central role in a different kind of assignment.
- Collaborative Activities (one at the beginning of the chapter and another at the Testing Your Choice stage of invention work) enable students to rehearse the writing situation they are beginning to explore and let them try out their tentative essay plans on each other.

Readings and Accompanying Activities

- Readings, Analyzing Writing Strategies, and Commentaries indicate the range of writing strategies used to achieve various purposes for particular audiences.
- Connecting to Culture and Experience sections following each reading draw students into discussion of a main idea in the reading in terms of their own experiences.
- Considering Topics for Your Own Essay sections start students generating possible topics and speculating about how they might develop them.

Analysis of Purpose and Audience and Summary of Basic Features

- An analysis of Purpose and Audience followed by a Summary of Basic Features and the kind of prose they illustrate provides an overview of the readings.

Guide to Writing

- The Guide to Writing helps students solve the problems they encounter during the process of writing each kind of essay, beginning with Invention and Research and Planning and Drafting.

- The Critical Reading Guide helps students read each other's drafts critically and constructively.
- Revising and Editing and Proofreading leads students to revise their writing thoughtfully and systematically.

A Writer at Work

- A Writer at Work profiles one student's attempt to solve a particular writing problem.

Thinking about What You Have Learned

- Reflecting on Your Writing invites students to review their writing process and to recognize that they now have the resources to solve problems they encounter in particular kinds of writing.
- Reviewing What You Learned from Reading urges students to recognize the important role reading plays in writing, both for content and form.
- Considering the Social Dimensions of the kind of writing studied in the chapter engages students in thinking about writing as both a social/political act and a way of knowing.

In the chapter-by-chapter discussion later in this section, we will suggest ways of approaching each individual assignment. Here, we examine each of the components listed above to suggest ways of handling them in the classroom.

CHAPTER INTRODUCTION

The Writing Situations

Each chapter opens with three Writing Situations, briefly illustrating the kind of writing covered in the chapter. They are natural discussion openers illustrating a range of academic and world-of-work contexts in which each of the kinds of writing in Part I might be required. These situations also suggest the primary features of each kind of writing, features highlighted again in the readings, in the Summary of Basic Features, and throughout the Guide to Writing.

You might lead a discussion of the Writing Situations, helping students understand the special writing requirements of the rhetorical situations. Or you might divide your class into small groups of three or four, asking them to analyze the Writing Situations in order to discover their common features. Someone in each group could report to the whole class. Or you might have each group work together to invent a writing situation. The students could then read aloud these writing situations and discuss them. These classroom activities give students a sense of control over the upcoming assignment. They begin to see its constraints and possibilities. They tentatively explore topics they might pursue later. These activities might be done before students read any further in the chapter or just prior to their choosing topics of their own as they work through the Guide to Writing.

Writing in Your Other Courses

Each chapter includes three or four typical assignments from college courses across the disciplines. All of these assignments came from current academic texts or instructor's manuals. We did revise several of them to foreground aspects of the rhetorical situation, making explicit what the student is expected to know and do. Unfortunately, not all academics consistently make clear to students what is required in essay-exam questions or paper topics.

As with the chapter-opening writing situations, there is much you can do to involve students in analyzing these academic assignments:

- you can analyze one for them, emphasizing all of its thinking/writing demands, and then they can analyze another (either in small groups or as a class)
- you can ask each student to find another assignment in a textbook in another course or to construct a likely one based on information in the text

A Collaborative Activity

A Collaborative Activity early in each chapter engages students immediately in an interactive, oral rehearsal of the situation they will encounter when they write the chapter's essay assignment.

You'll notice that each collaborative activity divides distinctly into two parts: first, the rehearsal of the writing situation and, second, a reflection on what happened and what students learned. You may have to help students make this shift. The whole activity need not take more than twenty minutes or so. Because students *experience* the writing situation early in the chapter, we have found they are much more interested in the readings and questions. It starts them into a chapter in a surprisingly productive way. Don't skip this activity!

READINGS AND ACCOMPANYING ACTIVITIES

In each of the chapters of Part I, there are four or five short readings illustrating the kind of writing that the chapter presents. Some of the readings are complete essays, while others are edited pieces. Most are by recognized authors, but we have included in each set one essay written by a college freshman using earlier versions of this book. At the end of each chapter in *A Writer at Work*, we include part of the writing process (invention, draft, or revision) of one of these student essays.

Each of the readings is followed by these sections:

- Connecting to Culture and Experience: a topic for small-group or whole-class discussion of an idea in the reading
- Analyzing Writing Strategies: two or three questions for analysis requiring close reading
- Considering Topics for Your Own Essay: suggestions for topics students can consider writing about
- Commentary: our comments on the reading, pointing out noteworthy features, without answering any of the questions in the Analyzing Writing Strategies section

As a set, the Commentary sections present all of the rhetorical concepts students need to understand and produce the kind of writing treated in the chapter. Moreover, the Commentary and Analyzing Writing Strategies sections make cross-references to specific writing strategies discussed and illustrated in Part III of the *Guide*.

The following chart indicates some of the Connecting to Culture and Experience and Considering Topics for Your Own Essay sections in the chapters in Part I that are particularly useful for generating ideas about the thematic strands "identity and community" and "work and career."

	Identity and Community	*Work and Career*
2. Events	Dillard: Connecting	
3. People	Angelou: Considering	
4. Profile	"Soup": Connecting	"Soup": Connecting
5. Explanation	Toufexis: Connecting	Castro: Connecting; Considering
		Passell: Considering
7. Proposal		Frankel: Considering
8. Evaluation	Rafferty: Connecting	Etzioni: Connecting; Considering
	Romano: Connecting	
9. Cause	Berger: Connecting	
	Putnam: Connecting	

Readings

We have selected the readings carefully to represent a variety of examples of each kind of writing. They illustrate the full range of features and most of the strategies that characterize the type of writing. The readings in each chapter, therefore, work together as a set, and we try to assign as many of them as we can.

The purpose of the readings is to introduce writers to each kind of writing, showing them how various good writing of that kind can look, before they begin their own essays. Novice writers may be encouraged by seeing that other students have trod the way before them and used earlier versions of this book to learn to write.

Readings play an important role in each chapter of this book because we believe that writers benefit from studying good professional writing. We do *not* prescribe the readings as models for students to imitate but as examples of the many possible directions in which they can take their own writing. A few carefully chosen readings allow us to demonstrate some of the choices available to writers and also to point out the basic features of the type of writing as they appear in each of the readings. We can show students how the readings differ and also what they have in common. We believe that, used carefully, readings can inspire writers rather than intimidate them. Readings help them develop a sense of the problems they must face in each kind of writing and equip them with options for solving these problems.

Connecting to Culture and Experience

A Connecting to Culture and Experience section following each reading lets students engage the ideas in the reading before analyzing it rhetorically. The discussion task is set so that students can connect their personal experience to an idea in the text. It gives students practice in talking about ideas in texts, something few of them do every day, and we believe it increases their interest in a text and makes them more willing to analyze it.

We have had excellent results with this follow-up assignment: Immediately after the discussion, students take notes about their ideas; later they draft an extended journal entry; then at the next class meeting they share their ideas with members of their discussion group. This activity extends, refines, and clarifies each student's ideas.

Analyzing Writing Strategies

The analysis questions draw students into many different talking and writing activities:

- locating and identifying features of the reading and strategies the writer has used
- analyzing the writer's use of these strategies and their effects
- putting themselves in the writer's position and considering reasons for the writer's choices and solutions to the problems
- evaluating these choices and solutions and suggesting alternatives and improvements

The analysis questions aim to engage students actively with the readings, leading them to explore beneath the surface of each reading and to examine structural features and strategies they find there. The questions give students practice in thinking about the issues and problems that writers of each kind of writing must address as well as the decisions they must make. We find that this helps novice writers understand what they are trying to do in the assignment. Looking at what other writers have done to see what works and why it works helps them to set and pursue goals in their own writing.

Considering Topics for Your Own Essay

This section anticipates the first invention step in the Guide to Writing: listing topics and choosing one. Even before they arrive at invention, students begin generating possible topics and considering the possibilities and constraints of the assignment. If they read all four readings and consider the writing possibilities following each one, they will be well prepared to identify their own essay topics.

You can profitably approach this activity as an occasion for whole-class brainstorming. Each student can contribute at least one topic and speculate about its appeal and requirements. You can then single out topics that seem especially promising. Each student could then take any topic and rehearse it briefly in writing.

Commentary

The purpose of the commentary on each reading selection is to introduce the basic features and strategies illustrated in the readings. The commentaries complement the Analyzing Writing Strategies questions. In most cases, a particular feature or strategy identified in one commentary becomes the subject of a question in succeeding readings. Sometimes an analysis question introduces a feature or strategy that is taken up in the commentary for the next reading. This recursiveness is designed to reinforce students' learning.

The commentaries also introduce concepts discussed in further detail in other parts of the book, primarily the Writing Strategies in Part III. Page references have been set out in the margin to make cross-reference easier.

The commentaries are intended to model close rhetorical analysis of the readings and to stimulate further discussion. They are neither exhaustive nor definitive. We expect you and your students to find places where you can extend, illustrate, or disagree with our analysis. The point is to get students thinking and talking about how writing is put together. We encourage our students to imagine themselves in the writer's place in order to speculate about why the writer might have made particular choices. We also urge students to think about the wisdom of those choices and to consider ways in which the essay could be revised.

Using the Readings and Analysis Questions in Class.   The readings and questions are adaptable enough to suit a variety of class plans. To cover all the readings and questions in depth takes at least two class periods and some homework assignments, so in each chapter you may want to concentrate on just one or two of the readings and discuss the others briefly. Another way to save time is to address only one of the questions following each reading.

If you follow the sequence of each chapter, discussion of the readings precedes students' work on invention for their own essays, ensuring that they will have a solid grounding in each kind of writing before they attempt it. They will have read several good examples and thought about the issues raised by the analysis questions. The Summary of Basic Features then reviews and consolidates the important issues for each kind of writing, preparing students to begin the invention process.

An alternative scheme would be to have students begin their invention while they are reading the selections. You could introduce the invention activities by discussing particular readings. If you choose to integrate the invention task with discussion of the readings, the Summary of Basic Features, which follows the readings in each chapter, can be a preview for students before they begin invention and a review before they begin their first drafts. You may also want to save one of the readings—perhaps the student essay—to discuss at this point.

When we discuss the readings in class, we use the analysis questions in two formats: an open forum, with the instructor acting as moderator, or small groups of three or four students, each group discussing a question about one of the texts. Discussion by the whole class allows you to steer the discussion of the readings directly. One good way to ensure that everyone has something to contribute to the discussion is to assign an informal, one-page response to one of the analysis questions, in their journals if you have students keep journals. You can then call on some students to read aloud what they have written. This response can be written as homework before the class, or it can be written in five or ten minutes at the beginning of the class period.

These short written responses to the analysis questions can also help to initiate discussion in small groups, with one student in each group reading his or her response to the others in the group. In large classes this format allows more students to participate, and it can elicit responses from students who would not speak in front of the whole class. After ten or fifteen minutes, a student from each group can make a brief oral summary of the group's discussion for the rest of the class. These summaries can lead naturally into a whole-class discussion of the readings or a brief lecture by the instructor on some specific writing issue that appears in the readings.

Successful Class Discussions of the Readings.   Since the primary purpose of discussing the readings is to help students write essays of the same kind, we make frequent connections between the features we find in the readings and those students will be generating in their invention writing. We usually make these connections as we summarize the main points of the discussion. Often we summarize by listing discourse features and strategies on the chalkboard, inviting students to help us make the lists. Students then have a visual reminder of the key points they are learning, and the instructor can happily avoid the role of Inspector of Responses in favor of being the leader and recorder of the discussion.

In our most successful class discussions, the students do most of the talking and talk to each other rather than just to us. The best discussions also have momentum: Students are able to sustain discussion instead of merely answering our questions. This is why the analysis questions focus on important writing issues but do not ask students simply for facts. We intend the questions to open up discussion and engage students with the problems they will be facing in their own essays, not merely test their comprehension of the readings.

ANALYSIS OF PURPOSE AND AUDIENCE AND SUMMARY OF BASIC FEATURES

Between the Readings and the Guide to Writing sections, each chapter contains a discussion of the rhetorical possibilities and a summary of the basic features for that kind of writing. The purpose and audience analysis draws students' attention to the rhetoric of the selections and helps them think about their own purposes and potential readers. This section summarizes the main points raised in the readings by the analysis questions and the commentaries, thus giving students a chance to review and consolidate the information they have learned so far before trying to apply it in their own essays. If students understand the basic features of each kind of writing and have seen how they work in the readings, it should be easier for them to respond to the invention tasks. Student writers often have difficulty coming up with much useful material until they learn the value of the features that the invention tasks ask them to generate. Referring students to the Purpose and Audience and Summary of Basic Features sections during the composing process reminds them of the key rhetorical issues for their writing.

GUIDE TO WRITING

The Guide to Writing assists the student in learning how to write the type of prose under consideration. Each Guide to Writing is tailored to consider special challenges the student will meet during the writing process. This section of the manual presents overall advice and specific teaching strategies for each of the sections that appear in the nine Guides to Writing: Invention and Research, Planning, Drafting, Critical Reading Guide, Revising, and Editing and Proofreading.

Invention and Research

Each Guide includes a sequence of invention activities designed specifically to help students ask themselves questions and generate ideas and information useful for their essays. Since so few students have ever participated in systematic invention, we are especially careful to introduce them to the invention activities. We ask the students to open their books to the invention section and then briefly explain the purpose of each activity. By having students turn the pages and skim the invention exercises while you preview them orally, you will be able to reduce students' apprehension about these unfamiliar activities and greatly increase the probability that they will successfully complete the invention section before beginning their drafts.

This is also the time to remind students of the time-frame for invention: Suggest that they begin work right away, but spread the work out over several sessions; tell them what day the invention will be due and that you will be checking it on that day to ensure that their invention base is adequate to begin planning and drafting.

The first part of the invention, Listing Possible Subjects, includes suggestions for general topics as well as for specific ones drawn from two thematic strands, "identity and community" and "work and career." You could do part of the invention in class as whole-class brainstorming or in small groups, beginning by reading the lists in the book and moving to other topics the students can think of. Students then move to choosing a topic and exploring it. Students will progress through the invention sequence at different rates, but you can help them stay on track by requiring that they reach a certain point by a certain class meeting. If you ask them to bring their invention-in-progress to every class meeting, you can ask them to share certain sections with their peers in pairs or small groups, while you circulate and examine each student's work-to-date.

Research is comfortably included in our broad definition of invention—everything that happens before and during writing to produce ideas and evaluate them. Except for the writing activities in Chapters 2 and 3 on reflective writing, all the other writing activities (Chapters 4 through 10) can include formal research. In our discussion about how to teach these activities later in this chapter, we explain how students can complete these assignments either with or without formal research. For example, depending on their topics, students can explain a concept that they already know without using or documenting any sources, or they can research new topics, relying entirely on sources (Chapter 5: Explaining a Concept).

Where research is appropriate, the Guide to Writing invites it. You can decide how much research students should do or leave it to them to decide. We provide additional guidance in Chapter 20: Field Research, Chapter 21: Library and Internet Research, and Chapter 22: Using and Acknowledging Sources.

Planning and Drafting

The Planning and Drafting section in each chapter in Part I is organized as follows:

- Seeing What You Have
- Setting Goals (focused on each chapter's type of writing)
- Outlining
- Drafting

Invention may produce a number of complete paragraphs, several lists, freewriting, an interview, or notes on library research—a plethora of material that must be organized before the student can write a draft. This much material poses a new problem for many students: what to do with all of it.

The Guide to Writing in each chapter urges students to consider several alternative plans before settling on one. Often students are unaware of alternatives; we find it helpful to illustrate several, sometimes from the reading selections and sometimes from topics suggested by students.

Each planning section reminds students, as they go on to draft, that what they have developed is only a plan. In other words, it is expendable. The final test for the paper is not whether it follows the outline, but whether it works. Like many other parts of the Guide to Writing, this may demand from inexperienced writers a new approach, a new order of priorities.

Up to the drafting stage, the student has been dealing with pieces or facets; now for the first time the student will attempt to see the material as a whole. We suggest that students write their first rough drafts in a single sitting lasting about two to three hours. The drafting session resembles extended freewriting. It lasts longer, it allows the student to pause much more, and of course the writer is trying for a more ordered product, but as in freewriting, the writer should work as fast as possible and not worry too much about grammatical details or spelling.

The object of this approach is to keep the student focused on the larger shape of the essay, not on distracting details. Research shows that most competent writers occasionally write garbled sentences in their first drafts and that writers who struggle to perfect each sentence as it is written are inefficient. Of course, there are exceptions, and students should remember that the Guide to Writing is just that—a guide, not a set of inflexible orders.

Critical Reading Guide

The part of this section called Critical Reading Guide assists students in analyzing a classmate's draft. Like the invention sequence, this section is specific to the particular discourse type. Nevertheless, in the various chapters these guides follow a general pattern. First the student reads the draft straight through and gives a general impression in just a few sentences. During close reading and rereading, the student analyzes the discourse features and strategies of the particular kind of writing being worked on. This section consists of several close-reading tasks that ask the student to *describe* and *evaluate* the draft. The tasks mirror the discourse issues central to the readings, questions, and commentaries at the beginning of each chapter, the Summary of Basic Features, the invention activities, and the advice on drafting. This circling back again and again to the central discourse issues for a kind of writing makes each chapter an integrated system of reading, analyzing, inventing, drafting, critical reading, and revising. Attentive students who have come this far—and who are able to analyze their own and other students' drafts thoughtfully—are in a surprisingly strong position to produce a solid revision.

Students may use the analysis section in various ways: (1) to guide an in-class written analysis of another student's draft; (2) to guide an at-home written analysis of another student's draft, in order to prepare for a conference or class discussion or just to turn over the analysis to the other student; and (3) to guide their discussions of drafts in pairs, in small groups, or in a whole-class workshop.

We recommend starting with a written analysis. To eliminate problems of duplicating and exchanging papers in advance of class meetings, we schedule class time for a written analysis of each draft. (Then we move on to some form of talk about the drafts.

See Organizing Workshops in Chapter 2: Teaching Practices.) Students need fifteen to twenty-five minutes to complete a thorough analysis, though, of course, you could ask for a quicker analysis.

The written analysis—as homework or in class—adds still another piece of writing to the class, writing of a type generally different from the essay the student is writing. It holds students' attention closely to the written text as they search for evidence to substantiate their evaluations. It is a writing-to-learn exercise *par excellence,* requiring review and use of the discourse concepts presented in the chapter. We have found that it also produces better workshop discussions of drafts.

In each chapter, before students use the Critical Reading Guide, we recommend that you orient them to it carefully, even taking them through each step to ensure that they understand how to read and respond to the draft. Encourage them to write as much as they can, being as specific as possible without worrying about being right or straining to say something wise. Each student should just try to give a full response as one thoughtful reader.

Good papers pose a special problem: Often students find nothing to say about them. We try to encourage students facing a fine essay to figure out precisely what is fine about it, to tell the author what she or he did well. Often this exercise will lead readers to notice something that was not in fact so fine, something that can be improved. But this is not the only point of the exercise; it also helps readers learn to analyze, and it often points out to the writer features and strategies of the essay which she or he may not have noticed.

These peer critiques not only make it possible for every student to receive some reaction to a rough draft before revising, but they also help teach students the critical and editing techniques they need to use on their own papers. With coaching and practice, students can write apt, detailed, and insightful criticism. (See the example in A Writer at Work, Chapter 3: Remembering People.) As they realize their own successes, students will come to respect both themselves and their classmates as readers and helpers. This respect improves every other classroom activity; most particularly, it does wonders for small-group work when students must look to each other rather than to the teacher for help or ideas.

Revising

This section has a revising plan that is organized as follows:

> *Identifying Problems*
>> Getting an overview
>>
>> Charting a plan for revision
>>
>> Analyzing the basic features of your draft
>>
>> Studying critical comments
>
> *Solving the Problems* (focused on each chapter's type of writing)
>
> *Editing and Proofreading*

Students are now on their own, perhaps with advice from other students and from you, to improve their drafts. The second stage above, Solving the Problems, takes them back through the possibilities of the assignment they are working on. It gives very specific advice about how they can solve problems they recognize in their drafts.

It will be an excellent use of class time to ask students to make or at least begin their plan for revision under your guidance. If they are able to reread their drafts carefully, compose a scratch outline, and study their peer's comments while they are in the classroom with you available as a resource for question answering, they will be well launched into the process and able to complete it and then revise their drafts on their own. Alternatively, students could write out their revision plans outside of class and you could review them at the next class meeting to ensure that they're on track. Then you could select and duplicate the best revision plan and ask the writer to present it to the class as a model.

Editing and Proofreading

The last step in revising is editing and proofreading—locating and correcting errors in grammar, spelling, and punctuation. Included in this section are guidelines for finding and editing sentence-level problems that, according to our research, are likely to occur in writing of the kind presented in each chapter. We also ask students to keep a record of the types of errors they habitually make and to check their writing for these errors. (See Responding to Error in Chapter 3: Evaluation Practices.)

A WRITER AT WORK

Each chapter includes among its readings one written by a first-year college student using this Guide to Writing. The Writer at Work section focuses on an earlier stage in the writing of one of those papers. The subject of the essay and the issues facing the student are discussed, followed by a typed version of the student's notes.

As a group, the selections cover many writing issues and all the key stages that a paper written according to the guidelines in this book will go through.

The Writer at Work sections also allow students to see what good work looks like before it is finished. A good essay bears few, if any, traces of its genesis; its surface is polished, smooth, impenetrable. Student writers can find no evidence there that they could do such work. To see a flawed first draft or jumbled invention writing—the sort of thing they can do—may help them believe that they can do the other as well.

THINKING CRITICALLY ABOUT WHAT YOU HAVE LEARNED

Coming at the end of the chapter after students have written and edited their final revisions, this section may seem to be merely an afterthought. But in our teaching, it has become an integral part of students' work in each kind of writing they do in Part I. These reflective or "metacognitive" activities bring closure to students' work in the chapter. They reinforce what students have learned and consolidate that learning—helping students remember and value their learning.

Three separate reflective activities are collected here: Reflecting on Your Writing, Reviewing What You Learned from Reading, and Considering the Social Dimensions of the kind of writing studied in the chapter. You probably won't have time to do all of them at the end of every chapter. Here we talk about some of the ways we use them; you will certainly think of many other possibilities.

We routinely ask students to write a page or so on the first two—Reflecting on Your Writing and Reviewing What You Learned from Reading—as part of the packet (invention writing, drafts, etc.) they hand in with the final revision of each essay. Because students sometimes view these two activities as make-work, we usually spend some class time discussing why we require them. You could have students write one or both of them in class on the day the final revision is handed in and then devote the rest of the class to discussing what students wrote.

When we grade and respond to the revised essay, we make a point of referring to the students' own reflections on how they discovered and tried to solve a particular problem in their writing. If their solution doesn't work very well, for example, we may be able to suggest other ways of reworking the essay. Often we can offer some additional ideas on how they can avoid the problem in the future. Sometimes, we point out another problem and invite the student to revise the essay one more time trying to solve that particular problem. We might also refer students to strategies used in one or two of the readings that they might be able to adapt to their purposes.

We also find students' written reflections useful for periodic conferences and for midterm class discussions. Often in conference we can suggest specific ways a student could use the invention activities to avoid a recurrent kind of problem or the strategies in the readings to solve the problem. Midterm discussion with the entire class could reinforce students' images of themselves as problem solvers, capable of learning from reading as well as from others. These two activities are especially useful if you are asking students to assemble a portfolio with a self-reflective statement evaluating what they have learned during the course. Chapter 24 of *The St. Martin's Guide to Writing* suggests how students can use these metacognitive activities for that purpose.

The third activity, Considering the Social Dimensions of the kind of writing studied in the chapter, introduces students to a new way of thinking about writing. We want them to understand that each genre has a social context, that writers and readers have certain assumptions about what a particular kind of writing can do as well as what it can say. For example, we point out in Chapter 2 that what we value in autobiography may be influenced by our society's preference for thinking of people in psychological rather than in cultural and political terms. We invite students to reflect on the autobiographies they have read as well as those they have written and to consider how thinking about autobiography in these different ways may affect their understanding of the genre.

If you've discussed in class some of the Connecting to Culture and Experience questions following the readings in the chapter, your students will be familiar with some of the issues raised in the Social Dimensions activity. But most students will need coaching before they feel comfortable theorizing about writing and society. This activity is meant to get them started thinking. We put it at the very end of the chapter because we think students need to have the intensive experience of reading and writing in a genre before they can reflect on how it works and what its broader social implications might be.

The best way to use the Social Dimensions activity, we've found, is in class discussion. You may be able to use small groups once you've gotten students started thinking provocatively about these issues, but only after they've had some experience thinking and talking about them in class.

Here is one student's response to the Reflecting on Your Writing questions for the Speculating about Causes assignment:

One of the main problems that I encountered while writing this essay was presenting the information that I felt was relevant to the topic in a way that did not confuse the reader. In this essay, I hoped to explain what exactly sexual harassment is, prove that there has been a significant increase in the reported incidents of sexual harassment, and present (as well as refute) a few suggested causes for this trend.

My first draft was unsuccessful. My readers could not even understand what I was writing about, as I discovered from my peer review. I followed what seemed to me to be a simple format—first defining sexual harassment, then presenting the trend, and then speculating about causes of the trend, but, unfortunately, I found that I spent too much time with the definition of sexual harassment early in the paper and my readers got lost. To remedy this situation in my final draft, I changed the format just a little bit. I first presented proof that the trend exists and then incorporated my definition of sexual harassment into the first of my causes. This format should be somewhat easier to follow since the definition is no longer such a major part of the essay.

This student focuses on a single major problem with her essay—her readers' inability to identify the point of her essay because she devotes too much space to defining sexual harassment at the beginning. She describes here how she reorganized her essay, presenting proof for the existence of a trend first and then defining sexual harassment. As she suggests, this reorganization makes clearer that she is speculating about causes rather than defining a concept. Writing this reflection allowed her to analyze her own writing process and to recognize the importance of readers' responses in revision. Although she doesn't address the issue directly, she also seems to have learned something about the relationship between purpose and audience, about the need to clarify one's purpose to meet the expectations of readers.

CHAPTER 1: INTRODUCTION

This brief introductory chapter begins by arguing that writing makes important contributions to thinking, learning, success, personal development, and communication. It then explains how writing is learned by identifying three things students need to know: how written texts work, how the writing process works, and how to think critically about writing. Each of these sections discusses how we can learn what we need to know and includes one or two exercises that could be used along with the quotations as the basis for class discussion.

How Written Texts Work introduces the concepts of purpose, audience, and genre or kind of writing. These are concepts central to the writing assignment chapters in Part I, each of which focuses on a different genre. We define genres as social acts: Different rhetorical situations call for different genres. We talk about the predictability as well as the variability of genres. The point is that genres have conventions, patterns that help readers understand them, but they should not be thought of as formulaic or static. By placing genres in their social context, we can see how they reflect as well as affect the values and assumptions of the people who use them. Different kinds of discourse privilege different kinds of experience, different ways of knowing. At the end of each Part I chapter, there's a critical thinking activity, Considering the Social Dimensions, that invites students to think more about the genre they have been studying in terms of its social context, what kinds of knowledge it validates, and how it authorizes some people and silences others.

If you want to read more about genres, see the articles by Berkenkotter and Huckin ("Rethinking Genre from a Sociocognitive Perspective") in the background readings section of this manual. There's also a list of additional sources on genre theory in the selected bibliography.

The second section, How the Writing Process Works, introduces the idea that writing is a complex and recursive process. We refer here to writing as creative problem solving, a notion that we come back to in another critical thinking activity at the end of each Part I chapter, Reflecting on Your Writing. We also introduce the important idea that writing is not always a solitary activity, but often involves collaboration. Since *The St. Martin's Guide to Writing* offers many opportunities for collaboration, you might want to reinforce this idea by putting students into small discussion groups and having them exchange the metaphors and similes they've thought of for Exercise 1.3.

Under the heading How We Develop a Writing Process That Works, we introduce the Guides to Writing in each of the Part I chapters. The Guides, as we explain, provide procedural scaffolding to help students recognize the full potential of the writing process. They help students resist the impulse to be done even before they've begun exploring their topic. They also make the process somewhat less imposing by suggesting how students might break it into smaller, more focused tasks.

Exercise 1.4 could be used to get students to reflect on what they typically do when they write. Many students will say they are satisfied with the process they currently use, even if that involves what we've called the "dangerous method." The Guides to Writing try to increase their repertoire of strategies for invention, planning, revising, and editing. They offer an array of heuristic questions specific to the genre that encourages students to think more about their subject as well as to think more systematically. If you would like to read more about the writing process, see "A Cognitive Theory Process of Writing" in the background readings and the section in the selected bibliography.

The third thing students need to know is How to Think Critically about Their Writing. What we are talking about here is metacognition, thinking about thinking. There's ample evidence to suggest that learners learn better when they reflect on what they are learning. Conscious reflection seems also to help writers in the process of writing. As Linda Flower points out in "Taking Thought: The Role of Conscious Processing in the Making of Meaning" (excerpted in Chapter 8 of this manual), writers often can rely on strategies they have used many times before. But when the subject is especially challenging or they are writing in a genre that is new to them, writers—no matter how expert—shift to a heightened state of awareness so they can use all of the resources at their command.

The section called Using This Book forecasts the plan of the book, emphasizing the Guides to Writing in the writing assignment chapters of Part I. Some general advice about invention, drafting, revising, and editing concludes the chapter.

A CHART CROSS-REFERENCING PARTS I AND III

The following chart indicates two things: where a particular Part III strategy is referred to in Part I (denoted by *Cross-ref.* in the box at the juncture of the corresponding chapters), and where Part III exercises refer to particular readings in Part I (exercise numbers are given in the box at the juncture of the corresponding chapters). This chart does not exhaust the cross-reference possibilities; it is intended simply as an aid when you first begin to use this book.

	2: Events	3: People	4: Profile	5: Explanation	6: Position	7: Proposal	8: Evaluation	9: Cause	10. Interpretation
13: Cueing the Reader				*Cross-ref.* Toufexis 13.1 All essays 13.2 Toufexis 13.6	*Cross-ref.* Estrada 13.1	*Cross-ref.* Weisman 13.5 Kaus 13.6		*Cross-ref.* King 13.1	
14: Narrating	*Cross-ref.* All essays 14.3 All essays 14.5	*Cross-ref.* Angelou 14.6 Haslam 14.8	*Cross-ref.* Noonan 14.10 Cable 14.10 Cable 14.12						
15: Describing		*Cross-ref.* Gray 15.3 Haslam 15.5 Gray 15.8 Angelou 15.14	*Cross-ref.* Noonan 15.6 Cable 15.16						
16: Defining			*Cross-ref.* Noonan 16.2 Noonan 16.4			*Cross-ref.* Weisman 16.6			
17: Classifying					*Cross-ref.* Estrada 17.4	*Cross-ref.* Frankel 17.4 Weisman 17.4			
18: Comparing	*Cross-ref.* Wolff 18.2		*Cross-ref.* Noonan 18.2	*Cross-ref.* Passell 18.3 Toufexis 18.2	*Cross-ref.* Ehrenreich 18.2				
19: Arguing					*Cross-ref.* All essays 19.2 All essays 19.3 Statsky 19.5 Statsky 19.6 Estrada 19.6 Ehrenreich 19.9 All essays 19.11 All essays 19.13	*Cross-ref.* All essays 19.3 Weisman 19.4 Weisman 19.5 O'Malley 19.7 O'Malley 19.12	*Cross-ref.* All essays 19.3 Ansen 19.6 Ansen 19.6	*Cross-ref.* All essays 19.3 Dartnell 19.4 Dartnell 19.9	*Cross-ref.* Essays on "Araby" 19.10

CHAPTER 2: REMEMBERING EVENTS

THE WRITING ASSIGNMENT

Write an essay about a significant event in your life. Choose an event that will be engaging for readers and that will, at the same time, tell them something about you. Tell your story dramatically and vividly, giving a clear indication of its autobiographical significance.

The Nature of the Writing Assignment

This assignment has two pedagogical goals: to teach students to write a coherent narrative and to introduce the rhetorical concepts of purpose and audience. This chapter, in conjunction with Chapter 14: Narrating, presents the basic strategies of effective storytelling. Students learn how to sequence the action chronologically, to shape the structure of their narratives meaningfully around a central conflict, and to use a con sistent point of view.

By focusing the writing assignment on the significance of the event, the chapter also draws students' attention to the way in which purpose and audience control the selection as well as the presentation of details. Students writing about significant events must decide how much they want to disclose about themselves and must discover ways of connecting to their readers' experience. This assignment involves students, sometimes for the first time, in reflecting seriously about their own experience and about human experience in general. It encourages students to make discoveries about themselves and to share these insights with others through writing. For inexperienced writers, this use of writing as discovery can lead to an important new commitment to writing, a commitment that subsequent assignments attempt to foster.

Autobiographical writing is treated here not merely as an exercise in storytelling but as a meaningful intellectual activity. In learning about autobiographical writing, students discover the basic process of all writing—making meaning from experience. That is, they learn how to present their experiences so that readers can recognize, believe, and understand what has happened and why it is important.

Chapter 2: Remembering Events pairs with Chapter 3: Remembering People to form a unit on reflective writing, writing that relies on the invention strategies of memory search and analysis as well as the writing strategies of narration and description. Many instructors like to begin writing courses with a unit on reflective writing, assigning both chapters if there is time or choosing between the two if there is not. We open with autobiography because students can use a fairly straightforward narrative organization for their essays.

Writing about a remembered person usually requires students to discover another way of organizing the hodgepodge of anecdotes, descriptive detail, and other information that they have gathered about the remembered person.

Special Problems of This Writing Assignment

We have noticed that students facing this assignment for the first time may have problems developing a well-paced, dramatic narrative and achieving the self-disclosure necessary to reveal the event's significance.

In their first drafts of essays about events, student writers tend to draw on what they know of storytelling conventions. Typically this involves beginning with a general introduction, setting the scene or declaring the significance of the event in broad terms. The succession of events is then played out in the body of the paper without much alteration in pace to include descriptive details, the writer's feelings at the time, and reflections with hindsight. A writer often forgets to show as well as tell, to bring an experience alive with sensory detail rather than merely to record the sequence of events.

Many writers have initial difficulties managing the pace of a narrative, not realizing that the climax of an event can easily be undercut if pages of incidental events have misdirected readers' expectations. We find it useful to spend some time explaining ways to adjust the flow of time and create suspense. As the commentaries show, the readings offer good examples of ways to order and shape narratives, and the examples and exercises in Chapter 14: Narrating address these issues directly.

For many writers, the companion to the convention of beginning a story with a general introduction is the convention of ending it with a moral. Unused to probing the personal significance of events they write about, inexperienced writers tend to translate this convention into a moralistic conclusion. Again we use the readings to point out ways in which reflection on the significance of an event can be woven into the narrative and how to avoid simplistic conclusions. We encourage them to go deeper—to look at reasons for their actions and reactions, to explore the humorous or absurd possibilities of their topics and the personal insights that these can provide.

Promising and Unpromising Topics

The writing assignment in this chapter gives students a wide choice of topics. This latitude, as students soon discover, presents problems as well as opportunities. The chief problem comes when students choose events from which they do not have enough distance or events in which the significance is too obvious.

When asked to choose a significant event, students frequently want to write about the first topic that comes to mind, often a recent experience or a traumatic one. An event that happened very recently may only appear to be important because it is on the writer's mind. While writing about such an event will help the writer understand it, the event may turn out not to have much meaning after all. Traumatic events may also be problematic as topics, not because they lack significance but because they are too meaningful. Writing about a traumatic event may involve more self-disclosure than seems appropriate given the writing situation.

Looking back over the events of their lives for possible topics, writers understandably tend to think big. Major emotional landmarks readily suggest themselves: graduation, making the team, having an accident, passing or failing the big test. In the Guide to Writing, we suggest that students also consider events from other categories including topics from the "identity and community" and "work and career" strands.

Some of the peak experiences we suggest are initiations or rites of passage. They are prominent in the minds of many students and can make excellent autobiographical topics. The events featured in all the readings in this chapter also may be said to involve rites of passage.

A problem, however, with these topics is that many of them are common experiences, familiar to almost everyone. The challenge in writing about such an event is to avoid the cliché, to find something distinctive in the experience, or to give readers a new perspective on it. We encourage students to think twice before writing about their first experience on the ski slopes, the prom that was not all it promised to be, the event that would have embarrassed anyone. Experiences such as these that exactly match expectations contain nothing surprising for readers, no new insights or discoveries. Students would do better to look beyond the obvious and consider some of the subtler experiences they may have had—moments of intense awareness, realizations, important changes that took place within themselves.

CHAPTER INTRODUCTION

The Writing Situations

The three brief descriptions of writing situations for remembered events show students a range of possible occasions for this sort of writing. You may want to use the three situations to address the problems mentioned above by pointing out how the writers have chosen personally significant topics, how they have enough distance from these topics to be able to discuss their significance, and how they achieve the depth of insight for which students writing this assignment should aim. All three examples involved the writers in stress and anguish: handling a large and potentially dangerous animal, feeling racial prejudice in a graduation speech, and fearing a father's rejection. We tell students that although they need not write about traumatic events, autobiographical writing often explores events that were uncomfortable at the time. The writers in these three situations demonstrate that we often learn most about ourselves from times when we are under some kind of pressure and that writing about a painful experience can transform it into a valuable one. Chapter 14: Narrating can be used to explain the value of creating conflict and tension in a narrative.

Writing in Your Other Courses

We wouldn't want to overemphasize the number of times students will be asked to write about their personal experience in their college courses. In fact, you may want to take this opportunity to discuss with them the value of writing about personal experience. Freshmen, both the eighteen-year-old variety and the older student, are often struck by the abstractness of their college studies. Some instructors may even appear to disdain self-examination even though Socrates taught us that the unexamined life is not worth living. The three sample assignments—from psychology, political science, and linguistics—suggest ways in which personal experience can inform our studies of academic subjects. You might point out that connecting what one is learning to one's own life, though certainly not a requisite of learning, can be a stimulant.

Practice Remembering an Event: A Collaborative Activity

If you decide to have your students do this collaborative activity, you will find that their interest in the chapter will be enhanced along with their confidence that they will be able to write an interesting remembered event essay. This activity guides them through a rehearsal for the essay they will write later and prepares them to think seriously about the genre.

If you are beginning the course with this chapter, this particular collaborative activity provides a good starting point. It has students tell each other stories, which is always fun. And it gives students a chance to get to know one another and begin to form a good working relationship.

READINGS

All of the readings in this chapter involve childhood experiences. That is not to say, of course, that students must be limited in their own topic choice. But since most students using this book are still quite young and relatively inexperienced, we thought the focus on childhood would have the widest appeal. We also wanted to give instructors an opportunity to compare and contrast the readings' themes.

One recurrent theme in autobiography appears to be the struggle to acquire a sense of identity, to define one's self. All the writers in this chapter contend with this issue. Dillard's self-definition hinges on her discovery of pursuits that are hers alone. She assumes her parents care about what she's been doing in the basement and is at first surprised and then relieved to find that they are basically uninterested. Wolff fashions an image of himself that leads him to play a dangerous game that he must hide from his mother and her boyfriend. Auster explores his adolescent identity through his first traumatic experience with death. And Brandt, the student author in the collection, comes to understand herself and her relationship with her parents after shoplifting an inexpensive button. The Writer at Work section demonstrates Brandt's growing awareness of the role her parents play in making this event significant for her.

Other themes are suggested in the Connecting to Culture and Experience and Considering Topics for Your Own Essay sections following each reading, and you will undoubtedly see still other thematic connections worth making.

Topics in Analysis Questions and Commentaries

These lists can serve as a quick reference to help you to plan your discussion of discourse features either in class or in conference.

Dillard

Analyzing Writing Strategies	*Commentary*
1. features of a remembered event essay	arousing curiosity
2. naming and detailing	giving the story a point
	dramatic structure
	autobiographical significance
	reflection on experience
	describing strategies: naming, detailing, and comparing

Wolff

Analyzing Writing Strategies	*Commentary*
1. significance	pacing
2. specific narrative action and action verbs	specific narrative action
	cueing devices: verb tense and time markers

Auster

Analyzing Writing Strategies	*Commentary*
1. organization: beginning	autobiographical significance
2. naming, detailing, and comparing; dominant impression	telling and showing
	past and present perspective
	dominant impression

Brandt

Analyzing Writing Strategies	*Commentary*
1. dialogue	deciding what to disclose
2. framing	dialogue: summarizing and quoting
3. significance	

HANDED MY OWN LIFE
Annie Dillard

Dillard's story might surprise some students because it is not particularly dramatic, and it is certainly not traumatic or even disturbing. Students need to realize that to be significant an experience does not have to be earth-shattering, nor does it have to be sad. Dillard writes about a liberating experience, one that helped to make her the confident, independent, hard-working person she has become.

The questions ask students to consider why Dillard wrote this piece and what she wanted readers to think of her after reading it. This issue of self-presentation goes to the heart of writing autobiography and may be relevant to the very act of writing. It is especially pertinent for students who are concerned about exposing themselves to their classmates and their instructor.

Connecting to Culture and Experience

This activity, which might be handled in small groups or by the class as a whole, is designed to get students thinking about the significance of Dillard's remembered event. We want students to understand that autobiographical writing is not only personal but also has a social dimension. It connects the writer's and readers' experiences and says something about what people value and how their values may be in conflict—even within themselves.

The instructions lead students from the specific to the general. They focus students' attention on the writer's perspective and ask them to compare it to their own. We basically want students to consider two issues: How might seemingly trivial experiences shape one's identity? And what cultural values and attitudes inform these experiences? This activity also invites students to speculate on the importance of events in their own lives that may seem trivial, but that actually may have some larger significance in terms of their growth as individuals or as members of specific communities.

Analyzing Writing Strategies

1. This question asks students to examine Dillard's essay in light of what we've said about the aims and characteristics of remembered event essays. By looking closely at Dillard's essay both for what is and is not there, students can get a better understanding of what this kind of writing tries to accomplish.

2. The aim of this question is to draw students' attention to Dillard's visual descriptions and to emphasize the importance of this writing strategy in remembered event essays. Students may notice that the details in the description of Dillard's parents relaxing after dinner suggest a pleasant domestic scene. You might refer students to the Naming and Detailing sections of Chapter 15: Describing.

Considering Topics for Your Own Essay

Here students are invited to respond to Dillard's essay by recalling related events in their own lives when they made a significant discovery or learned something important. You could ask them first to focus on academic sorts of learning, but to then go on to other kinds of learning—learning about oneself, about others, about how to get along in the world. You might encourage students to return to this section—and similar sections in the following readings—when they begin the invention process.

Commentary

This brief commentary introduces the basic features of writing about remembered events: a well-told story with autobiographical significance and vivid descriptions. Research suggests that by the time people are in college, they have had sufficient experience with narrative to allow them to internalize its general pattern. They may not have the vocabulary conventionally used to describe the pattern, however, and you may want to present it to them at this time so that the class shares a common terminology they can use when analyzing narrative texts as well as when composing them. You might take the time now to review the section on Shaping Narrative Structure in Chapter 14: Narrating.

Students may be divided about whether the discovery of the elusive amoeba or the parents' reaction on learning of the discovery is the climax. You might want to introduce the Aristotelian concept of *peripeteia* or reversal to indicate the role the parents' reaction plays. Reversal usually includes some kind of recognition or insight, what Aristotle calls *anagnorisis*. In this story, the narrator learns something about herself and about her relation to her parents as a result of their reaction to her discovery of the amoeba. She learns that they have a life of their own and that she too has a life of her own.

Dillard ends on a positive note, concluding that this recognition is liberating. But you might want to point out how another writer could have taken the same basic story and made the ending seem somewhat less upbeat. Some of your students may already suspect that Dillard's ending represses her more negative feelings—as endings are wont to do. They might even question the image she portrays of herself as a model child with model parents. If doubt about her place in her parents' life had been expressed in the ending, the tone of the story would have been significantly altered.

Like question 2 of Analyzing Writing Strategies, this commentary draws attention to Dillard's use of naming and detailing; it also introduces another strategy: comparing. Our experience in teaching this genre indicates that student writers often have difficulty incorporating visual descriptions in their own remembered event essays. Discussion of Dillard's descriptive language provides an opportunity to stress the importance of this strategy and to analyze techniques for using it. You might again refer students to Chapter 15: Describing.

See the following exercise based on this reading in Chapter 14: Narrating:

- Exercise 14.3 on the use of narrative time signals

ON BEING A REAL WESTERNER
Tobias Wolff

Wolff's is a compelling narrative, brilliantly told. In our experience, students respond strongly to this selection—some empathize with the boy, while others are repulsed by his behavior. The challenge with this piece is to use the initial responses to analyze it as a piece of autobiographical writing. The following activity for discussion tries to make this transition.

Connecting to Culture and Experience

This activity can be handled in small groups or by the class as a whole. Like the one on Dillard, it asks students to think about both the essay's personal and broader cultural significance. We begin by inviting students to look at what Wolff seems to be saying about playing soldier and cowboy. Then, in the second paragraph, we ask them to focus on their own role playing, the assumptions underlying these roles, and the ramifications of them for their own identity. Students may explore stereotypical gender roles, power relationships, and cultural values.

Be sure that students think about Wolff's statement in the final paragraph: "All my images of myself as I wished to be were images of myself armed. Because I did not know who I was, any image of myself, no matter how grotesque, had power over me."

Analyzing Writing Strategies

1. In their analysis of paragraphs 7–13, students should notice that the boy's first response is to hide. Then when his mother comes home, he plays a role. He pretends to be innocent and cries. (You might ask them why Wolff uses the word "blubbered" instead of "wept.") That night, he prays and blissfully goes to sleep. Students might argue over Wolff's tone here, but it seems to us that he is quite sardonic in this self-portrait.
2. Analyzing specific narrative action and action verbs will familiarize students with techniques for pacing stories. They should recognize that Wolff's use of specific narrative action heightens tension and increases suspense by emphasizing certain actions leading up to the climactic moment when he shoots the squirrel. Wolff conveys the significance of his exercise in power by *showing* what actions he and the others took. Students may learn more about specific narrative action in Chapter 14: Narrating.

Considering Topics for Your Own Essay

This may be a question to which only selected students will be able to respond. Most of us can readily recall occasions when power was used on or against us, but seldom recall occasions when we used or abused power. Students might recall occasions when one sibling had power over another, probably a younger sibling. Power situations also include occasions when decisions—however trivial—were made and one person had the deciding vote.

Commentary

This commentary gives you an opportunity to spend some time discussing and even practicing narrating strategies from Chapter 14: Narrating.

See the following exercise based on this reading in Chapter 14: Narrating:

- Exercise 14.3 on the use of narrative time signals

WHY WRITE?
Paul Auster

Students should find this dramatic story of an adolescent's first encounter with death compelling. Part of the effect of the narrative stems from the emotional distance that Auster maintains. He conveys the immediacy of the event and his perspective at the time it occurred. But he also provides his perspective thirty-four years later and reveals without sentimentality the lasting effect of this traumatic experience.

Connecting to Culture and Experience

Recent high school graduates, who are themselves still technically adolescents, may have difficulty achieving the distance necessary to answer these questions. Beginning this activity with a general whole-class discussion of the changes occurring during adolescence and then breaking into small groups to answer the remaining questions may help students to place their own adolescence into perspective.

Analyzing Writing Strategies

1. Here is a possible paragraph-by-paragraph scratch outline for this essay:
   - situates the event in a particular time and place in his life (1)
   - characterizes himself emotionally and intellectually at age fourteen (2)
   - introduces Ralph and describes his own reaction to him (3)
   - depicts the counselors and camp as atypical (4)
   - highlights the unusualness of the hike (5)
   - suggests the carefree nature of the hike (6)
   - describes the ominous shift in the weather that destroys the carefree mood (7)
   - describes the storm (8)
   - describes the boys' reaction to the storm (9)
   - recounts what appeared to happen to Ralph and his own reaction at the time (10)
   - reveals what actually happened to Ralph (11)
   - describes learning of Ralph's death and compares his reaction then and thirty-four years later (12)

   This question encourages students to speculate about the consequences of Auster's choice of beginning with background information that stresses his own vulnerability and sets the stage for the twist that occurs when the carefree summer excursion turns deadly. This opening resembles Brandt's in that both essays shift dramatically after the first few paragraphs. (See question 2 of the Analyzing Writing Strategies section for the Brandt essay.) Students should recognize that the opening paragraphs of Auster's essay contribute to the autobiographical significance by stressing his innocence and naiveté, thus establishing the context for the experience.

2. This question provides another chance for students to analyze ways in which writers incorporate vivid description in their writing. You might again point them toward Chapter 15: Describing, specifically to the sections on naming, detailing, and comparing. Students may differ in their views of the dominant impression, but they will probably note the fury of the storm and its biblical overtones.

Considering Topics for Your Own Essay

This activity calls students' attention to the possible pitfalls of writing about traumatic events—too much self-disclosure, too little emotional distance. It also offers an alternative way of viewing Auster's essay as a model for student writing, as the retelling of an event that is significant because the outcome is different from the expectation of it.

Commentary

This commentary introduces students to the distinctions between showing and telling to convey the autobiographical significance. Students are also encouraged to see the distinction between Auster's remembered thoughts and feelings about the event and his adult perspective on it. The invention activity Reflecting on the Event's Significance asks students to explore their own past and present perspectives, and you might refer back to this commentary and Auster's essay when the students begin this invention exercise.

The discussion of showing and telling also expands on question 2 of Analyzing Writing Strategies by focusing on Auster's use of descriptive language to create a dominant impression. You might refer students to Chapter 15: Describing, specifically the sections on showing and telling, at this point.

CALLING HOME
Jean Brandt

This selection is written by a first-year college student about an event that occurred when she was thirteen. Brandt is writing about an embarrassing event and with a good deal of honesty. By focusing on what she felt at the time of the event, Brandt avoids the predictable moral about crime not paying. She boldly presents her changing feelings: naive optimism, humiliation, excitement, shame, worry, relief.

Some of Brandt's invention writing and the first draft appear at the end of the chapter in the Writer at Work section. You might want students to read these pages before they read the revised version of the essay printed here. If you assign the draft, you could begin your analysis of the essay with question 3, which refers specifically to the way Brandt refocused the essay as she revised it. You can use the Writer at Work section to prepare your own students to write an essay on a remembered event.

Connecting to Culture and Experience

Students may be hesitant to speak openly about some occasion that made them feel ashamed, especially if the remembered event essay is the first assignment of the course and they have not established working relationships with their classmates. This activity might work best if students form small groups. You might instruct them to write briefly about such an occasion on a piece of paper that they need not share with others. Then they may reveal as much about the occasion as they feel comfortable revealing and answer the questions in paragraphs 2 and 3.

Analyzing Writing Strategies

1. Brandt uses dialogue throughout this essay: a brief exchange with her sister (end of paragraph 3 and beginning of 4), a summarized dialogue with the man from the store in paragraph 6, an extended exchange with her sister in paragraphs 7–15, a summary of what the police officers said to her in paragraphs 16 and 18, the phone conversation with her father and mother in paragraphs 19–34, and the final comment by her father (and silence by her mother) in paragraphs 36–38.

   Students tend to be insightful about this parent–child relationship. Some will note that the father's anger is more open than the mother's reaction, and that he displaces the blame, converting his daughter into a victim of the authorities. As a victim, Brandt may consider herself freed from taking responsibility. Her mother, however, expresses disappointment and then appears to withdraw her love. When Brandt writes, in paragraph 9, about anticipating explaining to her parents, she focuses on her dread of her mother's reaction. Perhaps this is because she knows her mother will respond by withdrawing love. Students familiar with the concept of "tough love" may interpret the mother's reaction positively.

2. The strategy of framing an essay is simple but quite useful. Students will see that the story begins and ends with a car ride. You might ask them to contrast these two scenes. Many readers sense that not only was this experience sobering, but it also helped Brandt mature. In the opening scene she seems to be childish, and in the end she is much more reserved and chastened. You might ask them what Brandt seems to have learned at the time, and what she learned years later from writing about this remembered event.

3. This question pertains to Brandt's relations with her parents but also focuses on the process of clarifying the event's significance that Brandt went through as she drafted and revised the essay.

Considering Topics for Your Own Essay

The focus here is on actions that are atypical, times when you did something that surprised even you. We stress that these do not have to be negative experiences. In fact, many are likely to be quite positive, even liberating.

Commentary

Here we raise the issue of personal disclosure and point out that students must decide what they want to disclose about themselves. In the Writer at Work section near the end of the chapter, students see Brandt struggling not to oversimplify her feelings or whitewash her actions. They should note that it is through this struggle, during the writing process itself, that Brandt is able to discover the deeper significance of the event.

This commentary also focuses on Brandt's use of dialogue, on her choices to summarize or quote her own words and those of others. Student writers often hesitate to quote and instead rely exclusively on summary. Others often fail to discriminate between more significant and less significant quotations and instead write narratives that seem more like movie scripts. Chapter 14: Narrating discusses the use of dialogue as a technique for pacing a narrative. You might encourage your students to consult this section at this point. In this commentary, we also explain the conventions associated with the use of dialogue.

PURPOSE AND AUDIENCE

This section of the chapter reminds students that essays about remembered events have important rhetorical constraints. You might want to discuss the various motives autobiographers have for writing about their own experiences. A way to begin is by asking students about their own choices. Why are they willing to share some memories and not others? How much is their choice affected by their assumptions about readers?

In the reading selections, for example, Dillard presents herself and her parents in the rosiest possible light. Yet even this picture of middle-class domestic bliss can be interpreted another way, for example as an expression of Dillard's isolation from her parents and her desire for their approval. Many students are surprised that Brandt chose to relate an embarrassing experience like breaking the law and being arrested. One wonders what to make of her obvious pride when she thinks she has successfully stolen the Snoopy button. Is she writing to confess her guilt or to brag, or both?

Writers frequently have multiple and even contradictory motives. We want to show our weaknesses but be liked in spite of them or even because of them. Wolff risks alienating readers by scaring them, but at the same time, he appeals to their sympathy.

SUMMARY OF BASIC FEATURES

This section reviews the most important features of writing about autobiographically significant events:

- a well-told story
- a vivid presentation of significant scenes and people
- indication of the autobiographical significance

We discuss these features in detail and illustrate them with specific reference to the selections.

You might want to discuss them before students plan and draft their own essays and review them again before they read each other's drafts to see how well they used and developed these features in their own writing.

GUIDE TO WRITING

Throughout the Guide to Writing, students who use word processors will find specific advice in the left margin of the text.

Invention

We recommend the following invention activities to help students choose a promising subject and probe it fully:

- Choosing an event to write about
- Describing the scene
- Recalling key people
- Sketching the story
- Testing your choice
- Reflecting on the event's significance

We designed this sequence of invention activities to address the special problems that the assignment poses: choosing an appropriate event with autobiographical significance and telling a vivid, engaging story about it.

We offer a list of topics (in the Aristotelian sense)—kinds of events students might consider writing about. The Considering Topics for Your Own Essay section after each reading can also help them think of topics.

Once they have an event to work with, the guide invites them to recall specific sensory details and key people associated with it. These heuristics lead writers to imaginatively re-create the scene, inhabited with people and echoing with language. The idea is that this reenactment will allow them to gain insight into the event's significance. They then sketch out the story and test their choices, in part by rehearsing them for others in their group.

Next comes a set of heuristics designed to get them to systematically probe the event's significance. They try to recall their feelings at the time of the experience and contrast these remembered feelings with their present perspective. We find that this procedure, when performed thoughtfully, can be enormously powerful. It enables the writer to create the remembered self as the subject of discourse, often freeing the writer to present the thick texture of experience.

Testing Your Choice: A Collaborative Activity

Here students are urged to meet with other students to rehearse their stories. Trying out the story in this informal way can help students get a better sense of how to structure the narrative to make it interesting to readers. It also helps them decide whether their choices are good ones.

Planning and Drafting

You might help students plan their essays by conferencing with them about the goals they've set for the essay. In this conference, the student would do most of the talking. Your role would be primarily to help students clarify their global goals—those dealing with purpose and audience.

Critical Reading Guide

This section provides a guide that will help students read each other's drafts and respond constructively. Question 1 directs the reader to get an overall sense of the essay before looking at its basic features.

You will notice that questions 2 through 5 deal with the basic features. We don't expect students to point to everything we mention or to answer every question. They should focus on the areas that seem to them to need special attention. Or the writer could ask the reader to focus on certain questions.

Revising

These sections urge students to think of revising as problem solving. Analyzing specific features and considering readers' critical comments can help students focus on the aspects of the essay that need substantial revision. The idea of revising as problem solving is addressed in one of the concluding sections under Thinking Critically about What You Have Learned: Reflecting on Your Writing.

Editing and Proofreading

In this section, we direct students to proofread their essays and edit for errors commonly found in this particular genre. You might ask them to edit and proofread outside of class. Some instructors take class time on the day the revision is due to have students work through this section, making corrections neatly on the final draft. This is an appropriate time to discuss grammar and mechanics, with individual students or the class as a whole, within the context of their own writing.

A WRITER AT WORK

Since this is the first writing assignment, this Writer at Work section gives an overview of Jean Brandt's writing process from invention through drafting to revising. We recommend having students read Brandt's Writer at Work before or after they've studied her completed essay. You might also refer to it as a way of introducing the Guide to Writing.

THINKING CRITICALLY ABOUT WHAT YOU HAVE LEARNED

Because we have found that students' experience with each genre is made richer through retrospective examination, each assignment chapter in the text concludes with a series of activities for guided reflection on the students' writing and reading experiences. Once students have finished writing their own autobiographical narratives, we ask them here to reflect on their experiences with the genre through a series of three activities: reflecting on their own writing, reviewing what they've learned from reading, and, finally, considering the social dimensions of autobiography. Having just come through what they may consider an arduous writing process, students may need your special encouragement to approach these important activities thoughtfully before moving on to their next assignment.

RESPONDING TO ESSAYS ABOUT REMEMBERED EVENTS

Here are some of the kinds of problems you can expect to find in students' writing about remembered events:

Subject

- The essay does not meet the criteria for an event essay, but seems more like a person essay, reflections essay, or some other type of writing.
- The topic is too broad ("my childhood," "our championship season").
- The event does not seem important to the writer.
- The essay either trivializes a major event or overstates a minor one (this second case can be effective if handled humorously).

Narrative Structure of the Event

- The event sprawls out over too much time or space.
- The event is not clearly framed for the reader; it should begin or end at another point.
- The narrative drags in places, or skips over important episodes too quickly.
- The narrative lacks dramatic tension or suspense.
- The dialogue is undramatic and uninteresting; it does not move the action forward.

Anecdotes and Scenes

- Are either too brief, or much too extended.
- Do not seem to relate well to the event, are poorly chosen or badly framed.
- The essay lacks telling details to build a dominant impression.
- The writer has not selected relevant details, or includes too many trivial, irrelevant ones.
- People do not seem believable in their actions or dialogue.

Significance to the Writer

- There is no apparent significance, stated or implied.
- The significance is heavy-handed, inflated, oversimplified, or sentimentalized; the writer moralizes about the event.
- The essay is not very thoughtful in exploring the event's significance; the writer may come off as a hero or a blameless victim.
- The essay has not given the reader a vivid impression of the writer.

PREPARING FOR CONFERENCES

If you hold conferences with your students on their drafts, you could have them prepare for the conference by filling in the form on the following page.

PREPARING FOR A CONFERENCE: CHAPTER 2

Before the conference, write answers to the questions below. Bring your invention-writing and first draft to the conference.

1. Briefly describe the event you are writing about. How did you come to choose it? Why is it important in your life?

2. List the scenes (locations) and people in your essay. Be prepared to talk about which ones are most vividly presented and which may need further detailing or less.

3. Explain briefly how you organized your telling of this event. What other possibilities could you consider for beginning, ending, and organizing the essay?

4. Event essays involve both self-discovery and self-presentation. What, if anything, has writing this draft led you to discover about yourself? What kind of self does your draft now present to readers?

5. What are you most pleased with in this draft? Be specific.

6. What specifically do you need to do next to revise your draft? List any problems you see in the draft or problems that another reader has pointed out. Say briefly how you might attempt to solve these problems. Use the back of this form for these notes. (If you have completed the text's Revising plan, bring it with you to the conference instead of answering this question.)

CHAPTER 3: REMEMBERING PEOPLE

THE WRITING ASSIGNMENT

Write an essay about a person who has been important in your life. Strive to present a vivid portrait, one that will let your readers see the person's character and the significance of the relationship to you.

The Nature of the Writing Assignment

This assignment has several goals: to teach students to make interpretations about a person and give substance to them through the use of description and narration, to reinforce the rhetorical concepts of purpose and audience introduced in Chapter 2: Remembering Events, and to help students learn how to select and organize their material to serve their purpose.

Students who studied Chapter 2 have developed some mastery in these areas. From their study of the selections in Chapter 2 and the strategies in Chapter 14: Narrating, they already know how to tell a story purposefully. With further support from Chapter 15: Describing, students also master the strategies of describing people and scenes vividly. They understand how purpose and audience determine the selection as well as the presentation of narrative and descriptive details. In addition, they have learned how to use narrative to organize a series of incidents into a dramatically significant essay. In moving from the remembered event to the portrait, students face a somewhat more complex and challenging task in selecting and organizing details, usually from a much larger pool of information over a greater span of time. They may discover that the organizational strategies that worked well for the event are inadequate for their purposes in this essay.

Special Problems of This Writing Assignment

Students attempting this task for the first time often encounter difficulties in these areas: choosing a person to write about, conveying the person's significance, and describing the person vividly.

The primary difficulty in topic choice is grasping the relationship's significance. We find that student writers are tempted to choose people with whom they still have deep emotional bonds. This tendency can be advantageous when students experience a sense of discovery in their writing, but it is disadvantageous when they are too caught up in their feelings to analyze them. The result often is eulogy or vitriol—with nothing in between.

Ambivalence tends to be a difficult concept for some students, and it is always hard to express in writing. It is valuable to get students to recognize that many of the writers in this chapter—whether they present generally positive or negative images of their subjects—attempt to convey their mixed feelings. For instance, Angelou indicates that her Uncle Willie sometimes scared her, and Gray acknowledges that she felt responsible for her father even though he disgusted and frightened her.

Few students use the full repertoire of describing strategies presented in Chapter

15: Describing. Their writing frequently lacks the richness of detail and the evocativeness of language required for vivid description. (See Naming, Detailing, Comparing, and Using Sensory Description in Chapter 15: Describing.) In addition, many fail to appreciate the importance of selecting images that create a dominant impression while at the same time allowing for mixed feelings. (See Creating a Dominant Impression in Chapter 15: Describing.) But the most important problem is that some student writers think it is inappropriate to analyze, evaluate, or otherwise generalize about a person's character. They need to be shown that biographers are interpreters, not just reporters, of human behavior, that they make generalizations and provide illustrative detail—anecdotal and descriptive—to support their generalizations.

Promising and Unpromising Topics

Usually, students can readily think of people who have been significant in their lives. The greatest difficulty comes when they present the person or relationship in terms of extremes—either highly idealized or vilified—rather than seeing the complexity or ambiguity in the relationship.

Students tend to think immediately of people whose roles in their lives have been momentous, such as parents and grandparents, and those who are important to them right now. We encourage students to avoid writing about a person with whom they have a very close relationship at the present time, such as a current boyfriend or girlfriend or even an immediate family member. To help students consider other possibilities, we suggest they consider a wider range of individuals: people they knew long ago and those they knew more recently, people they knew well and those they knew only superficially, people they liked and those they disliked.

We also present, in the invention section of the Guide to Writing, several categories to suggest the kinds of significance students might look for. If your students are working with one of the thematic strands "identity and community" or "work and career," they will also find lists of related subjects in this section. You might encourage students to generate a list of possibilities in these categories rather than choose the first possibility that comes to mind.

When students do make the choice of writing about a parent or teacher, they should be urged to discover meaning in the small details, the behavior that is typical rather than unusual. As in remembering events, it is not necessary to write about what was traumatic. Nor should they feel obligated to demonstrate the person's uniqueness. The writing task does not ask students to describe the most important person in their lives, merely someone who was significant at one time.

CHAPTER INTRODUCTION

The Writing Situations

These writing situations suggest the principal features of essays remembering a significant person, in particular, ways of using description and anecdote that point to the significance of a relationship. The football player, for example, finds significance in a paradox: He still wants to gain his former coach's approval even though he realizes the coach was immature and cruel to him. The novelist locates significance in a resemblance: She not only looks like her prevaricating aunt, but also shares her vivid imagination. The political science student finds significance in a dissimilarity: Whereas he feels bitterness and anger, the candidate maturely accepts defeat. You might ask students to write their own scenarios illustrating situations, other than assignments for English classes, in which one would write about a significant person. [Assignment suggested by Sandy Cavanaugh, Hopkinsville Community College] These scenarios could be assigned as journal entries and then discussed in small groups or by the whole class.

Writing in Your Other Courses

Students sometimes wonder how these autobiographical (or more personal) forms of writing relate to their work in other academic courses. They may have the impression that writing about a remembered person is less rigorous than either explanation or argument. The examples provided here demonstrate a range of typical academic assignments in several disciplines (education, history, philosophy, and nursing), all of which require a serious application of the writing and thinking strategies they will learn in writing a remembered person essay.

You could have students read these illustrative assignments and discuss how to handle the question or problem posed by each one. Then they could generate a similar assignment for a course in another discipline, such as psychology, anthropology, or science.

Practice Remembering a Person: A Collaborative Activity

The group inquiry activity is based on current research in collaborative learning and composing. Students have an opportunity to begin exploring the rhetorical situation of firsthand biography, even before they have started the invention work for choosing a topic. The activity prepares them to approach the readings from the perspective of a writer, studying the ways that various writers have negotiated this rhetorical situation. As they try out an idea with two or three fellow students, they become aware of the important dimensions of purpose and audience. Then they step back to examine the rhetorical situation of telling about a remembered person.

Students find this activity quite engaging, and you can expect lively discussion. After about fifteen minutes, remind students to shift from telling about their subjects (Part I) to discussing the rhetorical situation (Part II). This will help them think about the larger context for the essay.

It is important that students understand that this activity is not designed to help them choose a topic; their final subject may very likely be a different person from the one they talk about in this activity. Rather, we are simply establishing a context for thinking about this type of writing and recognizing the significant ways it is shaped by purpose and audience.

READINGS

This set of readings portrays an uncle (Angelou), a great-grandmother (Haslam), a mother (Wu), and a father (Gray). The writers of these selections express such feelings as fear, empathy, anger, jealousy, disappointment, admiration, love, and shame. Some writers have the relationship in perspective, while others are trying to work it out as they write. Together they illustrate the full array of descriptive and narrative strategies.

If you must choose among these selections, we recommend you begin with Angelou because her portrait of Uncle Willie introduces most of the essential features of writing about remembered people. In our commentary, we draw attention to the way Angelou reveals her relationship with her uncle and tells us about herself. She uses carefully selected anecdotes together with incisive description to show what Uncle Willie was like.

You might compare Angelou's portrait of Uncle Willie to student Jan Gray's description of her father. Like Angelou, Gray organizes her essay around description and anecdote. Also like Angelou, Gray writes about a relationship about which she had ambivalent feelings. Neither writer falls into the trap of sentimentalizing. Wu's essay contrasts her perspective on her relationship with her mother with her friends' view of it. She seems much less ambivalent than Angelou or Gray about her feelings and willing to accept her mother's approach to love and discipline. Haslam's essay on his great-grandmother will strike a chord with many students. They may have similar experiences with elderly relatives or with distant relatives who share their home.

Topics in Analysis Questions and Commentaries

For your convenience as quick reference, we list below the discourse topics addressed in each of the Analyzing Writing Strategies and Commentary sections. You might refer to the list in class or in conference to direct a student's attention to particular discourse features which they should review before revising. For example, if a student's draft needs help with using dialogue, you could suggest reviewing Angelou's essay, specifically question 2.

Angelou

Analyzing Writing Strategies	*Commentary*
1. basic features	showing significance
2. dialogue	description
	word images
	organization

Haslam

Analyzing Writing Strategies	*Commentary*
1. specific narrative action	anecdotes
2. anecdotes (Angelou)	dialogue
	cumulative sentences
	sentence variety, narrative action, and dramatic emphasis

Wu

Analyzing Writing Strategies	*Commentary*
1. comparison	anecdotes
2. significance	recurring activities
	conversation with others

Gray

Analyzing Writing Strategies   *Commentary*

1. dominant impression: naming and   organization
   detailing   significance
2. dialogue
3. organization

UNCLE WILLIE   In our introduction, we quote Angelou's statement, "I speak to the black experience;
Maya Angelou   but I am also talking about the human condition." You might ask your students to
consider *how* this portrait speaks to "the black experience" since it seems at first to have
very little to do with race. The only explicit reference is in the first sentence of paragraph 5 where Angelou mentions the economic status of able-bodied black men and
their cruelty toward Uncle Willie. Students might observe that Uncle Willie's story allows Angelou to say something about self-representation. Rather than be stereotyped
by others, Uncle Willie gets to project the "self" he chooses.

Connecting to Culture and Experience

This activity, which may be done in small groups or as a whole class, asks students to
look at the social and personal dimensions of pretense. Some students may not be comfortable revealing a time when they were motivated to pretend to be someone else.
You might ask them to write briefly about such a time, but not require them to share
what they've written with other students. In small groups, students can then discuss
personal and social motivation in general terms.

Analyzing Writing Strategies

1. This question reminds students of the basic features of this particular genre and
   asks them to analyze Angelou's essay with these features in mind. This exercise
   will help to focus the students' attention on these features as they read the essays
   in the text and those written by classmates. In addition, it will make them mindful of the features as they begin their own writing. Students may have differing
   opinions about whether these assertions are true of Angelou's essay.
2. Dialogue is also discussed extensively in Chapters 14 and 2. The dialogue in this
   selection is artfully done. We can see Uncle Willie trying to control his stutter (what
   Angelou calls his "thick tongue") and making small talk that completely ignores
   his condition. Angelou also describes the impatience in his face and his attempt to
   laugh off the woman's question about having children of his own. Students may
   note the tension between what Uncle Willie says and Angelou's comments on his
   physical appearance as he speaks.

Considering Topics for Your Own Essay

This section shifts attention from the reading to the student's own plans to write a firsthand biography. Our suggestions ask students to recall adults who significantly influenced their lives. This activity works particularly well with the thematic strand "identity and community." You might encourage students to return to this section—and
similar sections following the other readings—when they begin the invention process.

Commentary

This selection demonstrates the importance of narrating and describing to writing about remembered people. Since the major concepts of narration were discussed extensively in Chapter 2: Remembering Events, students are asked in these questions for analysis to apply what they have learned. Describing, which was touched on briefly in Chapter 2, takes center stage in our commentary here. We introduce and illustrate the basic describing strategies of naming, detailing, and comparing. You might want to spend some time discussing these strategies by using the illustrations and exercises in Chapter 15: Describing.

Among the other points covered in the commentary is the importance of combining showing with telling. Angelou, as we point out, tells us that Uncle Willie was proud and defiant, but she also shows us how these attitudes manifested themselves. Without the vivid anecdotes and descriptions, readers would not really know what she means by these generalizations. Some students avoid making generalizations. It's important for them to appreciate the role of generalizations in portrait writing, but they also need to understand that without specific detail, generalizations are difficult to comprehend and also may be hard for readers to accept.

We also point out that writing about remembered people very often involves ambivalent feelings. Students need to recognize that portraits that show only the good or the bad side of a person lack credibility and offer little insight to readers. Even so, the impulse to whitewash or vilify is strong. This is especially true, we find, when students write about influential adults. You might discuss the problem with students and even ask them to write a paragraph citing bad as well as good points about an adult who has been important to them.

We want students to notice that writing about a remembered person is autobiographical. Writers not only present the other person but also their relationship with the person. Angelou expresses embarrassment, vulnerability, resentment, and empathy. She reveals her feelings and lets us glimpse what must have been a difficult relationship.

Finally, we offer one possibility for organizing essays about remembered people by analyzing Angelou's plan. We demonstrate that she has followed a simple plan using two anecdotes to structure her narrative. Students may have difficulty making decisions about structuring their own narratives, and you may want to refer back to this commentary when they begin to plan their essays.

See also the following exercise on this selection in Chapter 14: Narrating:

- Exercise 14.6 on specific narrative action

GRANDMA
Gerald Haslam   In Haslam's essay, as in Maya Angelou's, students are confronted with the writer's ambivalent feelings for an older relative. Here, too, anecdotes and dialogue are central to the vivid presentation of the subject. This essay, however, focuses on an important change in the writer, from a powerless *malcriado* to a person with wisdom, a voice, and an influence on adults. It also raises interesting issues about cross-cultural and cross-generational families.

Connecting to Culture and Experience

Once again, the activities in this section give students an opportunity to respond to the reading, either in a whole-class or small-group discussion. The personal and social issues surrounding care of the elderly invite lively discussion. We suggest that students interview elderly family members in order to answer the questions in paragraph 2. This activity will give them a taste of the kind of field research that will be necessary for some of the later assignments—in particular, for the profile.

Analyzing Writing Strategies

1. Students will have different views on which narrative actions are the most vivid, but they may notice, for example, that the verbs used to describe the great-grandmother eating the gumdrop paint a particularly clear picture complete with sounds. If students need help identifying the specific narrative actions in the passage, you might refer them to Chapter 14: Narrating.

2. Effective portraits are built with memorable anecdotes. Where the Angelou essay was centered on the contrast between two anecdotes, Haslam's essay has four key anecdotes which show a progressive change in the young boy and in his relationship with Grandma. Here we ask students to identify the anecdotes and analyze how each contributes to the portrait of Grandma. The first anecdote opens the essay, the second occurs in paragraphs 17–28, the third in paragraphs 32–42, and the final anecdote closes the essay. Some students might include some or all of the numerous smaller incidents between these as well, such as the arrival of Grandma in paragraph 11. In assessing the significance of each anecdote, students should consider why the writer selected this particular incident to include here, and what would be lost if the anecdote were deleted from the essay. The anecdote in paragraphs 17–28, for example, provides readers with a good sense of a small boy's frustration, shock, and feeling of betrayal, yet it signals a change for the better in his relationship with Grandma, and reveals her as a bit of a tease.

Considering Topics for Your Own Essay

We suggest that students recall adults who influenced their early childhood and then passed out of their lives. Students may assume they must choose someone who has died, as in Haslam's essay. Remind them that people may pass from our lives in a number of ways: They may move away; there may be a dispute or disagreement which separates us; they may change (or we might); or we may simply move on (as we do with elementary school teachers, coaches, and babysitters). You might handle this as a whole-class brainstorming activity in which students fire ideas for listing on the blackboard. Then you might choose several from the list and discuss how essays could be developed for each of them. You might also assign it as a journal question (either in-class or outside of class) in which students pick one person and rehearse how they might use certain anecdotes to frame up an essay for a specific audience. Again, the purpose of this activity is not to choose a topic, but rather to help students to make the transition from close reading to thinking about their own writing, anticipating the invention work which lies ahead.

Commentary

The commentary reiterates the key role of anecdotes in creating vivid, memorable portraits and notes Haslam's use of an anecdote to open his essay as an effective strategy that students might consider for their own papers. Dialogue is also discussed, and the problem of remembering precisely what was said is addressed.

The commentary also draws students' attention to the cumulative sentence, in which phrases follow a main clause but do not modify a specific word in the clause. It provides examples, as well as a rationale for sentences such as these, which give rhythmic variety, compression of narrative action, and dramatic emphasis in the writing. This part of the commentary is particularly helpful for some student writers, who tend to write sentences with little variety, whether short and simple ("primer prose") or complex and rambling. The cumulative sentence is a useful alternative in either case.

See also the following exercise on this selection in Chapter 14: Narrating:

- Exercise 14.8 on dialogue

A DIFFERENT KIND OF MOTHER
Amy Wu

In our introduction to Wu's essay, we suggest that students take note of her reliance on contrast to present her mother and her special relationship with her mother to her readers. Students may respond to Wu's mother as her friends did, by expressing surprise at the harshness of her mother's reprimands. You might ask students to compare Wu's feelings for her mother with the feelings of Angelou for her uncle and of Haslam for his great-grandmother.

Connecting to Culture and Experience

This activity should stimulate lively discussion since students will probably have strong opinions about Wu's beliefs. You might have students share information about their own ethnic backgrounds in small groups in order to give each student a chance to speak. The questions in paragraph 3 might then be answered in a whole-class discussion. This activity would be particularly useful to students who are writing on the thematic strand "identity and community."

Analyzing Writing Strategies

1. This question builds on the Connecting to Culture and Experience section in which students were asked to compare their ethnic backgrounds with those of others. It introduces them to the use of comparison and contrast in firsthand biography and encourages them to focus on specific language in order to draw general conclusions about Wu's relationship with her mother. You might also ask students to comment on the way in which Wu organizes her extended comparison. Chapter 18: Comparing and Contrasting provides a detailed discussion of structuring comparisons.
2. This exercise illustrates the differences between showing and telling by asking students to make a table aligning the anecdotes or recurring events and their explanatory statements. Students might complete this exercise as a journal entry or in-class writing activity and then discuss their findings as a class. You might ask students to comment on how the statements that explain the significance of each anecdote or recurring event affect them as readers and on whether these statements are essential to convey the significance of each.

Considering Topics for Your Own Essay

This section invites students to begin to think about ways in which they could convey the significance of their own relationships with others using details and anecdotes. Students might write out this activity and then choose one anecdote to share with other students, who could then comment on what the anecdote reveals to them about the relationship.

Commentary

In this commentary, we continue the discussion of anecdote and recurring activities and draw attention to the rhetorical role of each. We want students to recognize that each serves a particular function in this genre and that both can be employed fruitfully in their own writing. They may choose to relate anecdotes that provide strikingly vivid portraits of their subjects at specific points in their relationships, or they may want to stress the importance of a repeated behavior or interaction. You might stress that the choices a writer makes depend on his or her purpose and audience. Chapter 14: Narrating addresses the use of anecdote in more detail, and you might encourage students to consult this chapter at this point.

We also discuss a particular use of dialogue to report conversations with others as a means of revealing important aspects of the remembered person. Students frequently have difficulty incorporating effective dialogue in their writing; understanding that it has distinct possible uses may lessen their hesitation to try it and may help them employ it more judiciously.

FATHER
Jan Gray

This student essay is the subject of the Writer at Work section in this chapter, which shows how a classmate's critique of her draft helped Gray work toward a deeper understanding of her ambivalent feelings. The revision also shows considerable mastery of description and organization.

Connecting to Culture and Experience

This activity explores the ambivalence present even in seemingly simple relationships, a concept which will probably make some students a bit uncomfortable. The idea that we may harbor resentment at times against even a loving parent or the idea that a powerful dislike might be colored with pity or even affection is sometimes difficult to accept. Our recognition of this fact may come only with maturity and a certain amount of experience. The discussion, though focusing on students' responses to the reading, forecasts the issues they will face in their own writing. These questions might be discussed in small groups or with the whole class.

Analyzing Writing Strategies

1. Students will already be familiar with the concept of a dominant impression created by the writer, a key idea in both this chapter and Chapter 2: Remembering Events. This question highlights the role of naming and detailing in creating a dominant impression; both naming and detailing and the dominant impression are discussed in detail in Chapter 15: Describing.
2. Students will undoubtedly notice the father's use of parental clichés (such as "I did this for your own good" in paragraph 14) and may sense his patronizing tone ("I don't think that's a very good idea, *dear*" in paragraph 10). You might also point out the way Gray contrasts her father's posture ("leaning against the door jamb," paragraph 13) with his offer to help her right her dresser.
3. This question helps students to focus on the complex organization of Gray's final draft. Most students will agree that Gray's use of an anecdote-within-an-anecdote in the revised version of her essay is far more satisfying than the organization of the first draft presented in the Writer at Work section near the end of the chapter. For a discussion of the use of flashback, see Chapter 14: Narrating.

Considering Topics for Your Own Essay

Here we ask students to consider the difficulty of writing about people with whom they are in conflict. The problem in writing about such feelings is that they are often deeply disturbing. Focusing on the strategies one could use to present the person and dramatize the conflict might help the writer gain the distance necessary to engage in this kind of writing. In addition, the writer may achieve some degree of insight and relieve burdensome feelings.

Commentary

This section draws students' attention to the roles of anecdotes and flashbacks in writing about remembered people, as well as to the challenges for the writer of dealing with ambivalent or unresolved feelings toward the person in question. The first part of the commentary invites students to explore further Gray's use of anecdotes and flashback, already touched upon in the third question in the Analyzing Writing Strategies section. We want to encourage students to consider the possibility of shaping their own essays using flashbacks if they seem appropriate. Frequently, students are reluctant to take risks in writing, but the example of another student writer successfully using a complicated plan for her essay may alleviate some of their fears of failure.

The Commentary section concludes by asking students to consider Gray's handling of her rather complicated feelings about her father. In several of the activities connected with this reading, we have dealt with the issue of ambivalence. Many students will want to write about people with whom they have close, emotional relationships. This commentary gives you the opportunity of addressing the advantages and disadvantages of such a choice.

PURPOSE AND AUDIENCE

You might remind students of the discussion in Chapter 2 of the purpose and audience for writing about remembered events. Some students think that their writing about events and people is purely expressive, but it is important that they understand the rhetorical aspect of autobiographical writing. They need to appeal to readers by making their descriptions vivid and their anecdotes interesting. They also have to help readers understand the significance of the relationships and experiences they write about. They will discover that in the process of trying to communicate to others, writers usually make discoveries for themselves as well.

SUMMARY OF BASIC FEATURES

Here we review the most important features of firsthand biography:

- a vivid portrait
- detailed anecdotes, scenes, and recurring activities

   • an indication of the person's significance

   These are basically the same features discussed in Chapter 2: Remembering Events, the only difference being a shift in emphasis from narration to description.

GUIDE TO WRITING

Throughout the Guide to Writing, students who use word processors will find specific advice in the left margin of the text. We leaf through the pages of the Guide to Writing section of the chapter in class, commenting briefly on each section, to help students prepare for the work ahead.

Invention

Here is a list of the invention activities:

   • Choosing a person to write about
   • Describing the person
   • Testing your choice
   • Defining the person's significance

   The Invention section guides students through a variety of activities designed to help them develop a large list of potential subjects, make a thoughtful and informed choice, try out their choice with a sample audience, and generate a wealth of details that will be useful to them in the drafting stage. Most students will have had no experience with the kind of thoughtful, carefully sequenced invention work central to this text. They may resist it in various ways, based on the belief that these are just make-work activities which only delay their getting down to the real business of writing the essay. To help them see the value of invention, you might give them an overview of the specific activities, making the significance of each one clear. For example, the first activity is Choosing a Person to Write About. Students are anxious to settle on a topic as soon as possible, ending the uncertainty they see as an obstacle to moving ahead. Some students will be convinced that they know exactly whom they want to write about; others will look for a quick solution. However, there are good reasons why we ask students to list here as many possible subjects as they can. We often use a focused brainstorm session to generate a large list on the board, to help students expand the range of their thinking about possible subjects. Often the first person who comes into the student's mind is not the best choice: The student may have such strong feelings about the person that emotional distance is impossible. Or she may discover, once she begins testing her choice, that her first idea does not make a very good subject. When students have a very large list to choose from, they are less likely to settle on safe, predictable choices, they can be more comfortable that they have made a good choice, and they will be less anxious if their first choice doesn't work out.

   We consider this invention work so important in preparing students for drafting that we often collect and quickly review their invention writing, noting when it seems too sketchy to generate a fully developed draft.

   Testing Your Choice asks students to write briefly about their proposed subjects. If students are unable to write easily about a subject for five minutes or if they have been unable to recall enough details during the previous listing activities, it should be obvious that the subject is not very promising for a full-length essay. Since they have some time already invested in this subject, students will naturally resist a change of subject. You will want to remind students that they have a large list of alternative possibilities and that the time they have already spent is not wasted if they change topics. They've saved themselves a great deal of work by discovering this problem early. Moreover, the work they've done up to this point gives them a good idea of what makes a promising topic.

Testing Your Choice: A Collaborative Activity

This activity involves students in another way of testing their choices: trying out their subjects on a sample audience of two or three students. This gives the writer a chance to rehearse what he or she might say about the subject. Remind students that their role here is not to give the writer advice or to provide a critique, but to play the part of a responsive, curious audience.

Planning and Drafting

When students have worked through the invention sequence thoughtfully, planning and drafting usually go much more easily. Students already have generated a substantial amount of writing about their subject, from listing physical details and anecdotes to exploring the person's significance. They've also had an opportunity to get a sense of their audience's needs and expectations.

The key to effective planning and drafting lies with this section's goal-setting activities, which help students think carefully about what they are trying to accomplish in their essays. These goal-setting questions might form the basis for a conference with the writer. We usually ask the writer to come to the conference with some brief written responses to some or all of these questions. Another possibility is to use the goal-setting questions as the basis for a group activity just before students begin drafting. As in the collaborative activity, you will want to remind students that their role is not to provide a critique, but to help writers clarify their goals for the draft.

Students who find themselves struggling at this stage may find it productive to do some more invention. This is particularly true if the invention work has been done hastily or carelessly. Often just rethinking these activities will provide students with the help they need to move ahead.

Critical Reading Guide

We have found that the Critical Reading Guide works best as an in-class workshop in which students work in pairs; students generally need thirty to forty-five minutes to complete this activity.

We often ask students to prepare for the workshop by writing out responses to questions defining their purpose and audience. They bring these responses, together with copies of their draft, to the workshop and give them to the reader. The guidelines provide questions which direct the student's attention to the following features of the draft: the description of the person, the use of anecdotes, effective dialogue, the subject's significance to the writer, the beginning and the ending. Students will have a better idea of what you expect them to do if you are able to reproduce an example of a thoughtful, fairly extensive response as a handout. In the Writer at Work section there is a good student model: critical comments on Jan Gray's draft, written by fellow student Tom Schwartz. Students should write out their comments and exchange them at the end of the workshop period so writers will be able to consult them when revising.

Revising

Here again, you may want to give students an overview of the sequence of activities in Revising. Although these activities are designed so that students can readily work through them on their own, they also lend themselves to various kinds of group work, from whole-class analysis of a single draft to small-group revision workshops where two or three students work together on some or all of the activities in any one of these stages.

These activities will also help students to prepare for a conference, if you plan for one at this stage. If students have thought carefully about the draft and prepared brief written responses to the questions and activities in this section, their questions will tend to fall into two categories: What problems have I overlooked or failed to identify correctly? and How can I solve this particular problem? Often, we refer the student back to specific readings or to sections of the chapter which cover the specific features of the student's essay.

Editing and Proofreading

This section asks students to focus on the kinds of errors common to this particular genre. Students might edit and proofread their essays outside of class or in class, under your direction, on the day the revision is due.

A WRITER AT WORK

This section focuses on Jan Gray's writing process as she drafted and revised "Father." It shows how one reader responded to her draft and how she incorporated his suggestions into her revision. Key issues for revising were improvements in describing, reorganization of anecdotes, and a reexamination of the subject's significance.

THINKING CRITICALLY ABOUT WHAT YOU HAVE LEARNED

As in Chapter 2: Remembering Events, we conclude this chapter by giving students an opportunity to reflect in some detail on their experiences with the type of reading and writing presented in the chapter. Students are first asked to reexamine their own writing processes; then they are asked to review what they have learned from the reading selections in the chapter. Finally, they are invited to consider the social and cultural dimensions of this type of writing. They are encouraged to articulate what they have learned about empathy for and distance from others, as well as about the formation and construction of the self, both through relationships with others and through the act of writing.

RESPONDING TO ESSAYS ABOUT REMEMBERED PEOPLE

Following are some problems you can expect to find in students' writing about remembered people:

Subject

- The writer does not know, care, or remember enough about the subject to write in any depth.
- The essay does not meet the criteria for a person essay, but seems more like an event essay, reflections essay, or some other type of writing.

Presentation of the Subject

- The subject is not presented at all: The essay consists of the writer's reactions to and interpretation of the relationship.
- The subject is described briefly, but without sufficient detail.
- The anecdotes, dialogue, or descriptions do not reveal the subject well; they may be lacking entirely, poorly chosen, badly presented, or too general.
- The subject is presented without sufficient depth or complexity.

Anecdotes and Scenes

- Do not reveal anything about either the subject or his or her relationship with the writer.
- Are not framed well and so lack any dramatic or narrative effect.
- Lack dialogue altogether, where dialogue would obviously be appropriate.
- Include dialogue that is awkward or unnatural.
- Are either too brief or much too extended.

Significance to the Writer

- The subject appears to have no significance to the writer, either stated or implied.
- The significance is oversimplified or sentimentalized.
- The significance is trite and overly generalized ("I learned what friendship is all about"; "I learned not to trust everybody.").
- The essay is not very thoughtful in exploring the relationship.
- The essay does not really disclose anything about the writer.

PREPARING FOR CONFERENCES

If you hold conferences with your students on their drafts, you could have them prepare for the conference by filling in the form on the following page.

PREPARING FOR A CONFERENCE: CHAPTER 3

Before the conference, write answers to the questions below. Bring your invention-writing and first draft to the conference.

1. Which person have you selected for your essay? What is your relationship with this person? How has your relationship with this person been important in your life?

2. How do you want your readers to view this person? How have you avoided either condemning or idealizing the person and sentimentalizing your relationship? Explain.

3. List the concrete, one-time anecdotes included in your draft. After each one, indicate what it reveals about the person or your relationship. Do you need all these anecdotes? Do you need more?

4. Describe briefly how you've organized your essay—how you begin, end, and sequence your presentation of the person. What advantages do you see in your plan? Note one or two ways you might strengthen the organization.

5. What are you most pleased with in this draft? Be specific.

6. What specifically do you need to do next to revise your draft? List any problems you see in the draft or ones pointed out to you by other readers. Say briefly how you might attempt solving these problems. Use the back of this form for these notes. (If you have completed the text's Revising plan, bring it with you to the conference instead of answering this question.)

CHAPTER 4: WRITING PROFILES

THE WRITING ASSIGNMENT

Write an essay about an intriguing person, place, or activity in your community. Your instructor may offer you a choice of options: a brief profile of an event, a place, or an activity observed once or twice; a brief profile of an individual based on one or two interviews; or a longer, more fully developed profile of a person, a place, or an activity based on several observational visits and interviews. Observe your subject closely, and then present what you have learned in a way that both informs and entertains readers.

The Nature of the Writing Assignment

A profile is an informative and entertaining report based on a writer's firsthand observations and interviews. It is an engaging way to introduce field research. It asks students to rely not on their memories or books they've read, but on their abilities to attend to what they see and what they hear.

When students write profiles, they seek primarily to inform readers but also to engage their interest and entertain them. Just by singling out a place, person, or activity as a subject, a profile writer tells readers that it is important and worth their attention. Profiles are openly interpretive; they do not pretend to be objective reporting.

Writing a profile can be an unusually interesting project, since it takes students out into the community to meet new people and observe unfamiliar activities. Students practice observing, interviewing, notetaking, and writing activities basic to the work of investigative reporters; to naturalists, ecologists, geologists, anthropologists, sociologists, pollsters, and other academic researchers; and to doctors and psychologists. When students write up the results of their observations and interviews, they learn how to organize information gathered in firsthand research. This activity helps students develop their research and analytic skills.

All or most of the information in a profile comes from students' own observations. In the two preceding chapters, students were asked to rely on their memories of events or individuals important in their personal lives. In this assignment, they must take notes at the time of the interview or observation or just after, so they are using a different kind of memory. This chapter also forms a bridge to the next chapter, in which students study and do another kind of explanatory writing, explaining concepts, which relies primarily on well-established information they've learned from books and articles, rather than on firsthand observations.

Since a profile may involve several trips off campus, students should choose a subject as soon as possible, and they will need help from you in scheduling their research. Advise them on the size and scope and the amount of time you want them to spend on this project. A profile may be simple or complex, based on a single observation or interview (such as a sporting event, poetry reading, or boat show) or on several observational visits and interviews (such as to an emergency room, law court, or local television studio).

The Guide to Writing in this chapter provides support for planning, researching, and writing a profile based on multiple observations and interviews; but it will also be very useful for students who do a smaller project. In addition, Chapter 20: Field Research provides helpful advice on observing, interviewing, and writing up what is learned. You might want to have students read that chapter in order to discover how to plan and conduct observations and interviews.

Special Problems of This Writing Assignment

There are essentially two problems students have with this assignment. The first has to do with scheduling the research and the other with focusing the information.

To deal with the scheduling problem, the Guide to Writing recommends that students establish their own research schedules. But you might also set up deadlines for various stages of the project—such as deciding on a subject and arranging an interview or observation, writing up notes on observational visits and interviews, or writing the first draft—to help students keep on schedule. You could easily have students follow the guidelines for writing up their observations and interviews in Chapter 20: Field Research and then use class time for peer workshops on these notes and writeups. The Writer at Work section for this chapter illustrates one student's interview notes and writeup.

Writing up these notes and exchanging these writeups with others in the class can also help students focus their profiles. The focusing problem results from the overwhelming quantity of information students usually gather. The more they work with their material—analyzing it, writing about it, finding connections and patterns in it—the more likely they are to develop an interpretation with which to organize the information.

Promising and Unpromising Topics

For many novice writers who have just arrived at a university (or a new city), the profile offers an ideal chance for exploration. Students should be encouraged to seek out unusual activities, people, or places. When you make the profile assignment, tell them to avoid topics with which they are overly familiar (for example, the summer job they have had for the last four years, their college dorm, etc.). If your students are writing a longer profile, they will need to pick a topic with plenty of activity, enough people for several interviews, and a place that can be described specifically (profiles about "the beach" or "downtown" generally don't work, for instance).

You should also be aware that this assignment may pose problems for some students. Those who do not have ready access to transportation may be encouraged to choose their subjects from the campus community. However, you should avoid limiting your students to campus choices, especially if you have a significant population of commuting students, who might instead be encouraged to focus their attention on subjects in their own neighborhoods. Extremely shy students pose a different kind of problem. Although this assignment does not lend itself well to collaborative writing, you might suggest that students conduct their observations together if they are focusing on the same place or activity. They could then work separately on the observation writeup.

Two other problems with selecting a profile topic are those of accessibility and security. Subjects that may sound exciting in theory may not be possible or appropriate in practice: A doctor or scientist may not be available for interviews; a military installation or a nuclear power plant may be off-limits to the general public.

Similarly, you should discourage students from exploring topics that are potentially dangerous. Students should think twice about profiling something like the county jail (which may be off-limits anyway), a neighborhood with a high incidence of crime, or some activity that presents a health or safety hazard. On the one hand, you don't want your students to select mundane or drab topics, but on the other hand, you should urge them to use discretion when picking a subject to profile.

You can spend class time exchanging topic choices or you can circulate topic sheets. At the top of a sheet of paper students write a tentative title for their profiles. Then they describe in two or three sentences the person, location, or activity that will be the subject of their profile. In one sentence they identify possible readers (class members, readers of a particular newspaper or magazine, or perhaps a special group of readers with a need to know what the writer will discover). These sheets then circulate around the class, with students writing questions or comments and even commenting on other students' comments.

We think it's a good idea for teachers to discuss and even approve students' topic choices because students are unlikely to foresee the possibilities and problems of a topic.

CHAPTER INTRODUCTION

The Writing Situations

The three writing situations that open the chapter suggest some of the possibilities for this kind of writing. Students can see right away that a profile may focus on a place (radio station, rare-book room), a person (artist), or an activity (selling produce at a farmers' market). But they also see that these categories overlap: Writing about a place involves presenting personalities and their activities; writing about a person involves describing his or her activities and the places in which they occur. Finally, these situations show that profiles generally emphasize the incongruous or unexpected, centering on the contrast between expectation and reality (the personal discovery about a radio station or farmers' market, for example). But sometimes what is revealed is simply a new and fascinating experience (such as mural painting).

You could analyze one situation fully for students, identifying all aspects of its rhetorical situation and playing out some of the possibilities in it. Then students could analyze another with you or in small groups. The writing situations are also useful for introducing the basic features of this kind of writing and for discussing the process for writing profiles.

Writing in Your Other Courses

The profile lends itself to a wide range of academic assignments which require first-person research: Observations, interviews, and interpretation are central to these actual assignments drawn from business, education, and anthropology textbooks. You could analyze with students one of these academic assignments. Students might discuss how they could go about putting such a report together—how to get information and whom to get it from. Ask students to find examples of observational/interview assignments from their current courses by reviewing their own textbooks or talking to instructors.

Practice Choosing a Profile Subject: A Collaborative Activity

This collaborative activity enables students to explore the rhetorical situation of the profile. The activity prepares them to approach the readings from the perspective of a writer, studying the ways that various writers have negotiated this rhetorical situation, and it also prompts them to begin thinking about their own topics. As they try out an idea with two or three fellow students, they become aware of the important dimensions of purpose and audience. Then they step back to examine the rhetorical situation of profiling a subject, and to think about the ways in which readers' expectations about and knowledge of the subject affect a writer's approach to it. Because students find this activity so engaging, you will need to remind them to shift from telling about their subjects to answering the questions in the text.

READINGS

Like the writing situations, the readings suggest a range of possibilities for profile writing. Noonan focuses on an activity (brain surgery), while "Soup" focuses on a person (Albert Yeganeh), and Cable on a place (the Goodbody Mortuaries). The longest selection in the chapter, by Catherine S. Manegold, might be said to focus on a situation—that faced by teens in urban schools. You might contrast the degrees of objectivity Noonan and the anonymous author of "Soup" bring to their writing and compare the ways they use interpreters (the surgeons in Noonan's piece and the customers in the "Soup" essay) to make their subjects comprehensible to their readers. Whereas Noonan and Cable use narrative to organize their information, Manegold and the author of "Soup" rely on the juxtaposition of different types of information.

Topics in Analysis Questions and Commentaries

These lists can serve as a valuable quick reference, enabling you in class or in conference to direct a student's attention to a particular feature in an essay question or Commentary. The student may find ideas for addressing a particular problem in revising his or her draft. For example, if a student has difficulty integrating quotations, you might refer him or her to Cable's reading, particularly question 3 of Analyzing Writing Strategies.

Soup

Analyzing Writing Strategies	*Commentary*
1. basic features	organization: topical
2. details and dominant impression	point of view

Noonan

Analyzing Writing Strategies	*Research Commentary*
1. organization: chronological	research
2. quotations	organizing information
	narrative pace
	defining

Manegold

Analyzing Writing Strategies	*Commentary*
1. narrative and descriptive strategies; dominant impression	research: observation and interviews judgments or conclusions
2. organization: topical	

Cable

Analyzing Writing Strategies	*Commentary*
1. opening strategies	point of view
2. descriptions and dominant impression	
3. quotations	

SOUP
The New Yorker

"Soup" is a lively profile of an unusual take-out restaurant and its owner. We ask students to pay close attention to the use of dialogue in the essay. You might also ask students to imagine what kind of person would run a restaurant that serves only soup. What would they want to know about a person like this?

Connecting to Culture and Experience

This activity, which might be handled in small groups or by the class as a whole, asks students to consider a central issue in the reading—dedication to quality on the job. Students may draw from their own experiences in school or at work to answer the questions and probably will have developed definite opinions about values in either environment. If you are asking your students to focus on the "identity and community" thematic strand, you might encourage them to address the issue of excellence in school. If you've chosen to focus on "work and career," you might ask them to limit their discussion to work experiences.

Analyzing Writing Strategies

1. This question asks students to measure "Soup" against the criteria for an effective profile. It encourages them to focus analytically on this particular essay and this genre. It also makes them conscious of the basic features of this kind of writing to prepare them to critique their own and others' profiles.
2. The restaurant is described as a tiny storefront in New York City, marked by an awning and an electric signboard. The key description of the interior occurs in paragraph 5, which details the cramped quarters, the case filled with fresh vegetables, and the prices of the soups, as well as a typical order for "any well-behaved customer." Students' impressions of the place will vary, but they will probably notice that it contributes to the portrait of Mr. Yeganeh, reflecting his single-minded drive.

Considering Topics for Your Own Essay

Students will generate some very interesting or surprising possibilities in response to reading "Soup." Here again we help the students to make the transition between reading and planning their own writing. Interesting or unusual people and places make promising profile topics for students (and readers). You might encourage students to return to this section—and similar sections in the following readings—when they begin the invention process.

Commentary

The commentary discusses a special type of organization—topical. Students may be surprised to realize that there is a most careful plan behind a profile like "Soup" that does not proceed chronologically. We explain in some detail how "Soup" is organized to help students see this topical structure. If they decide to profile a person or a place, it's likely they will use this method for organizing their essays.

The discussion following the scratch outline demonstrates the logic behind the organization of this profile and identifies and distinguishes between material derived from interviews and from observation. It further encourages students to think ahead to the process of writing a profile and choosing an appropriate plan for their own essays. You might ask students to come up with a chronological scratch outline for a profile of Yeganeh and to consider the relative advantages and disadvantages of each plan.

You might also ask students to find or bring in to class other examples of topical organization, either from readings in this text or from another class they are taking. They should make some notes about how the piece is organized so that they can share their understanding with other students, either in small groups or as part of a class discussion.

The Commentary section concludes by helping students to focus on the writer's position in a profile. Students will want to begin considering whether they will be "visible" or "invisible" in their own profiles; this commentary should help them recognize that this decision is dependent on their particular subjects and purposes.

INSIDE THE BRAIN
David Noonan

In this piece, David Noonan describes a team of surgeons operating on a human brain. To alert students to the rhetorical situation in which Noonan is writing, we ask them to notice how he presents graphic detail and technical terminology. You might ask students to explore their associations with surgery, and brain surgery in particular, before they read this piece. What do they expect to find? What do they think would interest them? What might repulse them?

Connecting to Culture and Experience

The questions for discussion, which might be handled as a small-group or a whole-class activity, raise interesting issues concerning the uses—and costs—of disassociation. Using the attitudes of the surgeons in Noonan's piece as a starting point, this section asks students to consider their own experiences with disassociating themselves from their feelings.

Analyzing Writing Strategies

1. Here is one possible scratch outline for Noonan's piece:
   - description of patient on operating table (1)
   - the difficulty of neurosurgery (2–3)
   - preparing to open the skull (4–6)
   - drilling into the skull (graphic and jarring—drill like a worker's tool) (7–8)
   - exposing the brain, retracting the *cerebellum* (9–13)

- looking for the tumor (14–15)
- finding and diagnosing the tumor (16–18)
- attitude towards the patient (seeming indifference) (19–20)
- explanation, defense of surgeon's activity (21–23)

"Inside the Brain" is a somewhat lengthy piece about a complicated and eso-teric subject. A predominantly technical description of brain surgery would have been too difficult to comprehend and more than a little boring for Noonan's au-dience (the general public). He wants to emphasize how meticulously painstaking the procedure is and still show that there are dramatic moments. He succeeds by providing detailed description of preparation for the surgery punctuated by the surprisingly earthy comments from the surgeons. Students who have written ei-ther the remembering an event or remembering a person essay will have little trou-ble identifying the narrative elements in the essay. You might suggest that they com-pare the organization of Noonan's profile with that of the one on Yeganeh.

2. Students might look at this question from two points of view: how dialogue enhances the dramatic quality of the profile and how it helps establish the surgeons as distinct possibilities. This issue of individuality relates to the stereotype of the surgeon as an impersonal technician that Noonan explores in the last part of the profile.

Considering Topics for Your Own Essay

Here students might be encouraged to think about the common conceptions and mis-conceptions we hold about various types of specialists. They might also think about the different aspects of a specialist's work. Are all the aspects of equal importance? Do all require the same degree of training and expertise? Which would readers find most interesting? Students should also be made aware that both library research and per-sonal interviews may be necessary in learning about a specialist's work.

You might use a focused brainstorming session here, or ask students to work in small groups, to list a wide variety of specialists as potential topics. You could then dis-cuss what information they would need to write a profile for one or two of these ideas.

Commentary

One of the points we make is that Noonan gathered information for this profile in var-ious ways—by observing at least one actual operation, by interviewing several surgeons, and probably also by reading about brain surgery. The surgeons he interviewed may have suggested that he look at one or more medical books to review the terminology and procedures. Students often have difficulty imagining what kind of readings they should do for their profiles. You might want to ask your students to speculate on which information Noonan may have gotten from books.

We also stress the way Noonan organizes the information in the profile. We dis-cuss narrative pacing in Chapter 14: Narrating. But here we refer to two types of pac-ing, the parceling out of information as well as the duration of narrative time. You might want to spend some class time exploring the concept of pacing as exemplified in this and the other profiles in this chapter.

See also the exercises on this reading in Chapter 14: Narrating, Chapter 16: Defin-ing, and Chapter 18: Comparing and Contrasting:

- Exercise 14.10 on point of view
- Exercise 16.2 on types of definitions

- Exercise 16.4 on extended definitions
- Exercise 18.2 on using comparisons

SCHOOL SERVES NO PURPOSE
Catherine S. Manegold

This lengthy but engaging selection profiles the case of Crystal Rossi, whom the author has identified as a fairly typical urban teenager struggling with various academic and social pressures. Students will recognize many of the narrative and descriptive strategies Manegold uses; you might also have them ask themselves as they read whether the piece is, as its title suggests, an indictment of the school system or of a whole complex of social and economic factors.

Connecting to Culture and Experience

As usual, this section can be used in either a small group or a larger class setting or in a combination of the two. Here, students are invited to reflect on their own past experiences, noting the presence or absence of a figure who might have "guided" them through adolescence. In addition to considering this question in terms of their own experience, students are asked to comment on the various social and economic conditions that make such guidance possible.

Analyzing Writing Strategies

1. This question helps students focus on the narrative and descriptive strategies Manegold uses in presenting her subject. As the note in the left margin of the text suggests, you may want to take this opportunity to review with students the narrating and describing strategies discussed in detail in Chapters 14 and 15. Few students will miss the figurative language at the beginning of the piece, in which the dyed streaks in Crystal's hair are compared to Kool-Aid—an image which serves at once to set Crystal apart and to identify her with the stereotype of the rebellious teenager, as well as to suggest, through the comparison to the sweetened drink, that Crystal is in many ways still a child. Students who have had some experience with the issues of self-representation raised in the previous two chapters of the text will readily note the discrepancy between what Crystal says about herself and the ways in which she is perceived by others.

2. As they begin to plan their own profiles, students will need to consider whether to organize their material chronologically, as Noonan and Brian Cable, the author of the following profile, do, or topically, as Manegold and the author of "Soup" do. In Manegold's case, the use of topical organization allows her to incorporate different types of information, from a wide variety of sources, without interrupting or disrupting a chronological narrative.

Considering Topics for Your Own Essay

This section encourages students to consider writing about a particular child or youth, portraying him or her in interaction with a variety of other people. This might be a good opportunity to discuss the differences between the profile and the assignment presented previously in Chapter 3: Remembering People. It may be necessary to warn students that family members, whom the students know intimately, are less likely to be willing to sit for interviews because they may assume that the students know all there is to know about them.

Commentary

This section focuses on the profile as a serious research project, requiring the writer to gather material from different types of sources. Chapter 20: Field Research provides a starting point for the two types of research that are fundamental to profile writing: observation and interview. As this commentary suggests, profile writers may also, like Noonan, draw on more standard research sources; Chapter 21: Library and Internet Research provides detailed guidance here. Students should note that different profile writers use lesser or greater proportions of each type of material and that they may, like Manegold, use a variety of different materials within each type of source, observing several scenes and/or interviewing multiple sources. Finally, the commentary points up the role of the writer as commentator in the profile, reminding students that writers may choose to guide their readers' judgments and reactions more or less directly.

THE LAST STOP
Brian Cable
Brian Cable profiles the Goodbody Mortuaries. His humorous tone is likely to please readers and encourage students to try humor in their own profiles. You might wish to discuss the difficulties inherent in controlling tone, especially humor. Cable's essay is the subject of the Writer at Work section, which discusses his interviewing notes and writeup.

Connecting to Culture and Experience

The questions here point to an interesting aspect of American culture: our attitudes toward death. If students have experienced death and attended funerals, these questions could lead to interesting discussions about different cultural traditions and attitudes concerning death. If Cable is correct, though, you may find students a bit reluctant to respond to these questions. That reluctance, of course, could present another topic for discussion. You might ask students to list, either as a whole class or in small groups, the various terms we use for death and dying and then explore the metaphors that lie behind the terms. What does it mean when we say someone "passed away," "croaked," was "iced," or was "wasted"?

Analyzing Writing Strategies

1. The opening quotation announces the topic of death and dying and, by mentioning the undertaker, even forecasts the specific focus of the profile. The attribution of the epigraph to Mark Twain may lead students to expect that the topic will receive a somewhat humorous treatment. Students will probably agree that whether the profile writers in this chapter begin their pieces with vivid images (Noonan, Manegold) or unusual or surprising quotations (Cable, the author of "Soup"), the purpose is the same: to capture the reader's interest and suggest the topic of the profile. But we want students to recognize also that different subjects require different rhetorical strategies.

2. This question encourages students to make the connection between the specific details used to describe each room and the dominant impression Cable conveys. Students will probably note the contrast between the "homey, lived-in look" of the lobby and the "showroom" atmosphere of the casket room with its bright lights

highlighting the advantages of each coffin, especially the " 'top of the line' " model. These rooms contrast with the chapel with its "musty" smell and dim light. Students may note that the three rooms underscore the impression that the mortuary is above all a business dealing with the practical, physical aspects of death.

3. The list of descriptive details in Cable's notes appears in the left-hand column, where he lists details about Howard ("weird looking," "Tall," "long fingers," "big ears," "Low, sloping forehead," "plays with lips") and about the mortuary itself ("musty, old stained glass," "sunlight filtered," "wooden benches," "contrast brightness," "fluorescent lights," "plexiglass stands"). You might point out in discussing this question the difference between a vague impression like "weird looking" and a specific detail, like "low, sloping forehead." This distinction will be an important one when students are taking notes for their own profiles.

Considering Topics for Your Own Essay

This task asks students to think about the role of preconceptions in profile writing. You might invite students to discuss their preconceptions of a variety of subjects as a way of helping them to find subjects for their own profiles.

Commentary

Here we comment on Cable's use of the first person in profiling the Goodbody Mortuary, compared with the use of the second-person pronoun in the other profiles. Some students have been taught never to use first-person pronouns in formal or academic writing, but the commentary makes it clear that there are valid reasons for its use here. You might discuss this commentary in class in order to help to clear up students' misconceptions about the use of the first-person point of view.

This commentary also discusses tone and the necessity of matching tone with subject matter. We emphasize that Cable's humor does not come at the expense of the mortuary workers, who are treated respectfully and presented objectively. You might point out that some of the humor comes directly from the quotations—from Cable's presenting, without comment, exactly what Deaver and Tim say.

See the following exercises on this reading in Chapter 14: Narrating:

- Exercise 14.10 on point of view
- Exercise 14.12 on using process narrative

PURPOSE AND AUDIENCE

Remind students that awareness of purpose and audience should guide their work in developing a profile, in deciding what to include in the draft and revision, and in choosing how to organize the material. Whether they include visual details, dialogue, or metaphor, whether they organize narratively, whether they focus on a person or an activity, what dominant impression they convey—all these crucial decisions are influenced by what they want to achieve with particular readers.

SUMMARY OF BASIC FEATURES

In this section, we summarize our analysis of the reading selections, distilling four essential features of profile writing:

- an intriguing, well-focused subject
- a vivid presentation of the subject
- a dominant impression and interpretation
- an engaging and informative plan

We illustrate our discussion of these features with extensive references to the readings.

GUIDE TO WRITING

We turn the pages of the Guide to Writing section of the chapter in class, commenting briefly on each section, to help students prepare for the work ahead.

Invention

Here is a list of the invention activities:

- Choosing a subject
- Exploring your preconceptions
- Planning your project
- Posing some preliminary questions
- Finding a tentative interpretation

The Invention section guides students through a variety of activities designed to help them develop a large list of potential subjects, make thoughtful and informed choices, try out their choices with a sample audience, and generate a wealth of details that will be useful to them when they draft. We always give students an overview of the specific invention activities, making the significance of each one clear. The invention work for the profile is extensive. It includes not only the listing, collaborative, and exploring activities, but also activities to help students plan and execute the field research as well.

The first activity is Choosing a Subject. Students are anxious to settle on a topic as soon as possible, ending the uncertainty they see as an obstacle to moving ahead. Some students will be convinced that they know exactly what they want to write about; others will look for a quick solution. However, there are good reasons why we ask students to list here as many possible subjects as they can. We often use a focused brainstorm session (as described earlier in this manual) to generate a large list on the board, to help students expand the range of their thinking about possible subjects. When students have a large list to choose from, they are less likely to settle on safe, predictable choices, they can feel more comfortable that they have made a good choice, and they will be less anxious if their first choice doesn't work out. We consider invention work so important in preparing students for drafting that we sometimes devote class time to reviewing the invention work.

Exploring Your Preconceptions helps students see what they already know or think about the subject. Sometimes these preconceptions are later woven into the profile itself, as in Cable's piece; sometimes they help the writer frame the essay as a contrast to common perceptions of their subject, as in Noonan's piece. In any event, you might discuss with students the way our preconceptions about a subject determine not only our starting point, but also our approach, our selection of details, and even our ability to make sense of what we observe.

Planning Your Project is a useful guide for writers who are confused about how to start their research. It offers suggestions for planning and refers students to Chapter 20: Field Research for additional guidance in observing and interviewing. Field research is quite challenging and interesting for students. Few have had any experience with it, but most students really enjoy it. We require students to revisit their subject several times, in order to gather a rich array of details and impressions. They might focus on sensory details during their first visit, followed by interviews on the following visits. Or they may interview several people on several different visits to get different points of view.

In Posing Some Preliminary Questions, we invite students to think carefully about the questions they will want to ask in their interviews. At this point in the invention process, you might consider arranging for your whole class to conduct an interview with an interesting campus figure, such as a teaching assistant from another country or the director of a campus program. You might also take your class on a field trip, on or off campus, to observe a place or activity. Students may choose to do follow-up interviews or observations and write their profiles on these subjects, or they may choose other subjects. Either way, this activity will give students a model to follow in pursuing their own research.

Finding a Tentative Interpretation helps them reflect on what they've learned about the subject and through exploratory writing to discover a possible focus for their draft.

Testing Your Choice: A Collaborative Activity

Once students have a tentative subject in mind, the group inquiry will provide an opportunity to try it out on a sample audience of two or three students. The responses will help the writer see whether the subject is inherently interesting to a potential audience or whether interest will need to be created through an unexpected angle or an offbeat treatment. You might write some questions on the board to help students focus the discussion, for example:

- What is likely to be most interesting or surprising about your subject?
- How might you get the information you need to write about it?
- What made you choose this subject?
- What unusual twist or angle might you develop?

Planning and Drafting

If students have worked through the invention sequence thoughtfully and have revisited their subject several times, taking notes on each visit, they will be surprised at how much material they have collected. Sometimes students are overwhelmed by the task of turning this mountain of observations, impressions, and reflections into a coherent essay. The activities in this section are especially designed to help students to absorb and analyze the material they have and set goals for organizing, outlining, and drafting the profile.

This is an excellent opportunity for a planning workshop, where students in small groups can try out different alternatives for organizing their material, explore potential readers' interest in certain aspects of or details in the material collected, and experiment with possible ways of shaping the essay. Encourage them to have an open and wide-ranging discussion about their plan and questions for drafting.

If students find themselves struggling at this point or if the material they've collected seems thin and unpromising, there are five suggestions you might make:

1. They might review the invention activities to see where they could be developed further.
2. They might revisit their subject to gather more information.
3. They might do some library research to find background material on the subject.
4. They might tell another student what they've learned about the subject as a way to see how they might present it in a draft.
5. They might review the reading selections for ideas about organizing their own material.

Critical Reading Guide

We often set up an in-class workshop in which students work in pairs. You will want to allow extra time for this workshop, perhaps as much as fifty minutes or an hour, since drafts tend to be fairly long, often longer than the final essay will be. We encourage readers to write comments on the draft and on a separate sheet of paper so that writers will remember what they said. If you have made this a full-blown research project, you might schedule two or three workshops to review successive drafts focusing perhaps on vividness of description first and organizational issues in later drafts.

Revising

Students need time to think about the critical comments from readers and to review the draft with some objectivity. The activities in this section will help them to develop a plan for revising by rereading the draft, focusing on readers' comments, identifying problems in the draft, analyzing the features of the profile, and working to solve the problems. Students may work alone to complete these activities, but several of them can be productive for students working in small groups. For example, once students have a sense of the problems in the draft, they might work with two or three other students to develop solutions, using the problem-solving suggestions as a guide.

To help students to make substantial rather than superficial revisions, we try to arrange a conference and require them to complete the outline and problem-solving chart and to bring it in with them. On this occasion, we often remind them that the chapter readings might now be maximally useful—as they return to them to consider the ways other writers have solved the problems they now face. After they've finished their essay, they'll have an opportunity in Thinking Critically about What You Have Learned to reflect both on how they solved problems in their drafts and how the profiles they read may have influenced their own writing.

Editing and Proofreading

At this point, students will proofread to polish their final drafts, correcting errors of mechanics, usage, punctuation, and spelling. You might ask students to edit outside of class or in class with your guidance. You might also put students in pairs and ask them to proofread each other's essays.

A WRITER AT WORK

The profile is an extremely ambitious project for any writer. So much legwork is involved—observing, conducting interviews, writing up notes—that the prospect of controlling and shaping the mass of information into a cohesive, focused essay may seem a bit overwhelming. By looking at Cable's accumulated field research, students can see how specific details (the personal traits of the funeral director, unusual features of the mortuary) quickly establish themselves in the writer's mind. Cable's observation and interview notes, along with his writeups, provide a useful overlay of invention for the profile draft.

THINKING CRITICALLY ABOUT WHAT YOU HAVE LEARNED

Like the previous two chapters, this chapter concludes by asking students to reflect carefully on their experiences with the type of reading and writing introduced in the chapter. First, we ask students to reexamine the process of writing their own profiles; then they are asked to review what they have learned from the reading selections in the chapter. Finally, students are encouraged to consider the social dimensions of profiles. This section discusses the dual purpose of profile writing (to inform and entertain) as well as the role of the profile writer as interpreter; in particular, the section calls students' attention to the necessity of reading profiles critically, not as objective or neutral documents, but as pieces whose writers have made distinct and significant choices in selecting and presenting their material.

RESPONDING TO PROFILES

Problems like the ones listed below are typical of students' writing of profiles:

Subject
- The essay simply reports information and does not reveal a point of view or an angle on the subject.
- The angle is too pat and predictable, and offers nothing new about the subject: Hell's Angels are actually just ordinary folks like you and me, with families, picnics, and so on.
- The treatment of the subject is superficial; the essay reads like an advertisement for the place or person.

Presentation

- The essay tells rather than shows what happened at the site or in an interview.
- The organization is problematic: Narrative structure breaks down, topical structure is unpredictable, or organization is lacking altogether.
- Too much of the essay is concerned with the writer's process: ("I cautiously turned the glistening knob of the main door, approached the receptionist, and blurted out, 'I am writing an assignment. I had an appointment to speak with Ms. Simpson.' ").
- There is a wealth of information but no effective organization of it, or conversely, there is too little detail.
- The essay lacks continuity; it seems as though the writeups have simply been "stapled" together.

Pace

- Too much irrelevant information in some places slows the pace.
- The narrative rushes over places where the reader would like more information.
- The pace is uneven or does not build tension or interest as a narrative.
- The pace is slowed by the unnecessary description of the writer's activities ("We were late because we stopped for lunch before we met Mr. Sanchez, and the service in the restaurant was very slow.").

PREPARING FOR CONFERENCES

If you hold conferences with your students on their drafts, you could have them prepare for the conference by filling in the form on the following page.

PREPARING FOR A CONFERENCE: CHAPTER 4

Before the conference, write answers to the questions below. Bring your invention-writing and first draft to the conference.

1. What subject are you profiling? Why did you choose it? What is the single most surprising thing you've learned about it?

2. Who are your readers? How did your awareness of them influence the way you wrote this draft? Be specific.

3. Explain briefly the plan of your essay—your beginning, ending, and sequencing of observations and comments. Why is this plan especially appropriate for your readers? Note one or two ways to improve your plan.

4. What is your interpretation? How did you discover it, and how has it helped you to focus and unify your draft?

5. If you were to return for one more visit, what would you like to find out? Whom would you try to talk to? What information do you still need about the subject?

6. What are you most pleased with in this draft? Be specific.

7. What specifically do you need to do next to revise your draft? List any problems you see in the draft as well as any that have been pointed out by other readers. Say briefly how you might attempt to solve these problems. Use the back of this form for these notes. (If you have completed the text's Revising plan, bring it with you to the conference instead of answering this question.)

CHAPTER 5: EXPLAINING A CONCEPT

THE WRITING ASSIGNMENT

Write an essay that explains a concept. Choose a concept that interests you and that you want to study further. Consider carefully what your readers already know about it and how your essay might add to what they know.

The Nature of the Writing Assignment

This assignment gives students practice in the most common kind of writing they are likely to encounter: writing to convey helpful and interesting information. We like to give students a fairly free rein in choosing their concepts. We urge them to be guided by their academic or extracurricular interests, but we require that their subjects be significant and their information new and interesting for a number of readers.

Aside from requiring fresh, interesting information, this assignment's main demand of a writer is clarity. Reporting information is an exercise in organization, in marshaling available information into a pattern that will be easy for readers to see. The Summary of Basic Features reviews for students a set of strategies including definition, classification, process narration, comparison and contrast, and cause and effect. The assignment invites the student writer to use these strategies in a combination that suits the subject, the readers, and the writer's point.

The essay that explains a concept may be used to introduce students to techniques of library research and to styles of documenting sources (Chapter 22: Using and Acknowledging Sources), and it can become an extended term paper. This chapter introduces students to strategies that they will need again when they write arguments in subsequent chapters, as well as essay exams or reports for classes. As they gain control of these writing strategies, students learn new ways to organize information, to phrase it in their own words, and thus to make it their own. The strategies are the basic tools with which they can make writing a way of learning, of assimilating new knowledge.

If your students are going from Chapter 4 to Chapter 5, you might want to point out some of the similarities and differences between observational and explanatory writing. Both aim to present information in a way that readers will find intelligible and interesting. Observational writing derives mainly from the writer's firsthand experiences and observation, and it often relies on narrative and vivid description to communicate what the writer has seen or learned about the subject. Explanatory writing, on the other hand, typically derives from a variety of sources that may include the writer's personal experience and observation, but it usually depends heavily on what the writer has learned from others through reading and listening. Writers of explanation analyze and synthesize, interpret and summarize the work of others. They present information, draw connections, and discuss implications.

In this chapter, we focus on a particular aim of explanatory writing—writing to explain concepts. This focus enables students to work on the kind of explanation they are reading and writing in most of their courses. Throughout the disciplines, particularly in introductory courses, students are learning basic concepts. They learn by reading and by writing. Understanding the rhetoric of explanatory discourse can help them to become better learners as well as more effective explainers.

Special Problems of This Writing Assignment

In our experience, the main problems that student writers have in this assignment fall into two categories: choosing an appropriate concept and then analyzing and synthesizing the available information on it. One solution to the problem of topic choice is to encourage students to write about subjects introduced in their other courses. In the section Invention and Research, some academic subjects are suggested. This assignment lends itself well to cross-disciplinary writing. We also suggest possible concepts associated with the thematic strands "identity and community" or "work and career." If you are not limiting your students to one of the thematic strands, and if students lack confidence in writing about academic subjects, you might allow them to write about concepts drawn from their extracurricular interests.

Students may ask you "What *is* a concept?" We propose an answer which paraphrases the dictionary definition: *a general idea derived from specific instances.* Each reading in this chapter enables students to understand that concepts are formed from many specific observations or instances. It is also interesting to consider that certain concepts can be intuited or fully recognized long before they are named.

Students will need your help in finding a focus for their essays. Most concepts are too big—too much is known about them—for a college essay, even a long research paper. Consequently, you may want students to write about only one *aspect* of the concept. The readings are useful in illustrating how one narrows a concept to a specific aspect and focus. For example, Toufexis explains the concept of love narrowed to a specific aspect, sexual love. She focuses even more narrowly on the chemistry of love. You might encourage students to see their own search for a topic as a process of moving from a large concept to a specific aspect with a specific focus. Notice how the invention activities are set up to lead students first to a broad overview of the concept and then to a focus on one interesting aspect of it. Only with a focus in mind do they begin collecting research information.

When we teach this assignment, we discuss with students their concept-choice and the concept-focus. We involve the whole class in assessing each other's topic choices and foci.

Presenting a technical concept in a way that is clear and interesting to a general audience challenges student writers. Students may become very concerned with the specificity and accuracy of the information they report and, in the process, forget about engaging readers' interest. The purpose of the essay is to give readers interesting new knowledge. The greatest challenge of this assignment may not be the analysis and selection of information, but the presenting of information in a way that allows readers to understand key terms, follow the organization of the essay, and remain interested in the topic. To succeed with this challenge, students will need to pay particular attention to the tone they use, the cues they provide for readers (see Chapter 13), and the defining and classifying strategies they use (see Chapters 16 and 17).

The assignment can also be a good way to introduce students to library research. The student who knows little about a concept but is curious about it can gather information from the library or by talking with experts. You may want to require some library research from all students, referring them to Chapter 21: Library and Internet Research and Chapter 22: Using and Acknowledging Sources.

The most important problem students have with this writing task is that they may allow themselves to be eclipsed by their sources. Their essays then become dumping grounds for unprocessed information, leaving readers to guess at its significance. One of the hardest things for student writers to do is to discover what they want readers to learn about the information. Without this particular purpose, the essay will be a point-less collection of facts, drifting like an abandoned ship. An essay explaining concepts needs to be organized around a main point or thesis.

Related to discovering an informative purpose is the problem of selecting and arranging the information, using the range of available strategies to achieve the purpose. Student writers often have difficulty designing a plan that will organize the information in a way readers will find interesting and comprehensible. A common problem is the essay that grasps at a simple, ready-made structure, often following the writer's process of discovering the information and ignoring what readers know or need to know about the subject. Again, analyzing the structure of the readings can show students how to avoid this problem. Further advice on essay structure can be found in Chapter 13: Cueing the Reader. Defining, classifying, and comparing and contrasting are explained in Chapters 16 through 18.

Promising and Unpromising Topics

The least problematic topics are those which are established concepts, such as existentialism or bilingualism. Students who choose such topics will probably have little difficulty finding and maintaining a conceptual focus. Other kinds of topics are no less promising, but they can be problematic in different ways:

- *Concepts undergoing change:* Some concepts may be treated from a static and historical perspective. For example, the concept of musical harmony can be considered to be stable and fixed. It might appear this way if one researched it only through reference sources and books. On the other hand, if one researched extensively in specialized periodicals, one could discover challenges by avant-garde musicians to traditional concepts of harmony. In this case, either treatment seems justified, depending on the purpose and audience. For certain other concepts, however, acknowledgment of recent developments and rapidly evolving trends seems vital to an accurate portrayal of the concept; notions of mental illness and democracy, for example, have undergone major transformations in recent years.
- *Concepts about controversial issues:* If your course will cover both explanatory writing (Chapter 5) and persuasive writing (Chapters 6–10), now is the time to begin discussing with your students the differences between the two genres. For this essay, we emphasize that their opinions should not be foregrounded or obviously stated, though it will certainly guide their selection and presentation of material. Students who have chosen a concept they have strong feelings about, e.g., racism

or recycling, will need your guidance to help them shape a balanced, informative treatment of the topic, rather than a partisan, argumentative one. Suggest that students save the argumentative approach for the next assignment, the position paper.

- *Concepts about personal life:* Some students may be attracted to concepts for which personal experience will be their sole resource. Topics in this category from the Collaborative Activity section include friendship, success, and maturity. Students may be more likely to choose these topics if the class has already done personal experience writing (Chapters 2–4). While this focus is certainly valid, you may want to encourage students to move beyond personal experience to published sources. Your guidance here can be supportive and enlightening: Many students will be surprised to discover that library sources are available on such concepts as friendship and maturity and that material from these sources may be interwoven with personal experience anecdotes to create an effective essay.

CHAPTER INTRODUCTION

The Writing Situations

The writing situations that open this chapter demonstrate a range of academic and nonacademic occasions for explaining concepts and educating readers about a subject. The situations involve a variety of sources of information as well as writing strategies. Students can readily see why readers will need or want to know the information explained by each writer. They can also see how these writers purposefully seek to increase their readers' knowledge and appreciation of a concept.

You might use these writing situations as an opportunity to discuss choosing a specific aspect of a concept. For example, in order to illustrate how the first writer might have narrowed his concept further, you could ask your students to think of a specific aspect of religious fundamentalism in a specific time and place. Students could then discuss the particular sources the writer would need to consult in order to focus more narrowly.

Writing in Your Other Courses

These examples of explaining concepts come from college courses in disparate academic domains: hard science, social science, and humanities. Working through this chapter and writing their own essays on a concept will familiarize students with the central role concept definition and explanation play in all fields of inquiry.

Practice Explaining a Concept: A Collaborative Activity

This activity gives students their first classroom opportunity to explain a concept, in this case orally, briefly, and informally, to a small group of their peers. This activity shouldn't take more than fifteen minutes. If the list of possible concepts does not allow sufficient choice, you could lead a class brainstorming session to come up with other possible concepts. Before they begin the activity, you could review with students the interactive nature of the exercise: Following the mini-presentations, listeners ask questions that elicit additional information necessary to clarify the concept. The questions at the end of the activity help students to recognize the importance of audience in shaping their explanations.

READINGS

Topics in Analysis Questions and Commentaries

For your convenience, we list below all the discourse topics addressed in each of the Analyzing Writing Strategies and Commentary sections. This list can serve as a quick reference in class or in conference to direct a student's attention to an essay question or commentary which addresses an area the student needs to work on in revising his or her draft. For example, if a student's draft would benefit from more examples, you could suggest reviewing Passell from the perspective of question 2 and the commentary.

Toufexis

Analyzing Writing Strategies	*Commentary*
1. features of concept explanations	cueing the reader
2. transitions	using sources
	writing strategies

Castro

Analyzing Writing Strategies	*Commentary*
1. defining key terms	using sources
2. readability	organization
	sentence structure

Passell

Analyzing Writing Strategies	*Commentary*
1. organization	definition
2. examples	examples
	focus

Murayama

Analyzing Writing Strategies	*Commentary*
1. source use	engaging readers
2. framing	forecasting plan
3. source use: A Writer at Work	strategies for explaining concepts
	strategies for incorporating quoted material

LOVE: THE RIGHT CHEMISTRY
Anastasia Toufexis

Students usually find this to be an informative and entertaining essay: It shows that explanatory writing need not be dry or dull. Toufexis comes across as an expert on her subject, but she is not a professional scientist. Her authority, like that of students themselves as they write their own essays, comes from research into secondary sources.

Connecting to Culture and Experience

This section, which is particularly useful for students focusing on the thematic strand "identity and community," asks students to respond to Toufexis's essay on a personal level first and then to consider the cultural dimensions of sexual attraction. This section could be assigned first as a written journal entry; in-class follow-up could include whole-class or small-group discussion.

Analyzing Writing Strategies

1. This question asks students to examine Toufexis's essay in light of what we've said about the aims and characteristics of concept explanations. By looking closely at Toufexis's essay both for what is and is not there, students can get a better understanding of what this kind of writing tries to accomplish.
2. This question forecasts the following commentary, asking students to look at Toufexis's use of a key cueing device: transitions. While most students will be familiar with the use of transitions, analyzing their use in Toufexis's essay should help them see the rhetorical value of these devices and use them more confidently in their own writing. Students may note that Toufexis's transitions range from simple linking words such as "but" and "still" to the more sophisticated weaving together of different types of information.

Considering Topics for Your Own Essay

This activity could function as a pre-invention exercise, perhaps for a journal entry. Though you need not present it to students as a way of generating possible topics for their own essays (indeed, to do so might inhibit their listing), you might ask them to refer back to these lists during invention.

This section offers rich possibilities for student writing in an area that will be of interest to many students. The subject of love or romance also lends itself to a pleasing complementarity of printed sources and of personal experience anecdotes.

Commentary

This commentary helps students focus on three fundamental elements of concept explanation: cueing the reader, using sources, and choosing appropriate and effective writing strategies. While students have already examined Toufexis's use of transitions in the second question for analysis, the commentary points out other types of cues and refers students to Chapter 13: Cueing the Reader for a more detailed discussion of these important devices.

The commentary also discusses Toufexis's use of sources, pointing out that she makes use of both printed sources and interviews in gathering information for her essay. While most students will rely primarily on printed sources in gathering material for their own essays, you might refer those who will use interviews as well to Chapter 20: Field

Research for valuable advice on interviewing. You may also want to remind students that they will need to document their sources considerably more thoroughly than Toufexis needs to; this point can bear quite a bit of emphasis, as few students have extensive experience with the thorough and formal citation of sources demanded in academic writing. Chapter 21: Library and Internet Research and Chapter 22: Using and Acknowledging Sources will be particularly valuable resources for this assignment.

Finally, the commentary calls students' attention to three specific types of writing strategies as they appear in Toufexis's essay: narrative strategies (see Chapter 14: Narrating), classification (see Chapter 17: Classifying), and analyzing effects.

See the following exercises based on this reading in Chapter 13: Cueing the Reader and Chapter 18: Comparing and Contrasting:

- Exercise 13.1 on the thesis statement
- Exercise 13.6 on topic sentence strategies
- Exercise 18.2 on analyzing comparisons

CONTINGENT WORKERS
Janice Castro

Because many students—particularly older ones—may have experience as "contingent" workers, they are likely to have strong opinions about the impact of this trend and Castro's evidence for its existence. Some may share Castro's somewhat bleak outlook, while others may see the trend as an opportunity for increased flexibility in the workplace.

Connecting to Culture and Experience

This section, which could be assigned first as a written journal entry and then used as a basis for small-group or whole-class discussion, asks students to reexamine Castro's essay—particularly its disturbing predictions—in light of their own hopes and plans for the future. These questions will be particularly helpful for students writing on the thematic strand "work and career." If you will eventually be assigning Chapter 9: Speculating about Causes, you might find that this essay provides a useful introduction to the concept of a *trend*.

Analyzing Writing Strategies

1. Defining, whether of key or peripheral terms, is a crucial strategy in explaining concepts. Students will probably note that Castro's definition of "contingent workers" is itself somewhat contingent—a developing definition for a still-developing concept. For a thorough discussion of strategies of definition, the text refers students to Chapter 16: Defining.
2. Among the elements that contribute to the readability of Castro's essay, students are likely to identify her definitions of terms (discussed in the previous question), the pace at which she presents information, her use of transitions and other cues (see the second question in Analyzing Writing Strategies and the Commentary following the previous reading selection), and her use of specific statistics and examples, including direct quotations from those affected by the trend.

Considering Topics for Your Own Essay

Here, students are invited to consider writing about some aspect of the world of work, ranging from a variation on the concept explained in Castro's essay to a completely different concept such as the "glass ceiling." As many students will have had limited firsthand experience with the concepts mentioned in this section, you might point out that students who choose to write about this type of topic will be particularly reliant on secondary sources. Again, this section links up nicely with the thematic strand "work and career."

Commentary

This section discusses the use of sources, organization, and sentence structure. Students are once again asked to consider the variety of sources cited in Castro's essay; they are also reminded that they will be expected to document their sources more thoroughly than Castro needs to. The following section of the commentary highlights the ways in which writers organize the information they have gathered and plan their essays. This discussion will prepare students to answer question 1 in the Analyzing Writing Strategies section for the next reading. As students proceed with their own writing, they will find valuable guidelines for selection and organization in the Invention and Planning and Drafting sections of the Guide to Writing later in the chapter. Finally, the commentary discusses the use of specific types of sentence structure in presenting information; you might reassure students that they do not need to know the technical grammatical terms for these types of sentences in order to use sentence combining to good effect in their own writing.

PATH DEPENDENCE: WHY THE BEST DOESN'T ALWAYS WIN
Peter Passell

This selection challenges a notion that most of us accept: The best always wins. In defining an economic term, "path dependence," Passell provides familiar and convincing examples to illustrate his point that the best does not always win. Students may find Passell's examples convincing but his conclusion hard to take.

Connecting to Culture and Experience

This section asks students to think more broadly about the theory that the best does not always win and to practice finding examples to illustrate a general point. This activity might start out as a journal entry or as an in-class writing exercise and then move to small-group discussions.

Analyzing Writing Strategies

1. Here is one possible scratch outline for Passell's essay:
   - opening example of Apple and Microsoft computers leading to general statement that the best does not always win (1–2)
   - example of typewriter keyboard configuration leading to definition of path dependence (3–4)
   - returns to first example of Microsoft to flesh out the definition (5)
   - example of Betamax and VHS videocassette recorders (6–7)
   - example of the automobile engine, path dependence with greater consequences for the environment and the economy (8–11)
   - example with even higher stakes, "light-water nuclear technology" (12–15)
   - concludes with suggestion that path dependence functions in his own field of economics (16)

Students may notice that Passell begins with a recognizable and well-known (to computer users) example of path dependence to get the attention of his readers before he makes his general assertion that the best does not always win. They may also notice that he provides two examples before he gives the technical definition of path dependence in paragraph 5. They may identify various patterns in the remaining paragraphs, including that Passell moves from less to more consequential examples, in terms of the global environment and economy. And they may have different perspectives on the advantages and disadvantages of Passell's organization.

2. These questions allow students to build on the work done for question 1. They may notice, for example, that some examples, like the one in paragraphs 6 and 7, focus mainly on the economic consequences for a single company and others, like the one in paragraphs 8–11, show a heavier cost for all of us. Students will differ in their views of the most informative and memorable examples.

Considering Topics for Your Own Essay

If you are asking your students to draw essay topics from the thematic strand "work and career," this section will be useful in generating possible topics. Since it relies on the interests of individual students, you will probably want to assign it as a journal entry. You might ask students to return to this section during the invention process.

Commentary

In this commentary, we compare Passell's definitions with those provided in the two previous readings. At this point, you might direct your students to Chapter 16: Defining to learn more about the types of definitions that they can incorporate into their own writing. You might also ask them to identify the types of definitions that the three examples given here illustrate.

Paragraph 2 of this commentary develops the issues covered in question 2 of the Analyzing Writing Strategies section. We can't emphasize enough the importance of examples in this kind of writing. Students will probably have experience using examples in previous writing courses, but we want to stress the central role of examples in clarifying concepts as well as in gaining and keeping the attention of the reader.

Finally, we point out that Passell's essay focuses on a specific aspect of his topic, and that his choice of focus is closely related to his purpose of introducing the concept to a general audience. We also remind them that they will need to choose an appropriate focus for their own essays. You may want to refer back to this commentary when they reach the Focusing the Concept section of the Guide to Writing.

See the following exercise based on this reading in Chapter 18: Comparing and Contrasting:

SCHIZOPHRENIA: WHAT IT LOOKS LIKE, HOW IT FEELS
Veronica Murayama

• Exercise 18.3 on analyzing comparisons

This student essay provides a strong model for student writers because Murayama successfully focuses on a narrow and manageable aspect of her concept. She demonstrates that a writer need not cover all areas of a topic in order to write an informative and engaging essay.

Connecting to Culture and Experience

Notice how this section shifts midway from commenting on the subject of Murayama's essay to asking for the students' opinions on this subject. This activity earnestly solicits the students' views; it validates their prior knowledge and their beliefs about mental illness as useful background for understanding the essay. It also teaches students how to talk about ideas in texts. Following class discussion—conducted in small groups or with the whole class—you could give students a few minutes to jot down some notes about the discussion to serve as the basis for a journal entry they will write outside of class.

Analyzing Writing Strategies

1. This question asks students to analyze Murayama's use of summary, paraphrase, and quotation in order to make them aware of the range of possibilities for using sources. They will probably readily note that Murayama allows the schizophrenics to speak for themselves because their words are more compelling than a summary or paraphrase would be. They will also recognize that she does not quote her sources when providing statistics, but that she does quote when the language of the source is technical or particularly strong. You might remind students that the choices they make in determining how to use their sources will depend on their own purposes and readers.

2. By examining the beginnings and endings of these two essays, students will see that framing an essay brings a sense of closure and completion. In an essay explaining a concept, it may highlight the importance of the concept. Murayama's essay, for example, is framed by references to the fact that many homeless people are untreated schizophrenics, certainly a compelling reason to motivate a reader to learn more about schizophrenia. Toufexis's framing is more playful, addressing readers' expectations for an essay explaining love.

3. This analysis activity directs students to the Writer at Work section to examine the strategies Murayama used to narrow her focus after surveying her sources. It also includes a helpful discussion of her integration of sources. You might discuss this section with your students during the invention process.

Considering Topics for Your Own Essay

This section expands from the essay's focus on schizophrenia to the general subject of mental illness. Students can then refocus on different smaller topics; all mental disorders can be considered concepts and would be good choices for this essay. You could conduct a brief but lively whole-class brainstorming session and follow it up with a journal question giving students the opportunity to pick a topic and rehearse it.

Commentary

The commentary concentrates on writing strategies, forecasting, engaging readers, and incorporating quoted material. We first ask students to see a connection between Murayama's purpose for writing on the symptoms of schizophrenia and her techniques for engaging readers. She attempts to engage her readers by offering reasons for learning about schizophrenia and reveals that her purpose is not just to inform her readers but also to influence their attitudes toward homeless schizophrenics. This might be a good time to remind students that they will need to define their own purposes clearly during the writing process.

This commentary also discusses forecasting as a cueing device in Murayama's essay and points out that readers of explanatory essays need such helpful cues. You might refer students to Chapter 13: Cueing the Reader, particularly the section on thesis and forecasting statements.

We also direct students' attention to Murayama's use of the writing strategies classification, cause, and comparison and contrast. Again, in analyzing these strategies, we point out that her use of them hinges on her purpose and audience. We further suggest that students will have to make similar decisions in their own writing.

Finally, we discuss Murayama's strategies for incorporating quotations. Students may have had experience in previous assignments with using dialogue cues, but they may be less familiar with the use of the colon or the noun clause. You might refer students back to this commentary when they are revising and editing their essays if they have trouble smoothly integrating quotations.

PURPOSE AND AUDIENCE

This section highlights the goals of explanatory writing and stresses that writers must take on the role of expert in order to engage and inform readers.

SUMMARY OF BASIC FEATURES

Here is a list of the features covered in this section. It is useful to have students read this section once before they begin work on invention and then to reread it as they are making their revision plans.

- a focused concept
- an appeal to readers' interests
- a logical plan
- clear definitions
- appropriate writing strategies
- careful use of sources

GUIDE TO WRITING

Invention and Research

Here is a list of the invention activities:

- Finding a concept
- Researching the concept
- Focusing the concept

- Testing your choice
- Considering explanatory strategies

It will be a good idea to familiarize your students with these steps before they actually begin the invention process. Suggest that they begin work right away, but spread the work out over several sessions. You can help them stay on track by requiring that they reach a certain point by a certain class meeting.

Testing Your Choice: A Collaborative Activity

At the Testing Your Choice stage of invention, we invite students to meet in small groups to try out their ideas on each other.

Planning and Drafting

The purpose of this section is to help students move smoothly from invention to drafting. After students take time to review their invention writings, they should set some goals for their essays. If there is time, students could explain their goals to you in a brief conference, or they could explain them to one another in small groups.

Critical Reading Guide

We usually urge students to write out comments and suggestions. Students who have participated in peer review of drafts in the past may have made only marginal comments on the draft itself and may have exchanged oral comments with another student. Getting comments in writing helps later when the writer is trying to make a revising plan.

Revising

Working with this section will enable your students to decide what changes they want to make and to carry out these revisions effectively. During this phase of the writing process, you might remind them that they can review the Summary of Basic Features or look at how the writers in this chapter solved similar problems, study the critical comments they received from their peers, or discuss their plans for revisions with you.

Students who seriously question their drafts in light of the guidelines in this section will probably revise their essays substantially. You could point out to students how recursive the process is; as we move from examining readings to doing invention to getting critical comments to making our revision plans, we lead ourselves back through the possibilities for developing an essay of this type, though the tasks are posed differently now.

We find it useful to emphasize to students the importance of rereading and considering the draft *as a whole* before contemplating specific revision changes. Some students resist this step; once they have secured feedback from their classmates, they want to proceed directly to revising their drafts.

You might ask students to make or at least begin their plan for revision under your guidance. If they are able to study their peers' comments, reread their drafts carefully, and compose a scratch outline while they are in the classroom with you available as a resource, they will be well launched into the process and able to complete it and then revise their drafts on their own. Alternatively, students could review them at the next class meeting to ensure that they're on track. Then you could select and duplicate the best revision plan and ask the writer to present it to the class as a model.

Editing and Proofreading

At this point, we suggest that students read through their essays at least three times to check for errors in paragraphs, sentences, and words. You might assign this section to be completed outside of class or in class on the day the revision is due.

A WRITER AT WORK

This section is connected to the last essay in the chapter, the student essay written by Veronica Murayama. It discusses her use of sources: finding them, deciding which ones to use, and integrating them into her essay.

THINKING CRITICALLY ABOUT WHAT YOU HAVE LEARNED

Once students have completed their own essays, we ask them to reflect carefully on their experiences with reading and writing concept explanations. First, students are asked to reexamine the process of writing their own essays; then we ask them to review what they have learned from the reading selections in the chapter. Finally, students are encouraged to think critically about the social dimensions of concept explanation. This section discusses the role of the writer as authoritative interpreter; in particular, the section calls students' attention to the necessity of reading concept explanations critically, not as neutral documents, but as pieces whose writers have made distinct and significant choices in selecting and presenting their material.

RESPONDING TO ESSAYS EXPLAINING CONCEPTS

Here are some typical problems you might find with students' concept explanations:

Concept

- The essay is unfocused. It is not clear what point the writer is trying to make about this concept.
- The writer apparently has not mastered the concept—relies too much on sources and jargon, lacks authority.
- The explanation seems inappropriate for the audience—telling them too much or too little.

Plan

- The essay is hard to follow.
- The writer neglects to forecast the plan and provide transitions.
- The information needs to be rearranged to make more sense.

Definitions and Other Writing Strategies

- Definitions of terms likely to be unfamiliar to readers are inadequate.
- The writer has not made use of clearly relevant strategies of presenting information—comparison and contrast, classification, cause and effect, for example.
- Examples don't seem to have a clear purpose or point.
- The writer concentrates on recent developments, when readers need background information or historical information.
- Instead of reporting on a concept, the writer takes a position on an issue related to the concept.

Sources

- The citations and sources reveal a superficial or incomplete search for information.
- Certain sources are inappropriate, dated, or peripheral.
- The essay relies too much or too little on quoted material.
- Quoted material is not integrated smoothly into the writer's text.
- Sources cited are not in the reference list.
- Citations and references do not consistently follow an accepted documentation style.

PREPARING FOR CONFERENCES

If you hold conferences with your students on their drafts, you could have them prepare for the conference by filling in the form on the following page.

PREPARING FOR A CONFERENCE: CHAPTER 5

Before the conference, write answers to the questions below. Bring your invention-writing and first draft to the conference.

1. What concept are you explaining? How did you come to choose it?

2. Who are your readers? What do you assume they already know about your concept? How did these assumptions influence how you decided to focus your explanation?

3. What main point do you make about your concept?

4. Explain briefly what writing strategies you decided to use—defining, classifying, comparing and contrasting, examining cause and effect, narrating a process—and why they seem appropriate.

5. Describe your organizational plan. How does the essay begin and end? How is the body of information presented?

6. What are you most pleased with in this draft? Be specific.

7. What specifically do you need to do next to revise your draft? List any problems you see in the draft or any that have been pointed out by other readers. Say briefly how you might attempt to solve these problems. Use the back of this form for these notes. (If you have completed the text's Revising plan, bring it with you to the conference instead of answering this question.)

CHAPTER 6: ARGUING A POSITION

THE WRITING ASSIGNMENT

Write a position paper on a controversial issue. Present the issue to readers, take a position, and develop a convincing, well-reasoned argument.

The Nature of the Writing Assignment

With this assignment, students begin the third and perhaps most challenging kind of writing featured in this book—argumentation. The sequence of five types of argumentative writing includes the position paper (Chapter 6), proposal (Chapter 7), evaluation (Chapter 8), speculation about causes (Chapter 9), and literary interpretation (Chapter 10). Whether you teach all or a selection of these chapters, Chapter 6 along with Chapter 19: Arguing will serve as an excellent introduction to the basic rhetorical concepts and strategies of argumentative writing.

As the first chapter in the sequence, Chapter 6 introduces the idea of developing an argumentative strategy that reflects the writer's purpose given the particular audience being addressed. This strategy informs the whole range of writing decisions from choosing an issue to anticipating opposing arguments to establishing a credible tone. Chapter 6 shows the full rhetorical context for such decisions. It is linked through a system of cross-references to the argumentative strategies in Chapter 19: Arguing, where making claims, presenting evidence, refuting opposing arguments, and avoiding logical fallacies are discussed and illustrated in detail.

When students take a position on a controversial issue, they discover not only that people differ in their opinions but also that they have good reasons for their different views. They learn to respect the complexity of these issues and the subtlety of others' reasoning. Because these chapters emphasize the rhetorical aspects of argumentation, they help students to avoid polemics.

The writing assignment requires that students examine the issue critically. Instead of framing an argument to support an already-formed opinion, we encourage students to analyze and evaluate the pros and cons of the issue before reaching their own conclusions. We urge them to examine their own underlying assumptions as critically as they would those of their opponents. We want them to recognize the value of thinking through the issue and of basing their position on solid reasoning and evidence, not merely to convince others but for their own sake as well.

Special Problems of This Writing Assignment

Probably the greatest problem students encounter when they begin writing position papers is mistaking assertion for argumentation. This problem manifests itself in sweeping generalizations unsupported by reasons and evidence. Students with little experience developing an argument usually assume that all they need do is state what they think. They don't realize that they have to give the reasons for their position or offer evidence to support it. Nor do they recognize how important it is to anticipate readers' opposing arguments and either to modify their own position by acknowledging good points or to defend it by refuting arguments with which they disagree.

For some students, the essential problem is lack of experience setting out their reasons in a way that others can follow. For them, reading a diversity of arguments will provide instructive illustrations. If, however, the problem stems from the habit of relying on unexamined assumptions and biases, then the solution becomes more difficult. These students need first to accept the value of introspection and reasoning. They must recognize that the aim of argumentation is not merely to voice your own opinion but to examine it critically.

The root of the problem might be cognitive as well as emotional immaturity. Students who have not yet overcome their own egotism have little experience with other points of view; therefore, they have few strategies for self-analysis, let alone for audience analysis. They may be able to assert their own opinions forcefully, but tend to have difficulty looking critically at their own assumptions or presenting to others a train of thought. In our experience, students with this kind of problem respond well when argumentative writing is presented as an act of communication rather than as an act of aggression. When the emphasis is on creating common ground instead of squashing your opponents into the ground, students feel less defensive and more open to alternative ways of seeing.

Promising and Unpromising Topics

We have found that there is no simple rule for prejudging the promise of topics for position papers. Many experienced instructors feel differently. For example, they often eliminate from consideration issues having to do with matters of faith like abortion and creationism. We find, however, that students can often handle issues such as these if they take seriously other points of view. What we find most limiting is lack of information. If students are not well informed about a topic and do not have the time or inclination to inform themselves, then their argument is likely to be fatuous—full of generalization and lacking in reasons and evidence.

Without making the assignment a full-blown research project, you might encourage students to discuss the issue with others and to do some reading about it. Exploring opposing views should be a routine part of the invention process. Sometimes, however, students make their research one-sided. It is good to seek reasons and evidence to support a position, but students also need to learn about the other side. They need to be able to anticipate opposing arguments and to recognize values and concerns they may share with others.

In the Guide to Writing, we offer a list of possibilities to get students thinking about issues they could write about. Many of the topics we suggest are ones we think students will know and also care about. Caring about the topic is essential for good writing, particularly for argumentative writing. This requirement comes as a surprise to some students and may even be threatening to them. We have been amazed at how many students are reluctant to express an opinion. Sometimes there is a cultural basis to their resistance. They may have been taught that it is inappropriate for them to argue assertively. Some have been made to feel that they know too little to have an opinion worth sharing. Others believe that they are in college to consume ideas and opinions, not to produce them. For these students, we emphasize the process over the product. We explain that taking a position teaches them to analyze issues critically and to evaluate arguments pro and con. With experience, students gain confidence in their reasoning abilities and come to enjoy developing a thoughtful, well-supported argument.

CHAPTER INTRODUCTION

The Writing Situations

The three brief situations that open the chapter show the range of contexts in which people write position papers—for publication in a newspaper, as part of business and community life. The situations also suggest some of the issues debated in position papers—fraternity hazing, corporate responsibility for the environment, and dealing with conflict in schools. You might ask your students to brainstorm a list of other issues even before reading further in the chapter. Or you might come back to these writing situations just before asking students to list topics on which they would consider writing.

Writing in Your Other Courses

Reading and writing about controversial issues is common throughout the curriculum. The examples included here suggest a range of courses—pre-law, health sciences, and business—where students can expect to encounter such assignments. Notice that these assignments do not ask students simply to summarize other people's arguments, but to present and support their own as well. You might ask students to collect similar assignments from their classes and describe them as a journal entry. An in-class discussion of these entries will stress the significance of this genre.

Practice Constructing an Argument for a Position: A Collaborative Activity

This activity gives students a preview of the process of writing a position paper. The most important part of the activity is the reflection at the end. Students are likely to discover that researching their topics will be essential to making a convincing argument. You might ask students from each group to speak to the class for a few minutes about their experiences.

READINGS

These four readings, three of which are new to this edition, should be interesting and challenging to students. Two of them deal with language: one with racially offensive language, the other with political discourse. Another treats the controversial issue of television talk shows. The last essay, written by a first-year college student, deals with children's participation in competitive sports. All are on important, controversial topics. From these examples, students can see how position papers deal with fundamental ethical questions.

See the following exercises based on these selections in Chapter 19: Arguing:

- Exercise 19.2 on making claims
- Exercise 19.3 on the use of fact
- Exercises 19.13 and 19.14 on refutation

Topics in Analysis Questions and Commentaries

These lists can serve as a quick reference to help you plan your discussion of discourse features either in class or in conferences.

Estrada

Analyzing Writing Strategies	*Commentary*
1. features of position papers	basic features
2. anecdote	argumentative strategy
	purpose and audience

Ehrenreich

Analyzing Writing Strategies	*Commentary*
1. example: case	defining the issue
2. tone	using dashes

Molyneaux

Analyzing Writing Strategies	*Commentary*
1. argumentative strategy	writing strategies
2. quotations	cohesive devices: word repetition and synonym

Statsky

Analyzing Writing Strategies	*Commentary*
1. cueing devices	defining the issue
2. citing sources	qualifying the position
3. counterargument	

STICKS AND STONES AND SPORTS TEAM NAMES
Richard Estrada

Estrada's essay deals with a controversial issue: the institutionalization of ethnic slurs. Students will be interested in the controversy and will probably have strong opinions about this subject. In our introduction, we ask students to consider the appropriateness of Estrada's title.

Connecting to Culture and Experience

This section invites students to enter the debate. We ask them to begin by examining their personal experiences with name-calling. You might assign this part of the activity as a journal entry followed by a discussion, in groups or with the whole class, of the larger issue. Students may not have thought in terms of power relationships and may need guidance from you to frame the issue in these terms.

Analyzing Writing Strategies

1. As we always do with the first analysis question of the first reading, we ask students to measure Estrada's essay against the criteria for this genre. This question will increase students' awareness of the basic features of position papers as they read the other essays in the text, other students' essays, and their own.

2. This question asks students to recognize the child's situation and the father's reaction to it as an example of insensitivity rather than hypersensitivity, as some readers might believe. In order to answer this question, students will need to analyze Estrada's readers; you might want to refer them to paragraph 2 of the commentary where we discuss the *Dallas Morning News* readers. Students should be encouraged to look critically at Estrada's argument here and at arguments in the other essays they read for this assignment.

Considering Topics for Your Own Essay

You might assign this section as a journal entry or use it for a whole-class brainstorming activity. Students are likely to have strong opinions about these issues, so discussion should be lively. As a follow-up activity to an in-class brainstorming session, you might ask students to choose an issue and write out arguments and counterarguments for it as a journal entry.

Commentary

In this commentary, we discuss Estrada's essay in terms of the basic features of this genre, stressing the importance of audience. We ask students to consider again the readers of his essay and to think further about how their values and assumptions shape his argumentative strategy. You might spend time discussing his counterarguments and the specific ways in which he accommodates his readers' views, since student writers often have difficulty stretching to consider opposing arguments.

We also include a scratch outline emphasizing the basic features. You might suggest that students return to this commentary when they begin to organize their own essays.

The focus on audience continues in the comparison of Estrada's tempered argument in a conservative newspaper with Churchill's in a liberal journal. In small groups, students could examine the Churchill passage and paragraphs 11–13 of Estrada's essay, adopting the perspective of the readers of each, and discuss the choices the writers make given their specific purpose and audience. This exercise may require students to suspend their views in order to recognize the values and assumptions of others, which will be good practice for their own writing.

See the following exercises based on this reading in Chapter 13: Cueing the Reader, Chapter 17: Classifying, and Chapter 19: Arguing:

- Exercise 13.1 on thesis statements
- Exercise 17.4 on classification
- Exercise 19.6 on anecdote

IN DEFENSE OF TALK SHOWS
Barbara Ehrenreich

Many students will be familiar with television talk shows, but should find Ehrenreich's position new and thought-provoking. We ask students to determine whether her portrayal of talk shows is faithful and whether she provides enough specific detail about talk shows to make them vivid to her readers.

Connecting to Culture and Experience

Students will enjoy doing this activity in small groups. Allow about ten minutes for groups to identify specific television programs, and then encourage them to move into the discussion of class and stereotypes about class. Many students will not recognize the existence of a class structure in the United States, but the specific examples of programs that we provide may increase their awareness.

Analyzing Writing Strategies

1. In the Analyzing Writing Strategies section for the first reading, we introduce students to the possibility of using anecdote in this kind of essay; in this question, we focus on case as a specific type of example available to writers of position papers. Students might notice that Ehrenreich moves from the specific case of Susan to a number of brief examples to make a generalization about these talk shows: that they all follow the same moralistic plot. Students may decide that the case and examples are necessary to provide sufficient evidence to support Ehrenreich's argument.

2. In this question, we return to the subject of tone, which is such an important element of argumentative writing. Students may see more than one tone in this passage: a sarcastic tone in words like "co-crusader" and "dithered" as applied to political leaders, and a serious, earnest tone in the description of the talk show guests as "so needy." In order to answer this question, students will need to analyze Ehrenreich's readers.

Considering Topics for Your Own Essay

In the Considering Topics section for the Estrada reading, we asked students simply to list issues, but in this section we ask them to move beyond listing to construct an argument for a particular position. This activity moves them a little closer to actually writing their own essays. You might assign this section as a journal entry or in-class writing.

Commentary

In this commentary, we focus on one feature of essays arguing a position, the well-defined issue. Comparing Ehrenreich's essay with Estrada's, we discuss the ways in which a writer defines or redefines an issue depending on his or her purpose and audience. We also point out that Ehrenreich's redefinition of morality incorporates aspects of the definition acceptable to those who take the opposing view. You might discuss the advantages and disadvantages of this strategy with your students.

We also draw students' attention to the usefulness of the dash. You might refer students back to this section during the revision process, when they may be ready to focus on refining their writing styles.

See the following exercises based on this reading in Chapter 18: Comparing and Contrasting and Chapter 19: Arguing:

- Exercise 18.2 on comparison
- Exercise 19.9 on case

THE DECLINING ART OF POLITICAL DEBATE
Guy Molyneaux

Our questions in this introduction encourage students to apply Molyneaux's argument about political debate to arguments that may be more familiar to them. Students may need help understanding some of the references, so you might want to conduct a class discussion of them before they read the essay.

Connecting to Culture and Experience

This section asks students to bring the issues discussed by Molyneaux to a personal level. You might ask students to write out an experience that they can then share with a small group of students. Individual students from each group could report their collective findings to the whole class.

Analyzing Writing Strategies

1. Here is one scratch outline of Molyneaux's essay:
   - presents the issue using several examples (1–2)
   - defines the issue and asserts his position (3)
   - acknowledges a different perspective on the issue and appeals to both sides of the political debate (4)
   - identifies causes for the decline of the art of political debate (5)
   - uses comparison to reassert his position (6)
   - contrasts current style of political debate with the art of persuasion (7–8)
   - gives anecdote to exemplify failure to seek shared values (9–10)
   - compares current political rhetoric with great political rhetoric (11–13)
   - suggests causes of decline (14)
   - places blame for decline on both sides of political debate and on the media (15)

   You might have students outline this essay in small groups and then conduct a whole-class discussion to determine how effectively Molyneaux establishes common values. Individuals could then summarize the findings of the class in writing, perhaps for a journal entry.

2. This question encourages students to look closely at Molyneaux's use of quotations. In the essay assignment for this chapter, students will be applying what they have learned so far about choosing and incorporating quotations to a new kind of writing. It might be useful to answer this question with them in a whole-class discussion.

Considering Topics for Your Own Essay

This section invites students to narrow possible topics to issues prominent on the local level, either on campus or in their community. It also asks students to think specifically about conducting research on a particular issue. You might ask students to do this activity in small groups; then you could talk about strategies for researching an issue with the whole class.

Commentary

In this commentary, we discuss Molyneaux's use of writing strategies. As we point out, he uses a wide variety, and you might want to stress that students need not feel compelled to use as many in their own writing. Students who wrote an essay explaining a concept will be familiar with these strategies, but you might want to refer them to Chapter 17: Classifying and Chapter 18: Comparing and Contrasting at this point.

We also point to Molyneaux's use of cohesive devices, specifically word repetition, synonyms, and pronouns. This section gives you the opportunity to address the problem of ambiguous pronouns, like *this,* which frequently turn up in student essays. You can use their own confusion over Molyneaux's meaning to illustrate the problems that may arise when their own pronouns are not clear. This might also be a good time to consult Chapter 13: Cueing the Reader.

CHILDREN NEED TO PLAY, NOT COMPETE
Jessica Statsky

This essay treats a topic with which some students may have had personal experience: organized sports for children. The headnote invites them to reflect on their experience, and you might make this the subject of class discussion.

Connecting to Culture and Experience

This activity focuses on Statsky's basic assumption about traditional American values. Once again, the discussion can take place in small groups or with the whole class. Students are invited to test her assumption against their own experience and observation. They are asked specifically to think about how the educational system deals with the ideas of cooperation and competition and also to examine their treatment in the media and advertising. The point is to get them to come up with specific instances to support one point of view or the other.

Analyzing Writing Strategies

1. You can expect students to notice the following cueing devices. Statsky does some forecasting, but her essay could be improved on this score. She forecasts the first reason at the end of paragraph 1, and repeats it again at the end of paragraph 2, where she also forecasts the second reason. Students should question this repetition. You might ask them to suggest language Statsky could have used to concisely forecast all three of her reasons.

   She does a good job with topic sentences both to introduce the topic of the paragraph (as in paragraph 3) and to provide a summary/transition (as in paragraph 4). You might want to emphasize her use of explicit transitions: "For example" (paragraphs 3 and 8), "another reason" and "Consequently" (paragraph 7), and "Indeed" (paragraph 8).

2. Statsky refers to as many as twelve authorities, including Dr. Tutko (paragraph 3), the mother of a Pee Wee Football player (paragraph 4), Rablovsky and several unidentified studies (paragraph 5), and so on. Since there are so many authorities cited, you might divide them among the students (working in pairs or small groups) and have them report their conclusions to the class.

3. This question directs students' attention to the Writer at Work section. In particular, it focuses on Statsky's purpose and audience analysis and how it changed as she drafted and revised the essay.

Considering Topics for Your Own Essay

Students will be surprised at how many controversial issues related to childhood and adolescence they can come up with. You might generate the list in a class brainstorming session and then invite students to choose a topic and discuss it with the other students who chose that topic.

Commentary

This commentary treats important aspects of two basic features of this kind of writing.position: defining the issue and qualifying the position. Statsky is careful (some readers may think overly careful) to state the issue precisely. You might ask students to consider whether each of her distinctions is really needed. For example, she specifies non-contact as well as contact sports. This distinction would be important if someone argued that contact sports might be dangerous to children but non-contact sports are not.

See the following exercises based on this reading in Chapter 19: Arguing:

- Exercise 19.2 on evaluating claims
- Exercise 19.5 on using authorities
- Exercise 19.6 on the use of anecdote
- Exercise 19.13 on analyzing a refutation
- Exercise 19.14 on writing a refutation

PURPOSE AND AUDIENCE

This section treats purpose and audience in position-paper writing. Purpose and audience are basic concepts for every type of writing, but are essential for argumentation. The argumentative strategy that writers devise depends on how well they can anticipate their readers' assumptions and values and adjust their purpose to their particular audience. We identify a spectrum of purposes and audiences. You might ask students to try to infer the writers' aims and assumptions about readers from the selections in this chapter.

SUMMARY OF BASIC FEATURES

In this section we review the important characteristics of the position paper:

- a well-defined issue
- a clear position

- a convincing, well-reasoned argument
- an appropriate tone

As you move through the argumentative writing chapters, you might want to point out that many of the same features are considered essential.

GUIDE TO WRITING

Invention and Research

We recommend the following invention activities to help students to analyze the issue and develop an argument for particular readers:

- Choosing an issue
- Exploring the issue
- Considering your purpose and audience
- Testing your choice
- Developing your argument
- Developing your counterargument
- Deciding on an argumentative strategy

Under the first heading, we propose a list of possible topics to get students thinking of issues in which they have an interest. Throughout the *Guide*, we encourage students to consider their purpose and audience, and we also emphasize the deliberative aspects of argumentation, asking students to explore all sides of the issue.

Testing Your Choice: A Collaborative Activity

This collaborative activity really serves as a further way for students to test their choice of topic. Students are asked to tell the others about the issue they have chosen to address in their essays. The task of briefly explaining an issue is not as simple as it may sound. To explain the issue, students need to have given it considerable thought and also need to have some sense of how much their listeners may know about it. If students find that their group members see the issue differently than they do, they may need to redefine it for the others, indicating why they see it as they do.

If the issue is one that the others in the group feel strongly about, they may wind up debating it. Although such a discussion could take up more time than your schedule allows, debating can be a very productive invention and critical thinking exercise.

Planning and Drafting

If you have students working in groups, you might give them an opportunity to discuss their goals and plans. You could have them bring to class a tentative outline to present to the group. The group members could then query the writer as to how certain elements of the outline embody the writer's purpose and expectations about readers. Students, for example, might ask the writer what made her decide on a particular sequence of reasons or why she chose to refute a particular argument. Explaining her plans might lead the writer to clarify or even modify them. The group could also help the writer consider other possibilities. Such a discussion could help the writer not only develop her thinking on the issue but also possibly develop a better sense of audience.

Critical Reading Guide

Students are likely to take lightly the request that they identify their purpose and audience for their readers. For example, they may assume that all they need to say about purpose is that they are trying to convince readers to accept their position. Since readers seldom adopt writers' positions completely, however, writers dealing with highly controversial issues usually have more limited—and realistic—aims. They might aim, for example, to get readers to accept certain arguments even if they won't accept the writer's conclusion. You might want to spend some time discussing purpose so that students can better prepare their readers.

Since position papers are difficult intellectually as well as rhetorically, you might want to organize more than one reading, focusing each time on different features. A first reading, for example, might focus on presentation of the issue and statement of the thesis, while further readings might focus on the points in the argument and their organization.

Revising

You might want to point out to students that the guides for the reader in the previous section and the plan for revising presented here both center on the basic features of position papers. The plan for revising leads them to identify problems having to do with the basic features in their drafts. The advice under Solving the Problems is also organized by the basic features. The rationale for organizing all of this material around the basic features is that it gives students a way to focus their revision on one thing at a time.

Although the advice for solving problems is quite detailed, it is meant only to be suggestive. You might also remind students of how the writers they have read handled potential problems. If students have been working in groups, it might be profitable to have them discuss with their group members one or two of the problems with their drafts and their ideas for solving those problems. Getting students involved in actively discussing their drafts should encourage them to do some substantial revision.

Editing and Proofreading

This section provides an opportunity for students to focus on issues of grammar and style and for you to address these issues within the context of their writing. You might have students complete this section out of class before they turn in the revision. Or you might set aside time in class for students to proofread and edit their own essays or exchange papers and proofread and edit each other's.

A WRITER AT WORK

This section focuses on Jessica Statsky's invention process, specifically those activities that help her to clarify the rhetorical situation in which she is writing. The first activity involves exploring the issue by rehearsing both sides of the argument. Some students may resist examining both sides, feeling that they should concern themselves solely with developing an argument for their own side, whatever that happens to be. You might want to discuss why it is important intellectually as well as rhetorically to examine both sides.

Statsky decides, as a result of her exploration of the issue, to address her essay to parents who are undecided about involving their children in organized, competitive sports. Students may observe that in making this choice, Statsky avoids addressing questions about cultural attitudes toward competition and winning. You might point out, however, that her final, and most important, argument focuses on competition and winning.

THINKING CRITICALLY ABOUT WHAT YOU HAVE LEARNED

As students complete their own projects, we ask them to reflect carefully on their experience with reading and writing essays that take positions on controversial issues. First, students are asked to reexamine the process of writing their own essays; then we ask them to review what they have learned about taking a position from the readings in this chapter. Finally, students are encouraged to think critically about cultural attitudes about public debate and controversy as reflected in position papers. This section begins by pointing out that writing that takes a position plays an important role in a democracy—especially in American democracy, which is based on a model of citizen participation. We suggest that, unlike "brawling," the goal of argument is to find a workable common ground, and that careful argument requires its participants to scrutinize their own assumptions, as well as taking the assumptions of their opponents into account. However, the section continues, the ideal of rational, objective argument may not be so ideal after all: Not only may objectivity be an illusion and rationality a mask for rationalization, but the privileging of "rational" discourse may serve to exclude and even repress opinions which are different either in style of presentation or in content. When individuals or groups who hold these opinions are made to conform to the model of "objective" argument in order to be heard, the "common ground" that is the goal of rational debate can easily become a damaging compromise that maintains the status quo. These ideas may be somewhat difficult for students to grasp; the For Discussion section following this commentary should help to facilitate class discussion.

RESPONDING TO ESSAYS TAKING A POSITION

You might expect to find problems like the ones listed below in student essays taking a position on a controversial issue.

Issue

- The issue the student is writing about is not really an issue—no one is debating it.
- The issue is not adequately described or opposing views are not clearly explained.

Position

- The writer does not assert a position on the issue; the writer may waffle, agreeing with one side and then the other, but never taking a stand.
- The writer merely reports opposing positions.
- The thesis is asserted too soon or too late.
- The key terms of the thesis do not seem appropriate and are not carried through the essay.

Argument

- It is difficult to see exactly why the writer takes the position; the reasons would be difficult or impossible to list.
- There is no explicitly cued, logical progression to the argument.
- The argument would be stronger if the points were arranged in a different order.
- Support is thin—relatively few examples, anecdotes, statistics, etc.
- The argument is adequately supported but seems flat, uncommitted, lacking surprises or insights, and likely to bore readers.
- The writer ignores readers—no objections or opposing arguments accommodated or refuted.

Tone

- The tone seems inappropriate to the writer's purpose and assumed readers.

PREPARING FOR CONFERENCES

If you hold conferences with your students on their drafts, you could have them prepare for the conference by filling in the form on the following page.

PREPARING FOR A CONFERENCE: CHAPTER 6

Before the conference, write answers to the questions below. Bring your invention-writing and first draft to the conference.

1. Which controversial issue are you writing about? How did you come to choose it? Why are people still debating it?

2. What is your position on the issue?

3. Who are your readers and how do you want to influence them?

4. For what reasons do you take this position? Be prepared to talk about their relation to each other, their sequence in your essay, and ways you might anticipate readers' objections to them.

5. What are you most pleased with in this draft? Be specific.

6. What specifically do you need to do next to revise your draft? List any problems you see in the draft or any that other readers have noticed. Say briefly how you might attempt to solve these problems. Use the back of this form for these notes. (If you have completed the text's Revising plan, bring it with you to the conference instead of answering this question.)

CHAPTER 7: PROPOSING A SOLUTION

THE WRITING ASSIGNMENT

Write an essay proposing a solution to a problem. Choose a problem faced by a community or group to which you belong, and address your proposal either to one or more members of the group or to an outsider who might help solve the problem.

The Nature of the Writing Assignment

Proposal writing reinforces the aim of argument as positive and constructive—to convince readers to solve a common problem in a particular way. This view of argumentation (sometimes called Rogerian because it is based on the work of psychologist Carl Rogers) assumes that, in order to get readers to consider alternatives, it is necessary to reduce their sense of threat. Hence, argumentation becomes an effort not to defeat an opponent but to bridge differences by finding or creating common ground.

Learning to write a proposal directly engages students in learning to write for particular readers. For this reason, we have narrowed the scope of the writing task by asking students to propose solutions to problems plaguing communities or groups to which they belong. We want students to practice writing for particular readers whose interests and values they could imagine. In the Guide to Writing, we urge students to anticipate their readers' possible objections, foresee their alternative proposals, and figure out which reasons and evidence they would find most persuasive.

Since many proposals written in the workplace are collaborative, it would be a valuable experience for students to work through this assignment in collaboration with others. Small groups might work together to research a problem and solution and write individual essays, or a group might write a collaborative essay, with each student responsible for a specific section. You could limit them to problems on your campus. Or you might incorporate a service learning project into this assignment and send them out into the community to solve a local problem.

Special Problems of This Writing Assignment

Special difficulties students sometimes encounter as they write proposals involve topic choice and the need to establish the problem's existence and seriousness. Even though students are asked to write about a problem faced by a group to which they belong, they sometimes take on problems that are too abstract or complicated for them to handle effectively in a short time. It is understandable that students should want to solve some of the major problems we as a society face—such as the threat of nuclear annihilation, the lack of shelter for the homeless, or the deterioration of our industrial urban centers. As much as we do not want to discourage students from trying to understand these problems and even possibly contributing to their solution, we also do not want them to fail in their attempts to write successful proposals because their writing is too general. This chapter is designed to teach students how to gather the information they need to make their writing more specific.

A good proposal does two things: it defines a problem and argues for a particular solution. We have found that even the student who argues effectively for a solution may sometimes fail to establish that the problem exists and is serious. Defining the problem actually requires careful assessment of the rhetorical situation. The student must decide just how aware of the problem the readers are and how best to convince them that it is worthy of their attention and possibly their time and money as well.

Promising and Unpromising Topics

Choosing an appropriate topic is probably the hardest part of proposal writing. Some students know immediately what they want to write about, while others are at a loss. Perhaps the greatest stumbling block is abstractness. The more distant the problem is from the writer's personal experience, the harder it is to write about. That is why we urge students to choose a problem plaguing a community or group to which they belong. Even the most abstract problems can be treated in the context of a local group. Those concerned with broad educational problems, for example, might find evidence of the problem in their own high school or college. Those concerned with social and economic problems like homelessness and unemployment might look in their communities. In order to encourage students to localize abstract problems, you could have them each write down on a sheet of paper a national or international problem that concerns them. Each then passes his or her problem to another student, who then writes down a local, personal version of the problem. As a class, you could discuss the ways in which they've narrowed the topics. [Activity suggested by Joan Costello, Inver Hills Community College]

Writing about a problem in a group to which they belong will also help students with the crucial task of analyzing their readers. They can more easily anticipate possible objections to their solutions and alternative solutions others might offer. They can also draw on common values, interests, and experience to establish the seriousness of the problem and argue for the feasibility of the proposed solution.

CHAPTER INTRODUCTION

The Writing Situations

The chapter opens with three writing situations that suggest a range of occasions when proposals might be written. The first proposal, written for a national newsmagazine, deals with educational policy. The second situation involves writing for a college political science course. Another kind of proposal commonly written in colleges and universities treats administrative problems, exemplified by the third situation, a proposal for a handbook for predentistry students.

You could give a brief presentation to your students on the rhetorical features of one of the situations. Using your presentation as a model, students could then work in small groups to develop their own presentations on the rhetorical features of the remaining situations, each small group taking one situation. After all the groups have given their presentations to the class, discussion could center on the similarities and differences among the rhetorical features of the situations. Here is our rhetorical analysis of the second situation, the proposal written in a political science class:

- topic: the four-year presidency
- writer: college student
- audience: the professor, hypothetical policymakers

- problem: presidents are only productive for half of their four-year terms
- reason: they spend too much time getting organized, running for reelection, or being lame ducks
- evidence: examples from recent history
- solution: a six-year nonrenewable presidential term
- reason: it would give presidents 4–5 years of good time
- objection: it could make presidents less responsive to the public will
- refutation: the system of legislative checks and balances would prevent this problem
- alternative solutions: none

Writing in Your Other Courses

These essay assignments from college classes in three disciplines all require analyzing a problem and proposing a solution to it. For all three cases, an audience is specified. You will want to discuss with students how the language of the assignments makes it clear that analyzing, researching, and explaining the problem are important steps for this writing purpose, but that they are all preliminary to and supportive of the main emphasis: the presentation of the solution.

Practice Proposing a Solution: A Collaborative Activity

Conducting this group activity so early in the process, long before they begin to consider their own topics and even before they discuss the chapter readings, students will be drawn surprisingly quickly into the complexities and possibilities of proposing solutions to problems. This activity has the benefits of preparing the students for the readings and anticipating the entire chapter. After about fifteen minutes, shift the students to the set of questions in Part 2 that ask them to step back and reflect together on the experience. After a few more minutes, shift the focus to whole-class discussion to share reflections on and reactions to the process of proposing solutions.

READINGS

These four readings should have appeal to most of your students. All are on important and controversial topics, and all make lucid and well-reasoned proposals to solve serious problems.

Topics in Analysis Questions and Commentaries

This list can serve as a quick reference, indicating where each rhetorical concern is addressed. In class or in conference, you can use it to direct a student's attention to a particular area the student needs to work on. For example, if a student's draft lacks alternative solutions, you could point him or her to Kaus—Commentary and Weisman—Commentary.

Frankel

Analyzing Writing Strategies	*Commentary*
1. features of proposals	organization
2. support	argumentative strategy

Kaus

Analyzing Writing Strategies	*Commentary*
1. strategies of argument	anticipating and evaluating alternative solutions
2. cueing the reader: forecast and transitions	research
	partial or interim solutions
	tone

Weisman

Analyzing Writing Strategies	*Commentary*
1. titling and opening	acknowledging an alternative solution
2. find common values	objection
	argumentative strategy

O'Malley

Analyzing Writing Strategies	*Commentary*
1. solution: define and qualify	taking readers seriously
2. reasons and support	organization
3. revision—A Writer at Work	

UNIVERSAL E-MAIL: WORTHY OF A "NEW FRONTIER" COMMITMENT
Max Frankel

Although your students may not have had access to e-mail before, their entrance into an academic community will probably make it available to them. Consequently, they may have a particular interest in the subject of Frankel's article and his proposal that universal access to e-mail be the focus of political leaders.

Connecting to Culture and Experience

This activity could be done in small groups with a whole-class discussion as a follow-up. Most students will have strong opinions about government intervention in general, which could lead to lively exchanges. Depending on the economic backgrounds of your students, they may have had ready access to e-mail or none at all. As a class, you might discuss the role that economic class plays in making the Internet available.

Analyzing Writing Strategies

1. With the first analysis question of this chapter, we want to focus students' attention on features of this genre. You should encourage students to look critically at Frankel's essay and justify their views on his effectiveness in meeting the criteria we've outlined.
2. This question requires students to look closely at the kind of support Frankel uses. It may be necessary to profile the typical *Times* reader with your students in order for them to judge the effectiveness of the support for Frankel's audience. You might also help students recognize that the effectiveness of the instance of support depends on its location in the article. For example, the Sputnik comparison functions as a kind of call to action in the conclusion of the proposal.

Considering Topics for Your Own Essay

This section draws attention to the real-world possibilities of this genre and will be particularly relevant to working students. In addition, if you are encouraging your students to write on the thematic strand "work and career," this activity can launch them into the invention process. You might assign this section as a journal entry; students could write their proposals in letter or memo form.

Commentary

In this commentary, we outline Frankel's essay to call attention to his organization, which is simple, effective, and works as a model for students' proposals. You might stress the importance of defining the subject, as Frankel does, in case readers are not familiar with it. Students may note that he does not explicitly state his solution, but instead suggests it in paragraph 6 by pointing out the importance of government intervention in mail and telephone services.

We also discuss the relationship between the structure of Frankel's essay and his argumentative strategy and specifically address the function of framing and analogy. Students looking for ways to begin and end their essays may be directed to this reading and commentary during the drafting and revision process. You might also want to have students consult the section on analogy in Chapter 18: Comparing and Contrasting.

In paragraph 5, we continue a discussion begun in question 1 of Analyzing Writing Strategies and stress the importance of anticipating readers' questions. You might ask students to refer back to this list when they begin to anticipate their own readers' questions. They could formulate their own lists using this one as a model.

Finally, we give you an opportunity to address the issue of tone. Students who are emotionally involved with the problem they choose may have difficulty achieving a balanced tone. You can help them recognize tone as an argumentative strategy and realize the ramifications of the tone they adopt.

STREET HASSLE
Mickey Kaus

Both male and female students are likely to find this essay interesting and even provocative, and it is sure to provide for plenty of spirited class discussion. As the introductory note suggests, Kaus redefines the problem in question, locating it not in a conflict between the rights of individuals, but in a conflict between individual rights and a larger ideal of "civility." We ask students to consider especially Kaus's treatment of other proposed solutions to the problem of public verbal harassment.

Connecting to Culture and Experience

This section, which could be assigned first as a written journal entry and then used as a basis for small-group or whole-class discussion, asks students to consider their own experiences with "street hassles." You may find that female students have considerably more to say on this subject than males since verbal harassment is usually defined as uninvited remarks of a sexual nature. You could ask students to discuss other kinds of invasions of personal space as well.

Analyzing Writing Strategies

1. A scratch outline of this essay might look like this:
   • introduces problem by referring to Bowman's article (1)
   • criticizes what he feels to be Bowman's excesses in presenting the problem (2–3)

- by comparing problem to panhandling, criticizes conservative hypocrisy in dealing with the problem of verbal harassment of women (4)
- establishes existence and seriousness of problem (5–8)
- refutes alternative solutions (reeducation, civil litigation) (9–10)
- presents own solutions (criminal prosecution) (11–12)

    Students may note that Kaus's plan allows him to appeal to his more conservative readers by spending the first quarter of his essay criticizing Bowman's feminist stance, even though his own solution—criminal prosecution of those who engage in the verbal harassment of women—may seem to some readers considerably more extreme than Bowman's own suggestion of legal recourse on a civil level.

    Students will probably see quickly that, in presenting the problem in the first eight paragraphs, Kaus criticizes—at least implicitly—both conservative (Limbaugh, Wilson) and liberal (Bowman, Galston) commentators. Like his presentation of the problem, his proposed solution may appeal obliquely to both camps. If you have not yet reviewed with your students Chapter 19: Arguing, this question might provide a good opportunity for doing so.

2. This fairly simple question reminds students once again of the importance of cueing the reader. Kaus forecasts his presentation of three possible solutions in the first sentence of paragraph 9; each of the following two paragraphs begins with a simple numerical transition ("Second . . . ," "The third . . .").

Considering Topics for Your Own Essay

This section asks students to use this essay as a springboard to other writing topics about social problems. It asks students to make a list of possible topics; one possibility would be to construct the list on the board, with all class members participating. Then students, working in small groups, could briefly rehearse an argument proposing a solution to a problem they choose from the list.

Commentary

This section discusses several important elements of proposal writing as they appear in Kaus's essay: dealing with alternative solutions, using research, and proposing partial or interim solutions. First, we deal with the strategy of anticipating and evaluating alternative solutions, reminding students that, as writers of their own proposals, they will have certain options in responding to solutions proposed by others. Then we briefly mention the role of research in this type of writing, suggesting that it serves his purpose well. We try to reassure students that it is not always possible to present a complete and conclusive solution—perhaps especially in the case of social problems. Instead, like Kaus, many writers propose "solutions" that amount to steps in the right direction.

    We also return to the subject of tone and compare Kaus's aggressive, sharp tone with Frankel's more inviting one. As we point out, political discourse is often harsh, a risky tone if one's aim is to gain an ally. You might ask students to find examples of political discourse with an aggressive tone and describe the effect such discourse has on their willingness to accept the solution proposed. This activity could be assigned as a journal entry with a follow-up in-class discussion.

    See the following exercise based on this reading in Chapter 13: Cueing the Reader:

- Exercise 13.6 on using rhetorical questions

BIRTH CONTROL IN THE SCHOOLS
Adam Paul Weisman

This essay deals with a problem students should be somewhat familiar with—teenage pregnancy. Weisman advocates a solution to the problem that is controversial. He proposes that birth-control clinics be located on high school campuses to provide students with contraceptives. We point out that the idea of school-based birth-control clinics is not original with Weisman. Your students may be surprised to find a proposal advocating someone else's idea. They should realize, however, that this often happens. The fact that a proposal has been tried already and has had some success should increase its chances of being accepted by readers.

Connecting to Culture and Experience

This activity seeks to involve students in the debate. The discussion can take place in small groups or with the whole class. Since many of your students will have just come from high school, they are likely to have something to say about the problem and whether basing clinics on high school campuses is likely to help ameliorate it.

Analyzing Writing Strategies

1. Writers are always concerned with the writing problem of how to begin an essay. Experienced writers have a repertoire of potential opening gambits they can draw upon. Inexperienced writers, however, tend to get stuck when they don't know just how to begin an essay. It is important for students to develop a set of strategies for beginning and to understand the strategies' advantages and disadvantages in particular rhetorical situations.

   Weisman combines two common strategies in his opening paragraph: beginning with a rhetorical question and citing authorities. His title identifies the proposed solution (birth-control clinics) and combines with the opening paragraph to orient readers and prepare them for the argument, which is the body of the proposal.

2. This question focuses attention on the need to bridge a gap between the writer and readers by establishing common ground through shared values. Students may note that Weisman recognizes objections to the use of schools as the agency to cure all social problems but points to successful nonacademic services performed by schools, such as immunization programs. They may express different opinions about his success.

Considering Topics for Your Own Essay

This activity turns students' attention to the prospect of writing a proposal. It takes a somewhat unusual tack by asking students to consider what problems a particular group—high school or perhaps college students—could help solve. Our intention is to get students to tap their own experiences. This question will inspire good class discussion.

Commentary

We begin our commentary with the concept of the argumentative strategy. This concept helps students understand the rhetoric of writing a proposal. By analyzing the argumentative strategies of writers like Weisman, they begin to see how purpose is affected by the values and assumptions of readers, and to apply this knowledge to their own writing. Moreover, they consider strategically how they might present the problems and argue for their solutions. They also take seriously the need to anticipate and respond to objections others might make to their arguments. In addition, they recognize how central to proposal writing it is to anticipate alternative solutions.

See the following exercises based on this reading in Chapter 13: Cueing the Reader, Chapter 16: Defining, Chapter 17: Classifying, and Chapter 19: Arguing:

- Exercise 13.5 on analyzing topic sentences
- Exercise 16.6 on stipulative definition
- Exercise 17.4 on classification
- Exercise 19.4 on the use of statistics in argument
- Exercise 19.5 on the use of authorities in argument

MORE TESTING, MORE LEARNING
Patrick O'Malley

This student essay shows students the advantages of careful invention, research, and revision. They should also note O'Malley's considerate treatment of readers' objections and alternative solutions. He adds to his credibility by his responsible use of publications from educational psychology and his reference to a Harvard study.

Connecting to Culture and Experience

This activity connects students' personal experiences with the subject of the essay. As they discuss their own experiences with frequent exams, their interest in O'Malley's proposal will be heightened and they will be more receptive to the subsequent rhetorical focus in the questions for analysis. Once again, this discussion can take place in small groups or with the whole class.

Analyzing Writing Strategies

1. This question asks students to underline words or phrases in paragraph 3 that show how O'Malley defines and qualifies his solution. One possibility for getting students started on the questions for analysis would be to discuss the questions briefly after you have discussed the reading. You could even give students a few minutes in class to underline. (Question 2 also calls for underlining.) By providing time for your students to begin this work in class under your guidance, you can help them learn how to annotate a text, an essential strategy of critical reading. Then you could ask them to write out answers to the questions outside of class—to be turned in at the next class meeting.

    A careful underlining of paragraph 3 will reveal that O'Malley explains his solution, gives examples of how it could work in two disciplines, and specifies frequency, length, and question type.

2. O'Malley presents the different parts of his argument—in this case the reasons for or benefits of his proposal—so clearly that they really stand out for the reader. This is the heart of his essay—the changes for the better which will ensue if his proposal is adopted. In each paragraph, the topic is introduced quickly and directly, with brief transitions for paragraphs 5 and 6.

    paragraph 4: "the main reason . . . students learn more"
    paragraph 5: "Another reason . . . improve their study habits"
    paragraph 6: "Frequent exams should also decrease anxiety . . ."

    Students will probably note that the studies conducted by university researchers would carry particular weight with college professors, but they may differ in their views of what is most and least convincing about the support.

3. This challenging question asks students to compare one paragraph of O'Malley's draft with one paragraph of his revision. The most obvious change is elaboration; the revised version elaborates much more extensively on the positive effects of frequent testing, while the draft devotes only two sentences to this. We also see better use of sources, with the well-integrated quotes from the Harvard study and the paraphrase from Frederiksen. Finally, the revision exhibits greater felicity of expression. Ask the students to compare the second sentences of each paragraph, which are on the same topic, for clarity, precision, and elegance.

Considering Topics for Your Own Essay

This section asks students to write about a problem they have encountered in learning something new. You could generate some potential topics for it through whole-class brainstorming and then assign a brief rehearsal of a chosen topic as journal writing.

Commentary

This commentary accentuates the extreme care O'Malley takes with objections and alternative solutions. O'Malley did not merely speculate about his readers' responses to his solution; he also interviewed those directly involved to discover their objections, questions, and preferred solutions. Some instructors encourage or require their students to do interviews as part of the research for this essay. Useful information about conducting interviews is included in Chapter 20: Field Research.

This section also presents the strengths of O'Malley's organization. You might ask students to compare this outline with Frankel's simpler one, discussed in the commentary for his essay. Students may also consult both outlines when they begin to plan their own essays.

See the following exercises based on this reading in Chapter 19: Arguing:

- Exercise 19.7 on analyzing the use of scenario
- Exercise 19.12 on accommodating readers

PURPOSE AND AUDIENCE

As we have suggested, proposal writing, perhaps more than any other kind of writing, requires sensitivity to readers and careful thought to purpose. Throughout the chapter, we discuss the role the argumentative strategy plays in realizing the writer's understanding of the rhetorical situation. Here we remind readers of some of the problems proposal writers encounter with their readers and the ways in which they might try to solve them.

SUMMARY OF BASIC FEATURES

Here we review the most important features of proposals:

- a well-defined problem
- a proposed solution

- a convincing argument
- a reasonable tone

These are basically the same features discussed in Chapter 6: Arguing a Position, the only difference being the shift from issue and position to problem and solution.

GUIDE TO WRITING

Invention and Research

Here is a list of the invention activities:

- Choosing a problem
- Analyzing and defining the problem
- Identifying your readers
- Finding a tentative solution
- Defending your solution
- Testing your choice
- Offering reasons for your proposal
- Considering alternative solutions
- Doing research

You might want to give students an overview of the invention activities and discuss how much time you expect them to spend on them. You could do the first part of the invention, listing problems, in class as whole-class brainstorming or in small groups, beginning with the problems the students have generated in the section Considering Topics for Your Own Essay and moving to other problems the students can think of. Students will progress through the invention sequence at different rates, but you can help them stay on track by requiring that they reach a certain point by a certain class meeting. If you ask them to bring their invention-in-progress to every class meeting, you can ask them to read aloud from it to begin class discussion or to share certain sections with their peers in pairs or small groups.

Testing Your Choice: A Collaborative Activity

This activity will give your students the opportunity to rehearse their plans before an actual audience. By talking with one another in small groups, they will clarify the meanings they have created through the invention exercises. As group members discuss their essay plans, they should question one another about their intentions: "How will you convince readers that the problem is serious?" "Whom do you plan to address your proposal to?" They will also be able to offer suggestions: "Let me tell you one alternative solution I can think of. It would be to . . ." "You know, there's a group here in town working on that problem. It's called . . ."

Planning and Drafting

The purpose of this section is to help students move smoothly from invention to drafting. After students take time to review their invention writings, they should set some goals for their essays. If there is time, students could explain their goals to you in a brief conference, or they could explain them to one another in small groups. As students move into drafting, you can remind them to rely heavily on their invention for material; if they find that their invention is not providing them with enough material, they may need to do more invention writing.

Critical Reading Guide

Since we argue that proposal writing requires a strong sense of audience, getting comments on the draft is especially valuable. You might encourage readers in a draft workshop to pretend they are the readers addressed in the proposal. Role playing like this can be informative and fun. Having two or three students listen as the writer reads the draft aloud might enhance the fun. The listener/readers could discuss the proposal as if they were at a meeting to discuss its merits.

Revising

We find it useful to emphasize to students the importance of rereading and considering their draft as a whole before contemplating specific revision changes. We know that successful writers take time to review their drafts from a global, holistic perspective prior to considering what modifications they will make. Some students resist this step; once they have secured feedback from their classmates, they want to proceed directly to revising their drafts. It would be an excellent use of class time to ask students to study their peers' comments, reread their drafts carefully, and compose a scratch outline while they are in the classroom. They can then discuss their revision plans in small groups with the students who listened to or read their drafts.

Editing and Proofreading

In this section, we suggest that students proofread their essays and edit for errors common to this particular genre. You might ask students to complete this section out of class, but you might also use it as an opportunity to address issues of mechanics and usage in class within the context of their own essays.

A WRITER AT WORK

This section deals with the revision process of the student essay by Patrick O'Malley on frequent testing. It asks students to compare part of O'Malley's draft with his revision. Question 3 in the Analyzing Writing Strategies section also relates O'Malley's essay and this section.

THINKING CRITICALLY ABOUT WHAT YOU HAVE LEARNED

Now that students have completed their own essays proposing solutions, we ask them to reflect on what they have learned about this genre. In addition to reviewing what they have learned about the genre through the reading selections in the chapter and through their own writing, we invite students to consider in some depth the social and economic dimensions of proposals. This section helps students to understand that both of the main components of proposal essays—presenting the problem and proposing the solution—involve ideological considerations and that proposal writers may often be pitting their arguments against the forces of inertia, expediency, or both.

RESPONDING TO ESSAYS PROPOSING SOLUTIONS

You might expect to find problems like the ones listed below in students' proposal essays.

Problem

- It is not clear to whom the proposal is being presented and what the writer expects readers to do about it.
- The problem is much too large or complex for the student writer to enter the debate on it authoritatively: poverty in America, terrorism.
- The problem is too insignificant or temporary to matter to readers (noise in the dorms, lack of school spirit, bad cafeteria food).
- The problem shifts in mid-essay to something different, usually a result of not framing the problem clearly enough in the beginning.

Alternative Solutions

- Alternative solutions are not presented, where there are obvious alternatives.
- The alternative solutions are represented unfairly.
- Alternative solutions are not effectively refuted or accommodated.

Proposed Solution

- The essay focuses on causes or effects of the problem rather than proposing a solution.
- The writer complains about the problem at length and only expresses a demand that it be solved, rather than presenting a feasible solution.
- The essay offers too many solutions, without arguing effectively for one, or for a two-pronged or three-pronged attack on the problem.
- The essay naively proposes an entirely inadequate solution to a large, complex problem, or the proposed solution does not seem workable (it may be frivolous, too complex or costly).
- The essay does not argue effectively for the proposed solution: the proposed solution may lack reasons or evidence, or there may be logical fallacies in the argument.
- The essay ignores obvious or major obstacles or objections to the proposed solution.
- The solution doesn't match the problem (solving the problem of children's excessive TV watching by having teachers assign a weekly environmental project) or proposes a solution which has been tried unsuccessfully in the past (without showing why it could work this time).

Tone

- The essay moralizes, editorializes, or rails about the problem, lecturing the reader.
- The essay denounces those seen as causing the problem.
- The essay seems confused or unclear about the problem, lacks authority.

PREPARING FOR CONFERENCES

If you hold conferences with your students on their drafts, you could have them prepare for the conference by filling in the form on the following page.

PREPARING FOR A CONFERENCE: CHAPTER 7

Before the conference, write answers to the questions below. Bring your invention-writing and first draft to the conference.

1. What problem are you trying to solve? Why is it significant? Who is affected by the problem, and how much do they know about it?

2. What solution are you proposing to solve the problem?

3. Who are your readers? (An individual, committee, group?) Be very specific in identifying your readers. What action do you want them to take?

4. Which of your reasons do you think would be most convincing to these readers? Briefly explain why. How have you anticipated readers' objections to your proposed solution? What else could you do?

5. What alternative solutions do you think your readers might be considering? How have you handled these alternatives? What else could you do?

6. What are you most pleased with in this draft? Be specific.

7. What specifically do you need to do next to revise your draft? List any problems you see in the draft or any problems pointed out by other readers. Say briefly how you might attempt to solve these problems. Use the back of this form for these notes. (If you have completed the text's Revising plan, bring it with you to the conference instead of answering this question.)

CHAPTER 8: JUSTIFYING AN EVALUATION

THE WRITING ASSIGNMENT

Write an essay evaluating a particular subject. State your judgment clearly, and back it up with a convincing argument based on standards of value that your readers will be likely to agree are appropriate for judging this kind of subject.

The Nature of the Writing Assignment

Evaluation essays are so well understood, their features so well established, that we can hold students to a standard of performance that may surprise them in its fullness and preciseness. The evaluation essay is the third in a series of five argumentative writing assignments in this book:

Chapter 6: Arguing a Position

Chapter 7: Proposing a Solution

Chapter 8: Justifying an Evaluation

Chapter 9: Speculating about Causes

Chapter 10: Interpreting Stories

Writing an evaluation requires students to consider carefully their reasons. Sometimes they must bring criteria to the surface, examining their appropriateness for the subject and readers. Students also may need to consider whether their criteria must be justified. Writing an evaluation nearly always draws students into comparison or contrast. Both this chapter and the exercises in Chapter 18: Comparing and Contrasting provide an opportunity to work seriously with students on this basic writing strategy.

Special Problems of This Writing Assignment

This seems like a straightforward assignment: Say whether you like or dislike something, and then say why. It can, nevertheless, go wrong in many ways the first time student writers try it. Students may not be willing to assert firm judgments, or they may not understand that they need to defend their judgments. In addition, because they are unaccustomed to being held to the rhetorical requirements of a specific writing situation, student writers may overlook the requirement to describe the subject for readers who are unfamiliar with it. They may also unwittingly merge or blur their reasons because they lack confidence in them.

These problems suggest that, before you ask students to analyze each other's drafts, you may want to have the class discuss sample essays to see how the writers meet the rhetorical requirements of the assignment. Furthermore, the problems of the assignment make the evaluation a good choice for a double assignment in which you ask students immediately to do a second essay on a different subject. For the first essay, you could give them two or three choices of subjects, such as the same story or movie, and then they could choose their own subjects for the second essay.

Perhaps the biggest problem of all arises when students risk doing this assignment from memory. To support an argument, writers need specific details. A subject to be evaluated needs to be studied and restudied before and during invention and drafting. Students should not evaluate a movie unless they can see it two or three times, nor should they evaluate a novel unless they have time to reread it.

Promising and Unpromising Topics

The first step in the Invention and Research section for this chapter asks students to list possible subjects for their evaluation essays. We provide a list of general topic areas to get students started, a list drawn from our own experience with successful and unsuccessful topics. As you can see, we suggest a range of possible topic areas—including culture, written work, education, government, and leisure—that extends far beyond the few examples we have provided through the chapter readings. We also suggest subjects from the two thematic strands "identity and community" and "work and career."

Our experience has shown us that the most successful essays are those that draw heavily on the writer's interests and expertise. Students who express an avid interest in skateboarding often write fine essays on skateboard magazines, skateboard parks, or skateboard models. Not only are they familiar with the standards usually applied to that field of interest, but they are also able to make comparisons and contrasts to related subjects (for example, other skateboard magazines, parks, or models) with some ease. The topics themselves can be quite ambitious—we have had some remarkable essays evaluating such things as strategic nuclear arms treaties and UAW contracts—but they are successful only when the student has expertise in the topic. You should, by all means, encourage your students to draw on their own strengths, knowledge base, and interests when choosing topics.

By and large, students have the least amount of difficulty evaluating consumer products. Criteria are fairly easy to establish, the essays themselves are not difficult to structure, and comparisons can often be found in personal experience. Students, however, have a tendency to slip into a kind of Madison Avenue prose, uncritically touting the virtues of their chosen product and making claims of "comfort" or "style" that are unsupported by evidence. Personal taste often takes the place of more objective bases for evaluation in essays about consumer products. We discourage essays about consumer products; some instructors forbid them.

We are also wary of topics that try to evaluate abstract concepts such as "friendship" or "greed." Though it is theoretically possible to write such evaluations, it is extremely difficult to decide upon appropriate standards for judgment. Even more difficult is determining the kind of evidence that might be brought to bear on such a topic. Our students have occasionally written creditable essays evaluating "capitalism" or "democracy," but the key to their success seems to lie in the fact that these concepts can be illustrated by referring to specific examples of free market economics or democratic government.

Easily the most promising topics are discrete, tangible objects or events that can be revisited and analyzed—a story or novel, movie, musical recording, concert, play performance, essay in this book, magazine, restaurant, college program or service. Before drafting, students can revisit the subject, taking careful notes. They can revisit once again before revising, keeping the subject *present* throughout the writing process. The immediate presence of a subject makes it easier for a student to amass the evidence or examples required in a strong evaluation essay.

CHAPTER INTRODUCTION

The Writing Situations

The three writing situations that introduce this chapter illustrate a range of on-the-job and academic evaluations. Subjects being evaluated include a college course, an educational television series, and a factory. One of these situations, the course evaluation, permits you to introduce the basic features of evaluation essays:

- The writer provides enough information to give readers a context for judging the course.
- She gives a clear, authoritative judgment: She recommends the course, criticizing the professor, but praising the TA.
- She supports her judgment by contrasting the professor's lectures with the TA's discussion sessions and the professor's remoteness with the TA's accessibility. She concludes that the value of the course material and the effectiveness of the TA make the course worth taking.

This situation thus illustrates judgment, criteria, reasons, and evidence. The only major feature of evaluation not mentioned is refutation.

Writing in Your Other Courses

These three assignments represent some of the kinds of evaluative writing students may encounter in courses in the natural and social sciences and the humanities. You might begin by asking students to add to the list assignments from their own courses requiring evaluation. Be careful to discriminate between assignments requesting evaluation and those simply asking for analysis.

Students may be surprised to learn that academics tend to be more concerned with analysis—what we often call criticism—than evaluation. Analysis, of course, may implicitly include some evaluation. But students will seldom find assignments in literature courses, for example, that ask them to evaluate a poem or novel. Even a request to analyze the artistry of a particular poem should not be misread as a request for evaluation. The question assumes that the poem is artistic. Students are being asked to demonstrate in what ways the poem displays artistry, not to judge whether or not, or even to what degree, it is artistic. Questions asking students to agree or disagree with a critical statement about a work of literature may also be misread as a request for evaluation. Although the answer will involve judgment of the statement or idea as it is applied to the text, the essay should focus more on elucidating the text than on evaluating the statement.

Practice Evaluating a Subject: A Collaborative Activity

This group inquiry activity is designed to engage students in the most basic and yet most difficult aspect of evaluative writing: choosing appropriate criteria or standards for judgment. Notice that the activity has two parts. First, students discuss the criteria they would use for evaluating the subject they have chosen. Then, they reflect on the process of choosing standards. The second part of the task will likely be new for them because few students—indeed, few people other than experts in a field—think about the standards by which they judge things. Normally, we just make judgments without thinking seriously about the values underlying our judgments. Through this group inquiry activity, you can lead students to recognize the importance of self-reflectiveness and critical analysis.

If students have difficulty coming up with reasons, you might advise them to think of a particular instance they are all familiar with and to consider how they would judge that. The group inquiry activity asks them to arrive ultimately at a consensus about the reasons, but not about the judgment. Because the process of consensus building often involves argument, they should expect to disagree and they need to see how such disagreement can help them to anticipate and handle the rhetorical situation in which they will be writing.

READINGS

Topics in Analysis Questions and Commentaries

Two of the reading selections in this chapter deal with popular culture—film and television. Terrence Rafferty evaluates the film *Devil in a Blue Dress*. Amitai Etzioni's essay deals with a topic familiar to most students: jobs for teenagers at fast-food restaurants. James Wolcott reviews the television program *Night Stand*. Finally, Christine Romano evaluates the essay "Children Need to Play, Not Compete," a student essay by Jessica Statsky included in Chapter 6: Arguing a Position.

For your convenience as a quick reference, we list below the discourse topics addressed in each of the Analyzing Writing Strategies questions and in the Commentary. You might use this list in class or in conference to refer students to particular discourse features they need to review.

Rafferty

Analyzing Writing Strategies	*Commentary*
1. features of evaluative essays	argumentative strategy
2. comparison	presentation of the subject
	thesis statement
	arguing for judgment
	standards

Etzioni

Analyzing Writing Strategies	*Commentary*
1. presentation of the subject	thesis statement
2. support	argumentative strategy
	forecasting
	standards

Wolcott

Analyzing Writing Strategies	*Commentary*
1. framing	comparison and contrast
2. examples; quotations	argumentative strategy

Romano

Analyzing Writing Strategies	*Commentary*
1. forecasting	standards
2. writer's credibility	judgment
3. anticipating and accommodating readers' standards	topic sentences

BLACK EYE
Terrence
Rafferty

In this introduction, we ask students to focus on the first basic feature of evaluations and to consider whether Rafferty has presented his subject sufficiently well for them to make their own judgments about the film. We also ask them to pay attention to the kinds of choices that he and other film reviewers must make in presenting the subject, specifically in determining what to reveal and what to withhold in describing the film.

Connecting to Culture and Experience

This activity, which ties in neatly with the thematic strand "identity and community," could be done in small groups with a large-group follow-up discussion. The images that students arrive at will depend in part on their ethnic and economic backgrounds. It might be necessary for you to provide them with specific information to increase their awareness of cultures that differ from theirs.

Analyzing Writing Strategies

1. This question asks students to measure Rafferty's evaluation of the film against the criteria for this particular genre. We want to make students aware of the basic features of an evaluation essay early in this assignment and to give them practice in analyzing these features to prepare them for their own writing. You might have students write out the answers and then discuss them with the whole class.
2. In this question, we focus on the ways in which Rafferty establishes his authority as a movie reviewer, in particular by using comparison. Many students, particularly younger ones, may be unfamiliar with the detective novels and film that Rafferty refers to, so you may want to give them additional information. But we also want them to analyze their own responses as readers approaching the essay with diverse knowledge bases.

Considering Topics for Your Own Essay

You might assign this section as a journal entry or refer students to it during the invention process. In this section, we stress the importance of thoroughly knowing the subject of the evaluation, which might require viewing a movie several times. We also draw students' attention to the need to analyze their own assumptions about their readers when they set the standards against which they will evaluate their subjects.

Commentary

In this commentary, we focus on the relationship between the purpose of the essay and the argumentative strategy. We point out that since Rafferty's purpose is to give readers enough information to determine for themselves whether to see the film, he must develop a strategy that identifies and describes the film, places it in the context of other films of its genre, asserts a judgment of its value, and supports the judgment. We show how his argumentative strategy works by outlining it. As we point out and the outline demonstrates, Rafferty saves his thesis for the end of his essay. We discuss placing the thesis in the conclusion further in Chapter 13: Cueing the Reader.

We also return to the discussion of audience begun in question 2 of Analyzing Writing Strategies. You might show your students copies of the *New Yorker,* if they are not familiar with the magazine, to give them an idea of the context for Rafferty's essay and the perspectives of his readers. It would be interesting to discuss whether your students see themselves as members of his audience and whether they share the standards of this audience.

WORKING AT MCDONALD'S
Amitai Etzioni

In the introduction to this reading, we point out that Etzioni relied on his children for help in his evaluation of fast-food jobs. We ask students to determine the effect his admission that he relied on his children has on his credibility. Students may recognize that consulting those who actually hold these jobs adds to his credibility.

Connecting to Culture and Experience

If you are asking your students to draw their subjects from the topic strand "work and career," this activity is particularly appropriate. You might have them write down the skills that they see as essential for their own individual job or career goals. Then, in small groups, they could review Etzioni's essay and discuss the skills cited there that seem important to them. A follow-up discussion with the entire class would enlarge the perspectives of all the students.

Analyzing Writing Strategies

1. This question requires students to look closely at Etzioni's essay with their own experiences with fast-food restaurants in mind. Those who have worked at these jobs may find fault with Etzioni's presentation of them. We ask them to speculate about why Etzioni may have left out specific details. If they consider his omissions significant, you might ask them to think about how Etzioni might have argued against their objections.
2. Students will discover that Etzioni uses the two studies to support an evaluation of these jobs that in some ways contradicts the conclusions of the researchers. They may note, for example, that although Charper and Fraser see value in the skills that teenage workers learn, like how to use a cash register, Etzioni sees these skills as insignificant in helping them gain higher-paying jobs.

Considering Topics for Your Own Essay

This section will be useful to students writing on a topic from the "work and career" strand. This activity will increase their awareness of the need for establishing standards with which to measure their subjects. It will also help students realize that they will need to research their topics in order to support their judgments.

Commentary

Here we return to the discussion of cueing devices begun in the commentary for Rafferty's essay. You might encourage your students to compare the rhetorical situation of Etzioni's essay with that of Rafferty's to determine the reasons for their choices in positioning their thesis statements and point out that the students will need to make similar decisions when they write their own essays. We also discuss Etzioni's forecasting statement and speculate about why he chose to reverse the order of his first two reasons. We again discuss standards for judging and the need to ensure that they are shared by the writer and readers.

This commentary also focuses on Etzioni's reasons for making his judgment. We include a chart of one of Etzioni's reasons and its support; you might suggest that students use this chart as a model when they reach the Developing an Argumentative Strategy section in Invention and Research. Finally, we discuss the strategies that Etzioni uses to explain his reasons—specifically, defining terms and contrasting job skills.

TALKING TRASH   This entertaining essay evaluating a television series provides abundant examples for
James Wolcott   the benefit of readers who may not have seen the series. In this introduction, we ask the students to decide whether Wolcott provides enough information about his subject to allow readers to understand his evaluation. If your students have not read the Ehrenreich essay in Chapter 6, you might suggest that they do so before they read Wolcott's essay.

Connecting to Culture and Experience

This activity will be fun for students and should lead to lively discussions. With the entire class, you might discuss the meaning of Wolcott's statement; then, in small groups, students can complete the activity. A follow-up session with the whole class will allow them to compare lists and share experiences and influences.

Analyzing Writing Strategies

1. This question gives you and your students an opportunity to look at strategies for beginning and ending essays in preparation for their own writing and for critiquing others' papers. You might ask students to write out their answers; then you could lead a class discussion examining the beginnings and endings of the other essays and evaluating the effectiveness of each.
2. By analyzing Wolcott's quotations, students will increase their understanding of how writers use quotations to support judgments and present their subjects. This question also gives you the opportunity to review techniques for integrating quotations.

Considering Topics for Your Own Essay

This section provides students with another chance to explore subjects for their own essays. They also must consider the standards that they would use in their evaluations. You might remind them that they should analyze their readers to ensure that they accept the same standards for judgment. This activity could be assigned as a journal entry or small-group discussion.

Commentary

Our focus in this commentary is on the writing strategy comparison and contrast. Students should be familiar with this strategy, but if necessary, you could refer them to Chapter 18: Comparing and Contrasting.

"CHILDREN NEED TO PLAY, NOT COMPETE" BY JESSICA STATSKY: AN EVALUATION
Christine Romano

This essay, written by a first-year college student, demonstrates how standards drawn from the *Guide* may be used to evaluate a written text. The appeal of this approach to this assignment is that students will find standards readily acceptable to readers. In addition, this exercise should fix the standards firmly in their minds and ultimately enhance their ability to read critically and to argue effectively. In this introduction, we again stress the importance of considering the intended readers when evaluating.

Connecting to Culture and Experience

This section provides students with another opportunity to explore the thematic strand "identity and community." Students might do this activity in small groups; then you could bring them together as a class to discuss their definitions of community.

Analyzing Writing Strategies

1. By analyzing the cueing strategies of forecasting and repeating key terms, students will increase their awareness of the necessity of providing these devices for readers. This question would work well as a small-group activity. You might refer students to Chapter 13: Cueing the Reader before assigning this question.
2. In order to answer this question, students will need to read the section Judging the Writer's Credibility in Chapter 12. You might ask students to write the answer to this question and then discuss it with the entire class. Students may notice that Romano's understanding of Statsky's essay is thorough, her tone is fair and respectful, and she acknowledges the arguments of those who would agree with Statsky.
3. This question sends students to the Writer at Work section for a view of Romano's writing process. It emphasizes the value of getting readers' responses at every step. You might ask students to answer this question in small groups.

Considering Topics for Your Own Essay

This section suggests another subject for an essay, one that may appeal to students because the standards for evaluating could be adopted from the text. You could refer students to this section when they begin the Choosing a Subject section of Invention and Research.

Commentary

In this commentary, we return to the topic of standards and the need to consider the point of view of readers. We also stress that evaluations need not exclusively praise or condemn the subject and that writers making unqualified judgments risk alienating readers. You might point out that most evaluations are qualified, citing both strengths and weaknesses.

We also focus again on cueing strategies, specifically on topic sentences. You might ask students to identify the cueing devices—as listed in Chapter 13—in one of the other essays in this chapter or in *Free Falling and Other Student Essays*. Students could complete this activity in small groups or as a journal entry.

PURPOSE AND AUDIENCE

This section gives you an opportunity to focus class discussion on the concepts of purpose and audience as they pertain to the writing of evaluation essays. The writing situations that open the chapter, together with the illustrative academic assignments in the introduction, should suggest the range of situations in which evaluative essays may be written.

Two of the essay selections exemplify a special use of evaluation: to review instances of popular culture such as films and television programs. If you ask students about the purpose of reviewing cultural artifacts like these, most students will answer in market terms: to help consumers decide which film to see. Although that is undoubtedly the way that readers of newspapers and magazines typically use reviews, the essays presented here attempt to do something more. In the Connecting to Culture and Experience sections, we attempt to make students aware of the ideological underpinnings of the evaluations.

SUMMARY OF BASIC FEATURES

This section summarizes what students have learned from analyzing the readings. We emphasize three basic features:

- a well-presented subject
- a clear, authoritative judgment
- a well-supported argument for the judgment

This discussion of basic features forms a bridge from the readings to the student's own writing. The same features reappear in the Invention and Research activities, in the Critical Reading Guide, and in the Revising section. You may want to refer students back to this summary if they have problems with a particular feature.

GUIDE TO WRITING

Invention and Research

We recommend these activities to help students choose a subject, determine what they think about it, and develop a reasoned argument supporting their judgment for their particular readers:

- Choosing a subject
- Considering your judgment
- Analyzing your readers
- Testing your choice
- Reconsidering your judgment
- Developing an argumentative strategy

You might want to spend class time brainstorming possible subjects for evaluation. You could, of course, assign the whole class the same subject—an evaluation of a short story (possibly chosen from the anthology in Chapter 10: Interpreting Stories), an essay from a chapter in this book, or a film you show on video. If you want to allow greater choice but also want to give students the benefit of collaborative learning, you could invite students to work together in small groups of three to five. These groups could discuss the subject they've chosen, debate their different judgments, and read each other's drafts. Some instructors have found it especially instructive for students to write the essay collaboratively. If you are attracted by this idea, be sure to consider—in advance—how you will grade the essay. Collaborative projects of this kind can be very productive, but they require careful planning and sensitive guidance to make them work well for everyone.

Probably the most difficult invention activity is Developing an Argumentative Strategy. Students tend to have two kinds of difficulty: identifying the standards underlying their judgment and finding evidence. You can address the first problem by having students (working together in pairs or small groups) explain to one another why they think the reasons are appropriate. If students are already working together on the same subject, the topic of what standards they are applying will probably come up. Even if students are not familiar with the particular subject, the writer could describe the subject as fitting into a general class of things (e.g., horror films) and then the group could discuss the question: What makes a horror film good?

The second difficulty—finding evidence—requires that the writer have ready access to the subject being evaluated. If it is a film, the videotape should be available for students to replay. Also, students need to develop a system of notetaking that allows them to refer specifically to the film (for example, by quoting or paraphrasing particular bits of dialogue).

Testing Your Choice: A Collaborative Activity

This group activity allows students to discover the needs and assumptions of their readers. Writers will present their subjects to other students, who will in turn point out gaps in the information provided and suggest standards with which to evaluate.

Planning and Drafting

This section offers advice on reviewing invention writings, setting goals, outlining, and drafting. You may want to spend some class time discussing the goals. Then refocus the basic features in terms of actions students can take, given their particular rhetorical situation, to present the subject effectively and make the argument understandable and convincing.

Critical Reading Guide

This guide to critical reading helps students analyze each other's drafts the way they analyzed the readings at the beginning of the chapter. Once again, all the basic features of evaluation essays are the center of attention. Students are specifically asked to look at these features in the context of the writer's audience and purpose.

Revising

This section urges students first to get an overview of their own essays and a sense of their problems before attempting to solve any single problem. We also encourage students to put off considering readers' critical comments until they have made their own assessments of their essays' strengths and weaknesses.

Editing and Proofreading

In this section, we focus on errors common to this kind of writing. You might ask students to complete this section outside of class or in class under your supervision.

A WRITER AT WORK

This section illustrates Christine Romano's attempts to anticipate her readers' standards of judgment and the revisions she makes to accommodate them. This section is the focus of question 3 of Analyzing Writing Strategies.

THINKING CRITICALLY ABOUT WHAT YOU HAVE LEARNED

As students complete their own evaluation essays, we ask them to reflect on what they have learned from the reading and writing they've done in this genre. After reviewing their own writing processes and examining what they have learned from the reading selections in this chapter, students are invited to consider the social and cultural dimensions of writing evaluations. This section begins by reiterating the centrality of evaluation in our society; it continues by pointing out the power of evaluative writing to foster an all-or-nothing thinking. Students may not have considered that a large part of the power of evaluative writing lies neither in its capacity to praise nor in its capacity to damn, but in its tendency to ignore completely those subjects that fall outside its interests, thus "excluding and silencing" works or products produced by marginalized groups or individuals. As this section continues, discussing the "hidden assumptions of evaluation," it reiterates for students the extent to which evaluations, rather than being neutral, objective documents, are informed by specific ideologies.

RESPONDING TO ESSAYS MAKING EVALUATIONS

You might expect your students' evaluation essays to have problems like the ones listed below.

Subject

- The subject is not within the limits set by your assignment (you assigned reviews of current movies and the student evaluates a fast-food place).
- The subject is too broad (jazz music rather than a particular jazz recording).
- The subject does not lend itself to evaluation (the homeless, cigarette smoking, school spirit).

Judgment

- The essay describes the subject or merely identifies its strong and weak points but does not express a clear judgment based on evidence.
- The judgment is overstated, without appropriate qualification or clarification.

Argument

- There is too much descriptive, historical, or biographical background, distracting from the argument.
- The argument consists of a string of unsupported value judgments ("The acting was good. The directing was excellent. The cinematography was well done.").
- There are too many reasons or too few.
- The reasons seem arbitrary and inappropriate, not based on standards usually applied to a subject of that kind.
- The reasons are not organized logically.
- The reasons do not support the judgment.
- The essay fails to provide enough evidence about the subject to be convincing.
- The essay falls back on "advertising language" or PR style.
- Faulty or circular logic: Something is "good" because it is entertaining; something is "good" because it presents contemporary issues.
- Similarly, something is not necessarily "good" because it is "realistic," or "bad" because it is not. Conversely, something is not "good" simply because it is "unusual," "offbeat," or "strange" (e.g., rock stars).

PREPARING FOR CONFERENCES

If you hold conferences with your students on their drafts, you could have them prepare for the conference by filling in the form on the following page.

PREPARING FOR A CONFERENCE: CHAPTER 8

Before the conference, write answers to the questions below. Bring your invention-writing and first draft to the conference.

1. What have you chosen to evaluate? How did you decide on this subject? What is your judgment of it?

2. Who are your readers, and what can you assume they know and think about your subject? How, specifically, do you hope to influence their thinking through your essay?

3. List the reasons for your judgment. Be prepared to talk about their appropriateness, sequence, and relationship.

4. What are you most pleased with in this draft? Be specific.

5. What specifically do you need to do next to revise your draft? List any problems you see in the draft or ones others have pointed out. Say briefly how you might attempt to solve these problems. Use the back of this form for these notes. (If you have completed the text's Revising plan, bring it with you to the conference instead of answering this question.)

CHAPTER 9: SPECULATING ABOUT CAUSES

THE WRITING ASSIGNMENT

Think of some important or intriguing phenomenon or trend, and explain why it might have occurred. Describe your subject, demonstrate its existence if necessary, and propose possible causes for it. Your purpose is to convince your readers that the proposed causes are plausible.

The Nature of the Writing Assignment

This writing assignment requires students to demonstrate that a phenomenon or trend exists and to argue for its possible causes. Essays analyzing cause or effect are assigned together in some rhetorics, students choosing the type they want to write. For reasons we explain in the next section, we want students in this assignment to carry out a *causal* analysis. More than that, we want them to explain the causes of a *phenomenon* or *trend*, not an event or a fad. A phenomenon is a notable and fairly constant fact of life, while a trend is an increase or decrease in some activity over an extended period of months or years. Speculating about the causes of a trend or phenomenon adds a challenging dimension to causal analysis, a challenge we believe college freshmen should be offered.

This essay is the fourth in a series of five argumentative writing assignments in this book:

Chapter 6: Arguing a Position

Chapter 7: Proposing a Solution

Chapter 8: Justifying an Evaluation

Chapter 9: Speculating about Causes

Chapter 10: Interpreting Stories

The position paper (Chapter 6) engages students in all the issues of convincing argumentation, especially establishing common ground with readers and anticipating their arguments. The proposal (Chapter 7) is a comfortable introduction to argumentation through personal experience: Students write to propose solutions for problems of groups they participate in. The evaluation (Chapter 8) involves students in arguing the worth of something. Speculating about causes (Chapter 9) teaches students the strategies of causal analysis and argumentation. Finally, analyzing and interpreting stories (Chapter 10) teaches students how to argue for an original interpretation on the basis of textual evidence.

Explaining causes requires students to do library research, at least to document the trend or phenomenon and perhaps to learn about alternative causes that they may reject or accept in their essays. Students learn how to evaluate causes, considering whether they are necessary, sufficient, immediate (or precipitating), remote (or background), perpetuating, obvious, or hidden.

Special Problems of This Writing Assignment

This assignment challenges every student and stretches even the very best students. Perhaps better than any other writing assignment in *The St. Martin's Guide,* this one demonstrates that with proper guidance nearly all students can attempt intellectually demanding writing and succeed. Because students will be struggling at first with this assignment, you may want to discuss the readings with particular care and thoroughness. You might also work closely with students throughout the process of writing.

Some students have difficulty seeing how a trend or a phenomenon is different from a fad or an event.

A trend is a change over time. It identifies an activity that is *increasing* or *decreasing*. Though life follows predictable patterns, we occasionally see changes in these patterns. If these changes have direction and momentum over a long period of time, we consider them trends. Changes that become trends are usually begun and sustained by a combination of causes.

In contrast to trends, fads are temporary, insignificant changes in people's preferences and actions. Fads enjoy brief popularity and then fade quickly after fulfilling the human desire for novelty. They are too short-lived to be considered trends.

Phenomena are permanent patterns of activity. They continue to happen, and the ways they happen do not change. Neither phenomena nor trends should be confused with events, which happen only once.

To add to what we say about these distinctions under Finding a Subject in the Guide to Writing, you might use these illustrations:

- Bird migration is a phenomenon, but a long-term change (continuing or completed) in migration habits or patterns is a trend. A causal-phenomenon essay would explain why birds migrate. A causal-trend essay would explain a noticeable *change* in migration patterns. (Other phenomena students mistakenly consider trends include popular activities like windsurfing, scuba diving, and mountain biking. Though students *could* treat these activities as trends by tracing the increasing participation in them since their beginnings, students tend to treat them as phenomena, explaining only why they are popular.)
- This year's clothing styles are a fad, but a change in clothing styles over several years is a trend. A causal-fad essay (which we do not assign) would explain why this year's styles have become popular. A causal-trend essay would explain a particular direction of change in clothing styles over many years. (Other fads students mistakenly consider trends include new dances, new hairstyles, new music, new car designs, new ski-boot designs, and so forth.)
- An airplane crash is an event, but a long-term change in air-safety statistics, the quality of air traffic control, or the crashworthiness of an aircraft is a trend. A causal-event essay (which we do not assign) would explain why one airplane crashed. A causal-trend essay would explain a *change* in air-safety conditions or records.

Another problem you should look for is that some students who choose to write about a trend are reluctant to demonstrate that a trend is actually a trend, that it is *increasing* or *decreasing* over a specific time period. This task really requires a double argument: The writer must first argue that a trend exists and then argue for some possible causes of it. You will need to give those students who have chosen to write about trends special encouragement and help with this first argument—demonstrating the existence of the trend.

Other problems students may encounter with this task include:

- choosing a widely recognized trend or phenomenon and presenting only predictable or obvious causes for it so that the reader thinks "So what?"

- choosing a trend that has very recently changed direction or lost momentum (such as the divorce rate) and thus may be difficult to interpret or project
- devoting considerable attention to establishing the existence of the phenomenon or trend and neglecting to mention any causes for it
- failing to consider alternative causes
- mentioning alternative causes but not refuting or accepting them
- failing to consider readers' objections to the writer's proposed causes
- shifting the focus from causes to effects

Though this writing assignment is challenging, with your help nearly all students can succeed at it and experience the very great satisfaction of meeting an intellectual challenge. The Guide to Writing has been devised to forestall all the problems we mention in this section. Later, when we discuss the invention sequence in the Guide to Writing, we will suggest specifically how you might support students' efforts during the crucial early stages of invention.

Finally, we should explain briefly why we insist that students write about causes rather than effects, thereby creating most of the problems we list above. We originally gave students a choice of a cause or an effect essay. Nearly all of them chose to write about effects of events, usually relying solely on conjecture, often choosing the scenario as the sole strategy for presenting effects. The papers were not very interesting, and students did not seem to be learning anything about argumentative writing.

Theorists of argumentation reminded us that causal analysis was an essential, basic strategy in argument, and so we decided to limit the writing assignment to the causes of events, phenomena, or trends. Most students chose to explain the causes of events, a worthy task, but the few students who chose trends or phenomena helped us see the possibilities in these choices. These were the choices that most challenged their powers of causal reasoning and argument, in part because of the need to argue for the existence of the trend or phenomenon, but also because of the dangers of confusing causes with effects in analyzing trends or phenomena. Hence, over years of trial and error we settled on analyzing causes of trends or phenomena as the way to pose an assignment certain to challenge and educate college students, who, after all, are ready to undertake serious intellectual work if given proper guidance and support.

After having made the best case we can for our assignment, we can now readily acknowledge that you might have very good reasons to think it is too difficult for many of your students. In that case, you could sidestep the problems raised with identifying and demonstrating trends or phenomena and have students write causal analyses of events. Possible topics for causal analyses of events include why a team lost a game, why someone lost an election, and why the state legislature raised college tuition.

Limit students to topics that must be argued. Steer them away from events with a single, obvious explanation, for which presenting the causes would involve only reporting, not arguing.

Responding to the challenge of this assignment, some instructors orient students to causal analysis by having them do a brief collaborative essay. Small groups (three to five students) work together to research and draft a causal argument.

Promising and Unpromising Topics

Students need careful guidance in choosing topics for this assignment. They should be able to demonstrate that their subjects are phenomena, involving patterns of behavior rather than one-time events; or that they are trends, involving long-term changes in patterns of behavior rather than short-term fads.

Some types of topics pose particular challenges for students:

- Historical phenomena or historically completed trends (for instance, an explanation of the increase in brain size during early human evolution): These subjects involve a different kind of research than that required by more current topics and tend to read like research reports of others' speculations rather than an argument for the student's own speculations.
- Phenomena observed in personal life (competitiveness, procrastination, popularity, laziness): Students writing about these topics tend to rely exclusively on anecdotal information drawn from their own experience, rather than generalizing from their own experience to reach larger conclusions about the phenomenon.
- Trends relating to technology (increased use of videocassette recorders, declining cost of handheld calculators, increasing use of cellular phones): Students often choose to write about these subjects because it is easy to document the existence of the trend itself; however, students may have difficulties going beyond the obvious explanation of technological advances in analyzing the causes of these trends.
- Subjects that could be approached as either phenomena or trends (teenage suicide, popular activities like windsurfing or rollerblading): Students will need to decide whether to treat the topic as a trend or as a phenomenon—to account for an increase or decrease (trend) as opposed to the simple fact that the phenomenon exists.

Since topic choice is a special problem, you might try the following activity. After discussing the readings in Chapter 9, list several possible phenomena or trends on the board. Ask students in groups of twos or threes to choose a topic and prepare a defense of it for the class. You can limit them to either phenomena or trends or let them choose. They must argue that

- the topic is actually a phenomenon or trend (and not an event or a fad)
- it is a researchable essay topic
- its causes are not already settled and therefore still require speculation
- the topic will interest some particular readers they identify

CHAPTER INTRODUCTION

The Writing Situations

These writing situations demonstrate that writers analyze and explain the causes of trends and phenomena outside of freshman English classes. The writers are journalists and anthropologists. The trends and phenomena they analyze are the decline of fixed pricing at auto dealerships, the period of reduced energy after the midday meal, and the small number of women choosing science as a career.

These situations will enable you to help students understand how trends and phenomena differ from fads and events. Note that all the writing situations involve analysis of two or more causes. Most involve disputing others' proposed causes. All are based on some research. These situations will inform students about the essay they will be writing, especially if you discuss the situations with them, emphasizing both the particular decisions the writers had to make and the unique features of this kind of writing.

Writing in Your Other Courses

These examples present cases in four different academic disciplines where causal analysis is required. As you discuss these representative writing assignments with students, they will realize that speculating about causes is a common undertaking in college writing.

Practice Speculating about Causes: A Collaborative Activity

Notice that this group inquiry invites students to speculate together on the causes of a trend and then to think about the process of speculating about causes. Specifically, it asks students to consider where their ideas come from, how they choose likely causes, and where they can find additional support. Students may be surprised to find that they have so many ideas and that their ideas do not come from an outside source but from their own observations and reflections. They may also recognize, however, that they need to do further research to strengthen their support.

READINGS

The four readings in the chapter illustrate a variety of trends and phenomena:

- King, "Why We Crave Horror Movies": the popularity of horror films
- Berger, "What Produces Outstanding Science Students": causes for high achievement in science
- Putnam, "The Strange Disappearance of Civic America": decline of civic engagement
- Dartnell, "Where Will They Sleep Tonight?": increase in numbers of homeless women

If students read these essays attentively and thoughtfully and consider the analysis questions, they will be able to avoid many of the problems we outlined earlier. They will come to see how writers describe and document trends, how they argue that trends really are trends, each with a beginning point and a noticeable change—an increase or decrease—over time. They will see how writers establish the existence of phenomena by identifying unchanging patterns of behavior. Students will discover how to evaluate and then reject or accept others' proposed causes. They will learn strategies for arguing the plausibility of their own proposed causes.

Topics in Analysis Questions and Commentaries

Here we list all the discourse topics in this chapter's Analyzing Writing Strategies and Commentary sections. You might find this list useful as a quick reference to particular rhetorical topics which you will want to emphasize with your students at different times during their writing process. For example, if you are conferencing with a student who needs to consider alternative causes before revising, you could glance at the list and ask him or her to reread the Putnam essay and the Dartnell essay from the perspective of the commentaries.

King

Analyzing Writing Strategies	*Commentary*
1. basic features	organization
2. support	argumentative strategy
	causes: obvious and hidden

Berger

Analyzing Writing Strategies	*Commentary*
1. argumentative strategy	presenting the subject
2. support for each cause	immediate and background causes

Putnam

Analyzing Writing Strategies	*Commentary*
1. presenting the subject	anticipating causes readers prefer
2. support	anticipating readers' questions or objections

Dartnell

Analyzing Writing Strategies	*Commentary*
1. organization	research
2. presenting the subject: defining a trend	alternative cause
	opening and closing

WHY WE CRAVE HORROR MOVIES
Stephen King

King's essay on the phenomenon of the appeal of horror movies has the advantages of a quick pace and a familiar topic—nearly everyone has squirmed through at least one horror film. Because students' attitudes toward horror movies are likely to vary from repulsion to indifference to the "craving" noted by King, this essay can introduce a discussion of how different readers may react to the same argument. King's essay also illustrates how moving from obvious causes to deeper or "hidden" causes is a convincing argumentative strategy and how an expressive, personal voice is appropriate in some argumentative writing situations.

Connecting to Culture and Experience

This activity asks for students' general reactions to the content of the essay. In this case, students are invited to react to King's assertions about the true function of horror movies and to reflect on some of the larger implications of these assertions. You could either lead a whole-class discussion or divide students into small groups. This activity is designed to help students discuss ideas in texts. It also stimulates their interest in the reading and increases the likelihood that they will want to analyze it closely.

Notice that the discussion topic connects to students' knowledge and experience and does not steer them toward a particular conclusion.

These discussions are nearly always engaging for students. We have also had excellent results with this follow-up assignment: immediately after the discussion, students take notes about their ideas; later they draft an extended journal entry; and then at the next class meeting, they share their ideas with members of their discussion group. This activity extends, refines, and clarifies each student's ideas about whether horror films and the arts in general have any social function.

Analyzing Writing Strategies

1. This question asks students to analyze King's essay in terms of the features of this genre. We want to make students aware of the specific requirements of this assignment early in this chapter to prepare them for analyzing others' essays and their own.

2. In order to answer this question, students will need to think first about the audience for King's essay. You might discuss his audience with them before you make this assignment. They will then look closely at the specific writing strategies he uses to support the proposed causes and determine whether they are effective given his audience. You might also suggest that they consult the section on analogies in Chapter 18: Comparing and Contrasting.

Considering Topics for Your Own Essay

This activity encourages students to start thinking about possible subjects and strategies for their own essays. Their answers will help them imagine how they might write about phenomena or trends that interest them. You might have students share their answers with the whole class or with small groups, and you can encourage them to imagine how they would present their subjects.

Commentary

The preceding essay questions and this commentary introduce most of the major issues in causal analysis, from presenting the subject, to identifying types of causes, to acknowledging the reader. In the commentary, we focus on King's organization and his argumentative strategy. We point out that a simple organization can support a sophisticated argument. We also discuss his use of obvious and hidden causes to achieve his purpose of convincing readers that horror movies have specific social value. Students may be encouraged by this essay and commentary to reach for less obvious causes for their own phenomena and trends.

See the following exercise based on this reading in Chapter 13: Cueing the Reader:

- Exercise 13.1 on thesis statements

WHAT PRODUCES OUTSTANDING SCIENCE STUDENTS
Joseph Berger

Students will no doubt have strong reactions to Berger's view that elite schools and special programs promote high achievement in science. In the introduction, we encourage them to enter the debate. They will likely draw from their own experiences in such programs or their own sense of exclusion from them. We also ask them to note that although Berger gives only two causes, he provides extensive support for them.

Connecting to Culture and Experience

This section gives students an opportunity to focus in depth on the issue of specialized education for a few gifted students. You might ask students to write for five or ten minutes on the topic, stating their views; then in small groups, they can exchange views with others and weigh the value of such programs to society. If your students are writing on topics from the strand "identity and community," this section would be particularly useful.

Analyzing Writing Strategies

1. Here is a sample scratch outline of Berger's essay:
   - introduces the subject of high achievement (or lack of achievement) in sciences and mathematics and suggests one cause (1)
   - presents the record of success of specialized programs—in particular, their success in producing Westinghouse Science Talent Search winners (2)
   - describes the Westinghouse Science Talent Search (3)
   - states the goals and philosophies of the Search (4)
   - indicates number of specialized and magnet science schools (5)
   - describes curriculum for these schools (6)
   - gives specific example of special science program (7–9)
   - cites long-lasting benefits of these programs to students (10)
   - gives two specific examples of students benefiting from such programs (11)
   - introduces second cause, the similar backgrounds of the successful students: immigrant background; refutes view of influence of foreign education (12)
   - gives reasons why immigrants succeed; refutes view that genetics is the reason (13)
   - cites another similarity in background of students: children of doctors or scientists (14)
   - gives causes for specialized science programs (15)
   - restates main cause: Specialized science schools and programs foster high achievement in science. (16)

   Students will probably find Berger's argumentative strategy more difficult to analyze than King's. You might ask students to outline the essay in small groups and then answer the questions. Or you might outline the essay as a class, writing it on the board. Students could then answer the questions in small groups, or you could continue with a whole-class discussion.
2. Before students answer this question, you might refer them back to the introduction to Berger's essay, where we briefly discuss his readers and ask them to consider the educational values of his conservative audience. Students may notice that in supporting his first cause, he describes the teaching methods by giving a specific example of a successful program, outlining the full four-year schedule of this program. Then he provides testimony from two successful scientists, both graduates of these special science programs.

Considering Topics for Your Own Essay

This section suggests that students draw on their experiences in educational programs to find subjects for their essays. They should be familiar with many of the programs listed here and probably will be able to name others. This activity could be conducted as a whole-class brainstorming session. You might also encourage students to return to this section during the invention process.

Commentary

In this commentary, we focus first on the need for Berger to devote a large section of his essay to presenting his subject. We stress that decisions about how extensively to present the subject are determined by the knowledge of one's readers.

In the commentary following King's essay, we discuss obvious and hidden causes. Here we introduce immediate and background causes; we provide definitions for these terms in the Considering Causes section of Invention and Research. You might return to this section during the invention process when students are analyzing their own causes.

THE STRANGE DISAPPEARANCE OF CIVIC AMERICA
Robert Putnam

Students will appreciate the engaging opening of Putnam's essay, although they may be uncomfortable with the implications of his argument. This introduction points out that Putnam focuses on a single cause. You might encourage students to think of alternative causes that he could have considered.

Connecting to Culture and Experience

This section asks students to apply Putnam's definition of civic life to their own lives. Students could list their civic activities as journal entries and then share them with others in small groups. A follow-up discussion with the whole class would allow all students to benefit from each group's insights.

Analyzing Writing Strategies

1. As Berger does, Putnam devotes several paragraphs of his essay to the presentation of his subject. Students will notice that he defines "social capital" and "civic engagement" and presents evidence to prove that the trend exists. They will also notice that he concedes that some people are still involved in their communities, thereby qualifying his claim. You will probably need to help students analyze his readers so that they can measure his success in presenting his subject.

2. This question asks students to analyze Putnam's use of studies of television viewing to support his contention that it has caused the decline in civic engagement. Students will note that he presents this evidence to prepare for his argument that viewing increased at the same time that civic engagement declined. Again, students will need to keep in mind the values and assumptions of his audience to determine the effectiveness of his support.

Considering Topics for Your Own Essay

This section suggests that students explore trends in civic life as possible topics for their own essays. You might assign it as a journal entry or refer students to it during the invention process. If you are asking your students to draw subjects from the thematic strand "identity and community," you might conduct a whole-class brainstorming session.

Commentary

In this commentary, we focus on Putnam's anticipation of his readers' concerns: their preference for other causes and likely questions and objections. Although he doesn't refute or accommodate alternative causes, he does acknowledge them in an extensive list. Students may need additional encouragement to address the issue of alternative causes since they will be primarily involved in coming up with and supporting their own. Multiple small-group sessions in which they exchange topics and discuss causes will help them recognize the possible concerns of readers, including questions and objections that readers might have.

We also point out that Putnam does not cite his sources because he is writing within a journalistic context. You might refer your students to Chapter 22: Using and Acknowledging Sources for the format that they should use.

WHERE WILL THEY SLEEP TONIGHT?
Kim Dartnell

While some writers rely on personal experience and familiar information to argue for proposed causes of phenomena or trends, Dartnell relies on library research. You will want to discuss with your students which of these sources of information is likely to be most fruitful for their own chosen essay topics. You may want to limit them to either research or personal observations—or leave it to them to decide. The Dartnell essay does illustrate nicely how the writing activities in Chapters 5 through 10 can involve library research. Our brief introductory note on Dartnell's essay asks students to notice how she bases her argument on library research. She uses the documenting style of the American Psychological Association. (This style is illustrated in Chapter 22: Using and Acknowledging Sources.)

Connecting to Culture and Experience

This activity asks students to reflect on the issue of homelessness itself. While most of them have encountered homeless people, many of them will not have considered very deeply either what it means to be without a home or what the problem of homelessness suggests about society in general.

Analyzing Writing Strategies

1. Here is a possible outline for this essay:
    - opens with Rebecca Smith anecdote (1)
    - demonstrates the existence of the trend (2)
    - describes homeless women; refutes alternative cause: homeless by choice (3)
    - cause: abuse (4)
    - cause: lockouts (5)
    - cause: lack of inexpensive housing (6)
    - refutes alternative cause: alcoholism (7)
    - major cause: deinstitutionalization (8)
    - main cause: economic decline (9)
    - ends with reference to Rebecca Smith (10)

    Encourage students to talk about the advantages or disadvantages of this ordering of causes. Point out that she puts her main cause at the end, the favored position in an argument. Students might compare this outline with that devised for Berger. Help them talk about differences, as those can be explained by the writers' subjects and purposes. We want students to see that there is no one best way to organize a causal analysis, but that a good analysis is carefully organized indeed.

2. This question asks students to focus on the way Dartnell defines homelessness in terms of women. Students will notice that she assumes that her readers are aware of the stereotypical view of homeless women, but that they need to be informed that many women attempt to hide the fact that they are homeless. Students may differ in their views of her effectiveness, but you should encourage them to keep her readers in mind as they evaluate her success.

Considering Topics for Your Own Essay

This activity asks students to imagine still another possibility for their own essays—a troubling social trend. You can help them generate a number of possibilities and test them to be certain they really are trends presently increasing or decreasing in severity. Push students to propose specific plans for documenting their trends and to come up with lists of possible causes for them.

Commentary

In this commentary, we point out to students how Dartnell relies on library research to document the trend and to gather causes. We emphasize that a social trend can often be documented quickly with just a few sources, thus reminding students that research can play an important role even in a brief essay—that research is not just for the long term paper. We teach research skills (Chapter 21: Library and Internet Research) and a documenting style (Chapter 22: Using and Acknowledging Sources) throughout the writing activities in Chapters 5 through 10, requiring library research with all or most of these assignments.

We also discuss the way in which Dartnell deals with her readers' preferences for an alternative cause. We point out that she relies on her own experiences as well as her research to project her readers' views and addresses them directly.

Finally, we focus on her use of framing to open and close her essay. You might ask students to compare her opening and closing with those in the other essays in this chapter.

See the following exercises based on this reading in Chapter 19: Arguing:

- Exercise 19.4 on using statistics
- Exercise 19.9 on using cases in argument

PURPOSE AND AUDIENCE

Students may need to be reminded that their purpose is not to prove that their causal explanation is right, but to convince readers that their proposed causes are plausible. This assignment requires students to be particularly aware of their readers from the earliest stages of the writing process. In addition to anticipating their readers' counterarguments, students should keep in mind that attentive readers will spot reasoning errors and hasty conclusions and are likely to find those arguments unconvincing. In order to win readers' confidence and respect, students must carefully think through and support their arguments.

SUMMARY OF BASIC FEATURES

We emphasize two basic features of these essays:

- a presentation of the subject
- a convincing causal argument

While this section summarizes what students have learned so far about essays speculating about causes, it also forecasts what is to come in their own invention, drafting, and revision. These features define the central thinking and discourse problems the student will be engaged in solving.

GUIDE TO WRITING

Invention and Research

The invention sequence for the essay speculating about causes includes these activities:

- Finding a subject
- Exploring what you know about your subject
- Considering causes
- Researching your subject
- Testing your choice
- Researching causes
- Considering your readers
- Developing your argument
- Anticipating and refuting objections
- Refuting alternative causes

There will be no surprises here for students who have considered the readings and analysis questions at the beginning of this chapter. Still, you will want to survey the invention activities with them, reminding them of the central importance of the rhetorical problem taken up by each activity, encouraging them to approach invention playfully, expecting to learn and be surprised.

Because some students will have difficulty distinguishing trends and phenomena from fads and events, you may want to work closely with them as they list possible topics and then choose trends or phenomena to write about. Do not hesitate to veto a topic that is not truly a trend or phenomenon or that might seem difficult to demonstrate. Some students will insist that events or fads are phenomena or trends; you will need to dissuade them gently of this belief. You may want to limit students to a certain kind of trend or phenomenon—continuing social or lifestyle trends, for example.

Once students have trends or phenomena to write about, we ask them—before they do any library research—to write out what they know about their subjects and to list possible causes for them. This step is important to give students confidence that they have some ideas of their own before they research others' ideas. We encourage them to make a table of causes and analyses, which they can add to when they begin research. Such a table is illustrated in the Writer at Work section from Dartnell's invention for her essay on homeless women.

Still another example of a table of causes and analyses is the following one for an essay on the trend of declining SAT scores. You might want to duplicate this table to discuss with students. (Note, however, that it is only a partial list of causes for this trend.)

Declining SAT Scores

Causes	Analysis
TV viewing	Not necessary, but maybe sufficient. Wouldn't affect everybody the same way—I watch TV and got high scores. Wouldn't necessarily lead to trends like this—you can learn things from TV. More TV equals lower scores. Two of my cousins watch TV all the time and got low scores. Don't know of any authorities right now. (Look it up?) Could it be a result of the trend, rather than its cause?
Broken homes	Not necessary but sufficient. Kids from broken homes make lower grades and so maybe would have lower SAT scores. Some kids are affected, some not. Some kids might try harder and have even higher scores (Tom). Divorces increased while scores were falling. Anecdote about Tom. Dr. Brothers on TV. Not a result.
Low standards in high schools	Might be necessary. Is sufficient. Grade inflation—similar trend. Would affect everybody by not preparing them for the test. This would always lead to trends like this. Must be statistical evidence on this—check it. Mrs. Cook. My experience in math. Not result, might be side effect.

If you want students to hold their essays to the usual essay length, explain to them that library research will be necessary only to document the trend (to prove to readers that something is increasing or decreasing) or phenomenon and quickly to survey causes proposed by two or three other writers on the trend or phenomenon. If you want to make this a full-scale research paper, then students can go much further in researching proposed causes. Even for a brief essay, students can document the trend or phenomenon and collect alternative causes from only two or three sources, as Dartnell does.

Help students understand that they are collecting causes for the purpose of *evaluating* them—weighing them within their own essays in order to accept or reject them. Students may consider causes others have proposed, accepting some, rejecting some, arguing for one as the most plausible cause. Or they may reject all other proposed causes and argue for their own original causes. Or they may see ways to regroup or combine others' proposed causes. Remind them that their purpose is not to report on others' proposed causes but to make arguments of their own that evaluate others' causes.

If you suspect that you may have to help students understand this crucial distinction between reporting and arguing, you could have them photocopy the pages in sources where they find any causes they consider in their own essays. They do not have to photocopy entire sources, just the page or pages used as sources for causes, whether actually referenced in their essays or not. (This request can do wonders for reducing plagiarism.)

Testing Your Choice: A Collaborative Activity

As group members discuss their subjects, they should question one another about their intentions: "Are you sure that this is a trend?" "Can you think of other possible causes?" They will also be able to offer suggestions: "I read an article about that last year in *Newsweek*." "I can think of one counterargument to your main cause." Thus, though writers present their plans to their classmates, the exchange is interactive and generative. At this important transition point in the writing process, students will be able to help one another make the shift from invention and planning to drafting.

Planning and Drafting

This section offers guidance for reviewing invention writings, setting goals, outlining, and drafting. You may want to discuss the goal-setting questions with students before they begin drafting. These questions review all the basic issues for essays explaining causes. They enable you to discuss logical fallacies within the context of a writing as-signment and at the point most helpful to students. Also encourage students to reread the general advice on drafting in Chapter 1: Introduction.

Critical Reading Guide

Be sure that writers identify their audience and purpose before handing a draft over for criticism. Encourage readers to evaluate the draft in terms of its intended audience and the writer's declared purpose. In this way, their criticism will be rhetorically based.

Revising

You might emphasize to students the importance of rereading and considering their draft as a whole before focusing on sentence-level changes. We often use class time to help students begin their plan for revision.

Editing and Proofreading

Again, we suggest that students finish by proofreading their essays and making any nec-essary changes in grammar and style.

A WRITER AT WORK

This Writer at Work section illustrates a key invention activity: Considering Causes, which includes Listing Possible Causes and Analyzing Promising Causes by setting up a convenient two-column table. Have students examine Kim Dartnell's table before they set up their own. (Dartnell's revised essay appears earlier in the chapter.)

First, review the questions Dartnell was responding to under Analyzing Promising Causes in Invention. Reviewing the questions will enable you to remind students of the wide range of types of causes that enter into speculation about phenomena and trends. The questions provide criteria for evaluating causes. They may enable students to avoid certain logical fallacies common to causal argument, such as confusing causes with effects and failing to identify a sufficient cause.

Second, help students see how Dartnell's analysis led her to a deeper understanding of the contribution each cause might make to her argument. This sort of analysis provides the starting point for a successful causal argument.

THINKING CRITICALLY ABOUT WHAT YOU HAVE LEARNED

As students complete their own essays, we ask them to reflect carefully on their experiences with reading and writing causal speculation. First, students are asked to reexamine the process of writing their own essays; then we ask them to review what they have learned about causal speculation from the readings in this chapter. Finally, students are encouraged to think critically about the social dimensions of writing that speculates about causes. This section discusses causal speculation as "persuasive writing *par excellence*"; in particular, the section calls students' attention to the necessity of reading concept explanations critically, not as neutral or objective documents but as pieces whose writers are guided by specific ideologies which lead them to make distinct and significant choices in selecting and presenting their material.

RESPONDING TO ESSAYS SPECULATING ABOUT CAUSES

Look for problems like the ones listed below in your students' causal speculation essays:

Subject

- The subject is not a trend or phenomenon, nor is it clearly defined or described.
- The subject does not lend itself to argument because it has an established or proven cause.
- If the subject is a trend: A significant change over time has not been demonstrated with evidence.

Argument

- The essay presents the trend or phenomenon, but it is not clear which cause the essay is arguing for.
- The proposed cause(s) is obvious or is neither necessary nor sufficient to explain the subject.
- There are no alternative causes presented.

- The causes are not presented in an organized or effective order.
- The argument contains obvious logical fallacies—such as confusing causes with effects.
- The essay does not offer enough evidence, examples, or anecdotes to support the argument.
- The essay evaluates the subject or proposes solutions for it, rather than speculating about its causes.
- The writer does not select or use sources effectively.
- If the subject is a trend: The argument does not show why there was a marked *increase* or *decrease* at the particular time.

Readers

- The essay does not consider possible objections to the argument or accommodate or refute them successfully.
- The writer's tone is too casual or frivolous for the subject and readers, or polemical rather than reasonable or speculative.

PREPARING FOR CONFERENCES

If you hold conferences with your students on their drafts, you could have them prepare for the conference by filling in the form on the following page.

PREPARING FOR A CONFERENCE: CHAPTER 9

Before the conference, write answers to the questions below. Bring your invention-writing and first draft to the conference.

1. What trend or phenomenon are you writing about? Why did you choose this subject? If it is a trend, when did it begin and to what extent has it increased or decreased over time?

2. Who are your readers? Describe briefly what you assume they already know about your subject and how your assumptions about your readers influenced the way you wrote this draft. Be specific.

3. List the cause or causes you propose to explain the trend or phenomenon. Be prepared to talk about why you've chosen these causes.

4. If you've considered and rejected other possible causes, list them here. Be prepared to talk about your reasons for rejecting them and how you handled alternative causes in your essay.

5. What are you most pleased with in this draft? Be specific.

6. What specifically do you need to do next to revise your draft? List any problems you see in the draft or any that other readers have pointed out. Say briefly how you might attempt to solve these problems. Use the back of this form for these notes. (If you have completed the text's Revising plan, bring it with you to the conference instead of answering this question.)

CHAPTER 10: INTERPRETING STORIES

THE WRITING ASSIGNMENT

Write an essay interpreting some aspect of a short story. Aim to convince readers that your view is insightful and can be supported by an imaginative reading of specific passages from the story.

The Nature of the Writing Assignment

This assignment gives you the opportunity to have your students write about literature. As you may know, there is a lively debate over whether to teach literature in a freshman composition course and, if so, how to teach it. In our view, writing about literature fits naturally into a writing program that emphasizes invention and critical reading. Apart from the intrinsic value of reading literature, writing about it teaches students to analyze the language of a text and to use textual evidence to support their ideas. Also, by sharpening students' receptivity to language, writing about literature heightens their sense of style.

Moreover, introducing college freshmen to the study of literature seems particularly important in this increasingly technological age when trust in objective facts and empirical study is in the ascendancy. Many students distrust literature for the very reason we admire it—it is complex and subtle. They tend to be impatient with ambiguity, eager for certainty, and overreliant on authority. Writing about literature gives students insight into both the way writers use language and the way readers interpret meaning from language.

This is the last in a set of five chapters on analysis and argumentation: position paper, proposal, evaluation, causal speculation, and literary interpretation. If your students have written any of these essays, they will know that writing to convince particular readers influences a writer's decisions. They will know how important it is to establish their credibility with readers by anticipating and refuting possible objections. The special contribution of this assignment is teaching students to interpret texts and marshal textual evidence to make a convincing argument.

This chapter's flexibility allows you to shape the assignment to fit your own and your students' needs. The chapter focuses on short fiction but could be used with a novel or film. You may wish to modify or supplement the Guide to Writing, and you will probably want to discuss one or more stories in class before students write interpretations on their own. You may also decide to narrow the writing assignment by assigning specific stories for the class to write about. You might even ask students to compare two works on the same theme or by the same author. We've included a brief anthology of short stories for your convenience.

Special Problems of This Writing Assignment

We have found that students tend to encounter several different problems as they try to write literary interpretations. Perhaps the most widespread problem is that some students simply retell the story, while others are satisfied with a superficial interpretation.

They state the obvious. We think this problem results not so much from lack of will as from lack of understanding. Many students are reluctant to probe their own responses. They fail to understand that reading must be an interactive process, an interplay between the words on the paper and their own knowledge, experience, beliefs, values, and feelings. We deal with this problem through class discussion and small-group activities.

Another problem involves the use of textual evidence. Many students do not understand that they need to support their assertions with evidence from the work. They often assume that what they are saying is self-evident and that anyone who has read the work will automatically know what they are talking about. Some students understand that they must cite evidence but do not realize that they should also explain how the particulars cited demonstrate the points they are making.

Others have an even more serious problem: They do not know how to take evidence from a text. These same students may be able to use evidence given to them in the form of raw data (a list of facts or quotations, for example). But when they have to crack the text apart like a walnut and dig out the meat, they are at a loss. All they can do is record their reading by presenting a running paraphrase with occasional commentary. They cannot extract details to use as evidence because they cannot wrench these details out of the order in the text and reorganize them to support their own ideas. We have found that annotating helps students overcome this particular problem.

Promising and Unpromising Topics

You may either give students a choice of stories to analyze or ask them all to work with the same story. This chapter includes a small anthology of short stories from which you could ask students to choose: "The Monkey Garden" by Sandra Cisneros, "The Use of Force" by William Carlos Williams, "The Hammer Man" by Toni Cade Bambara, and "Araby" by James Joyce. You might also consider allowing students to work in small groups with other students writing on the same story. They could discuss the various approaches to the story, share their interpretations, and exchange drafts with one another. Students also could work together in small groups to draft a collaborative essay interpreting a story.

If you want students to write on several stories by an author, here are some single-author collections of stories, all available in paperback:

Flannery O'Connor, *Everything That Rises Must Converge* and *The Collected Stories*

Raymond Carver, *What We Talk about When We Talk about Love* and *Fires*

Nadine Gordimer, *Selected Stories*

D. H. Lawrence, *The Woman Who Rode Away and Other Stories* and *The Complete Short Stories*

Nathaniel Hawthorne, *Selected Tales and Sketches*

Alice Walker, *You Can't Keep a Good Woman Down*

T. C. Boyle, *Greasy Lake and Other Stories*

James Joyce, *Dubliners*

Eudora Welty, *Collected Stories*

Gabriel Garcia Marquez, *No One Writes to the Colonel and Other Stories*

Julio Cortazar, *We Love Glenda So Much and Other Tales*

Tobias Wolff, *In the Garden of the North American Martyrs*

John Updike, *The Music School, Pigeon Feathers,* and *The Same Door*

Jayne Anne Phillips, *Machine Dreams*

Sandra Cisneros, *The House on Mango Street* and *Woman Hollering Creek*

CHAPTER INTRODUCTION

The Writing Situations

The chapter opens with three writing situations that give students a preview of the kind of writing they will be doing. These situations suggest that people do not write about literature solely in English classes. Writers may use literary texts in other college courses and even for nonacademic writing.

Of course, the way writers treat literary works depends on their purposes and readers. For example, a student writing for an introductory literature course is more likely to use the concepts and terminology he or she has learned in that course than a student writing for a history or science course. This would be so even if the same student were writing for both courses. Similarly, instead of writing a strict literary analysis of "The Yellow Wallpaper," the therapist uses the story to critique Mitchell's rest cure.

Writing in Your Other Courses

The sample assignments listed here suggest some of the ways instructors use interpretive writing in non-English courses. You and your students might have other examples to add to this list.

Practice Interpreting a Story: A Collaborative Activity

This activity engages students immediately in interpreting a story. Note that the activity asks students to do some exploratory writing on their own about the story in question before discussing the story with two or three other students. We don't expect—or necessarily want—students to reach a consensus; in fact, part of the point of this activity is to help students see that there can be a variety of plausible interpretations of the same story. As they continue their discussion in response to the questions that conclude this activity, we hope that they will become more aware of the ways in which they present and support their interpretations.

AN ANTHOLOGY OF SHORT STORIES

This brief anthology provides a rich variety of material for interpretation. You will probably want to limit your students to these stories for the Collaborative Activity discussed above; you may also want them to choose from among these selections as they prepare to write their own essays.

READINGS

In a departure from the preceding chapters in this text, we provide only two essay selections, both written by students. In addition, whereas earlier chapters follow each essay with Analyzing Writing Strategies and Commentary sections, here the first essay has an extensive Commentary, while the second has Analyzing Writing Strategies questions. As the following lists indicate, the Commentary following Crane's essay and the questions following the selection by Ratinov are parallel in focus. Since Crane and Ratinov both write about "Araby," you may want your students to read it before analyzing the student essays. But that may not be necessary if you focus solely on formal features as we do in the Commentary and Analyzing Writing Strategies sections. In fact, we find it helpful to separate considerations of form from content in this case because students have difficulty focusing on the essay's argumentative strategies. If they read "Araby," all they want to do is talk about the story. We have students read "Araby" *after* they've examined the student essays.

See the following exercise based on these selections in Chapter 19: Arguing:

- Exercise 19.10 on the use of textual evidence

Topics in Analysis Questions and Commentaries

These lists can serve as a quick reference to help you plan your discussion of discourse features.

Crane

Commentary
   thesis statement: key terms, forecasting
   argument: coherence, textual evidence, cueing the reader
   conclusion: "framing"

Ratinov

Analyzing Writing Strategies
1. thesis statement—key terms
2. forecasting—development
3. topic sentences
4. coherence
5. quotations
6. "framing" in conclusion

GAZING INTO THE DARKNESS
Sally Crane

To reach her interpretation of the final scene of "Araby"—an interpretation which conflicts with accepted readings of the scene—Crane focuses on the point of view of the narrator, suggesting that the voice in the story, rather than being that of a naive young boy on the threshold of adulthood, is the somewhat ironic voice of a grown man looking back on his youth.

Commentary

This section focuses on the fundamental elements of Crane's essay. As we note, the thesis statement (at the end of the first paragraph) and following material in Crane's essay serve not only to state the writer's interpretation of the story, but also to introduce the key terms she will use throughout her essay, as well as to forecast the order in which she will discuss these points. Marginal notes refer students to Chapter 13: Cueing the Reader for a more complete discussion of thesis and forecasting statements. Students may be surprised to learn that the thesis must be supported with an argument that is logical and coherent paragraph-by-paragraph as well as sentence-by-sentence. A scratch outline helps students see how the parts of Crane's argument cohere logically, and the discussion of the essay's third paragraph highlights the sentence-to-sentence connections that help Crane's argument flow smoothly. We then discuss the use of textual evidence, noting that, whether material from the text is quoted directly or paraphrased, it must be integrated smoothly into the writer's own text, and its relevance must be made clear to the reader. For a more complete discussion of using sources, including textual evidence, you might refer students to Chapter 22: Using and Acknowledging Sources. We end with a brief discussion of Crane's conclusion and the technique of framing.

FROM INNOCECE TO INSIGHT: "ARABY" AS AN INITIATION STORY
David Ratinov

Whereas Crane focuses on the narrator, Ratinov focuses on the role other characters play in the story. He uses his findings about these characters to argue that, through his self-delusion, the boy increasingly resembles the adult characters, and "later, at Araby, he realizes the parallel between his own self-delusion and the hypocrisy and vanity of the adult world."

Analyzing Writing Strategies

1. Ratinov sets forth his thesis in the opening sentence and elaborates it extensively in the first paragraph, which introduces the key terms and forecasts the main points of the essay and the order in which they are presented. The key terms in Ratinov's thesis are *initiation, self-delusion, hypocrisy,* and *vanity.* Most students will have little difficulty tracing these key terms throughout the essay, although some readers may find the transition from hypocrisy in paragraph 4 to vanity in paragraph 5 somewhat abrupt. For more on thesis statements, students may consult Chapter 13: Cueing the Reader.
2. This question helps students see how one element of Ratinov's argument—the hypocrisy of adults—is developed through the use of specific examples from the text: the priest with prurient tastes and the mercenary Mrs. Mercer.
3. Students should have no trouble recognizing that, following the thesis paragraph, each succeeding paragraph begins with a topic sentence that announces the point developed in that paragraph. In addition to introducing further evidence in support of Ratinov's thesis, the topic sentence in each paragraph provides a transition from the previous paragraph, either through the use of a simple transitional device

such as "although" (paragraph 3) or through a word or phrase that refers directly to the point covered in the previous paragraph ("Araby" in paragraph 6, for instance, or "Mangan's sister" in paragraph 7).

4. Using the second paragraph as an example, this question calls students' attention to connective devices not only between but within paragraphs. (For more on these devices, students can refer to Chapter 13: Cueing the Reader.) Students will probably note that the first four sentences following the topic sentence in this paragraph relate directly to the narrator's move from childhood to adulthood; the remaining three sentences relate to the other element introduced in the topic sentence: his infatuation with Mangan's nameless sister.

5. One of the most important features of literary interpretation is the use of textual evidence, often in the form of direct quotation. Here, we ask students to look closely at Ratinov's third paragraph, of which more than half is direct quotation from "Araby." Although Ratinov relies heavily on quotation in this paragraph, he is careful to incorporate each quotation smoothly into his own text and to show how each quotation supports the main point of the paragraph, which is to illustrate the narrator's "lust" for Mangan's sister. For more discussion of incorporating quotations, you might refer students to Chapter 22: Using and Acknowledging Sources.

6. Ratinov, like Crane, frames his essay by repeating the key terms of his argument in his conclusion. Students may note that, rather than simply restating his thesis in the concluding paragraph, Ratinov expands slightly on the idea that the narrator's disillusionment with love is "a metaphor for disillusionment with life itself" (paragraph 1).

PURPOSE AND AUDIENCE

Students may wonder not only why they themselves should be writing essays about literature but also what real purposes such essays fulfill. In this section we try to give them answers. We emphasize sharing interpretations in a community of readers in order to deepen everyone's understanding of a story (and of storyness). We try to give students confidence that whatever their ideas, if they can be convincingly argued, they are likely to be well received.

SUMMARY OF BASIC FEATURES

This section briefly summarizes the basic features of writing about literature:

- an insightful interpretation
- a well-supported argument

You may use this summary to orient students before they begin working on their own essays.

GUIDE TO WRITING

Invention and Research

We recommend seven basic invention activities for writing a literary interpretation:

- Choosing a story
- Analyzing the story
- Writing to explore your annotations
- Formulating a tentative thesis statement
- Testing your choice
- Revising the thesis statement
- Finding additional support for your thesis

This invention sequence emphasizes studying the story closely in order to generate a thesis that can be substantiated with evidence from the text. The sequence begins with suggestions for choosing a story. If your students are writing on one of the thematic strands, either "identity and community" or "work and career," they will also find lists of stories that they might choose to write about. If you have assigned a story for the class to write about, your students should skip this activity.

The second activity, Analyzing the Story, will be the most time-consuming part of invention. Students are urged to read the story several times, annotating it each time. We would also encourage you to do some work with students on annotation. We discuss annotation as a general reading strategy in Chapter 12: A Catalog of Reading Strategies. In the Writer at Work section of this chapter we also illustrate the way David Ratinov annotated a portion of "Araby" in preparation for writing "From Innocence to Insight: 'Araby' as an Initiation Story." You might ask students to discuss their annotations in small groups or show them your own annotation. After annotating the story, students are asked to explore their annotations.

In light of such intensive analysis of the story, students choose tentative thesis statements for their essays. Next, they search the story for evidence to support their thesis statements, clarifying the thesis in the process.

Like you, we have struggled to help students write workable thesis statements. Following, we share with you a handout we have developed for our students. It includes several thesis statements about "Araby" and outlines the features of successful theses: the right key terms, forecasting, concluding restatement. We discuss all the examples carefully with our students and believe that, as a result, we are seeing stronger thesis statements.

Remind students that a workable thesis comes from an interesting and supportable idea about a story and that such ideas are hard won from patient annotating and discussion.

WRITING A THESIS STATEMENT FOR AN ESSAY INTERPRETING STORIES

The following examples and discussion will help you with the challenging task of devising a useful thesis statement. All the examples come from interpretive essays on "Araby" by college freshmen·

In "Araby" the young boy's quest is motivated by his desire to correct the hypocrisy, constraints, and decay of life around him. Though merely a boy, he intuits that somewhere lies the secret to restoring purity and faith to the world.

Knowing the story, you probably find this thesis both clearly stated and plausible. The key terms—hypocrisy, constraints, and decay vs. purity and faith—seem workable. That is, you can readily imagine someone discussing the story in these terms. The key terms must be right or workable so that they can be repeated throughout the argument. They label the basic concepts in your interpretation of the story and provide coherence and focus for your argument. This thesis also forecasts the sequence of the argument: In the essay, the writer first demonstrates hypocrisies of certain characters, then religious and social constraints on the narrator, and then finally decay in the setting. The writer goes on to argue that the boy's awareness of evils sent him to Araby in search of something better, though he failed in his quest.

Workable thesis terms and an essay forecast are not easy to come by. Sometimes a thesis statement must go through several drafts, with revisions at the beginning to establish a solid starting point, during drafting as the argument does not work out or takes a surprisingly new direction, or before revising when the evidence can be reconsidered and peer reviewers' suggestions taken into account.

Here is an earlier draft of the thesis statement above. Words and letters dropped from the later draft are in italics. Words and letters added are in parentheses.

> In "Araby" the young boy's quest is motivated by his inherent desire to *isolate himself from* (correct) the hypocrisy, *restriction,* constraints, and decay of life around him. Though merely a boy, he *seems to* intuit(s) that somewhere *there* lies the *tool that will* (secret to) restore(ing) purity and *sanctity* (faith) to the world.

You can see that the writer dropped the terms *isolate, restriction, tool,* and *sanctity* in favor of more appropriate terms. The revised thesis is briefer and more direct.

This next thesis relies on the key terms transition, oppression, and realization. Notice the explicit forecasting of the essay's plan.

> James Joyce's "Araby" tells the story of a boy's transition from the instinctive knowledge of his oppression to his conscious realization of it. The boy is oppressed by the circumstances and the atmosphere in which he lives, by the influence of other characters in the story, and finally by his own feelings, thoughts, and reactions to them.

Forecasting is not a requirement of an acceptable thesis statement, but it enables the writer to test out a possible direction for the argument. Forecasting enables readers to read essays more confidently.

This following concise, workable thesis does not include a forecast. In fact, the writer does not forecast the essay's plan anywhere in the opening paragraph. A reader might guess, though, that the essay will be organized around either "darker aspects" or minor characters.

> The minor characters play a major role in "Araby." Through his interactions with them, the narrator comes to understand the darker aspects of human nature which adults try to hide.

This final example illustrates how a beginning thesis statement can be restated and expanded at the end.

Beginning thesis

In "Araby" Joyce reflects on two problems faced by Ireland at the time he wrote the story: Irish-Catholic decay and British greed and materialism. The narrator witnesses and endures these problems and is deeply influenced by them.

Ending thesis restatement

The story portrays Ireland as corrupted from inside by the church and dominated from outside by England. The narrator's final despairing insight reflects the country's hopeless situation. At the end of the story, the narrator understands that his natural desire for the girls is thwarted by his church's repressive morality and by his materialistic desires for money and possessions.

An effective strategy in any kind of argumentative writing is to repeat the thesis at the end. It frames the essay and brings the argument to an emphatic, memorable conclusion. Notice that this writer does not simply repeat the thesis. She restates it in slightly different terms and connects it explicitly to other ideas developed in the essay.

With these models in mind, draft a thesis statement for your essay. A useful thesis should offer an interesting idea about the story, be concise and well-focused, offer workable key terms, and preclude easy challenge. It may forecast the argument.

Try out your thesis statement on your instructor and classmates. You want to know not whether they agree with it (if they have read the story you are interpreting) but whether they find it clear and workable.

Consider your current best version tentative. Once you begin collecting and organizing evidence to support this tentative thesis, you may decide the evidence supports it only partially or even contradicts it. Be prepared to revise the thesis to fit your new understanding of the story.

Testing Your Choice: A Collaborative Activity

The purpose of this group activity is to help students clarify the role of the thesis statement in general and also to improve the tentative thesis statements they have drafted. Reading aloud (especially in the presence of others) can help to defamiliarize one's own writing and give the writer a much needed critical distance. Getting reaction from a group of peers engaged in the same activity, although somewhat intimidating, can also reinforce the idea of audience. The act of consulting with other writers reaffirms the writer's membership in the discourse community (in this case, a community of novices in literary criticism). Group members should interrogate the statement, asking what the key terms mean and how they relate to one another.

Planning and Drafting

In addition to leading students to make a tentative outline, this section urges them to consider their goals both before drafting the essay and as they draft. The research in composing suggests that goal-setting plays a crucial role in drafting for experienced writers. Yet it is difficult to get inexpert writers to pause as they draft in order to reflect about the rhetorical constraints under which they are writing. These heuristic questions are meant to remind students of some of these constraints. You might spend some class time discussing them or give students time to return to their small groups to discuss with one another their plans regarding some of these questions.

Critical Reading Guide

This section is designed for students to use as they read and comment on one another's drafts. It is not necessary that students cover every question. In fact, the writer could ask readers to focus on particular problem areas, or you could ask the readers to identify problem areas themselves. Interestingly, a writer's perception of what's problematic in a draft does not always correspond to readers' perceptions.

Notice that this section is organized around the basic features and strategies that were pointed out in the analysis questions and commentaries following the reading selections. These are the same topics that students will use to organize their plans for revision in the section that follows.

Revising

If writers are to revise their drafts productively, they need to get sufficient critical distance from their writing so that they can see it as an object (rather than as an extension of themselves). This section seeks to help students see their own drafts with a critical eye, just as they have been led to see another's draft in the preceding section.

Although we want to encourage students to read and respond to each other's drafts, we want also to remind them that the first responsibility they have as revisers is to themselves or to the draft itself, not to their readers. Consequently, we urge them to reread the draft and assess it for themselves before considering what other readers have to say about it.

Editing and Proofreading

In this section, we suggest specific errors of style and grammar that students should look for in their own essays.

A WRITER AT WORK

We have referred to the Writer at Work section often because it illustrates so well two immensely useful strategies of literary analysis and interpretation: annotating and exploring one's annotations.

Here we present one section of David Ratinov's annotation. Since it illustrates many of the possibilities of annotating, your students will learn from a careful review of it. Ratinov's writing to explore his annotations reveals how writing itself can lead to still further ideas. Our students have found this to be a convincing demonstration, and we believe yours will too. Keep in mind that these productive strategies must be demonstrated, taught, justified, practiced, coached, and rewarded.

THINKING CRITICALLY ABOUT WHAT YOU HAVE LEARNED

As in the preceding chapters in this text, when students have completed their own essays, we ask them to reflect in some detail on what they have learned from the reading and writing they've done in this genre. After reviewing their own writing processes and examining what they have learned from the reading selections in the chapter, students are invited to consider the social and cultural dimensions of literary interpretation.

Having worked through their own interpretations of short stories, students will readily accept the observation that we do not read stories for pleasure alone, but that there is a certain amount of satisfaction to be gained in the act of interpretation as well. The discussion in this section helps students to think about both the satisfactions of and the misconceptions surrounding literary interpretation. First, we address two common misperceptions about language and meaning—that there is "a simple, one-to-one correspondence between a word and its meaning," and that an author can tell us unequivocally what a story *"really* means." We point out that, in the same way that words have multiple meanings, a single story can have "a profusion of possible meanings," as Sally Crane's and David Ratinov's disparate interpretations of "Araby" illustrate. Next, we examine the specific implications of these misconceptions for reading stories, pointing out that the common assumptions that stories always convey meaning and that authors are final authorities on that meaning can actually limit our appreciation and damage our interpretations of literary texts. The questions for discussion following the commentary in this section should help to guide students through their own reflections on language and meaning, authority of interpretation, and the relation between stories and "reality."

RESPONDING TO ESSAYS INTERPRETING STORIES

You can expect your students' essays interpreting a story to have some problems like the ones listed below:

Thesis

- Thesis is too general, obvious, or not clearly stated.
- Instead of a thesis, there is only a summary of the story.

The Argument

- The points raised do not support the thesis adequately.
- The thesis is not supported by enough specific textual evidence.
- The essay seems to be a patchwork of quotes, summary, and paraphrase, without enough of the writer's analysis and interpretation.

Organization

- The essay lacks a clear organizing principle, explicit forecasting, or transitions.
- The essay is badly framed: The introduction does not prepare the reader, or the conclusion is too abrupt or contrived.
- The essay is unbalanced: The writer gives disproportionate space to very minor points or hurries over major ones.

PREPARING FOR CONFERENCES

If you hold conferences with your students on their drafts, you could have them prepare for the conference by filling in the form on the following page.

PREPARING FOR A CONFERENCE: CHAPTER 10

Before the conference, write answers to the questions below. Bring your invention-writing and first draft to the conference.

1. Which story have you selected for your essay? What made you decide to use this story?

2. What is your working thesis? What are the key terms of your thesis? Why have you chosen these particular terms?

3. Point to places in your draft where the evidence still seems weak to you. Be prepared to talk about how you've used textual evidence to support your thesis.

4. What are you most pleased with in this draft? Be specific.

5. What specifically do you need to do next to revise your draft? List any problems you see in the draft or any that have been pointed out by other readers. Say briefly how you might attempt to solve these problems. Use the back of this form for these notes. (If you have completed the text's Revising plan, bring it with you to the conference instead of answering this question.)

CHAPTER 11: A CATALOG OF INVENTION STRATEGIES

Because each writing-activity chapter in Part I has its own invention sequence, we do not discuss invention as a general topic early in our text. Instead, we engage students immediately in invention at the beginning of each Guide to Writing in Chapters 2 through 10.

In this chapter, we catalog the familiar all-purpose heuristics or strategies of invention and inquiry in two categories:

Mapping: These graphic means of recording discoveries and seeing connections include clustering, listing, and outlining.

Writing: The various ways to use writing itself to discover what one knows and needs to know include cubing, dialogues, dramatizing, quick drafting, journals, looping, and questioning.

You can orient students to this catalog and let them use it whenever they want, or you can make specific assignments from it, helping students learn to use some of the strategies. All of the strategies can support writing activities in Part I, and specific strategies are recommended in the Guides to Writing. For example, in the Guide to Writing in Chapter 2: Remembering Events, students *list, loop* (write and then stop to focus their thoughts), *write a dialogue,* and *outline.* In addition, as students revise and edit their essays, they might use activities in this chapter to explore their subjects further or to solve problems in their drafts.

CHAPTER 12: A CATALOG OF READING STRATEGIES

In this chapter, we present various ways of using writing to think critically about your reading. To illustrate these strategies, we refer throughout the chapter to a sample reading selection—an excerpt from Martin Luther King, Jr.'s "Letter from Birmingham Jail," provided near the beginning of the chapter.

The strategies include annotating, taking inventory, contextualizing, reflecting on challenges to one's beliefs, paraphrasing, summarizing, exploring the significance of figurative language, looking for patterns of opposition, evaluating the logic of an argument, recognizing emotional manipulation, judging the writer's credibility, and analyzing the writing in other disciplines.

As with the preceding chapter cataloguing invention strategies, you can introduce students to this catalog and encourage them to use it whenever they like, or you can make specific assignments from it. Some of these strategies, such as annotating, inventorying, evaluating the logic of an argument, and judging the writer's credibility, are integrated into the Guides to Writing in Part I and can support the reading that students do in that section of the text.

CHAPTER 13: CUEING THE READER

Whereas Part I introduces the possibilities and constraints of various kinds of nonfiction prose, Part III focuses on the craft of writing, the strategies a writer can use to achieve a particular purpose in a piece of writing. Of the seven chapters in Part III, five are devoted to what are commonly called the modes of writing: narration, description, definition, classification, and comparison/contrast. In addition to these, the opening chapter brings together several topics that are generally taught in isolation: thesis, paragraphing, and cohesion. We combine these topics in one chapter called Cueing the Reader because we want students to think of thesis statements, paragraphing, cohesive devices, and transitions as part of a signaling system that writers use to help readers read and comprehend their texts. In effect, these are strategies that writers use to establish and maintain focus in writing.

The chapter is divided into four sections:

Orienting Statements. To suggest how writers can provide a context so that readers will understand each succeeding sentence, we discuss thesis statements and forecasting statements.

Paragraphing. To indicate how writers can use paragraphing to help readers, we show how indention affects readers and also how writers can use topic-sentence strategies to orient readers.

Cohesive Devices. To show how writers can enhance coherence by connecting key words and phrases, we illustrate the following cohesive devices: pronoun reference, word repetition, synonyms, sentence-structure repetition, and collocation.

Transitions. To demonstrate how writers signal and identify connections for readers by linking ideas between sentences and paragraphs, we survey the following transition strategies: local, temporal, and spatial relationships.

We illustrate each of these strategies extensively with examples by professional writers. The exercises invite students to see how these cueing strategies work in longer pieces of discourse.

OVERVIEW OF THE EXERCISES

13.1   Analyze the thesis in Toufexis's "Love: The Right Chemistry" (Chapter 5), Estrada's "Sticks and Stones and Sports Team Names" (Chapter 6), or King's "Why We Crave Horror Movies" (Chapter 9)

13.2   Analyze forecasting in any of the essays in Chapter 5

13.3   Put paragraphing symbols in the Gould passage

13.4   Analyze paragraphing in the Gould passage

13.5   Analyze topic sentences in Weisman's "Birth Control in the Schools" (Chapter 7)

13.6   Analyze rhetorical questions in Toufexis's "Love: The Right Chemistry" (Chapter 5) or Kaus's "Street Hassle" (Chapter 7)

13.7   Analyze topic-sentence strategies in the Gould passage

13.8   Analyze cohesive devices in the Gould passage

13.9   Analyze transitions in the Gould passage

SUGGESTIONS FOR TEACHING THE EXERCISES

13.1　　Analyze the thesis in Toufexis's "Love: The Right Chemistry" (Chapter 5), Estrada's "Sticks and Stones and Sports Team Names" (Chapter 6), or King's "Why We Crave Horror Movies" (Chapter 9).

You may use this exercise in two ways: (1) to examine similarities and differences in thesis statements for reflective, informative, and argumentative writing; and (2) to analyze the way a thesis statement in a particular essay focuses details and orients readers. To appreciate how thesis statements guide readers, students might be encouraged to convert each of the thesis statements into questions.

13.2　　Analyze forecasting in any of the essays in Chapter 5.

Some students wonder whether giving a detailed preview is advisable since it gives so much away. You might use this opportunity to discuss when writers need to forecast and how much forecasting they need to give. But recognize that this writing problem usually involves a broader one—how explicit should a writer be? Many inexperienced writers are afraid of being too obvious when stating a thesis or forecasting an essay. They do not know what readers expect and what etiquette to follow.

13.3　　Put paragraphing symbols in the Gould passage.

If you do not want this exercise to be merely clerical, you might ask your students to paragraph the Gould passage in class before they find out how it was originally paragraphed. Reading the passage aloud may help them sense where closure and orienting occur.

13.4　　Analyze paragraphing in the Gould passage.

This exercise works well as a small-group activity because it encourages students to find explanations for Gould's paragraphing decisions or to justify their own choices. To stimulate analysis, you might play devil's advocate and suggest some alternative paragraphing possibilities if students do not propose any of their own. Students tend to think that there are no alternatives if the piece was written by a professional and published. You might try the same exercise with an unidentified piece of writing or a student draft. You might have students do Exercise 13.7 as a follow-up to this exercise.

13.5　　Analyze topic sentences in Weisman's "Birth Control in the Schools" (Chapter 7).

In an argumentative essay like this one, the topic sentences do more than announce the topics of paragraphs; they also advance the argument and set up contrasts among opposing views or an opposing solution to the problem. Since topic sentences—their placement, form, and function—are not at all obvious to students, talk them through this essay paragraph by paragraph. Decide whether the first sentence is the topic sentence (we think it is in every case) and discuss its function at that point in the essay. Do not overlook the transition role of many topic sentences.

After leading a discussion of the topic sentences in this essay, you could put students on their own in pairs or small groups to analyze topic sentences in another essay. To prepare carefully for such group discussion, they could first write out their analysis as homework in a journal.

13.6   Analyze rhetorical questions in Toufexis's "Love: The Right Chemistry" (Chapter 5) or Kaus's "Street Hassle" (Chapter 7).

Several paragraphs in these essays begin with questions—questions which serve both a rhetorical and a topical function. Discuss several of them with your students, noting their transitional and topical functions. Caution students about overreliance on questions as topic sentences. Some respected writers use them sparingly, others regularly. Argument seems to invite their use.

13.7   Analyze topic-sentence strategies in the Gould passage.

This exercise might be used as a follow-up to Exercise 13.4, with students analyzing their paragraphing decisions in terms of topic-sentence strategies. Students should find sentences 13, 24, and 28 fairly conventional topic-sentence strategies. Sentence 11, however, might surprise them. The object of this exercise is for them to examine how those topic sentences serve readers. To do this most effectively, students probably should work in groups.

13.8   Analyze cohesive devices in the Gould passage.

Students might find this easier to do if they work in small groups, each group looking for a different cohesive device. They also might find it easier to study cohesion within paragraphs. Students might repeat this exercise using sample student essays, perhaps from *Free Falling*, or they might exchange second drafts of their explaining a concept essays and analyze the cohesive devices as part of the revision process.

13.9   Analyze transitions in the Gould passage.

Students will find lots of logical transitions and several temporal transitions but very few spatial ones in this passage. You might want to have them also analyze a passage with more spatial description. The purpose of this exercise, however, is not simply to locate transitions; it is to examine how they help readers make sense of what they are reading. Students should probably work in groups on this exercise and might also be asked to supply some alternative transitions that Gould could have used.

CHAPTER 14: NARRATING

This chapter on narrative strategies focuses primarily on structure, the way writers string events together to give them form and meaning. We cover the following topics:

Sequencing Narrative Action. To indicate how events may be presented, we discuss chronological sequencing and narrative time signals.

Shaping Narrative Structure. To suggest how narrative attains meaningful form, we introduce conflict, tension, and pacing.

Taking a Point of View. To show how narratives are presented to readers, we discuss a point of view.

Presenting a Process. To indicate how processes are presented, we explain the essentials of process narration.

In this chapter, we illustrate these narrative strategies with numerous excerpts from published writers. Many of the exercises urge students to practice these strategies in isolation, without consideration for the larger writing issues of purpose and audience. These larger issues, however, are part of other exercises that invite students to analyze particular narrative strategies in readings in Part I.

OVERVIEW OF THE EXERCISES

An asterisk marks the exercises that could be assigned as full-length essays.

*14.1	Write a narrative following a timeline
14.2	Analyze time markers in the White passage
14.3	Analyze use of time signals in any of the essays in Chapter 2
14.4	Analyze use of time signals in your own essay
14.5	Identify the conflict and climax in the essay you read for Exercise 14.3
14.6	Analyze specific narrative action in Angelou's "Uncle Willie" (Chapter 3)
14.7	Analyze specific narrative action in your own essay
14.8	Analyze dialogue in Haslam's "Grandma" (Chapter 3)
14.9	Practice writing dialogue
14.10	Compare point of view in Noonan's "Inside the Brain" and Cable's "The Last Stop" (Chapter 4)
*14.11	Write a narrative from two points of view
14.12	Analyze process narrative in Cable's "The Last Stop" (Chapter 4)
*14.13	Write a process narrative

SUGGESTIONS FOR TEACHING THE EXERCISES

14.1   Write a narrative following a timeline.

This exercise could lead to a single paragraph or a whole essay. The point is to get students to practice constructing timelines for their own narratives as they are asked to do in Chapter 2: Remembering Events. To make a timeline before drafting, the writer must divide the incident into constituent events and determine the relative importance of each event. These decisions require some thought about the conflict and suspense as well as some consideration of pacing.

14.2   Analyze time markers in the White passage.

The paragraph preceding the exercise should get students started on this task. You might have students work in pairs to find the markers. Then you could discuss in class how these markers help readers. You might try reading the passage without some or all of the time markers.

14.3   Analyze use of time signals in any of the essays in Chapter 2.

This exercise invites students to see how writers use these three kinds of time signals—time markers, verb tense markers, and references to clock time—in narrating remembered events. They will find lots of examples of time markers in these readings, but hardly any references to clock time. (Brandt uses clock time twice: when she gives as justification for stealing the button that she would have had to wait in line 30 minutes and later when she describes the drive to the police station as only taking a few minutes.) You might ask your students why they think writers use clock time so sparingly. Verb tense may present a trickier problem since few native English speakers have studied verb tense. If your students are having a problem using complex tenses, you might want to review tense in the Handbook.

14.4   Analyze use of time signals in your own essay.

This exercise involves analysis of the narrative students wrote for Exercise 14.1. It may be that some students did not use temporal transitions in these narratives. If so, you might want to suggest adding transitions to see how they affect the narrative's coherence. Temporal transitions are treated also in Chapter 13: Cueing the Reader. They are, of course, crucial signaling devices, cueing readers to shifts in sequence. But students should also recognize that excessive or unvaried use of temporal transitions (especially *then, next, first, second,* and *after that*) can make their prose wooden. You might combine this exercise with Exercise 14.3, analyzing the use of time signals in narratives in Chapter 2: Remembering Events.

14.5   Identify the conflict and climax in the essay you read for Exercise 14.3.

The point of this exercise is to help students understand how narratives are structured. You might group students according to the Chapter 2 essay they read. Doing this exercise in a small group requires that the students figure out for themselves what the terms *conflict, tension, suspense,* and *climax* mean, not in the abstract, but in the context of an actual narrative. If you then invite the groups to report their findings to the class as a whole, the class can compare and contrast the different strategies used in the narratives in Chapter 2.

14.6   Analyze specific narrative action in Angelou's "Uncle Willie" (Chapter 3).

Have students underline each of Uncle Willie's physical actions in paragraph 18. Encourage them to talk about the way such precise presentation of action slows and focuses the narrative pace and at the same time invites readers to create vivid visual images of a character moving in a specific scene. Invite students' conjectures about the contribution of this paragraph to the essay. There is no right or best answer.

14.7   Analyze specific narrative action in your own essay.

Few students will have used specific narrative action in their narratives written for Exercise 14.1. Encourage them to try it on one action which they have merely named but failed to dramatize and make concrete through specific narrative action.

For many students, writing specific narrative action into their narratives enables them for the first time to bring their personal and fictional stories to life. It is a major breakthrough in their writing development. It is not at all hard to do—though difficult to do well, of course—and all students can learn to do it. The case of specific narrative action illustrates, we think, that most writing problems result from *text*-making, not cognitive, limitations: Students can think well enough to meet the demands of nearly any writing situation; if they have the information they need (from memory or research), then they must know *specific text-making strategies* appropriate to the writing situation. *The St. Martin's Guide* illustrates and teaches such strategies.

14.8   Analyze dialogue in Haslam's "Grandma" (Chapter 3).

Students cannot fail to notice the central role dialogue plays in this essay. They may be interested also in its bilingualism. The distance between the boy and Grandma is potentially great, but speaking enables them to bridge the gap. That Grandma initially speaks only in Spanish increases the estrangement. But as they get to know one another, the language barrier falls and they are able to communicate in Spanish as well as English. You might also want to point out how his conversations with Grandma enable the boy to relate to his distant father and that at the end, by speaking for his great-grandmother, the boy gains his own voice in the family.

14.9   Practice writing dialogue.

Here is a chance for students to construct a narrative which relies on dialogue, probably the first such narrative for many students. After class discussion, students could revise their dialogues to enable them to more faithfully and dramatically represent the relationship between the writer and the other person. Some students may be able to add dialogues to the narrative they wrote for Exercise 14.1.

14.10   Compare point of view in Noonan's "Inside the Brain" and Cable's "The Last Stop" (Chapter 4).

Rewriting exercises, like this one, can teach students a lot. They will enjoy reading their paragraphs aloud. Encourage them to discuss the effect of the change in point of view.

14.11   Write a narrative from two points of view.

This exercise should consolidate for students everything they have learned about point of view.

14.12   Analyze process narrative in Cable's "The Last Stop" (Chapter 4).

This exercise invites students to conjecture about the contribution of process narratives to profiles. We would assign this exercise as a journal entry and then begin class discussion by asking a few students to read their entries aloud.

14.13   Write a process narrative.

We ask students to describe a familiar process in order to inform and interest readers, even to entertain them, not to give them directions (or procedures or recipes) for enacting the process.

CHAPTER 15: DESCRIBING

This chapter on describing strategies focuses primarily on language choice. Its aim is twofold: (1) to heighten students' awareness of the words writers use and (2) to give students practice making word choices.

Creating a Dominant Impression. To indicate how successful descriptive writing works, we discuss the importance of choosing words that reinforce a single, unified mood and purpose.

Describing Strategies. To help students generate richer, more specific descriptions, we divide describing into three strategies: naming (nouns used for identification), detailing (modifiers used for particularization), and comparing (figures of speech used for evocation).

Using Sensory Description. To suggest the language possibilities for sensory description, we discuss some resources for naming and detailing different sense impressions.

Assuming a Vantage Point. To present ways descriptions may be organized, we discuss the effects of stationary, moving, and combined vantage points.

In this chapter, we offer basically two kinds of exercises: directions to analyze specific describing strategies used in reading selections from Part 1 and opportunities to practice these strategies.

OVERVIEW OF THE EXERCISES

An asterisk marks the exercises that could be assigned as full-length essays.

*15.1	Describe a room you know well
15.2	Name objects and then write a descriptive paragraph
15.3	Analyze naming in Gray's "Father" (Chapter 3)
*15.4	Describe a common household object
15.5	Analyze detailing in Haslam's "Grandma" (Chapter 3)
15.6	Analyze comparison in Noonan's "Inside the Brain" (Chapter 4)
15.7	List comparisons and then distinguish fresh comparisons from clichés
15.8	Analyze naming, detailing, and comparing in Gray's "Father" (Chapter 3)
15.9	Describe a person's face
15.10	Describe a place through its sounds
15.11	Describe a place through its smells
15.12	Describe a tactile sensation
15.13	Describe the taste of a particular food

SUGGESTIONS FOR TEACHING THE EXERCISES

15.1   Describe a room you know well.

When students have written their own descriptions, you might have them share their efforts with several other students. Ask the other students to reflect back to the writer the impression they think the description creates. They might simply offer their own adjectives to characterize the room as it is described.

15.2   Name objects and then write a descriptive paragraph.

The aim of this exercise and the one that follows is to get students thinking about the role of naming in description. This exercise makes students conscious of the words they use to name things. In observing a scene and considering what to name the things in it, students become more attentive to their surroundings and to language. Students might be encouraged to do this exercise in pairs or small groups, either making separate lists and then comparing them or collaborating on a list. By discussing alternative word choices, students help each other understand the concepts of specificity and concreteness.

15.3   Analyze naming in Gray's "Father" (Chapter 3).

"Father" is rich in naming. You could ask students to underline all the names in paragraphs 1–4. You could even do it with them in class. The exercise then asks students to conjecture about the function and effect of all this naming.

15.4   Describe a common household object.

This exercise stresses close observation and word choice, focusing on detailing as well as naming. You might make this a classroom activity by bringing in a household object for the whole class to work on together.

15.5   Analyze detailing in Haslam's "Grandma" (Chapter 3).

Students should have little trouble finding examples of Haslam's use of naming and detailing: "horned toad," "small beast," "breast pocket," "involuntary step," as well as his physical description of his great-grandmother in paragraph 11. Your students will begin to see many other examples of Haslam's powerful use of detailing once their attention is drawn to this strategy.

15.6   Analyze comparison in Noonan's "Inside the Brain" (Chapter 4).

You might start students off on this analysis by focusing on the set of comparisons Noonan uses to describe the procedure, beginning with his comparison of opening the skull to "cabinet work" (paragraph 4) and continuing with the image in paragraph 11 of the drill as something that "should be hanging on the wall of a garage."

15.7   List comparisons and then distinguish fresh comparisons from clichés.

This exercise could be done in small groups or with the entire class, but the important thing is that students discuss the comparisons they list and justify classifying them as comparisons or clichés. This activity engages students in making decisions about the effectiveness of figurative language and encourages them to decide for themselves which expressions lack freshness and evocativeness.

You might bring in, at this point, George Orwell's distinction (in "Politics and the English Language") between *newly invented, dead,* and *dying* metaphors. Newly invented metaphors are fresh and evoke a vivid image. Dead ones (such as "underhand") have reverted back to being ordinary words. Dying metaphors, on the other hand, are used as though they were still evocative but actually have lost their evocative power from overuse. Orwell suggests that mixing metaphors and incorrectly using them (such as "tow the line" for "toe the line") are "a sure sign that the writer is not interested in what he is saying."

15.8   Analyze naming, detailing, and comparing in Gray's "Father" (Chapter 3).

This exercise enables students to demonstrate everything they have learned so far in this chapter about description. You could send students off in pairs to develop collaboratively a careful written analysis, or you could use this exercise as an in-class exam.

15.9   Describe a person's face.

This exercise not only encourages students to use visual images, but it also introduces the idea that description should create a unified impression. Ernest Hemingway's description conveys an impression of Fitzgerald more than it gives an exact verbal reproduction of his face. Students might notice, for one thing, how often Hemingway uses evaluative terms such as *handsome, pretty,* and *beautiful.* An enjoyable and instructive classroom activity is to have each student describe someone else in the class. The students read their descriptions aloud while their classmates try to identify the person being described.

15.10   Describe a place through its sounds.

This exercise invites students to experiment with the language of auditory description. Students might exchange their descriptions to see whether they have conveyed the impressions they were trying to create.

15.11   Describe a place through its smells.

This exercise again invites students to experiment with sensory language—this time the description of olfactory sensation. In reviewing the paragraphs students produce, you might have the class discuss the accuracy of the assertion that opens this section: "The English language has a meager stock of words to express the sense of smell."

15.12   Describe a tactile sensation.

In reviewing their paragraphs, students might consider the assertion that opens the discussion of the sense of touch in the text: "Writers describing the sense of touch tend not to name the sensation directly or even to report the act of feeling. Probably this omission occurs because only a few nouns and verbs name tactile sensations. . . ." Students could examine their own writing to see what nouns and verbs they used. In addition, they might discuss consistency of impression and how their language choices create a particular effect.

15.13 Describe the taste of a particular food.

You might bring several kinds of food to class (including a can of sliced pineapple) and ask students to describe the tastes of these foods. They might classify particular foods as sweet, sour, bitter, or salty. You might also ask them to consider how much their descriptions rely on naming and evaluating foods as opposed to describing the sensation of taste.

15.14 Analyze the sensory description in Angelou's "Uncle Willie" (Chapter 3).

This is a good exercise for group work. Students will find that Angelou uses a range of sensory images; in addition to the multiple images that evoke the sense of sight, students will note that Angelou uses images evoking the senses of touch and smell (the stove in the first two paragraphs), as well as of hearing (Uncle Willie's stammer in the dialogue portion of the selection).

15.15 Analyze vantage point in Exercise 15.1.

Students will likely notice that in describing a room for Exercise 15.1 they naturally used particular vantage points. You might have them read their paragraphs aloud so that the class can identify the kinds of vantage points used. They might also rewrite their paragraphs using different vantage points.

15.16 Analyze vantage point in Cable's "The Last Stop" (Chapter 4).

Students will probably observe that, while Cable relies on a moving vantage point to provide a framework for his profile as he moves through the mortuary, he switches to a stationary vantage point when describing a particular person or scene.

CHAPTER 16: DEFINING

This chapter opens with a discussion of the writer's uses for a dictionary, thesaurus, and dictionary of synonyms. We distinguish among these three, warning especially of the limitations of a thesaurus. Next, we illustrate in some detail the syntactic strategies of brief sentence definitions. Then we illustrate the strategies of extended, historical, and stipulative definition. The exercises ask students to practice these forms of definition and to analyze the ways writers use these forms for particular purposes within full essays from Part I.

OVERVIEW OF THE EXERCISES

Asterisks mark the exercises that could be assigned as full-length essays.

16.1 Practice various forms of sentence definition

16.2 Analyze sentence definitions in Noonan's "Inside the Brain" (Chapter 4)

*16.3 Write an extended definition

16.4 Analyze an extended definition in Noonan's "Inside the Brain" (Chapter 4)

16.5   Write a historical definition

16.6   Analyze a stipulative definition in Weisman's "Birth Control in the Schools" (Chapter 7)

*16.7   Write a stipulative definition

SUGGESTIONS FOR TEACHING THE EXERCISES

16.1   Practice various forms of sentence definition.

This exercise invites students to try out some syntactic options for the one-sentence definitions that are so common in all writing, especially reports and textbooks. Students could check each other's exercises for the correctness of the definitions and the fluency of the sentences.

16.2   Analyze sentence definitions in Noonan's "Inside the Brain" (Chapter 4).

This exercise enables students to see sentence definitions at work in one essay from Chapter 4: Writing Profiles. We ask them to classify the sentence definitions in the essay, using the types in this chapter, a request that permits them one final review of the strategies we illustrate. Then we ask them to consider the purpose of the definitions in the selection as a whole. This last request is very important, we think, because it reminds students that defining serves a larger rhetorical purpose. Writers very rarely write essays or book chapters of definition. They use definitions to explain or argue or entertain. For that reason, we treat definition—and the other modes of writing in Part III—as writing strategies, not as separate kinds of writing.

Students could very readily and usefully do this exercise together in class in pairs or small groups. Groups could compete to find all the sentence definitions, classify *all* of them correctly, and come up with a plausible statement about the purpose of each.

Although Noonan's profile includes much information and description that defines, his major sentence definitions include the following:

Paragraph	Term Defined	Strategy
2	suboccipital craniectomy	direct or apparent
6	sterile field	direct or apparent appositive
9	dura	direct or apparent appositive
		direct or apparent
13	cerebellum	direct or apparent
		direct or apparent
18	brainstem glioma	appositive

16.3   Write an extended definition.

Here students write an extended definition—several sentences or a full essay. We specify readers (their peers) and writing situation (readers who do not know the term being defined).

As with all the extended writing exercises in this chapter, this one could be revised after a class workshop or conference. Or it could be only a one-draft journal entry.

16.4   Analyze an extended definition in Noonan's "Inside the Brain" (Chapter 4).

This definition of *sterile field* extends over the first three sentences in paragraph 6. You might want to point out that Noonan extends the definition in much the same way that the field itself extends—radiating outward from the incision to include everything in the room, the instrument table as well as the doctors themselves.

Once students have carried out the analysis and written down their conclusions, this exercise could be the basis for a brief, productive class discussion. Like Exercise 16.2, it ensures that students consider defining strategies within the context of a complete essay.

16.5   Write a historical definition.

This exercise enables students to do what they have just seen Adler do—from etymological information develop an extended historical definition. Students look up one of the words from our list—all chosen after several hours' search for good candidates in *A Dictionary of Americanisms*—and devise a coherent historical definition from the bare etymological facts. A secondary benefit of this exercise is that students learn about a very important specialized dictionary, *A Dictionary of Americanisms.*

You may make enemies in the library if hundreds of students simultaneously try to use the one copy of this dictionary. You can keep goodwill in the library by photocopying some or all of these definitions for your students. You might first want them to write about the same word, comparing the results in class, and then perhaps revising. They could then choose their own words from those remaining on the list in order to write a second historical definition.

16.6   Analyze a stipulative definition in Weisman's "Birth Control in the Schools" (Chapter 7).

Like Exercises 16.2 and 16.4, this exercise asks students to return to an essay in Part I and analyze the role of defining as a writer's strategy in the context of a full essay written for a particular purpose to specific readers. Encourage students to pay attention to the way Weisman organizes and develops his stipulative definition.

16.7   Write a stipulative definition.

This exercise, which could produce a full essay, requires students to write a stipulative definition. Students would almost certainly be interested in seeing each other's stipulations—since they most often define familiar concepts or aspects of popular culture. A stipulative definition can be judged like an argument: Does the writer convince you that the stipulation is plausible?

CHAPTER 17: CLASSIFYING

This chapter presents illustrations and exercises for various strategies of classifying—dividing, grouping, and naming information one intends to write about. This is a chapter about a basic operation of mind, as well as a basic writing strategy. We illustrate principles of division, strategies for presenting a division coherently in writing, and the use of division with other writing strategies.

Students do not have to learn to classify because their minds naturally do so. They do, however, need to learn how writers present the results of classifying, how classifying looks as text on the page, and what decisions writers make so that classifying is both engaging and readable.

OVERVIEW OF THE EXERCISES

Asterisks mark the two exercises that could be assigned as full-length essays.

17.1	Diagram a division
*17.2	Divide a topic
17.3	Analyze strategies of coherence
17.4	Analyze classifications in readings in Part I
*17.5	Divide a topic and write a coherent draft

SUGGESTIONS FOR TEACHING THE EXERCISES

17.1   Diagram a division.

This exercise asks students to analyze this chapter's opening illustration by Thomas Sowell. In this exercise, students decide whether the illustration observes the principles of classification. That the selection does, quite obviously, may make this a good opening exercise. Discussing the results of this analysis will help students understand the principles of classification.

17.2   Divide a topic.

In this exercise, students choose at least two topics from our list and divide each topic in two or three different ways. They diagram each division and decide whether the division observes the principles of classification, given the point it makes. This exercise should help students see that a topic can be divided in different ways depending on the writer's purpose. It also deepens students' understanding of the principles of classification. If you wish to assign a classification essay, you could have students write brief or extended pieces from one of the divisions each has diagrammed.

17.3   Analyze strategies of coherence.

This exercise returns students to the Hemingway passage to analyze the way the writer cues the readers. Hemingway prepares readers for the organization of his writing and the elaboration of his division by fully forecasting the division. Then he paragraphs for each main part of the division, naming the part in the first sentence of the paragraph. Each part is also mentioned in subsequent paragraphs. (Chapter 13: Cueing the Reader has more on these strategies of coherence.)

17.4   Analyze classifications in readings in Part I.

This challenging and important exercise asks students to analyze classifications in selections in Part I. From this exercise, students will learn how writers present the results of dividing information on their topics. They will see the role of division within the context of a full piece as well as its use with other writing strategies. You might divide the essays among several small groups, asking each group to report the results of its analysis to the whole class.

17.5   Divide a topic and write a coherent draft.

In this final exercise, we ask students to divide a topic and write a brief piece based on the division. You could, of course, ask them to develop it into a full essay.

CHAPTER 18: COMPARING AND CONTRASTING

This chapter illustrates the writer's strategy of comparing and contrasting. We provide examples of the two basic forms of comparison—chunked and sequenced—and we emphasize the importance of a limited, focused basis for any comparison. We also include several examples of analogy, as a special form of comparison. The exercises invite students to write comparisons and analogies and to analyze comparisons and analogies found in the readings in Part I.

OVERVIEW OF THE EXERCISES

Asterisks mark the exercises that could be assigned as full-length essays.

*18.1   Write a comparison
18.2   Analyze comparisons in readings in Part I
18.3   Analyze extended comparisons in readings in Part I
*18.4   Write an analogy

SUGGESTIONS FOR TEACHING THE EXERCISES

18.1   Write a comparison.

In this exercise students practice writing comparisons. You could ask them to write for others in the class. You might limit them to either chunked or sequenced comparisons or let each of them decide which format to use. Or you might want to have them write on one topic in the chunked form and another in the sequenced form. In pairs or small groups, students can evaluate their comparisons using criteria of coherence, basis of comparison, and informativeness.

18.2   Analyze comparisons in readings in Part I.

Here we ask students to consider comparison as a writer's strategy within the context of a reading. Students analyze specific comparisons in four personal, explanatory, or persuasive essays. They must analyze the format of each comparison, identify its role in the whole piece, and judge its effectiveness—quite a challenging task. For this exercise and Exercise 18.3, you might want students to work together in pairs or small groups and to compare their analyses with those of other students.

18.3   Analyze extended comparisons in readings in Part I.

Some essays are extended comparisons—like two of the essays in Part I, essays representing diverse genres and purposes.

18.4   Write an analogy.

This exercise requires students to write extended analogies, something many of them will never have done before. Each student must compare a principle or process that is unfamiliar to readers with something very common and familiar. The trick is to find this familiar "something" as the basis for the analogy. The writers of our examples have chosen the calendar and widespread human arms, a movie projector, and a basketball team to explain their unfamiliar ideas.

Writing an analogy wonderfully illustrates the principle that writing itself lets you find out what you have to say. Tell students that the only way to test an analogy that seems workable is to write it out. Then it is possible to see whether it works, that is, whether it holds up reasonably well on paper so that a reader would find it convincing. Students may make several false starts.

Because this challenging exercise has such unpredictable results, students will especially enjoy sharing the outcome. Have them evaluate each other's analogies to determine whether the analogies are plausible, consistent, and truly explanatory. You might challenge students in pairs to help each other revise to meet the criteria in order to ensure that both have workable analogies.

CHAPTER 19: ARGUING

This chapter complements Chapters 6–10, the text's writing activities that require explicit argumentation. Since Chapter 19 offers a comprehensive introduction to the basic strategies of argument, you could devote some time to it before introducing your first argument assignment from Part I. On the other hand, two chapters in Part I—Chapter 6: Arguing a Position and Chapter 7: Proposing a Solution—also provide comprehensive introductions to all the basic strategies of argument, but introduce them in a full rhetorical context. Consequently, you might want to have students begin Chapter 6 or 7 (or some other argument chapter) and work in Chapter 19 only to consolidate rhetorical concepts and argumentative strategies they are analyzing and practicing while working on a full essay.

Among the strategies in Chapter 12: A Catalog of Reading Strategies are three specifically designed for analyzing and evaluating argument: evaluating the logic of an argument, recognizing emotional manipulation, and judging the writer's credibility. Other critical reading strategies in this chapter will be useful as well.

In this chapter, we introduce students to the following strategies of argument:

- Making a Claim
- Supporting Claims with Reasons and Evidence (facts, statistics, authorities, anecdotes, scenarios, cases, and textual evidence)
- Counterarguing (acknowledging, accommodating, or refuting)

OVERVIEW OF THE EXERCISES

Since we assume students will be practicing (drafting, revising) these strategies as they write essays in Chapters 6–10, only a few exercises in this chapter ask them to practice a strategy. Instead, we ask them to analyze the strategies at work in the context of full essays in Part I.

19.1   Write a claim

19.2   Analyze the claim in any essay in Chapter 6

19.3   Evaluate the use of fact in an essay from Chapters 6–9

19.4   Analyze the use of statistics in one of the essays from Part I

19.5   Analyze the use of authorities in one of the essays from Part I

19.6   Analyze the use of anecdote in one of the essays from Part I

19.7   Analyze the use of scenario in O'Malley's "More Testing, More Learning" (Chapter 7)

19.8   Write a scenario

19.9   Evaluate the use of a case in Ehrenreich's "In Defense of Talk Shows" (Chapter 6) and Dartnell's "Where Will They Sleep Tonight?" (Chapter 9)

19.10   Analyze the use of textual evidence in one of the essays on "Araby" in Chapter 10

19.11   Evaluate the acknowledgment of readers in one of the essays in Chapter 6

19.12   Analyze the accommodation of readers in O'Malley's "More Testing, More Learning" (Chapter 7)

19.13   Analyze the use of refutation in an essay in Chapter 6

19.14   Write a refutation of an objection to an argument in the essay you chose in Exercise 19.13

19.15   Write a refutation of an objection to the claim you wrote in Exercise 19.1

SUGGESTIONS FOR TEACHING THE EXERCISES

19.1   Write a claim.

Writing an arguable, clear, and qualified claim is often a more challenging task than inexperienced writers can imagine. They may have difficulty in understanding the challenge, much less learning to meet it confidently, unless you help them one-by-one with their claims. A claim is a claim—rather than a topic or assertion in an essay reporting established information—if it is truly arguable, that is, of consequence to some readers and to the writer and if it can be argued on the basis of some evidence, even anecdotal evidence, but preferably facts, statistics, authorities, or textual evidence. A claim is not arguable if it derives solely from personal preference. Finally, a claim is arguable—and workable as an essay's thesis—if the terms are clear and exact and if they will sustain the argument as its key terms, to be repeated in nearly every paragraph right through to the conclusion.

The notion of "workable" is very important, in our experience. Unfortunately, a writer does not know whether the key thesis terms are workable without drafting the essay. Writers can, however, test a claim by projecting an essay's argument and direction. And that is what we would encourage them to do as you help them evaluate their claims. They will need to have specific readers in mind for a claim if they are to decide whether it is appropriately qualified.

We spend much time in class preparing for argumentative essays, going from student to student discussing claims, with the class contributing.

19.2   Analyze the claim in any essay in Chapter 6.

As in all Part III chapters, exercises here return students to full essays in Part I so that they can see how writers' strategies we survey in Part III can be used purposefully and shaped for particular readers. This exercise asks students to evaluate the claims in one of the four essays in Chapter 6, as a way of previewing that chapter. You might divide the class into four groups, assigning an essay in Chapter 6 to each group. Each student could evaluate the claim on his or her own, and then groups could take some time at the beginning of class to share results. However we posed the assignment, we would want to ensure that students understood how to find and evaluate a claim.

19.3   Evaluate the use of fact in an essay from Chapters 6–9.

Before you assign this exercise, you might want to identify facts and evaluate their use in one essay. Students would then know exactly what you wanted them to do on their own. Since class discussion is most profitable if students know well any essay being discussed, you might want to assign everyone the same one or two essays. Assigning two essays, each in a different chapter, would enable you to show how facts are used in different writing situations.

19.4   Analyze the use of statistics in one of the essays from Part I.

19.5   Analyze the use of authorities in one of the essays from Part I.

19.6   Analyze the use of anecdote in one of the essays from Part I.

Again, as we propose for Exercise 19.3, students will learn most from these exercises if you first carefully analyze one essay for them. Then they could analyze the other essay on their own. We make such assignments in a journal, and often begin class by asking two or three students to read their analyses aloud.

19.7   Analyze the use of scenario in O'Malley's "More Testing, More Learning" (Chapter 7).

Students should notice that O'Malley opens the essay with a scenario that helps define and lend credibility to the problem the proposal addresses. It dramatizes a familiar experience, reminding readers how they felt when they were only hours away from an important exam they were not quite ready to take. You might invite students to think of ways they could sharpen the scenario and make it even more convincing.

19.8   Write a scenario.

Students enjoy writing scenarios—imaginative narratives that argue for the beneficial or horrendous results of some trend, policy, or decision. As you make this assignment, have students identify specific readers for whom they will be devising their scenarios. In class, help students evaluate their scenarios in terms of narrative pacing and tension and drama (see Chapter 14: Narrating), appropriateness for their designated readers, and persuasiveness.

> 19.9 Evaluate the use of a case in Ehrenreich's "In Defense of Talk Shows" (Chapter 6) and Dartnell's "Where Will They Sleep Tonight?" (Chapter 9).

Students will recognize that the cases in these essays have both an informative and a rhetorical function. They are evidence for the argument, and they also draw readers into the essay and eventually frame it.

> 19.10 Analyze the use of textual evidence in one of the essays on "Araby" in Chapter 10.

If you analyze it carefully for them, students should be able to move confidently from the example to one of the essays in Chapter 10. You may want to limit them to just a few paragraphs in one of the two essays on "Araby." Be sure that students know the differences among the terms *quoted, paraphrased, summarized,* and *referred to.*

> 19.11 Evaluate the acknowledgment of readers in one of the essays in Chapter 6.
>
> 19.12 Analyze the accommodation of readers in O'Malley's "More Testing, More Learning" (Chapter 7).
>
> 19.13 Analyze the use of refutation in an essay in Chapter 6.

Each of these exercises enables students to observe how writers anticipate their readers' concerns. We are always surprised at how few students have ever *noticed* this strategy, though they have heard and read it countless times. Students seem never to have been asked to do it in their own writing. Since it is an easy and satisfying strategy to master, we give it special attention in our classes. In every Guide to Writing in Chapters 6–10, anticipating readers in various ways is a major invention activity.

> 19.14 Write a refutation of an objection to an argument in the essay you chose in Exercise 19.13.
>
> 19.15 Write a refutation of an objection to the claim you wrote in Exercise 19.1.

Both these exercises invite students to write out a refutation. Follow up in class, identifying characteristics of the most successful refutations.

CHAPTER 20: FIELD RESEARCH

This chapter introduces three essential techniques of field research: observing, interviewing, and surveying by questionnaires. Observations and interviews are required for Chapter 4: Writing Profiles but may be used along with questionnaires for other essays in Part I as well. Although field research is not likely to be as important in most freshman composition programs as library research, we urge you to introduce these techniques to your students. They will not only make students more observant but also heighten their sensitivity to readers' varying needs and interests. Field research will be central to the academic majors and careers of many students. It engages them in a basic form of inquiry in the social sciences.

OBSERVATIONS

This section is keyed to the Guide to Writing in Chapter 4: Writing Profiles. In that chapter, we refer students to the advice given here on conducting observational visits. You may also use this chapter in conjunction with the exercises in Chapter 15: Describing.

We recommend that any observation include these stages: observing and taking notes, reflecting on your observation, writing up your notes.

Whereas reflecting on observations should follow directly after the observational visit when the experience is still fresh in the observer's mind, writing up the notes can wait until the observer has considered what impression the description should give.

To help your students read their own and each other's observational notes and writeups analytically, here are critical reading guides they could use.

Reading Observational Notes with a Critical Eye

Even though notes are not finished writing, they are an interesting written artifact. They represent the immediate translation of firsthand experience into written language. They reveal what catches the observer's attention in a new scene. They are interesting for what they include and what they ignore, as well as for how they are patterned. Students reading each other's notes will see how someone else, faced with the same writing situation, recorded his or her experience.

1. What is centrally important about these notes? What general impression do they give you of the person, place, or activity being observed?
2. What is the single most surprising or incongruous detail in the notes? Try to explain why you find this detail so surprising.
3. Consider the notes as a collection of sensory images (sights, smells, sounds, tastes, and touches). Point to the single most evocative or suggestive image, and then briefly explain what feelings and associations this image evokes in you.
4. Try to imagine the notes accumulating on the page during the time the writer was observing the scene. What does the order of these notes tell you about the way the writer was looking at the scene?

Reading Observational Writeups with a Critical Eye

Composing observational notes into a report or writeup can be considered real writing because a writeup assumes particular readers and aims to create a specific impression. Writeups as part of the profile assignment in Chapter 4: Writing Profiles, however, do not serve as ends in themselves but as means to an end. In fact, the very process of writing up observational notes enables a writer to analyze and reorder them to reach a better understanding of how they might be useful in a profile.

1. What general impression of the place, person, or activity does this writeup give you? In one sentence, try to summarize your impression.
2. What order or pattern has the writer imposed on his or her observations? Are the details organized spatially, temporally, in groups, randomly, or some other way?
3. Where is the writer in relation to the subject? Does the writer use a moving vantage point, a stationary one, or a combination of the two? Does the writer move in close, remain at a distance from the subject, or shift perspectives?
4. What is the single most evocative image? Briefly explain what feelings or associations this image evokes in you.
5. Has anything you particularly liked in the notes been left out? Suggest where it could be included.
6. Are you left with any questions about the subject? List any information you would still like to have about this subject.

INTERVIEWS

Like the section on observations, this section on interviews is keyed to the Guide to Writing in Chapter 4: Writing Profiles. In that chapter, we urge students to study the advice offered here on conducting interviews. We recommend that students follow these steps: Set up and plan the interview, take notes during the interview, reflect on the interview immediately afterward, and write up the interview notes at a later time. We emphasize the need to plan an interview by writing questions, and we also discuss various kinds of questions.

Here are guidelines for reading interview notes and writeups. We urge you to offer these guides to your students to help them analyze their own and their classmates' interview material.

Reading Interview Notes with a Critical Eye

Like observational notes, interview notes are interesting to study in isolation and as raw material for an interview writeup. These guidelines assume that students have followed the suggestions for interviewing, written several questions in advance, and divided their notebook paper between Details and Impressions in the left-hand column and Information in the right.

First, read the interview notes and the writer's reflections directly following the interview. Then, briefly respond to these questions:

1. Compare the questions prepared in advance to the information received during the interview. Which of the questions were answered? What other questions seem to have been answered?
2. Study the information. Given the writer's reflections following the interview, identify what seems to you to be the most important bit of information the writer received in the interview.
3. Study the details and impressions. Identify one detail that is particularly evocative, helping you imagine the person and the scene. Then briefly explain what feelings and associations this detail evokes for you.

Reading Interview Writeups with a Critical Eye

Interview writeups are published in various forms in magazines and newspapers. In this chapter, we encourage students to compose a writeup that is more than a mere compilation of quotations and details. The writeup featured in the Writer at Work for Chapter 4: Writing Profiles shows the writer still trying to create order from the interview. Such a writeup is not really written to be read by others, nor does it have a specific aim other than to record the writer's thoughts on the interview. The following guide was written to enable students to evaluate each other's interview writeups.

1. What is your general impression of the person being interviewed? What details help you imagine the person? What else would you like to know about the person?
2. What particular angle of vision on the subject does this person give the writer? Do the person's comments raise any interesting new questions about the subject? Do they suggest any incongruities or surprises?
3. How much of the interview is quotation? Could the writer have paraphrased or summarized any of this quoted material without losing something of value?
4. Describe how the writer organized the quotations, paraphrases, summaries, descriptive details, and so forth. Is the description clumped together at the beginning, or is it interspersed with the other features? Advise the writer on possibilities for better integrating these features.

QUESTIONNAIRES

Our discussion of questionnaires focuses on the preparation of questions. We illustrate several kinds of closed and open questions. Then we briefly treat the topics of testing and administering the questionnaire. Finally, we suggest a plan for organizing a report of the results. Since questionnaire reports are not an integral part of any of the writing assignments in Part I, we do not supply guidelines for reading them with a critical eye. Students can work in pairs or small groups to complete survey projects. Working collaboratively, many students commit themselves energetically to survey projects. You might want to select two or three survey reports from the social sciences as models of the reports students will write.

CHAPTER 21: LIBRARY AND INTERNET RESEARCH

This chapter and the next present freshmen with all the information they need to do library and Internet research and document a research paper. Knowing, however, is not the same as doing. We urge you to arrange a library tour and Internet orientation for your students, one that not only follows the steps in the search strategy but also gives students actual experience with many of the research materials—encyclopedias, bibliographies, card and online catalogs, indexes, abstracts, computer databases, government publications—introduced here.

We also urge you to have your students do some library and/or Internet research for several of their papers in your course. The only writing activities in Part I that do not invite formal research are the reflective essays—remembering events and people. Research could be used for every other assignment. You would not have to make any of these essays a major research project. Research need not make writing seem more difficult or more time-consuming but should be viewed as a strategy used routinely, like clustering or reading a draft critically.

This chapter shows students how to approach library research and carry out all the stages of a research project. Besides describing many types of library-research sources and opening up access to academic sources, the chapter identifies sources useful for researching trends and their possible causes (assignment for Chapter 9: Speculating about Causes) and current controversies (assignment for Chapter 6: Arguing a Position).

In addition to guiding students in their use of the library, this chapter also introduces students to the Internet as a resource tool for research. In order to help students learn their way through the vast array of sources available online, consider conducting a "tour" of the Internet. Before students begin the online tour, it is best to assign Using the Internet for Research (see page 574) for them to read in advance. You can then go through each section in class while sitting at the computer, giving your students a hands-on experience. If you can, arrange to use an overhead projector that can display your computer screen. As you work through the section, students can get a look at various Web sites, learn what URLs and web browsers are, and even watch as you use a search engine. In order to encourage your students to try electronic sources, Vicky Sarkisian of Marist College suggests that you use the material on the Internet in conjunction with one of the writing assignments that may involve research in Part I. Once they have defined their topics and begun the invention work, students would then be responsible for locating material using the World Wide Web, Telnet, FTP, Gopher, etc. Stress that they should download and print their own material and learn to cite and document electronic sources properly. You might encourage them to create bookmarks for future reference.

Evaluating online text poses special problems. Instructors should start with traditional guidelines for evaluating text material and move from there (see Reading Sources with a Critical Eye). Because search engines prioritize information when they provide search results, you might do a model search with your students, noting the number of hits and the criteria the search engine uses for judging the sites. You should also point out to students that anyone with the knowledge and equipment can create a Web site and that it is important to deal with reputable sites such as those connected with libraries, museums, and universities.

As with any method of research, problems do arise when students use the Internet. Because hardware and software problems can be time-consuming, you should be knowledgeable about the Internet and willing to teach the system. In addition, make sure that technical support is available before beginning any Internet work with your students. In addition to problems with determining the credibility and reliability of sources, students need to be warned about plagiarizing online sources. Because information is so readily available, you will need to cover thoroughly your school's policy and stress the importance of documenting sources.

Finally, be flexible and be prepared with an alternate plan: if the Internet is down or unavailable, it can derail your plans for a class or delay your students' research. However, the Internet is a valuable tool for learning, and it can help students greatly if they learn to use it accurately and carefully.

CHAPTER 22: USING AND ACKNOWLEDGING SOURCES

The first of the three sections in this chapter, Using Sources, teaches students how to integrate source material into their writing. Next, Acknowledging Sources surveys MLA and APA documentation style and format. Then, An Annotated Research Paper illustrates MLA documentation style and format.

In this chapter, we briefly discuss plagiarism to clarify what is meant by the term and to bring into the open some of the reasons why writers plagiarize. We define plagiarism broadly as the "unacknowledged use of another's words, ideas, or information." You may wish to discuss these issues in class, and you probably also will wish to inform students of your own and your institution's policy regarding plagiarism.

Most students who plagiarize, we assume, do not understand that the acknowledged use of other people's ideas, information, and even words is not only acceptable but expected of educated people. For this reason, if for no other, we believe students should routinely be asked to consult sources when they write. If this is done, students will begin to understand that, for the most part, academic writing is a dialogue between the writer and other writers on a given subject.

Plagiarism is, we also assume, in many cases simply evidence of students' unfamiliarity with academic conventions. They plagiarize because they do not know how to integrate source material into their own writing. Using Sources surveys various acceptable methods of quoting, paraphrasing, and summarizing source material. In many cases, we use illustrations from essays in Part I so that students can see how these strategies are used in the context of a whole selection. You might take some class time to discuss these strategies and suggest others students might add to their repertoire.

CHAPTER 23: ESSAY EXAMINATIONS

This chapter offers a comprehensive introduction to the writing demands of essay exams. You could assign it at any time during the course, although just prior to midterm exams would be a good time. After their first essay exams in other courses, students might bring in their essay questions for the class to analyze and critique. We have organized the chapter as follows:

Preparing for an Exam: advice on keeping up with one's studies and directions for studying for an exam

Reading the Exam Carefully: strategies for figuring out the writing task posed by essay exam questions

Some Typical Essay Exam Questions: extensive illustrations and analyses of nine different types of essay exam questions

Planning Your Answer: strategies for planning under time pressure

Writing Your Answer: advice on specific techniques for presenting answers

Model Answers to Some Typical Essay Exam Questions: examples and analyses of short, paragraph-length, and long answers

This chapter is nearly all example, analysis, and discussion. The two exercises come at the very end of the chapter. After inviting some discussion from students about their successes and failures with essay exams, you can ask them to read the whole chapter down to the exercises. Ask them to come to class having identified what for each of them is the most puzzling or difficult essay exam question in the series of twenty-two sample questions. You can then extend your discussion of ways to handle the most difficult questions.

You might want to spend some time talking them through John Pixley's model long answer, helping them understand the decisions he made in composing the answer. You will want to point out that he relies on strategies of contrast, illustration, and coherence that we emphasize throughout the book, particularly in Chapter 5: Explaining a Concept, Chapter 13: Cueing the Reader, and Chapter 18: Comparing and Contrasting.

OVERVIEW OF THE EXERCISES

23.1   Analyze an essay answer

23.2   Analyze essay questions

SUGGESTIONS FOR TEACHING THE EXERCISES

23.1   Analyze an essay answer.

Students analyze a long essay answer written by a student in response to the same question Pixley answered. Summarizing the successful features of Pixley's essay and the criteria in Writing Your Answer would be a useful preliminary to this exercise. When students assess Hepler's answer, they could either write out their analyses or make notes for class discussion. Some students would benefit from your reading the essay aloud, commenting as you go on its successful features.

23.2   Analyze essay questions.

In this exercise, we ask students to analyze nine essay questions from exams in history, communications, and literature. We want them to decide what writing task is being posed in each of these questions and then, within the time constraints, to propose a general plan for answering the question. You could very usefully talk students through two or three of these and then have them develop plans for two or three more during class, evaluating their plans immediately while still in class. Then you could assign two or three more to be analyzed as homework.

CHAPTER 24: ASSEMBLING A WRITING PORTFOLIO

This chapter introduces students to writing portfolios and offers guidelines for assembling a portfolio of work from assignments in *The St. Martin's Guide*. Specifically, it offers students help in selecting work, reflecting on their work and learning, and organizing and presenting a portfolio. It also helps them understand how instructors read and evaluate portfolios.

For a portfolio to be a satisfying learning experience for students, you will have to allow time—some programs allow a week or two—for students to review their work, choose selections, perhaps revise an essay further, assemble the portfolio, and write an essay (or perhaps a letter to you) reflecting on their learning. They may need to confer with you and other students about their plans.

HANDBOOK

USING THE HANDBOOK

We conclude the complete edition of *The St. Martin's Guide* with a comprehensive handbook, one that can be used by students on their own or to illustrate class discussion. Designed for quick reference, the Handbook is divided into nine sections:

Sentence Boundaries

Grammatical Sentences

Effective Sentences

Word Choice

Punctuation

Mechanics

ESL Troublespots

A Brief Review of Sentence Structure

Glossary of Frequently Misused Words

In this Manual we offer specific advice on using the Handbook in Chapter 3: Evaluation Practices. In Chapter 3, see the section "Dealing with Error" and also Charles Cooper's student handout at the end of the chapter. We advocate an efficient procedure for teaching students how to use the Handbook by taking responsibility for correcting their own errors.

CHAPTER 7

A Selected Bibliography in Rhetoric and Composition

HISTORIES OF RHETORIC AND THE TEACHING OF WRITING

Applebee, Arthur N. *Tradition and Reform in the Teaching of English: A History.* Urbana, IL: NCTE, 1974.

Bender, John, and David E. Wellbery. *The Ends of Rhetoric: History, Theory, Practice.* Stanford: Stanford UP, 1990.

Berlin, James A. *Rhetoric and Reality: Writing Instruction in American Colleges, 1900–1985.* Carbondale: Southern Illinois UP, 1987.

———. *Writing Instruction in Nineteenth Century American Colleges.* Carbondale: Southern Illinois UP, 1984.

Brereton, John, ed. *Traditions of Inquiry.* New York: Oxford UP, 1985.

Connors, Robert J. "The Rise and Fall of the Modes of Discourse." *CCC* 32 (Dec. 1981): 444–63.

Connors, Robert J., Lisa S. Ede, and Andrea Lunsford, eds. *Essays on Classical Rhetoric and Modern Discourse.* Carbondale: Southern Illinois UP, 1984.

Corbett, Edward P. J., James L. Golden, and Goodwin F. Berquist, eds. *Essays on the Rhetoric of the Western World.* Dubuque, IA: Kendall/Hunt, 1990.

Crowley, Sharon. *The Methodical Memory: Invention in Current-Traditional Rhetoric.* Carbondale: Southern Illinois UP, 1990.

———. *Ancient Rhetorics for Contemporary Students.* New York: Macmillan, 1994.

Halloran, S. Michael. "Rhetoric in the American College Curriculum: The Decline of Public Discourse." *PRE/TEXT,* 3 (Fall 1983).

Horner, Winifred Bryan, ed. *The Present State of Scholarship in Historical and Contemporary Rhetoric.* Columbia: U of Missouri P, 1983.

Jarratt, Susan. *The Return of the Sophists: Classical Rhetoric Refigured.* Carbondale: Southern Illinois UP, 1991.

Johnson, Nan. *Nineteenth-Century Rhetoric: Theory and Practice in North America.* Carbondale: Southern Illinois UP, 1991.

Kennedy, George A. *Classical Rhetoric and Its Christian and Secular Tradition from Ancient to Modern Times.* Chapel Hill: U of North Carolina P, 1980.

Murphy, James J., ed. *The Rhetorical Tradition and Modern Writing.* New York: MLA, 1982.

———. *A Short History of Writing Instruction from Ancient Greece to Twentieth Century America*. Davis, CA: Hermagoras, 1990.

Phelps, Louise Wetherbee. *Composition as a Human Science: Contribution to the Self-Understanding of a Discipline*. New York: Oxford UP, 1988.

Royster, Jacqueline Jones. "Perspectives on the Intellectual Tradition of Black Women Writers." *The Right to Literacy*. Ed. Andrea Lunsford et al. New York: MLA, 1990.

Swearington, C. Jan. *Rhetoric and Irony: Western Literacy and Western Lies*. New York: Oxford UP, 1991.

Welch, Kathleen E. *The Contemporary Reception of Classical Rhetoric: Appropriations of Ancient Discourse*. Hillsdale, NJ: Erlbaum, 1990.

MODERN AND POSTMODERN RHETORIC AND DISCOURSE THEORY

Aronowitz, Stanley, and Henry A. Giroux. *Postmodern Education: Politics, Culture, and Social Criticism*. Minneapolis: U of Minnesota P, 1991.

Atkins, C. Douglas, and Michael L. Johnson, eds. *Writing and Reading Differently: Deconstruction and the Teaching of Composition and Literature*. Lawrence, KS: UP of Kansas, 1985.

Beale, Walter H. *A Pragmatic Theory of Rhetoric*. Carbondale: Southern Illinois UP, 1987.

Belanoff, Pat, Peter Elbow, and Sheryl I. Fontaine, eds. *Nothing Begins with N: New Investigations of Freewriting*. Carbondale: Southern Illinois UP, 1991.

Berthoff, Ann. *The Making of Meaning: Metaphors, Models, and Maxims for Writing Teachers*. Portsmouth, NH: Heinemann, Boynton/Cook, 1981.

Bitzer, Lloyd F. "The Rhetorical Situation." *Philosophy and Rhetoric* 1 (Winter 1968): 1–14.

Bizzell, Patricia. *Academic Discourse and Critical Consciousness*. Pittsburgh: U of Pittsburgh P, 1992.

Britton, James, et al. *The Development of Writing Abilities (11–18)*. London: Macmillan, 1975.

Bullock, Richard, and John Trimbur, eds. *The Politics of Writing Instruction: Postsecondary*. Portsmouth, NH: Heinemann, Boynton/Cook, 1991.

Clark, Gregory. *Dialogue, Dialectic, and Conversation: A Social Perspective on the Function of Writing*. Carbondale: Southern Illinois UP, 1990.

Crusius, Timothy W. *Discourse: A Critique and Synthesis of Major Theories*. New York: MLA, 1989.

Elbow, Peter. *Embracing Contraries: Explorations in Learning and Teaching*. New York: Oxford UP, 1986.

———. *What Is English?* New York: MLA, 1990.

Emig, Janet. *The Web of Meaning: Essays on Writing, Teaching, Learning, and Thinking*. Ed. Dixie Goswami and Maureen Butler. Portsmouth, NH: Heinemann, Boynton/Cook, 1983.

Faigley, Lester. *Fragments of Rationality: Postmodernity and the Subject of Composition*. Pittsburgh: U of Pittsburgh P, 1992.

Freedman, Aviva, and Ian Pringle, eds. *Reinventing the Rhetorical Tradition*. Urbana, IL: NCTE, 1980.

Giroux, Henry A. *Postmodernism, Feminism, and Cultural Politics: Redrawing Educational Boundaries.* Albany: SUNY P, 1991.

Kinneavy, James L. *A Theory of Discourse.* New York: Norton, 1980.

Lindemann, Erika, and Gary Tate, eds. *An Introduction to Composition Studies.* New York: Oxford UP, 1991.

Macdonell, Diane. *Theories of Discourse: An Introduction.* Oxford: Basil Blackwell, 1986.

Miller, Susan. *Rescuing the Subject: A Critical Introduction to Rhetoric and the Writer.* Carbondale: Southern Illinois UP, 1989.

———. *Textual Carnivals: The Politics of Composition.* Carbondale: Southern Illinois UP, 1991.

Moffett, James. *Teaching the Universe of Discourse.* Boston: Houghton Mifflin, 1968.

Perelman, Chaim. *The Realm of Rhetoric.* Trans. William Kluback. Notre Dame, IN: U of Notre Dame P, 1977.

Schilb, John, and Patricia Harkin, eds. *Contending with Words: Composition and Rhetoric in a Postmodern Age.* New York: MLA, 1991.

Secor, Marie, and Davida Charney, eds. *Constructing Rhetorical Education.* Carbondale: Southern Illinois UP, 1992.

Toulmin, Stephen. *The Uses of Argument.* New York: Cambridge UP, 1964.

WRITING AS A PROCESS

Emig, Janet. *The Composing Processes of Twelfth Graders.* Urbana, IL: NCTE, 1971.

Faigley, Lester. "Competing Theories of Process: A Critique and a Proposal." *CE* 48 (Oct. 1986): 527–42.

Flower, Linda, and John R. Hayes. "Problem-Solving Strategies and the Writing Process." *CE* 49 (1977): 19–37.

Flower, Linda, et al. "Detection, Diagnosis, and the Strategies of Revision." *CCC* 37 (1986): 16–55.

Gregg, L. W., and E. R. Steinberg, eds. *Cognitive Processes in Writing.* Hillsdale, NJ: Erlbaum, 1980.

LeFevre, Karen Burke. *Invention as a Social Act.* Carbondale: Southern Illinois UP, 1987.

Murray, Donald M. "Writing as Process: How Writing Finds Its Own Meaning." *Eight Approaches to Teaching Composition.* Ed. Timothy R. Donovan and Ben W. McClelland. Urbana, IL: NCTE, 1980.

Nystrand, Martin, ed. *What Writers Know: The Language, Process, and Structure of Written Discourse.* New York: Academic P, 1982.

Rose, Mike, ed. *When a Writer Can't Write: Studies in Writer's Block and Other Composing-Process Problems.* New York: Guilford, 1985.

Sommers, Nancy. "Revision Strategies of Student Writers and Experienced Adult Writers." *CCC* 31 (1980): 378–388.

Sudol, Ronald A., ed. *Revising.* Urbana, IL: NCTE, 1982.

COMPUTERS AND COMPOSITION

Cooper, Marilyn M., and Cynthia L. Selfe. "Computer Conferences and Learning: Authority, Resistance, and Internally Persuasive Discourse." *College English* 52 (1990): 847–69.

Hawisher, Gail E., and Cynthia L. Selfe. *Critical Perspectives on Computers and Composition Instruction*. New York: Teachers College P, 1989.

Holdstein, Deborah H., and Cynthia L. Selfe, eds. *Computers and Writing: Theory, Research, Practice*. New York: MLA, 1990.

Selfe, Cynthia L., and Susan Hilligoss, eds. *Literacy and Computers: The Complications of Teaching and Learning with Technology*. New York: MLA, 1994.

COLLABORATIVE LEARNING

Brooke, Robert E. *Writing and Sense of Self: Identity Negotiation in Writing Workshops*. Urbana, IL: NCTE, 1991.

Bruffee, Kenneth A. "Collaborative Learning and the 'Conversation of Mankind.' " *CE* 46 (Nov. 1984): 635–52.

———. *Collaborative Learning: Higher Education, Interdependence, and the Authority of Knowledge*. Baltimore: Johns Hopkins UP, 1993.

Gere, Ann. *Writing Groups: History, Theory, and Implications*. Carbondale: Southern Illinois UP, 1987.

Golub, Jeff, ed. *Focus on Collaborative Learning*. Urbana, IL: NCTE, 1988.

Haring-Smith, Tori. *Writing Together: Collaborative Learning in the Writing Classroom*. New York: HarperCollins, 1994.

Lunsford, Andrea, and Lisa Ede. *Singular Texts/Plural Authors: Perspectives on Collaborative Writing*. Carbondale: Southern Illinois UP, 1990.

METACOGNITION, READING, AND GENRE THEORY

Bereiter, Carl, and Marlene Scardamalia. *Psychology of Written Composition*. Hillsdale, NJ: Erlbaum, 1987.

Brown, Ann L. "Metacognitive Development and Reading." *Theoretical Issues in Reading Comprehension*. Ed. Bertram Bruce et al. Hillsdale, NJ: Erlbaum, 1980.

Cope, Bill, and Mary Kalantzis, eds. *The Powers of Literacy: A Genre Approach to Teaching Writing*. Pittsburgh: U of Pittsburgh P, 1993.

Dillon, George L. *Constructing Texts*. Bloomington: Indiana UP, 1981.

Freedman, Aviva. "Show and Tell? The Role of Explicit Teaching in the Learning of New Genres." *RTE* 27.3 (Oct. 1993): 222–51.

———. "Situating Genre: A Rejoinder." *RTE* 27:3 (Oct. 1993): 272–81.

Halliday, M. A. K., and Ruqaiya Hasan. *Cohesion in English*. London: Longman, 1976.

Kinsch, Walter. "The Role of Strategies in Reading and Writing." *Forum* III 67 (1982).

Kress, Gunther. "Genre as Social Process." *The Powers of Literacy: A Genre Approach to Teaching Writing*. Ed. Bill Cope and Mary Kalantzis. Pittsburgh: U of Pittsburgh P, 1993.

Miller, Carolyn. "Genre as Social Action." *Quarterly Journal of Speech* 70 (1984): 151–67.

Newkirk, Thomas, ed. *Only Connect: Uniting Reading and Writing*. Portsmouth, NH: Heinemann, Boynton/Cook, 1986.

Petersen, Bruce T., ed. *Convergences: Transactions in Reading and Writing*. Urbana, IL: NCTE, 1986.

Pianko, Sharon. "Reflection: A Critical Component of the Composing Process." *CCC* 30 (1979): 275–85.

Schank, R., and Abelson, R. *Scripts, Plans, Goals, and Understanding*. Hillsdale, NJ: Erlbaum, 1977.

Slevin, James F. "Interpreting and Composing: The Many Resources of Kind." *The Writer's Mind*. Ed. Janice Hays et al. Urbana, IL: NCTE, 1983.

Williams, Joseph M., and Gregory G. Colomb. "The Case for Explicit Teaching: Why What You Don't Know Won't Help You." *RTE* 27.3 (Oct. 1993): 252–64.

WRITING IN THE DISCIPLINES

Bartholomae, David. "Inventing the University." *When a Writer Can't Write*. Ed. Mike Rose. New York: Guilford P, 1985.

Bazerman, Charles. *Shaping Written Knowledge*. Madison: U of Wisconsin P, 1988.

Bazerman, Charles, and James Paradis. *Textual Dynamics of the Professions: Historical and Contemporary Studies of Writing in Professional Communities*. Madison: U of Wisconsin P, 1991.

Bullock, Richard. *The St. Martin's Guide to Teaching Writing in the Disciplines*. New York: St. Martin's, 1994.

Fulwiler, Toby, and Al Young, eds. *Programs That Work: Writing across the Curriculum*. Portsmouth, NH: Heinemann, Boynton/Cook, 1990.

Gere, Anne Ruggles, ed. *Roots in the Sawdust: Writing to Learn in the Disciplines*. Urbana, IL: NCTE, 1985.

Herrington, Anne, and Charles Moran. *Writing, Teaching, and Learning in the Disciplines*. New York: MLA, 1992.

MacDonald, Susan Peck. *Professional Academic Writing in the Humanities and Social Sciences*. Carbondale: Southern Illinois UP, 1994.

Maimon, Elaine P. "Collaborative Learning and Writing across the Curriculum." *WPA* 9 (1986): 9–15.

Russell, David R. *Writing in the Academic Disciplines, 1870–1990*. Carbondale: Southern Illinois UP, 1991.

Walvoord, Barbara, and Lucille McCarthy, eds. *Thinking and Writing in College*. Urbana, IL: NCTE, 1990.

GENDER, CLASS, ETHNICITY

Annas, Pamela J. "Style as Politics: A Feminist Approach to Teaching of Writing." *CE* 47 (Apr. 1985): 369–71.

Ashton-Jones, Evelyn, and D. Thomas. "Composition, Collaboration, and Women's Ways of Knowing." *Journal of Advanced Composition* 10 (1990): 275–92.

Belenky, Mary Field, et al. *Women's Ways of Knowing: The Development of Self, Voice, and Mind.* New York: Basic Books, 1986.

Caywood, Cynthia L., and Gillian R. Overing. *Teaching Writing: Pedagogy, Gender, and Equity.* Albany: SUNY P, 1987.

Eichhorn, Jill, et al. "A Symposium on Feminist Experiences in the Composition Classroom." *CCC* 43 (Oct. 1992): 297–322.

Flynn, Elizabeth A., and Patrocinio Schwickart, eds. *Gender and Reading: Essays on Readers, Texts and Contexts.* Baltimore: Johns Hopkins UP, 1986.

Fontaine, Sheryl, and Susan Hunter, eds. *Writing Ourselves into the Story: Unheard Voices from Composition Studies.* Carbondale: Southern Illinois UP, 1993.

Greco, Norma. "Critical Literacy and Community Service: Reading and Writing the World." *English Journal* 81 (1992): 83–85.

Heath, Shirley Brice. *Ways with Words: Language, Life, and Work in Communities and Classrooms.* Cambridge: Cambridge UP, 1983.

Hill, Carolyn Eriksen. *Writing from the Margins: Power and Pedagogy for Teachers of Composition.* New York: Oxford UP, 1990.

Langer, Judith A., ed. *Language, Literacy, and Culture: Issues of Society and Schooling.* Norwood, NJ: Ablex Publishing, 1987.

McCracken, Nancy Mellin, and Bruce C. Appleby. *Gender Issues in the Teaching of English.* Portsmouth, NH: Heinemann, Boynton/Cook, 1992.

McQuade, Donald A., ed. *The Territory of Language: Linguistics, Stylistics, and the Teaching of Composition.* Carbondale: Southern Illinois UP, 1986.

Rose, Mike. *Lives on the Boundary: The Struggles and Achievements of America's Underprepared.* London: Collier-Macmillan, 1989.

Rubin, Donnalee. *Gender Influences: Reading Student Texts.* Carbondale: Southern Illinois UP, 1993.

Shaughnessy, Mina. *Errors and Expectations.* New York: Oxford UP, 1977.

Smitherman-Donaldson, Ginevra, and Teun A. van Dijk, eds. *Discourse and Discrimination.* Detroit: Wayne State UP, 1988.

RESPONDING TO AND EVALUATING STUDENT WRITING

Anson, Cris M. *Writing and Response: Theory, Practice, and Research.* Urbana, IL: NCTE, 1989.

Belanoff, Pat, and Marcia Dickson. *Portfolios: Process and Product.* Portsmouth, NH: Heinemann, Boynton/Cook, 1991.

Black, Laurel, et al. *New Directions in Portfolio Assessment.* Portsmouth, NH: Heinemann, 1994.

Cooper, Charles, and Lee Odell, eds. *Evaluating Writing,* 2nd ed. Urbana, IL: NCTE, 1997.

Faigley, Lester, et al. *Assessing Writer's Knowledge and Processes of Composing.* Norwood, NJ: Ablex, 1985.

Freedman, Sarah W. *Response to Student Writing.* Urbana, IL: NCTE Research Report No. 23, 1987.

Greenberg, K. L., et al., eds. *Writing Assessment: Issues and Strategies.* New York: Longman, 1986.

Horvath, Brooke K. "The Components of Written Response: A Practical Synthesis of Current Views." *Rhetoric Review* 2 (Jan. 1985): 136–56.

Williams, Joseph M. "The Phenomenology of Error." *CCC* 32 (May 1991): 152–68.

CHAPTER 8

A Selection of Background Readings

Composition Theory in the Eighties: Axiological Consensus and Paradigmatic Diversity

Richard Fulkerson

Richard Fulkerson is director of English Graduate Studies at East Texas State University. "Composition Theory in the Eighties," which first appeared in College Composition and Communication *(December 1990), provides an overview of current composition theory and practice.*

When Alice asks the Cheshire Cat, "Would you tell me, please, which way I ought to go from here?" the sage Cat replies, "That depends a good deal on where you want to get to." The episode may be read as a parable for teachers, for it enunciates a fundamental principle about ends and means: without the end clearly in mind, it is pointless to ask how to get there.

BACKGROUND

In 1979, in a *CCC* article, I discussed four conflicting views about the ends of teaching composition, views which I called "philosophies of composition." Adapting the perspective of M. H. Abrams in *The Mirror and the Lamp*, I asserted that composition teachers, textbooks, and curricula could privilege any element in a communicative transaction and generate a "philosophy" of composition.

I need here to summarize that article briefly. Readers familiar with it are invited to skip the next three paragraphs.

If one privileges the text in a communicative transaction, I said, one adopts a formalist philosophy of composition. If the writer, an expressive philosophy. If the external reality, a mimetic philosophy. If the reader, a rhetorical philosophy. Each philosophy represents a view of the "end" composition values. Formalists value specified formal features, most often correctness at the sentence level, but conceivably a privileged style of sentence or a structure for a paragraph, or even the five-paragraph format for a paper. Expressivists value openness, honesty, sincerity, originality, authentic voice, and personal topics for writing. Mimeticists value accuracy of information, sound logic, and "truth" in prose (perhaps the best illustration being a "traditional" technical writing class). Finally, rhetoricists value "effectiveness," audience awareness, persuasiveness, and contextual flexibility. They see writing as a situated transaction and tend to say, "whatever works is right."

Clearly, writing always has all four dimensions; no teacher can ignore the ones he or she does not emphasize. But presumptively one's philosophical emphasis about what is valued in writing drives course design, textbook selection or creation, writing assignments, commentary on writing, and the day-to-day details of classroom interaction. And each of these could be examined semiotically in order to discover a teacher's *dominant* orientation.

Based on this four-part model, I preached two main messages: first, what is now a truism, that teachers who claimed to teach without any philosophy were deluding themselves. It is possible to be unconscious about philosophy, or to be inconsistent, but it isn't possible not to have one.[1] Second, and more important, I maintained, too often teachers were unaware of the philosophy they more or less adhered to and sent contradictory messages in the classroom. They either lacked a consistent view of the ends sought or followed paths that would not reach them. My moral was that the unexamined course is not worth teaching.

As I see matters now, the assertions that there are four major possible goals (ends) in teaching composition and that means can contradict ends still make sense. But the last decade has shown, I believe, an emerging consensus about which goal is most important and simultaneously growing complexity and conflict over means of reaching it.

To justify this view, I will first propose a metatheory about the components necessary to a "Theory of Composition." Then, using the metatheory, I hope to clarify the role of what I called in 1979 a "philosophy of composition." Finally, I will try to show by textual evidence that, in the eighties, Composition Studies has moved toward homogeneity of purpose within diversity of method. In the 1990s we may be ready to tell the Cheshire Cat where we want to go, but we don't agree about how to get there.

ELEMENTS OF A FULL THEORY OF COMPOSITION

As I examined the work of composition scholars through the eighties, I realized that in 1979 I had used the terms *theory* and *philosophy* quite loosely. In fact, I had often used them interchangeably to refer to any general propositions about writing and its teaching, yet at other times I had meant to designate only my primary concern with value position. My title, "Four Philosophies," referred specifically to four views of what makes writing good.

I now propose as a disciplinary paradigm that a full "theory" of composition would include four components, of which what I once called a "philosophy" is only the first:

1. A full theory necessarily includes a commitment about what constitutes good writing—not necessarily a simplistic one, but some analysis of what we want student writers to achieve as a result of effective teaching. This is an axiological component. (*Axiology* is a technical term in philosophy, introduced by French philosopher Paul Lapie in 1902. It means simply value theory conceived generally, as opposed to the more specific terms *ethics* or *aesthetics* [Reese 45].) Without some such aim, it is useless to teach composition since you can't know whether a change in student writing represents progress. Without the aim, the Cheshire Cat's advice holds: any road will do.
2. A full theory also necessarily includes a conception of how writers go about creating texts, and perhaps a conception of how they should go about it. That is, the theory has a *procedural* component describing the *means* by which writers can reach the *ends* specified by the axiology.
3. A full theory must include some perspective about classroom procedures and curricular designs suitable for enabling students to achieve the sort of writing one values, a *pedagogical* component. This component also concerns *means*, but the teacher's means rather than the writer's.[2]

Although ontologically different, a fourth element is necessary, an epistemology: our perceptions of how texts are created and of what classroom methods are effective depend on assumptions about what counts for knowledge. Moreover, writing itself requires epistemological assumptions, so teaching writing implicitly involves teaching epistemology (Berlin, "Contemporary Composition" 776). Yet, as Steve North has shown in *The Making of Knowledge in Composition,* our discipline scarcely shares a common epistemology.[3]

I maintain that these four elements are both necessary and sufficient for a theory of composition: these four, and only these four, are required, either conscious or not, to teach writing. Other matters may become part of one's theory of composition, such as a theory of invention or of style (see Gage, "Philosophies of Style") or of audience (see Coney) or of genre (see Kinneavy and Beale). None of these, oddly enough, is necessary, though good arguments exist that informed teachers will have views on each.

THEORY OF COMPOSITION A DECADE LATER: THREE AXIOLOGIES IN DECLINE

Ten years ago, genuine and extensive conflicts existed about what constituted good writing and thus about what sort of writing one ought to teach. We lacked shared axiological presumptions. But Composition Studies now shows the emergence of a significant consensus: the widely-held position today is a rhetorical axiology. Significant disparities, however, continue to exist about process, pedagogy, and epistemology. We are closer to agreeing on where we want to go, but not on how to get there.

Expressivism

In 1979 expressivism, which Jim Berlin ("Contemporary Composition" 771) and Karen LeFevre (49–50) both describe as deriving from Platonic individualism, was an expansive domain, with such charismatic leaders as Ken Macrorie, Don Stewart (author of *The Authentic Voice*), and Lou Kelly (author of *From Dialogue to Discourse*). Here, for example, is how Kelly described teaching writing: "the content of composition is the writer—as he reveals his *self,* thoughtfully and feelingly, in his own language, with his own voice. . . . We raise questions that we hope will help our students analyze and understand their own lives, their own beliefs, their own values" ("Toward Competence" 3).

And in a review article on the status of composition, Elizabeth McPherson answered the question "What do we teach writing *for?*" as follows:

> To help students grow—in their ability to understand themselves and their experiences, in their ability to share those experiences with other people. . . . When the main purpose of writing is seen as discovery, the job of the teachers shifts from laying down rules and formulas to finding ways that will help those discoveries take place. . . . The true content of the course became the students themselves, their attempts to use language to enlarge that vision. (180–81)[4]

We find nothing parallel in scholarly journals now, nor are new expressionist textbooks appearing. Works of the older writers like Macrorie are still in print, of course. And Don Murray's work sometimes seems expressionist, especially in the personal topics he stresses. Knoblauch and Brannon at times *seem* to take an expressionist position, such as when they say "the approximate goal [of the workshop approach] is to experiment with the making and sharing of meanings *that matter to the writers*" (105, emphasis added). Yet their stress on the collaborative response group might also reflect a rhetorical axiology. In fact, Brannon has written, "Writers need to be shown how readers might respond to their formulations. By internalizing readers' questions, writers can begin to locate possible problems within their own texts . . . taking into account the difference between . . . the effects they want to create and the actual reactions of their readers" ("The Teacher as Philosopher" 31).

Berlin ("Rhetoric and Ideology" 486) and others have called Peter Elbow an expression-ist, largely, I think, based on his famous *Writing Without Teachers*. But even in 1979 I disagreed with that view (346), as did William Woods in 1981 (406).[5]

Formalism

Even in 1979, the formalist axiology was hard to find in print: *no one* writing in our scholarly journals defended the most basic formalist assertion that good writing is correct writing, although we had plenty of evidence of its classroom existence.

- When I came to ETSU in 1970, the English Department had a set of printed grading reg-ulations which specified that any paper containing a single comma splice or five misspelled words would receive an F. It didn't matter how brilliant, moving, or persuasive. Such form meant failure.
- One of my honors students wrote about a high-school teacher in a Dallas suburb who re-quired that every essay have five paragraphs, that each body paragraph have exactly five sen-tences, that each sentence be footnoted, and that there be none of the student's viewpoint in the paper.
- Currently, in a nearby junior high school, English teachers are told to read a paper until they reach five of certain identified errors. Then they are to stop reading and return the paper for a rewrite. But the revision can receive a grade no higher than a 90. And the same five-error/stop rule applies.

Now those are instances of formalism with a vengeance. One did not find that sort of behavior advocated in print, not even ten years ago. I did, however, identify two formalist scholars at the time. E. D. Hirsch's empirical attempt to define "relative readability" (*Philosophy* 61) seemed an acontextual formalism. And Francis Christensen had come close to elevating the cumulative sentence into a self-justifying form. But Hirsch later repudiated his view when his research showed readability to be a contextual matter, based on audience background rather than on syntactic form ("Reading" 141–43). And it is rare now to find anyone advocating a rigid cumulative ap-proach to elaborating sentence textures.

In 1979, one could find a fair amount of overt defense of the five-paragraph essay, includ-ing a whole textbook entitled *The Five-Hundred-Word Theme* (Martin), with its example paper giving three reasons why dogs on the loose are a hazard (13). Today no self-respecting textbook focuses on such a form, even if a few discuss it.

My perception is that the major written presentation of a formalist axiology today exists in some traditional business-writing textbooks which stress the formal details of business corre-spondence and even prescribe rigid structures for both the bad-news letter (buffer, bad news, conciliatory close) and the sales letter (AIDA). But such approaches are under attack from a rhetorical perspective (see Mendelson).

Mimeticism

The strict mimetic axiology has never been common in writing courses. It more usually exists when teachers evaluate essay tests or research papers in their disciplines. Papers with inaccurate information or unacceptable conclusions are then judged seriously inferior.

I originally identified two mimetic varieties in English departments: one emphasized study-ing formal logic and fallacies; the other stressed writing from anthologized sources, on the ground that the problem with student prose was lack of information. Today formal logic has largely been replaced with argumentation models such as stasis theory and the Toulmin approach, which emphasize the rhetorical values of adapting to and persuading an audience (Toulmin's "argument field") by finding shared warrants for enthymemes.[6] We do, of course still have topically organized anthologies, such as Rottenberg's *Elements of Argument,* but the stress is on critical thinking and comparison of viewpoints, rather than on providing information for students to write from. And research casebooks, common then, are now largely out of print.

THE EMERGING CONSENSUS: RHETORICAL AXIOLOGY

Here are some recent and typical statements of the emerging rhetorical consensus on what constitutes good writing:

- In *Successful Writing,* Maxine Hairston tells advanced composition students "people must write to suit the particular needs of specific readers. . . . [P]eople whose business it is to evaluate writing almost all agree that the key element of good writing is that it communicates effectively with the readers for whom it is intended. . . . [E]ffective writers never work in a vacuum" (11).
- Richard Marius says, "In my teaching I have always told students that they must write for an audience. Student writers need to learn that they have to interest someone" (152).
- In her textbook, *Problem-Solving Strategies for Writing,* Linda Flower tells students, "Good writing is intensely functional. It goes beyond mere correctness to meet the needs of the reader" (1). She continues, "a writer has to communicate that understanding so a reader will see what the writer meant. Simply expressing one's ideas is usually not enough" (5).[7]

The consensus shows up in our textbooks, our books on teaching methods, our extensive scholarly discussion of audience and the social dimensions of discourse, plus one major view of writing across the curriculum.

Textbooks

The two best-selling college rhetorics in the country right now are Axelrod and Cooper's *St. Martin's Guide to Writing* and Trimmer's revision of McCrimmon's *Writing with a Purpose.* Both presume an essentially rhetorical axiology. In their general introduction about writing as a process, for example, Axelrod and Cooper give the following advice about revising.

> Before you read a draft in order to revise it, refocus on your readers and purpose. Ask yourself: how can I improve this draft to make it more readable and memorable for my readers? (11)

Each main chapter of the book presents a different sort of writing assignment, such as "Writing Profiles" or "Making Evaluations," and each of the ten main chapters begins by discussing purpose and audience for that type of writing, before leading a writer through both an extended writing process and peer review. These are hallmarks of a rhetorical approach in which readers and their responses are the final criteria of effectiveness.

Writing with a Purpose has been the preeminent rhetoric in the United States for the last three decades at least. And, according to Robert Connors's analysis, it was for most of that time a current-traditional (i.e., largely formalist) text. However, as Paul Kameen has pointed out, the eighth edition showed "the full impact of both audience-based approaches, and more particularly, problem solving" (176).

Another venerable text, still going strong, is Sheridan Baker's *The Practical Stylist,* now in its seventh edition. Baker, too, now adopts an overtly rhetorical orientation by including for the first time a section called "Consider Your Readers" (4–5). Of course, Baker's stress on the "argumentative edge" for all writing, which makes even exposition into persuasion, has always been an implicitly rhetorical focus, even though a number of features in his endpaper checklists suggest a perhaps inconsistent formalism (such as "Each paragraph begun with topic sentence?" and "Paragraph four or five sentences long?").

Books on Teaching Writing

In contrast to 1979, there are now probably a dozen full-length books about how to teach writing in college, including Irmscher, Lindemann, Williams, Huff and Kline, Bogel and Gottschalk, Neman, Graser, and Connors and Glenn. And whatever pedagogy they recommend, these books reflect an essentially rhetorical axiology.

Huff and Kline's book, *The Contemporary Writing Curriculum,* though a strange mixture of disparate elements (more on this later), eventually moves into analysis of rhetorically appropriate writing with an exercise in evaluating nine versions of a parent's letter urging a teacher to be more cooperative about a child's dyslexia (82–83). After listing rhetorical criteria for peer-group evaluation (122–23), the authors state the rhetorical axiology overtly: "real writing is judged by the effect that it has on a real audience" (183).

More recently James Williams, in *Preparing to Teach Writing,* has proposed a "pragmatic" view in which writing is a way of getting something done. Williams thus defines *rhetoric* as *"the conscious control of language to bring about an intended effect in an audience"* (27, emphasis in original). Journal keeping, a staple of expressive views, is omitted entirely.

Concern for Audience

Our disciplinary concern with audience and audience analysis, one reflection of a rhetorical axiology, has also grown dramatically. As Gordon Thomas put it in 1986, "writing teachers have become progressively more concerned with how writers shape their discourse to the demands of a particular audience" (580). He notes that practically the entire May 1984 issue of *CCC* was devoted to audience, including "Audience Addressed/Audience Invoked: The Role of Audience in Composition Theory and Pedagogy," for which Lisa Ede and Andrea Lunsford won the Braddock award.

Concern with audience has not abated since. Now virtually every textbook discusses audience analysis, and the first textbook focusing entirely on audience has appeared, Jan Youga's *The Element of Audience Analysis.* And many teachers require students to specify the audience. Both Lindemann (196) and Williams (239) recommend that all writing assignments should do so.

I do not wish to oversimplify the situation. We have an extensive and conflicting range of scholarly discussions about concepts of audience. The range is somewhat too simply illustrated by the polar opposites Ede and Lunsford criticize: audience addressed, a "real" audience that the writer tries to study and adapt to, vs. audience invoked, a "fictionalized" audience the writer attempts to create through textual cues, an audience any real reader is then invited to join. Barry Kroll has identified three alternate "perspectives" on audience, the informational, the social, and the rhetorical.

My point is that, no matter which view of textual adaptation to audience one takes, all such views imply the importance of "audience" to the writing. All *three* of Kroll's perspectives reflect variations on a rhetorical axiology.

The importance of audience may now seem *obvious* to us, as we have moved on to various ways of conceiving it. But what is obvious now stands in stark contrast to the concern with self expression, discovery, and actualization of the expressive axiology, as well as to the acontextualism of the formalist rules. A concern for audience was not standard in composition scholarship or textbooks a decade ago.[8]

The Social Conception of Writing

Directly related to our conceptualization of audience, our recent stress on the problematic but productive idea of writing as inherently social—what Marilyn Cooper calls "The Ecology of Writing"—also reflects a rhetorical axiology. As Cooper explains, the concepts of audience as addressed and of audience as invoked both presume that audience is the writer's cognitive construct (9). The "ecological" or social or collaborative model focuses on writing in situations in which authors actually *do* know their audiences and will, in fact, receive feedback from them during their writing process.

Axiologically, good writing is still what works for these readers. As Rubin puts it in "Social Dimensions of Writing," skilled writing performance "is enabled . . . most especially by the ability to anticipate readers' responses" (3). What *shifts* when writing is seen primarily as a social act is the *pedagogy* as well as the view of process, which now requires peer responses.

Similarly, other writers forward the idea of a "discourse community." Pat Bizzell has asserted that "discourse analysis goes beyond audience analysis because what is most significant about members of a discourse community is not their personal preferences, prejudices, and so on, but rather the expectations they share by virtue of belonging to that particular community" ("Cognition" 218). Bennett Rafoth proposes that the idea of a "discourse community" is conceptually superior to that of audience, which evokes a "static Aristotelian notion of writers acting to influence identifiable yet passive readers" (140). And most recently, building on Kroll's three perspectives on audience, R. J. Willey attacks the "rhetorical perspective," which he describes as "still the dominant perspective" (21), because it leads to seeing readers as passive and to stereotyping. He pushes students "beyond the rhetorical perspective into a more valuable social perspective" (23).

But such contrasts are based on a straw-man view of what audience analysis outside the classroom involves. If I write for the audience of *CCC*, I cannot know my readers' personal preferences and prejudices; and demographics of age, religion, sex, or political affiliation are both unavailable and useless. What I may be able to know are many of their community values and their shared background knowledge, as well as the conventions of discourse they accept, and a good deal about how they interpret texts. *Good* audience analysis thus involves directly the presumption of writing as a social act in a discourse community.[9]

Writing across the Curriculum

One model of writing across the curriculum involves a writer's learning to operate within the accepted practices of a discourse community: a biology major is supposed to learn to write like a biologist. That reflects a rhetorical perspective; a true expressivist would object to the enforcing of communal norms that might be uncongenial to the writer's sense of self.[10] And formalists might oppose features of the disciplinary discourse—such as the use of nominalizations and passive-voice constructions, or the use of the "you" attitude in a business letter.[11]

Those five sorts of evidence—despite their considerable disparity—suggest that most voices in the composition community share in 1990 an axiological core that was *not* shared a decade ago. Good writing, the sort of writing that we hope to enable students to produce, is contextually adapted to, perhaps even controlled by, its audience (or discourse community), addressed or invoked, or both.

AXIOLOGICAL CONSENSUS AND CONTINUING THEORETICAL DIVERSITY

If I am correct that Composition Studies is axiologically more unified than a decade ago, how then do I account for the apparent paradox of the obvious and widespread fragmentation one can see at any of our conferences?

The explanation lies in the fact that the four elements required for a complete composition paradigm are largely independent of each other, although we sometimes confuse the matter by using similar terms to describe different elements (e.g., a reference to the "expressive" view may mean an "expressive" epistemology, an "expressive" pedagogy, or an "expressive" axiology, or any combination thereof). Axiological commitments set up goals for pedagogy, but do *not* prescribe how best to reach them, and one's decision about how to reach the goal will be guided but not determined by views of writing as a process, just as both procedural and pedagogical theories will be based on whatever research or experience one's epistemology allows to constitute knowledge. There are many ways to skin a cat, even a Cheshire one—but the goal of cat-skinning does rule out some methods and privilege others.

This realization is crucial: while we can taxonomize alternate theories of process and alternate pedagogies, along with four axiologies, and several epistemologies, and while some of the same terms are used in each taxonomy, *no automatic one-to-one connection* exists between entries in each list.

Diverse Theories of the Writing Process

I am not prepared to offer a full analysis of variant views of writing process(es). But several alternatives are clear. The current-traditional viewpoint seemed to be a think/write oversimplification: first you thought of what you wanted to say and then you "put it into words." The writing-as-process movement was largely a reaction against such a view. But the reactions diverged into cognitive-process views, linear-stage views, expressive views, social views, etc.

Lester Faigley and Steven Lynn, in fact, have both proposed classifications of theories of the writing process. Faigley identifies three: expressive, cognitive, and social ("Competing Theories of Process"). A teacher holding a rhetorical axiology could certainly subscribe to either the cognitive or social views of process without fear of self-contradiction, and I'm not sure but what she could also accept the expressive view of process as being the one most likely to lead to writing of interest to readers, as Elbow does in "Closing My Eyes."

And in "Reading the Writing Process: Toward a Theory of Current Pedagogies," Lynn does a close reading of three scholarly works on process: Maxine Hairston's "The Winds of Change"; Knoblauch and Brannon's *Rhetorical Traditions and the Teaching of Writing;* and Ann Berthoff's *Forming Thinking Writing: The Composing Imagination.* Lynn sees Hairston and Knoblauch/Brannon as representing opposite ends of a process continuum. To oversimplify somewhat, Hairston is on the cognitive end and Knoblauch and Brannon represent the expressive end; Berthoff falls somewhere in the middle. Lynn calls for what he admits may be an impossible synthesis of the perspectives on process (909): impossible in my view because Knoblauch and Brannon differ from Hairston not only on process but also on axiology, not just on means but upon the ends desired as well.

The recent host of articles and books on the social nature of invention stresses that *all* writers use materials from their own social interactions. These views thus supply a more extensive analysis of one feature of Faigley's "social" view of writing processes. Karen Burke LeFevre in *Invention as a Social Act* identifies a four-part continuum of views on invention, ranging from the Platonic/Romantic, through "internal dialogic" and collaborative, to the collective view she supports. James Reither and Douglas Vipond similarly, in "Writing as Collaboration," argue that all writing should be seen as collaborative in one or more of three ways, again stressing the social nature of the process. And Bennett Rafoth and Donald Rubin have edited *The Social Construction of Written Communication,* which collects fourteen essays on different social features of writing, including social processing, rhetorical axiology, and pedagogical implications. (See also Cooper and Holzman's *Writing as Social Action.*)

These studies foreground social views of composing processes partly as correctives to the extreme stress on individualism in expressive theories. But they often make too easy an inferential leap from the premise that writing is a socially mediated process to the conclusion that it requires a collaborative pedagogy. If writing is by nature socially mediated (through shared cultural assumptions, the use of cultural allusions, intertextual citations, concern for audience understanding and acceptance, etc.), then whether taught by collaborative pedagogy or not, it remains social. Whether a collaborative pedagogy is the best means of enabling a necessarily social process in order to achieve a rhetorically effective product is a separate question.

Diversity in Pedagogical Theories

In general, one's axiological commitment and process theory will affect but need not determine large-scale classroom decisions. Certainly rhetorical axiology *can* be enacted in a collaborative pedagogy, but it can also be enacted through a models pedagogy, studying textual features of discourse accepted by a community, or through a presentational pedagogy carefully done.

By comparison to the scholarship on divergent axiologies and alternative theories of process, our classification schemes for classroom approaches are anything but systematic. Still, several books have at least catalogued some pedagogical variations. Donovan and McClelland assembled a collection of essays purporting to outline *Eight Approaches to Teaching Composition* in 1980. Later, to serve his own research purposes, Hillocks derived a four-part scheme, based only on teaching methods that had been the subject of empirical research. And White, after examining materials relating to California college courses, identified six "Approaches to Writing Instruction." The various schemes are shown in the following table:

Three Schemes of Composition Pedagogy

White (42–43)	Hillocks (194)	Donovan/McClelland (passim)
1. Peer Workshop	Natural Process	Writing as Process Experiential Approach
2. Text-Based Rhetoric	Presentational	Rhetorical Approach Prose Models Approach
3. Individualized Lab	Tutorial	Writing Conference
4. Basic Skills Approach		Basic Writing
5. Service Course		
6. Literary		
7.	Environmental	
8.		Epistemic
9.		WAC

I have attempted to line up what seem the closest similar approaches from the three sources, but the fit is poor, especially for Hillock's "environmental" approach, which is probably a specialized peer-workshop approach. And White has no slot for a "process approach" separate from peer review. Moreover, Hillock's presentational approach is broad enough that it probably matches several of White's categories, such as "service course" and "literary."

A rhetoricist who accepts a cognitive view of writing processes may still—without contradiction—employ a presentational classroom approach or a natural-process approach or a workshop approach. And a teacher committed to an expressive axiology and a social view of process could use the obvious workshop pedagogy but could also choose to examine model texts, including some written by other students. In fact, a workshop or collaborative pedagogy can harmonize with any of the major axiologies, depending on what students in the workshop are directed to emphasize. James Williams advocates a workshop approach with his "pragmatic" (rhetorical) axiology in *Preparing to Teach Writing*. Dowst advocates a workshop approach with his expressive/epistemic axiology. And I have heard of formalist classes in which workshops were genuinely used as "editing groups" to catch mechanical errors before the papers were submitted to the teacher.

In short, the connection between ends and means in the composition classroom is not simple and holistic. A full composition theory is less a package deal than an oriental restaurant menu: with some constraints, you can frequently choose one from column A, one from column B, one from column C. Shared axiology requires neither shared pedagogy nor shared epistemology.

CLASSIFYING DIVERGENT THEORIES

Failure to recognize the essential independence of pedagogy, epistemology, process theory, and axiology is one cause of problems and inconsistencies that crop up whenever scholars attempt to categorize approaches to teaching composition. For example, such a failure has led to difficulties in James Berlin's several attempts to taxonomize the major theories and theorists in composition, while defining his own "epistemic" perspective. Most of this epistemic perspective, in which a writer/rhetor cooperates with readers in the social generation of meaning, represents a version of the rhetorical axiology, as discussed above in connection with the concept of writing as a social act within a discourse community.

Berlin has, however, distinguished among three versions of epistemic rhetoric: psychological, transactional, and social. From the perspective of this paper, all three views actually and unfortunately merge axiology with epistemology and pedagogy. I agree with Berlin that psychological epistemicism, articulated mainly by Kenneth Dowst and following the work of William Coles, represents an excessive axiology joined with a subjective epistemology locating truth in the personal experience/perception of the language user ("Rhetoric and Ideology" 488) and thus valuing personally made meanings. For Coles and Dowst it also involves a unique pedagogy built around sequenced writing tasks on the same topic.

Transactional epistemicism, which Berlin identified in *Rhetoric and Reality* (1987), is a catch-all for a broad range of theorists marked only by agreement that at least some knowledge is socially created through discourse. Originally Berlin called this epistemic view "the new rhetoric," which he committed himself to as the best philosophy of composition ("Contemporary Composition: The Major Pedagogical Theories"). He identified Ann Berthoff, James Moffett, Linda Flower, Andrea Lunsford, and Barry Kroll as its leading exponents ("Contemporary Composition" 773). Later in *Rhetoric and Reality* this privileged status was granted to Janice Lauer, Ann Berthoff, Richard Ohmann, Ross Winterowd, and Ken Bruffee, certainly too diverse a group to be considered a school (see Crowley's review). The problem is that while these theorists may indeed share an epistemology,[12] they differ enormously in axiology, in process theory, and in pedagogy. It isn't helpful to say they represent the same theory of composition as a whole.

Most recently, in "Rhetoric and Ideology" (1988), Berlin has changed positions dramatically. In that article he defines both "cognitivist" and "expressive" positions, but rejects each in favor of "the social-epistemic" position. The latter includes "an explicit critique of economic, political, and social arrangements" ("Rhetoric and Ideology" 490). Modeled on Ira Shor's liberatory pedagogy (488), it makes "the question of ideology the center of classroom activities" (478). What Berlin and Shor describe strikes me as not so much a writing course but a course using writing to promote a single social agenda. Berlin says its *goal* is "to externalize false consciousness" (491), and that's a revealing remark: one would expect the goal of a writing course to at least refer to writing.

How much Berlin's view has shifted in this most recent article is highlighted by the fact that both Linda Flower and James Moffett, whom Berlin in 1982 placed in the honored epistemic/new-rhetoric camp, were moved in 1988 to the disreputable cognitive ghetto and labeled "heirs of the current-traditionalists" (480).

Berlin's criticism, however, conflates the different elements of a composition theory. Conceivably Flower shares some epistemological assumptions with the current-traditionalists (a belief that at least some features of reality can be studied empirically). But Flower accepts a rhetorical axiology and a complex cognitive rather than a think/write view of process. She devotes her research to answering descriptive questions about how writers produce prose for a specified audience. Her very comparison of an "able" writer's process to a novice's assumes a rhetorical standard of success within some discourse community. And Flower's famous distinction between "Writer-Based Prose" and its opposite is nearly a canonical text for those who share a rhetorical axiology. Thus Flower differs from current-traditionalists in axiology, in her view of process, and in her problem-solving pedagogy. And she differs from Moffett, who also differs from current-traditionalists, in epistemology and pedagogy both.

In his several taxonomies, Berlin presumes that axiology, process theory, pedagogy, and epistemology exist holistically, that if you commit to one, you commit to a package. But by seeing these elements as an ideological unit, Berlin and other composition taxonomists oversimplify, I believe, both the positions held and the complexities of "theories of composition."

THEORETICAL INCOMPATIBILITY

While axiology, pedagogy, process theory, and epistemology are not a tight-wrapped package, different elements in a theory of composition *can* still be logically incompatible. For the ends rule out some means, and some views of process conflict with some pedagogies. A natural-process pedagogy, for instance, does *not* harmonize with a formalist axiology. Such judgments are difficult to make *a priori*, however. The contradictions can be observed with certainty only in the full context of a writing classroom.

The most obvious inconsistency is subscribing overtly to one axiology and then evaluating writing from another. I, for example, claim to subscribe to a rhetorical axiology. Yet when a group of student readers (the audience identified by the writer) affirm that they find a paper very effective, I sometimes want to tear out my hair and scream, "Well you shouldn't have!" Often I have really judged the paper inadequate from a mimetic point of view since it was built on a factually false assumption about such matters as the number of student parking spaces at our university or state rules about nonresident tuition.

Also, it is possible to have conflicts across the elements of a theory: a theory isn't, finally, as indeterminate as the restaurant menu. Lil Brannon notes, for instance, that a handbook including both traditional grammar exercises and free writing "offers students two incompatible approaches to assist their development," based on contradictory assumptions about grammatical competence and how students learn ("Teacher" 26).

A real example of what seems to me a conflict between professed axiology and pedagogical practice is recounted in Robert Brooke and John Hendricks's *Audience Expectations and Teacher Demands*. Brooke wanted to teach a course using a rhetorical axiology and also dealing with the "pedagogical problem: how can we teach writing 'for an audience' in an institutional setting where students know that the teacher, not the addressed audience, assigns the grade?" (xv). Several features of the course trouble me, but one is especially salient. For the third of five writing assignments, students "were to write about the same subject in three different forms, making sure each was appropriate for an audience" (19). The forms suggested, however, were "an outline, an issue tree (Flower 1986), and a collage (Elbow 1981)" (19). But one doesn't write outlines or issue trees for audiences. Outlines and issue trees are processing devices to help writers generate and organize material, not finished texts for readers. Brooke "grew troubled by the degree of antagonism some students exhibited by the end of the course" (ix), but contradictions like this one (coupled with some equally inappropriate evaluation practices) seem virtually to guarantee student confusion and animosity.

As a final example, Huff and Kline seem to me to have included contradictory features within the workshop pedagogy advocated in *The Contemporary Writing Curriculum*. Essentially, the course stresses a rhetorical axiology, both in having writers analyze their audiences explicitly ("Texts exist for audiences and an audience is not an abstraction" [73]) and in having peer-workshop groups use criterion sheets that emphasize readers' reactions to the text. Yet the students must also pass usage tests over sentence fragments, subject-verb agreement, comma splices, punctuation, and pronoun referents, whether or not they have difficulties with these "basics" (161), and even though the peer-response groups are responsible for eliminating such editorial problems from student texts. The usage tests fit a formalist axiology and a drill pedagogy, not the axiology and pedagogy presented here.

Moreover, while Huff and Kline describe writing as an extensive and recursive cognitive process, four of the students' papers are written in class in three meetings each. One meeting is allowed for each stage of the writing process: zero drafting, problem-solving drafting, final drafting. The in-class papers are built from source sheets providing "25 divergent facts" about topics like inflation (92) or high-school illiteracy (111). Such three-day writing from fact sheets assumes a linear-stage view of process that neglects invention and is contradicted in other parts of the book. It also leads to texts that are essentially arhetorical, despite the supposed rhetorical axiology.

ON THE OTHER HAND

Let me acknowledge that a good deal of potential counter-evidence exists against my assertion of greater axiological unity today than a decade ago. The diverse essays collected from forty-eight leading composition teachers in William Coles and James Vopat's astounding anthology *What Makes Writing Good*, for example, might cast doubt on any claim that we agree about the nature of good writing, the central issue with which this article is concerned. Faigley has recently argued, however, that the collection consists primarily of the sort of personal writing most valued by axiological expressivists ("Judging" 404). Indeed, the teacher commentaries accompanying the essays in the collection often speak in the voice of the expressivist, as Faigley points out, praising the pieces for being "honest," having "authentic voice," or showing "integrity" (Faigley, "Judging" 404).[13]

He makes a good point. Probably the bias of English teachers, if left to select the sort of texts they prefer to read, leans toward the personal artistic essay. In fact, that same bias shows up in the anthology pieces they tend to select (e.g., Joan Didion, E. B. White, Annie Dillard, Russell Baker, Loren Eisely), so even the selections in our readers could be cited as evidence opposing my claim of a rhetorical consensus.

The continued sales of true handbooks also argue against my thesis, although even the handbooks now tend to contain chapters on process, invention, and audience.

The various stories one hears from students or teachers in the public schools also sometimes dispute my claim. In her despairing article, "Empty Echoes of Dartmouth: Dissonance between the Rhetoric and the Reality," Sharon Hamilton-Wieler says, the "paradigm shift described in the rhetoric of [our] journals . . . is simply not a day-to-day reality in the majority of classrooms" (31). In addition, such eminent scholars as Richard Larson (112) and Edward White (42–44) have both stressed the *variance* in current views of composition, as has Steve North.

Still, all such evidence of variation can easily be matched with even more extreme materials from a decade ago. I am not claiming that in the nineties we all accept a common paradigm. I *am* maintaining that we are much closer to accepting *one* portion of it than we were a decade earlier. Thus the major locus of our disagreements has shifted from axiology to process and pedagogy, where we have found plenty to fight about.

Even if you know where you want to go, a shrewd Cheshire Cat can point out more than one path to get you there, as well as some attractive ones that won't.

Notes

1. When made unreflectively, such judgments are enthymematic, with a major premise left tacit, below the surface, yet recoverable through examination.
2. In "Toward a Theory of Composition," Lil Brannon accepts the need for the procedural and pedagogical parts of this model, but surprisingly omits the axiological feature (6).
3. The process and pedagogical components of this metatheory are *theories* in the classical sense, as defined by Alan Brinton, drawing on the work of Carl Hempel: any classical theory involves (1) the identification or postulation of kinds of entities, (2) terms or predicates

denoting properties and relations of and between the entities, and (3) general statements about those properties or relations which are empirically testable and explanatorily powerful (Brinton 240). But the axiological and epistemological components are different. To "test" an epistemology would already presuppose an epistemology. And no way exists to "test" axiological commitments, although there certainly are ways to argue over them.

4. The most extreme statement of the expressivist view that I have encountered came from an article by McCracken and Ashby entitled "The Widow's Walk: An Alternative for English 101—Creative Communications":

> It is loving that is the problem. . . . Our students are not in love with anything. . . . [O]ur task must be to reach deeper and restore the lost connections between the sources of all love and the objects of love for it is these that have been severed—and the gap grows wider each year. . . . [W]e insist that there is not and should not be any way to evaluate writing! How would you evaluate a life? (61).

The viewpoint was symbolized for me in a textbook from 1972 entitled *It's Mine and I'll Write It That Way,* by Dick Friedrich and David Kuester. With its yellow pages and rounded corners, and its chapters alternating between rhetorical advice and a teacher's journal, it is an extreme version of what expressivism as an axiology of composition was all about.

5. Seeing Elbow as an expressionist rests on a restrictive reading of his work, as well as the fact that his views are complex, that, as reflected in the title of one of his books, he has a way of "embracing contraries." In 1968, Elbow identified his approach to teaching writing as traditional pretending to be iconoclastic ("Method" 123), and he committed himself explicitly to a rhetorical axiology by saying "the student's best language skills are brought out and developed when writing is considered as words on paper designed to produce a specific effect in a specific reader" (123). (He noted that his "essay would never sell under the title 'Getting Aristotle Back into Freshman English' " [123]). And even when writing "an argument for ignoring audience," Elbow manages paradoxically to base the argument on a rhetorical axiology: "What most readers value in really excellent writing is not prose that is right for readers but prose that is right for thinking, right for language, or right for the subject being written about" ("Closing" 54). So one often adapts best to audience by ignoring it, certainly a way to embrace apparent contraries. Elbow's newest book, *A Community of Writers* (co-authored with Pat Belanoff), seems largely rhetorical in its implicit axiology to me, but I'll grant that a reading of it as expressive is also possible.

6. See John Gage's *The Shape of Reason* or John Ramage and John Bean's *Writing Arguments* for textbooks built entirely around the notion of having students phrase enthymematic thesis statements for all their papers, with unstated warrants representing values shared by the intended audience.

7. See also Beth Neman, *Teaching Students to Write,* which says expository writing "expounds, explains, and sets forth information and ideas. . . . Its purpose, however, like that of all writing, is essentially persuasive" (21). Further statements of rhetorical axiology are easily located in current textbooks. See Booth and Gregory's *The Harper and Row Rhetoric* (34), Neeld's *Writing* (308–09), and Richard Coe's *Process, Form, and Substance* (145–65).

Sometimes this emerging rhetorical consensus is easily overlooked since it is expressed in different language. Martin Nystrand calls the perspective "reciprocity," saying, "A given text is functional to the extent that it balances the reciprocal needs of the writer for expression and of the reader for comprehension. Communicative homeostasis is the normal condition of grammatical texts" (71).

8. Lisa Ede made this point well in 1979 when she echoed an earlier remark from Ohmann that the reader "was a relatively minor element in the writing situation" as portrayed in popular composition texts. She noted that as of 1979 there were "a few notable exceptions." They represent the early presentations of the position I am arguing has now become the consensus ("On Audience" 292).

9. It's ironic that Willey, in rejecting the "rhetorical" view of audience and forwarding the "social" view, says that he has his students respond in writing to a four-question heuristic concerning the audience's prior knowledge.

   The superficial interpretation of classical conceptions of audience used by both Willey and Rafoth was well debunked by Lunsford and Ede in "On Distinctions between Classical and Modern Rhetoric": they note that "[f]ar from being 'one-way,' 'manipulative,' or 'monological,' Aristotle's rhetoric provides a complete description of the dynamic interaction between rhetor and audience, an interaction mediated by language. . . . We suggest that a much more accurate way to describe Aristotle's concept of the goal of rhetoric is as an interactive means of discovering meaning through language" (44).

10. See for example Donald Stewart's critique, "Collaborative Learning and Composition."

11. The other major approach to WAC, however, "writing-to-learn," does not reflect a rhetorical axiology, but probably an expressive one in which a student writes in order to make personal sense of materials studied. Patricia Bizzell discusses the two approaches in "Composing Processes: An Overview" (62–63).

12. Actually it is hard to see even epistemological agreement between Flower (a cognitive empiricist) or Lunsford (with her classical-rhetorical orientation), and Bruffee or Berthoff.

13. As it happens, many of the selections in Coles and Vopat's 1985 anthology were actually written a decade or more earlier and preserved in teachers' files.

Works Cited

Abrams, M. H. *The Mirror and the Lamp: Romantic Theory and the Critical Tradition.* New York: Norton, 1953.

Axelrod, Rise B., and Charles R. Cooper. *The St. Martin's Guide to Writing.* Short ed. New York: St. Martin's, 1986.

Baker, Sheridan. *The Practical Stylist.* 7th ed. New York: Harper, 1990.

Beale, Walter. *A Pragmatic Theory of Rhetoric.* Carbondale: Southern Illinois UP, 1987.

Berlin, James. "Contemporary Composition: The Major Pedagogical Theories." *College English* 44 (Dec. 1982): 765–77.

———. "Rhetoric and Ideology in the Writing Class." *College English* 50 (Sept. 1988): 477–94.

———. *Rhetoric and Reality: Writing Instruction in American Colleges, 1900–1985.* Carbondale: Southern Illinois UP, 1987.

Berthoff, Ann E. *Forming Thinking Writing: The Composing Imagination.* Rochelle Park: Hayden, 1978.

Bizzell, Patricia. "Cognition, Convention, and Certainty: What We Need to Know about Writing." *PreText* 3 (Fall, 1982): 213–43.

———. "Composing Processes: An Overview." *The Teaching of Writing: Eighty-Fifth Yearbook of the National Society for the Study of Education.* Ed. Anthony Petrosky and David Bartholomae. Part 2. Chicago: National Society for the Study of Education, 1986. 49–70.

Bogel, Fredric V., and Katherine K. Gottschalk. *Teaching Prose: A Guide for Writing Instructors.* New York: Norton, 1988.

Booth, Wayne, and Marshall W. Gregory. *The Harper and Row Rhetoric.* New York: Harper, 1987.

Brannon, Lil. "The Teacher as Philosopher: The Madness Behind Our Method." *Journal of Advanced Composition* 4 (1983): 25–32.

———. "Toward a Theory of Composition." *Perspectives on Research and Scholarship in Composition.* Ed. Ben McClelland and Timothy Donovan. New York: MLA, 1985. 6–25.

Brinton, Alan. "Situation in the Theory of Rhetoric." *Philosophy and Rhetoric* 14 (Fall 1981): 234–48.

Brooke, Robert, and John Hendricks. *Audience Expectations and Teacher Demands.* Carbondale: Southern Illinois UP, 1989.

Bruffee, Kenneth. "Collaborative Learning and the 'Conversation of Mankind.' " *College English* 46 (Nov. 1984): 635–52.

Christensen, Francis, and Bonniejean Christensen. *Notes Toward a New Rhetoric*. 2nd ed. New York: Harper, 1978.

Coe, Richard M. *Process, Form, and Substance*. 2nd ed. Englewood Cliffs: Prentice, 1990.

Coles, William. *The Plural I: The Teaching of Writing*. New York: Holt, 1978.

Coney, Mary B. "Contemporary Views of Audience: A Rhetorical Perspective." *Technical Writing Teacher* 19 (Fall 1987): 319–26.

Connors, Robert J., and Cheryl Glenn. *The St. Martin's Guide to Teaching Writing*. New York: St. Martin's, 1989.

Cooper, Marilyn. "The Ecology of Writing." *Writing as Social Action*. Ed. Marilyn Cooper and Michael Holzman. Portsmouth: Boynton, 1989. 1–13.

Cooper, Marilyn, and Michael Holzman. *Writing as Social Action*. Portsmouth: Boynton, 1989.

Crowley, Sharon. Rev. of *Rhetoric and Reality: Writing Instruction in American Colleges, 1900–1985*, by James Berlin. *College Composition and Communication* 39 (May 1988): 245–47.

Donovan, Timothy, and Ben McClelland, eds. *Eight Approaches to Teaching Composition*. Urbana: NCTE, 1980.

Dowst, Kenneth. "The Epistemic Approach: Writing, Knowing, and Learning." *Eight Approaches to Teaching Composition*. Ed. Timothy Donovan and Ben McClelland. Urbana: NCTE, 1980. 65–86.

Ede, Lisa. "On Audience and Composition." *College Composition and Communication* 30 (Oct. 1979): 291–95.

Ede, Lisa, and Andrea Lunsford. "Audience Addressed/Audience Invoked: The Role of Audience in Composition Theory and Pedagogy." *College Composition and Communication* 35 (May 1984): 155–71.

Elbow, Peter. "Closing My Eyes as I Speak: An Argument for Ignoring Audience." *College English* 49 (1987): 50–69.

———. "A Method for Teaching Writing." *College English* 30 (November 1968): 115–25.

———. *Writing Without Teachers*. New York: Oxford UP, 1973.

———. *Writing with Power: Techniques for Mastering the Writing Process*. New York: Random, 1989.

Faigley, Lester. "Competing Theories of Process: A Critique and a Proposal." *College English* 48 (Oct. 1986): 527–42.

———. "Judging Writing, Judging Selves." *College Composition and Communication* 40 (Dec. 1989): 395–412.

Flower, Linda. *Problem-Solving Strategies for Writing*. 2nd ed. New York: Harcourt, 1985.

———. "Writer-Based Prose: A Cognitive Basis for Problems in Writing." *College English* 41 (Sept. 1979): 19–37. *A Writing Teacher's Sourcebook*. Ed. Gary Tate and E. P. J. Corbett. New York: Oxford UP, 1981. 268–92.

Friedrich, Dick, and David Kuester. *It's Mine and I'll Write It That Way*. New York: Random, 1972.

Fulkerson, Richard. "Four Philosophies of Composition." *College Composition and Communication* 30 (Dec. 1979): 343–48.

Gage, John. "An Adequate Epistemology for Composition: Classical and Modern Perspectives." *Essays on Classical and Modern Discourse*. Ed. Robert Connors, Lisa Ede, and Andrea Lunsford. Carbondale: Southern Illinois UP, 1984. 152–69.

———. "Philosophies of Style and Their Implications for Composition." *College English* 41 (Feb. 1980): 615–22.

———. *The Shape of Reason*. New York: Macmillan, 1987.

Graser, Elsa R. *Teaching Writing—A Process Approach: A Survey of Research*. Dubuque: Kendall, 1983.

Hairston, Maxine. *Successful Writing.* 2nd ed. New York: Norton, 1986.

———. "The Winds of Change: Thomas Kuhn and the Revolution in the Teaching of Writing." *College Composition and Communication* 33 (1982): 76–88.

Hamilton-Wieler, Sharon. "Empty Echoes of Dartmouth: Dissonance between the Rhetoric and the Reality." *The Writing Instructor* 8 (Fall 1988): 29–41.

Hemple, Carl. *Philosophy of Natural Science.* Englewood Cliffs: Prentice, 1966.

Hillocks, George, Jr. *Research on Written Composition.* Urbana: NCTE, 1986.

Hirsch, E. D. *The Philosophy of Composition.* Chicago: U of Chicago P, 1977.

———. "Reading, Writing, and Cultural Literacy." *Composition and Literature: Bridging the Gap.* Ed. Winifred Bryan Horner. Chicago: U of Chicago P, 1987.

Huff, Roland, and Charles R. Kline, Jr. *The Contemporary Writing Curriculum: Rehearsing, Composing, and Valuing.* New York: Teachers College P, 1987.

Irmscher, William. *Teaching Expository Writing.* New York: Holt, 1979.

Kameen, Paul. "Coming of Age in College Composition." *The Teaching of Writing: Eighty-Fifth Yearbook of the National Society for the Study of Education.* Ed. Anthony Petrosky and David Bartholomae. Part 2. Chicago: National Society for the Study of Education, 1986. 170–87.

Kelly, Lou. *From Dialogue to Discourse: An Open Approach to Competence and Creativity.* Glenview: Scott, 1972.

———. "Toward Competence and Creativity in an Open Class." *College English* 34 (Feb. 1973): 644–60. Rpt. in *Ideas for English 101: Teaching Writing in College.* Ed. Richard Ohmann and W. B. Coley. Urbana: NCTE, 1975. 2–18.

Kinneavy, James. *A Theory of Discourse.* New York: Norton, 1980.

Knoblauch, C. H., and Lil Brannon. *Rhetorical Traditions and the Teaching of Writing.* Upper Montclair: Boynton, 1984.

Kroll, Barry. "Writing for Readers: Three Perspectives on Audience." *College Composition and Communication* 35 (May 1984): 172–85.

Larson, Richard. "Why It Is Unimportant How I Write." *Writers on Writing.* Ed. Tom Waldrep. Vol 2. New York: Random, 1988. 111–20.

LeFevre, Karen Burke. *Invention as a Social Act.* Carbondale: Southern Illinois UP, 1987.

Lindemann, Erika. *A Rhetoric for Writing Teachers.* 2nd ed. New York: Oxford UP, 1987.

Lunsford, Andrea, and Lisa Ede. "On Distinctions between Classical and Modern Rhetoric." *Essays on Classical Rhetoric and Modern Discourse.* Ed. Robert Connors, Lisa Ede, and Andrea Lunsford. Carbondale: Southern Illinois UP, 1984. 37–49.

Lynn, Steven. "Reading the Writing Process: Toward a Theory of Current Pedagogies." *College English* 49 (Dec. 1987): 902–10.

Macrorie, Ken. *Uptaught.* Rochelle Park: Hayden, 1970.

Marius, Richard. "How I Write." *Writers on Writing.* Ed. Tom Waldrep. Vol 2. New York: Random, 1988. 147–55.

Martin, Lee J. *The Five-Hundred-Word Theme.* 2nd ed. Englewood Cliffs: Prentice, 1974.

McCracken, Timothy, and W. Allen Ashby. "The Widow's Walk: An Alternative for English 101—Creative Communications." *College English* 36 (Jan. 1975): 555–70. Rpt. in *Ideas for English 101: Teaching Writing in College.* Ed. Richard Ohmann and W. B. Coley. Urbana: NCTE, 1975. 58–73.

McPherson, Elizabeth. "Composition." *The Teaching of English: The Seventy-Sixth Yearbook of the National Society for the Study of Education.* Ed. James R. Squire. Chicago: National Society for the Study of Education, 1977. 178–88.

Mendelson, Michael. "Teaching Writing Inductively." *Journal of Business Communication* 25 (Spring 1988): 67–83.

Moffett, James. *Teaching the Universe of Discourse*. Boston: Houghton, 1968.

Murray, Donald. *A Writer Teaches Writing: A Practical Method of Teaching Composition*. Boston: Houghton, 1968.

Neeld, Elizabeth Cowan. *Writing*. 3rd ed. Glenview: Scott, 1990.

Neman, Beth. *Teaching Students to Write*. Columbus: Charles Merrill, 1980.

North, Stephen. *The Making of Knowledge in Composition: Portrait of an Emerging Field*. Upper Montclair: Boynton, 1987.

Nystrand, Martin. *The Structure of Written Communication: Studies in Reciprocity between Writers and Readers*. Orlando: Academic, 1986.

Ohmann, Richard. *English in America*. New York: Oxford UP, 1976.

Rafoth, Bennett. "Discourse Community: Where Writers, Readers, and Texts Come Together." *The Social Structure of Written Communication*. Norwood: Ablex, 1988.

Ramage, John, and John Bean. *Writing Arguments*. New York: Macmillan, 1989.

Reese, William L. *Dictionary of Philosophy and Religion*. Atlantic Highlands: Humanities, 1980.

Reither, James A., and Douglas Vipond. "Writing as Collaboration." *College English* 51 (Dec. 1989): 855–67.

Rottenberg, Annette. *Elements of Argument: A Text and Reader*. 2nd ed. New York: St. Martin's, 1988.

Rubin, Donald C. "Introduction: Four Dimensions of Social Construction in Written Communication." *The Social Construction of Written Communication*. Ed. Bennett Rafoth and Donald Rubin. Norwood: Ablex, 1988. 1–33.

Shor, Ira. *Critical Teaching and Everyday Life*. 1980. Chicago: U of Chicago P, 1987.

Stewart, Donald C. *The Authentic Voice: A Pre-Writing Approach to Student Writing*. Dubuque: William C. Brown, 1972.

———. "Collaborative Learning and Composition: Boon or Bane?" *Rhetoric Review* 7 (Fall 1988): 58–85.

Thomas, Gordon P. "Mutual Knowledge: A Theoretical Basis for Analyzing Audience." *College English* 48 (Oct. 1986): 580–94.

Toulmin, Stephen. *The Use of Argument*. Cambridge: Cambridge UP, 1958.

Trimmer, Joseph, and James McCrimmon. *Writing with a Purpose*. Short ed. Boston: Houghton, 1988.

White, Edward. *Developing Successful College Writing Programs*. San Francisco: Jossey, 1989.

Willey, R. J. "Audience Awareness: Methods and Madness." *Freshman English News* 18 (Spring 1990): 20–25.

Williams, James. *Preparing to Teach Writing*. Belmont: Wadsworth, 1989.

Woods, William. "Composition Textbooks and Pedagogical Theory 1960–80." *College English* 43 (April 1981): 393–409.

Yonga, Jan. *The Elements of Audience Analysis*. New York: Macmillan, 1989.

A Cognitive Process Theory of Writing

Linda Flower and John R. Hayes

Linda Flower is professor of rhetoric at Carnegie-Mellon University and John R. Hayes teaches psychology at the same university. "A Cognitive Theory Process of Writing" appeared originally in College Composition and Communication *(December, 1981). In this shortened version of their classic article, Flower and Hayes show how the writing process is both recursive and goal-directed.*

There is a venerable tradition in rhetoric and composition which sees the composing process as a series of decisions and choices.[1] However, it is no longer easy simply to assert this position, unless you are prepared to answer a number of questions, the most pressing of which probably is: "What then are the criteria which govern that choice?" Or we could put it another way: "What guides the decision writers make as they write?" In a recent survey of composition research, Odell, Cooper, and Courts noticed that some of the most thoughtful people in the field are giving us two reasonable but somewhat different answers:

> How do writers actually go about choosing diction, syntactic and organizational patterns, and content? Kinneavy claims that one's purpose—informing, persuading, expressing, or manipulating language for its own sake—guides these choices. Moffett and Gibson contend that these choices are determined by one's sense of the relation of speaker, subject, and audience. Is either of these two claims borne out by the actual practice of writers engaged in drafting or revising? Does either premise account adequately for the choices writers make?[2]

Rhetoricians such as Lloyd Bitzer and Richard Vatz have energetically debated this question in still other terms. Lloyd Bitzer argues that speech always occurs as a response to a rhetorical situation, which he succinctly defines as containing an exigency (which demands a response), an audience, and a set of constraints.[3] In response to this "situation-driven" view, Vatz claims that the speaker's response, and even the rhetorical situation itself, are determined by the imagination and art of the speaker.[4]

Finally, James Britton has asked the same question and offered a linguist's answer, namely, that syntactic and lexical choices guide the process.

> It is tempting to think of writing as a process of making linguistic choices from one's repertoire of syntactic structures and lexical items. This would suggest that there is a meaning, or something to be expressed, in the writer's mind, and that he proceeds to choose, from the words and structures he has at his disposal, the ones that best match his meaning. But is that really how it happens?[5]

To most of us it may seem reasonable to suppose that all of these forces—"purposes," "relationships," "exigencies," "language"—have a hand in guiding the writer's process, but it is not at all clear how they do so or how they interact. Do they, for example, work in elegant and graceful coordination, or as competitive forces constantly vying for control? We think that the best way to answer these questions—to really understand the nature of rhetorical choices in good and poor writers—is to follow James Britton's lead and turn our attention to the writing process itself: to ask, "but is that really how it happens?"

This paper will introduce a theory of the cognitive processes involved in composing in an effort to lay groundwork for more detailed study of thinking processes in writing. This theory is based on our work with protocol analysis over the past five years and has, we feel, a good deal of evidence to support it. Nevertheless, it is for us a working hypothesis and springboard for further research, and we hope that insofar as it suggests testable hypotheses it will be the same for others. Our cognitive process theory rests on four key points, which this paper will develop:

1. The process of writing is best understood as a set of distinctive thinking processes which writers orchestrate or organize during the act of composing.
2. These processes have a hierarchical, highly embedded organization in which any given process can be embedded within any other.
3. The act of composing itself is a goal-directed thinking process, guided by the writer's own growing network of goals.
4. Writers create their own goals in two key ways: by generating both high-level goals and supporting sub-goals which embody the writer's developing sense of purpose, and then, at times, by changing major goals or even establishing entirely new ones based on what has been learned in the act of writing.

1. Writing is best understood as a set of distinctive thinking processes which writers orchestrate or organize during the act of composing.

To many this point may seem self-evident, and yet it is in marked contrast to our current paradigm for composing —the stage process model. This familiar metaphor or model describes the composing process as a linear series of stages, separated in time, and characterized by the gradual development of the written product. The best examples of stage models are the Pre-Write/Write/Re-Write model of Gordon Rohman[6] and the Conception/Incubation/Production model of Britton *et al.*[7]

STAGE MODELS OF WRITING

Without doubt, the wide acceptance of Pre-Writing has helped improve the teaching of composition by calling attention to planning and discovery as legitimate parts of the writing process. Yet many question whether this linear stage model is really an accurate or useful description of the composing process itself. The problem with stage descriptions of writing is that they model the growth of the written product, not the inner process of the person producing it. "Pre-Writing" is the stage before words emerge on paper; "Writing" is the stage in which a product is being produced; and "Re-Writing" is a final reworking of that product. Yet both common sense and research tell us that writers are constantly planning (pre-writing) and revising (re-writing) as they compose (write), not in clean-cut stages.[8] Furthermore, the sharp distinctions stage models make between the operations of planning, writing, and revising may seriously distort how these activities work. For example, Nancy Sommers has shown that revision, as it is carried out by skilled writers, is not an end-of-the-line repair process, but is a constant process of "re-vision" or re-seeing that goes on while they are composing.[9] A more accurate model of the composing process would need to recognize those basic thinking processes which unite planning and revision. Because stage models take the final product as their reference point, they offer an inadequate account of the more intimate, moment-by-moment intellectual process of composing. How, for example, is the output of one stage, such as pre-writing or incubation, transferred to the next? As every writer knows, having good ideas doesn't automatically produce good prose. Such models are typically silent on the processes of decision and choice.

A COGNITIVE PROCESS MODEL

A cognitive process theory of writing, such as the one presented here, represents a major departure from the traditional paradigm of stages in this way: in a stage model the major units of analysis are *stages* of completion which reflect the growth of a written product, and these stages are organized in a *linear* sequence or structure. In a process model, the major units of analysis are elementary mental *processes,* such as the process of generating ideas. And these processes have a *hierarchical* structure . . . such that idea generation, for example, is a sub-process of Planning. Furthermore, each of these mental acts may occur at any time in the composing process. One major advantage of identifying these basic cognitive processes or thinking skills writers use is that we can then compare the composing strategies of good and poor writers. And we can look at writing in a much more detailed way.

In psychology and linguistics, one traditional way of looking carefully at a process is to build a model of what you see. A model is a metaphor for a process: a way to describe something, such as the composing process, which refuses to sit still for a portrait. As a hypothesis about a dynamic system, it attempts to describe the parts of the system and how they work together. Modeling a process starts as a problem in design. For example, imagine that you have been asked to start from scratch and design an imaginary, working "Writer." In order to build a "Writer" or a theoretical system that would reflect the process of a real writer, you would want to do at least three things:

1. First, you would need to define the major elements or sub-processes that make up the larger process of writing. Such sub-processes would include planning, retrieving information from long-term memory, reviewing, and so on.

2. Second, you would want to show how these various elements of the process interact in the total process of writing. For example, how is "knowledge" about the audience actually integrated into the moment-to-moment act of composing?
3. And finally, since a model is primarily a tool for thinking with, you would want your model to speak to critical questions in the discipline. It should help you see things you didn't see before. . . .

The act of writing involves three major elements which are reflected in the three units of the model: the task environment, the writer's long-term memory, and the writing processes. The task environment includes all of those things outside the writer's skin, starting with the rhetorical problem or assignment and eventually including the growing text itself. The second element is the writer's long-term memory in which the writer has stored knowledge, not only of the topic, but of the audience and of various writing plans. The third element in our model contains writing processes themselves, specifically the basic processes of Planning, Translating, and Reviewing, which are under the control of a Monitor . . .

OVERVIEW OF A MODEL

The Rhetorical Problem

At the beginning of composing, the most important element is obviously the rhetorical problem itself. A school assignment is a simplified version of such a problem, describing the writer's topic, audience, and (implicitly) her role as a student to a teacher. Insofar as writing is a rhetorical act, not a mere artifact, writers attempt to "solve" or respond to this rhetorical problem by writing something.

In theory, this problem is a very complex thing: it includes not only the rhetorical situation and audience which prompts one to write, it also includes the writer's own goals in writing.[10] A good writer is a person who can juggle all of these demands. But in practice, we have observed, as did Britton,[11] that writers frequently reduce this large set of constraints to a radically simplified problem, such as "write another theme for English class." Redefining the problem in this way is obviously an economical strategy as long as the new representation fits reality. But when it doesn't, there is a catch: people only solve the problems they define for themselves. If a writer's representation of her rhetorical problem is inaccurate or simply underdeveloped, then she is unlikely to "solve" or attend to the missing aspects of the problem. To sum up, defining the rhetorical problem is a major, immutable part of the writing process. But the way in which people choose to define a rhetorical problem to themselves can vary greatly from writer to writer. An important goal for research then will be to discover how this process of representing the problem works and how it affects the writer's performance.

The Written Text

As composing proceeds, a new element enters the task environment which places even more constraints upon what the writer can say. Just as a title constrains the content of a paper and a topic sentence shapes the options of a paragraph, each word in the growing text determines and limits the choices of what can come next. However, the influence that the growing text exerts on the composing process can vary greatly. When writing is incoherent, the text may have exerted too little influence; the writer may have failed to consolidate new ideas with earlier statements. On the other hand, one of the earmarks of a basic writer is a dogged concern with extending the previous sentence[12] and a reluctance to jump from local, text-bound planning to more global decisions, such as "what do I want to cover here?"

As we will see, the growing text makes large demands on the writer's time and attention during composing. But in doing so, it is competing with two other forces which could and also should direct the composing process; namely, the writer's knowledge stored in long-term memory and the writer's plans for dealing with the rhetorical problem. It is easy, for example, to imagine a conflict between what you know about a topic and what you might actually want to say to a given reader, or between a graceful phrase that completes a sentence and the more awkward point you actually wanted to make. Part of the drama of writing is seeing how writers juggle and integrate the multiple constraints of their knowledge, their plans, and their text into the production of each new sentence.[13]

The Long-Term Memory

The writer's long-term memory, which can exist in the mind as well as in outside resources such as books, is a storehouse of knowledge about the topic and audience, as well as knowledge of writing plans and problem representations. Sometimes a single cue in an assignment, such as "write a persuasive . . . ," can let a writer tap a stored representation of a problem and bring a whole raft of writing plans into play.

Unlike short-term memory, which is our active processing capacity or conscious attention, long-term memory is a relatively stable entity and has its own internal organization of information. The problem with long-term memory is, first of all, getting things out of it—that is, finding the cue that will let you retrieve a network of useful knowledge. The second problem for a writer is usually reorganizing or adapting that information to fit the demands of the rhetorical problem. The phenomena of "writer-based" prose nicely demonstrates the results of a writing strategy based solely on retrieval. The organization of a piece of writer-based prose faithfully reflects the writer's own discovery process and the structure of the remembered information itself, but it often fails to transform or reorganize that knowledge to meet the different needs of a reader.[14]

Planning

People often think of planning as the act of figuring out how to get from here to there, i.e., making a detailed plan. But our model uses the term in its much broader sense. In the planning process writers form an internal *representation* of the knowledge that will be used in writing. This internal representation is likely to be more abstract than the writer's prose representation will eventually be. For example, a whole network of ideas might be represented by a single key word. Furthermore, this representation of one's knowledge will not necessarily be made in language, but could be held as a visual perceptual code, e.g., as a fleeting image the writer must then capture in words.

Planning, or the act of building this internal representation, involves a number of sub-processes. The most obvious is the act of generating ideas, which includes retrieving relevant information from long-term memory. Sometimes this information is so well developed and organized *in memory* that the writer is essentially generating standard written English. At other times one may generate only fragmentary, unconnected, even contradictory thoughts, like the pieces of a poem that hasn't yet taken shape.

When the structure of ideas already in the writer's memory is not adequately adapted to the current rhetorical task, the sub-process of organizing takes on the job of helping the writer make meaning, that is, give a meaningful structure to his or her ideas. The process of organizing appears to play an important part in creative thinking and discovery since it is capable of grouping ideas and forming new concepts. More specifically, the organizing process allows the writer to identify categories, to search for subordinate ideas which develop a current topic, and to search for superordinate ideas which include or subsume the current topic. At another level the process of organizing also attends to more strictly textual decisions about the presentation and ordering of the text. That is, writers identify first or last topics, important ideas, and presentation patterns. However, organizing is much more than merely ordering points. And it seems clear that all rhetorical decisions and plans for reaching the audience affect the process of organizing ideas at all levels, because it is often guided by major goals established during the powerful process of goal-setting.

Goal-setting is indeed a third, little-studied but major, aspect of the planning process. The goals writers give themselves are both procedural (e.g., "Now let's see—a—I want to start out with "energy"") and substantive, often both at the same time (e.g., "I have to relate this [engineering project] to the economics [of energy] to show why I'm improving it and why the steam turbine needs to be more efficient" or "I want to suggest that—that—um—the reader should sort of—what—what should one say—the reader should look at what she is interested in and look at the things that give her pleasure . . .").

The most important thing about writing goals is the fact that they are *created* by the writer. Although some well-learned plans and goals may be drawn intact from long-term memory, most of the writer's goals are generated, developed, and revised by the same processes that generate and organize new ideas. And this process goes on throughout composing. Just as goals lead a writer to generate ideas, those ideas lead to new, more complex goals which can then integrate content and purpose.

Our own studies on goal setting to date suggest that the act of defining one's own rhetorical problem and setting goals is an important part of "being creative" and can account for some important differences between good and poor writers.[15] As we will argue in the final section of this paper, the act of developing and refining one's own goals is not limited to a "pre-writing stage" in the composing process, but is intimately bound up with the ongoing, moment-to-moment process of composing.

Translating

This is essentially the process of putting ideas into visible language. We have chosen the term translate for this process over other terms such as "transcribe" or "write" in order to emphasize the peculiar qualities of the task. The information generated in planning may be represented in a variety of symbol systems other than language, such as imagery or kinetic sensations. Trying to capture the movement of a deer on ice in language is clearly a kind of translation. Even when the planning process represents one's thought in words, that representation is unlikely to be in the more elaborate syntax of written English. So the writer's task is to translate a meaning, which may be embodied in key words (what Vygotsky calls words "saturated with sense") and organized in a complex network of relationships, into a linear piece of written English.

The process of translating requires the writer to juggle all the special demands of written English, which Ellen Nold has described as lying on a spectrum from generic and formal demands through syntactic and lexical ones down to the motor tasks of forming letters. For children and inexperienced writers, this extra burden may overwhelm the limited capacity of short-term memory.[16] If the writer must devote conscious attention to demands such as spelling and grammar, the task of translating can interfere with the more global process of planning what one wants to say. Or one can simply ignore some of the constraints of written English. One path produces poor or local planning, the other produces errors, and both, as Mina Shaughnessy showed, lead to frustration for the writer.[17]

In some of the most exciting and extensive research in this area, Marlene Scardamalia and Carl Bereiter have looked at the ways children cope with the cognitive demands of writing. Well-learned skills, such as sentence construction, tend to become automatic and lost to consciousness. Because so little of the writing process is automatic for children, they must devote conscious attention to a variety of individual thinking tasks which adults perform quickly and automatically. Such studies, which trace the development of a given skill over several age groups, can show us the hidden components of an adult process as well as show us how children learn. For example, these studies have been able to distinguish children's ability to handle idea complexity from their ability to handle syntactic complexity; that is, they demonstrate the difference between seeing complex relationships and translating them into appropriate language. In another series of studies Bereiter and Scardamalia showed how children learn to handle the translation process by adapting, then eventually abandoning, the discourse conventions of conversation.[18]

Reviewing

Reviewing depends on two sub-processes: evaluating and revising. Reviewing, itself, may be a conscious process in which writers choose to read what they have written either as a springboard to further translating or with an eye to systematically evaluating and/or revising the text. These periods of planned reviewing frequently lead to new cycles of planning and translating. However, the reviewing process can also occur as an unplanned action triggered by an evaluation of either the text or one's own planning (that is, people revise written as well as unwritten thoughts or statements). The sub-processes of revising and evaluating, along with generating, share the special distinction of being able to interrupt any other process and occur at any time in the act of writing.

The Monitor

As writers compose, they also monitor their current process and progress. The monitor functions as a writing strategist which determines when the writer moves from one process to the next. For example, it determines how long a writer will continue generating ideas before attempting to write prose. Our observations suggest that this choice is determined both by the writer's goals and by individual writing habits or styles. As an example of varied composing styles, writers appear to range from people who try to move to polished prose as quickly as possible to people who choose to plan the entire discourse in detail before writing a word. Bereiter and Scardamalia have shown that much of a child's difficulty and lack of fluency lies in their lack of an "executive routine" which would promote switching between processes or encourage the sustained generation of ideas.[19] Children for example, possess the skills necessary to generate ideas, but lack the kind of monitor which tells them to "keep using" that skill and generate a little more. . . .

2. The processes of writing are hierarchically organized, with component processes embedded within other components.

A hierarchical system is one in which a large working system such as composing can subsume other less inclusive systems, such as generating ideas, which in turn contain still other systems, and so on. Unlike those in a linear organization, the events in a hierarchical process are not fixed in a rigid order. A given process may be called within another instance of itself, in much the same way we embed a subject clause within a larger clause or a picture within a picture.

For instance, a writer trying to construct a sentence (that is, a writer in the act of translating) may run into a problem and call in a condensed version of the entire writing process to help her out (e.g., she might generate and organize a new set of ideas, express them in standard written English, and review this new alternative, all in order to further her current goal of translating. This particular kind of embedding, in which an entire process is embedded within a larger instance of itself, is known technically in linguistics as recursion. However, it is much more common for writers to simply embed individual processes as needed—to call upon them as subroutines to help carry out the task at hand.

Writing processes may be viewed as the writer's tool kit. In using tools, the writer is not constrained to use them in a fixed order or in stages. And using any tool may create the need to use another. Generating ideas may require evaluation, as may writing sentences. And evaluation may force the writer to think up new ideas. . . .

A process that is hierarchical and admits many embedded sub-processes is powerful because it is flexible: it lets a writer do a great deal with only a few relatively simple processes—the basic ones being plan, translate, and review. This means, for instance, that we do not need to define "revision" as a unique stage in composing, but as a thinking process that can occur at any time a writer chooses to evaluate or revise his text or his plans. As an important part of writing, it constantly leads to new planning or a "re-vision" of what one wanted to say.

Embedding is a basic, omni-present feature of the writing process even though we may not be fully conscious of doing it. However, a theory of composing that only recognized embedding wouldn't describe the real complexity of writing. It wouldn't explain *why* writers choose to invoke the processes they do or how they know when they've done enough. To return to Odell's question, what guides the writer's decisions and choices and gives an overall purposeful structure to composing? The third part of the theory is an attempt to answer this question.

3. Writing is a goal-directed process. In the act of composing, writers create a hierarchical network of goals and these in turn guide the writing process.

This proposition is the keystone of the cognitive process theory we are proposing—and yet it may also seem somewhat counter-intuitive. According to many writers, including our subjects, writing often seems a serendipitous experience, an act of discovery. People start out writing without knowing exactly where they will end up; yet they agree that writing is a purposeful act. For example, our subjects often report that their writing process seemed quite disorganized, even chaotic, as they worked, and yet their protocols reveal a coherent underlying structure. How, then, does the writing process manage to seem so unstructured, open-minded, and explanatory ("I don't know what I mean until I see what I say") and at the same time possess its own underlying coherence, direction, or purpose?

One answer to this question lies in the fact that people rapidly forget many of their local working goals once those goals have been satisfied. This is why thinking aloud protocols tell us things retrospection doesn't. A second answer lies in the nature of the goals themselves, which fall into two distinctive categories: process goals and content goals. Process goals are essentially the instructions people give themselves about how to carry out the process of writing (e.g., "Let's doodle a little bit." "So . . . , write an introduction." "I'll go back to that later."). Good writers often give themselves many such instructions and seem to have greater conscious control over their own processes than the poorer writers we have studied. Content goals and plans, on the other hand, specify all things the writer wants to say or do to an audience. Some goals, usually ones having to do with organization, can specify both content and process, as in, "I want to open with a statement about political views." . . .

Goal directed thinking is intimately connected with discovery. Consider for example, the discovery process of two famous explorers—Cortez, silent on his peak in Darien, and that bear who went over the mountain. Both, indeed, discovered the unexpected. However, we should note that both chose to climb a long hill to do so. And it is this sort of goal-directed search for the unexpected that we often see in writers as they attempt to explore and consolidate their knowledge. Furthermore, this search for insight leads to new, more adequate goals, which in turn guide further writing.

The beginning of an answer to Odell's question, "What guides composing?" lies here. The writer's own set of self-made goals guide composing, but these goals can be inclusive and explanatory or narrow, sensitive to the audience or chained to the topic, based on rhetorical savvy or focused on producing correct prose. All those forces which might "guide" composing, such as the rhetorical situation, one's knowledge, the genre, etc., are mediated through the goals, plans, and criteria for evaluation of discourse actually set up by the writer.

This does not mean that a writer's goals are necessarily elaborate, logical, or conscious. For example, a simple-minded goal such as "Write down what I can remember" may be perfectly adequate for writing a list. And experienced writers, such as journalists, can often draw on elaborate networks of goals which are so well learned as to be automatic. Or the rules of a genre, such as those of the limerick, may be so specific as to leave little room or necessity for elaborate rhetorical planning. Nevertheless, whether one's goals are abstract or detailed, simple or sophisticated, they provide the "logic" that moves the composing process forward.

. . . Finally, writers not only create a hierarchical network of guiding goals, but, as they compose, they continually return or "pop" back up to their higher-level goals. And these higher-level goals give direction and coherence to their next move. Our understanding of this network and how writers use it is still quite limited, but we can make a prediction about an important difference one might find between good and poor writers. Poor writers will frequently depend on very abstract, undeveloped top-level goals, such as "appeal to a broad range of intellect," even though such goals are much harder to work with than a more operational goal such as "give a brief history of my job." Sondra Perl has seen this phenomenon in the basic writers who kept returning to reread the assignment, searching, it would seem, for ready-made goals, instead of forming their own. Alternatively, poor writers will depend on only very low-level goals, such as finishing a sentence or correctly spelling a word. They will be, as Nancy Sommers's student revisers were, locked in by the myopia in their own goals and criteria.

Therefore, one might predict that an important difference between good and poor writers will be in both the quantity and quality of the middle range of goals they create. These middle-range goals, which lie between intention and actual prose, give substance and direction to more abstract goals (such as "appealing to the audience") and they give breadth and coherence to local decision about what to say next.

GOALS, TOPIC, AND TEXT

We have been suggesting that the logic which moves composing forward grows out of the goals which writers create as they compose. However, common sense and the folklore of writing offer an alternative explanation which we should consider, namely, that one's own knowledge of the topic (memories, associations, etc.) or the text itself can take control of this process as frequently as one's goals do. One could easily imagine these three forces constituting a sort of eternal triangle in which the writer's goals, knowledge, and current text struggle for influence. For example, the writer's initial planning for a given paragraph might have set up a goal or abstract representation of a paragraph that would discuss three equally important, parallel points on the topic of climate. However, in trying to write, the writer finds that some of his knowledge about climate is really organized around a strong cause-and-effect relationship between points 1 and 2, while he has almost nothing to say about point 3. Or perhaps the text itself attempts to take control, e.g., for the sake of a dramatic opening, the writer's first sentence sets up a vivid example of an effect produced by climate. The syntactic and semantic structure of that sentence now demand that a cause be stated in the next, although this would violate the writer's initial (and still appropriate) plan for a three-point paragraph.

Viewed this way, the writer's abstract plan (representation) of his goals, his knowledge of the topic, and his current text are all actively competing for the writer's attention. Each wants to govern the choices and decisions made next. This competitive model certainly captures that experience of seeing the text run away with you, or the feeling of being led by the nose by an idea. How then do these experiences occur within a "goal-driven process"? First, as our model of the writing process describes, the processes of generate and evaluate appear to have the power to interrupt the writer's process at any point—and they frequently do. This means that new knowledge and/or some feature of the current text can interrupt the process at any time through the processes of generate and evaluate. This allows a flexible collaboration among goals, knowledge, and text. Yet this collaboration often culminates in a revision of previous goals. The persistence and functional importance of initially established goals is reflected by a number of signs: the frequency with which writers refer back to their goals; the fact that writers behave consistently with goals they have already stated; and the fact that they evaluate text in response to the criteria specified in their goals.

Second, some kinds of goals steer the writing process in yet another basic way. In the writers we have studied, the overall composing process is clearly under the direction of global and local *process* goals. Behind the most freewheeling act of "discovery" is a writer who has recognized the heuristic value of free exploration or "just writing it out" and has chosen to do so. Process goals such as these, or "I'll edit it later," are the earmarks of sophisticated writers with a repertory of flexible process goals which let them use writing for discovery. But what about poorer writers who seem simply to free associate on paper or to be obsessed with perfecting the current text? We would argue that often they too are working under a set of implicit process goals which say "write it as it comes," or "make everything perfect and correct as you go." The problem then is not that knowledge or the text have taken over, so much as that the writer's own goals and/or images of the composing process put these strategies in control.[20]

To sum up, the third point of our theory—focused on the role of the writer's own goals—helps us account for purposefulness in writing. But can we account for the dynamics of discovery? Richard Young, Janet Emig, and others argue that writing is uniquely adapted to the task of fostering insight and developing new knowledge.[21] But how does this happen in a goal-directed process?

We think that the remarkable combination of purposefulness and openness which writing offers is based in part on a beautifully simple, but extremely powerful principle, which is this: *In the act of writing, people regenerate or recreate their own goals in the light of what they learn.* This principle then creates the fourth point of our cognitive process theory.

4. Writers create their own goals in two key ways: by generating goals and supporting sub-goals which embody a purpose; and, at times, by changing or regenerating their own top-level goals in light of what they have learned by writing.

We are used, of course, to thinking of writing as a process in which our *knowledge* develops as we write. The structure of knowledge for some topic becomes more conscious and assertive as we keep tapping memory for related ideas. That structure, or "schema," may even grow and change as a result of library research or the addition of our own fresh inferences. However, writers must also generate (i.e., create or retrieve) the unique goals which guide their process.

In this paper we focus on the goals writers create for a particular paper, but we should not forget that many writing goals are well-learned, standard ones stored in memory. For example, we would expect many writers to draw automatically on those goals associated with writing in general, such as, "interest the reader," or "start with an introduction," or on goals associated with a given genre, such as making a jingle rhyme. These goals will often be so basic that they won't even be consciously considered or expressed. And the more experienced the writer the greater this repertory of semi-automatic plans and goals will be.

Writers also develop an elaborate network of working "sub-goals" as they compose. As we have seen, these sub-goals give concrete meaning and direction to their more abstract top-level goals, such as "interest the reader," or "describe my job." And then on occasion writers show a remarkable ability to regenerate or change the very goals which had been directing their writing and planning: that is, they replace or revise major goals in light of what they learned through writing. It is these two creative processes we wish to consider now. . . .

This process of setting and developing sub-goals, and—at times—regenerating those goals is a powerful creative process. Writers and teachers of writing have long argued that one learns through the act of writing itself, but it has been difficult to support the claim in other ways. However, if one studies the process by which a writer uses a goal to generate ideas, then consolidates those ideas and uses them to revise or regenerate new, more complex goals, one can see this learning process in action. Furthermore, one sees why the process of revising and clarifying goals has such a broad effect, since it is through setting these new goals that the fruits of discovery come back to inform the continuing process of writing. In this instance, some of our most complex and imaginative acts can depend on the elegant simplicity of a few powerful thinking processes. We feel that a cognitive process explanation of discovery, toward which this theory is only a start, will have another special strength. By placing emphasis on the inventive power of the writer, who is able to explore ideas, to develop, act on, test, and regenerate his or her own goals, we are putting an important part of creativity where it belongs—in the hands of the working, thinking writer.

Notes

1. Aristotle, *The Rhetoric,* trans. Lane Cooper (New York: Appleton-Century-Crofts, 1932). Richard Lloyd-Jones, "A Perspective on Rhetoric," in *Writing: The Nature, Development and Teaching of Written Communication,* ed. C. Frederiksen, M. Whiteman, and J. Dominic (Hillsdale, N.J.: Lawrence Erlbaum Associates, in press.)
2. Lee Odell, Charles R. Cooper, and Cynthia Courts, "Discourse Theory: Implications for Research in Composing," in *Research on Composing: Points of Departure,* ed. Charles Cooper and Lee Odell (Urbana, IL: National Council of Teachers of English, 1978), p. 6.
3. Lloyd Bitzer, "The Rhetorical Situation," *Philosophy and Rhetoric,* 1 (January, 1968), 1–14.
4. Richard E. Vatz, "The Myth of the Rhetorical Situation," in *Philosophy and Rhetoric,* 6 (Summer, 1973), 154–161.
5. James Britton et al., *The Development of Writing Abilities,* 11–18 (London: Macmillan, 1975), p. 39.
6. Gordon Rohman, "Pre-Writing: The Stage of Discovery in the Writing Process," *CCC,* 16 (May, 1965), 106–112.
7. See Britton et al., *The Development of Writing Abilities,* pp. 19–49.
8. Nancy Sommers, "Response to Sharon Crowley, 'Components of the Process,'" *CCC,* 29 (May, 1978), 209–211.
9. Nancy Sommers, "Revision Strategies of Student Writers and Experienced Writers," *CCC,* 31 (December, 1980), 378–388.
10. Linda S. Flower and John R. Hayes, "The Cognition of Discovery: Defining a Rhetorical Problem," *CCC,* 31 (February, 1980), 21–32.
11. Britton et al., *The Development of Writing Abilities,* pp. 61–65.
12. Sondra Perl, "Five Writers Writing: Case Studies of the Composing Process of Unskilled College Writers," Diss. New York University, 1978.
13. Linda S. Flower and John R. Hayes, "The Dynamics of Composing: Making Plans and Juggling Constraints," in *Cognitive Processes in Writing: An Interdisciplinary Approach,* ed. Lee Gregg and Erwin Steinberg (Hillsdale, N.J.: Lawrence Erlbaum Associates, 1980), pp. 31–50.
14. Linda S. Flower, "Writer-Based Prose: A Cognitive Basis for Problems in Writing," *College English,* 41 (September, 1979), 19–37.
15. Flower, "The Cognition of Discovery," pp. 21–32.
16. Ellen Nold, "Revising," in *Writing: The Nature, Development, and Teaching of Written Communication,* ed. C. Frederiksen et al. (Hillsdale, N.J.: Lawrence Erlbaum Associates, in press).
17. Mina Shaughnessy, *Errors and Expectations* (New York: Oxford University Press, 1977).
18. Marlene Scardamalia, "How Children Cope with the Cognitive Demands of Writing," in *Writing: The Nature, Development and Teaching of Written Communication,* ed. C. Frederiksen et al. (Hillsdale, N.J.: Lawrence Erlbaum Associates, in press). Carl Bereiter and Marlene Scardamalia, "From Conversation to Composition: The Role of Instruction in a Developmental Process," in *Advances in Instructional Psychology,* Volume 2, ed. R. Glaser (Hillsdale, N.J.: Lawrence Erlbaum Associates, in press).
19. Bereiter and Scardamalia, "From Conversation to Composition."
20. Cf. a recent study by Mike Rose on the power of ineffective process plans, "Rigid Rules, Inflexible Plans, and the Stifling of Language: A Cognitivist's Analysis of Writer's Block," *CCC,* 31 (December, 1980), 389–400.

21. Janet Emig, "Writing as a Model of Learning," *CCC,* 28 (May, 1977), 122–128; Richard E. Young, "Why Write? A Reconsideration," unpublished paper delivered at the convention of the Modern Language Association, San Francisco, California, 28 December 1979.

Rethinking Genre from a Sociocognitive Perspective

Carol Berkenkotter and Thomas N. Huckin

Carol Berkenkotter teaches at Michigan Technological University and Thomas N. Huckin teaches at the University of Utah. "Rethinking Genre from a Sociocognitive Perspective" was first published in Written Communication *(October 1993). This excerpt can help us begin to think about the social dimensions of writing genres. An expanded version of this article appears in* Genre Knowledge in Academic Writing *(Erlbaum, 1994) by Berkenkotter and Huckin.*

> The significance of generic categories . . . resides in their cognitive and cultural value, and the purpose of genre theory is to lay out the implicit knowledge of the users of genres. (Ryan, 1981, p. 112)

> The shapes of knowledge are ineluctably local, indivisible from their instruments and their encasements. (Geertz, 1983, p. 4)

A great deal has been written about literary genres, and in rhetorical studies, genre theory has had a healthy resurgence in the past 15 years. Much of this material can be seen as various attempts to develop taxonomies or classificatory schemes or to set forth hierarchical models of the constitutive elements of genre (for reviews, see Campbell & Jamieson, 1978; Miller, 1984; Swales, 1990). This taxonomical scholarship and theory building have been based largely on analyses of the features of written or oral texts. Although such an approach enables one to make generalizations about what some writers refer to as a genre's "form, substance, and context" (see, e.g., Yates & Orlikowski, 1992), it does not enable us to determine anything about the ways in which genre is embedded in the communicative activities of a discipline. Nor does a traditional rhetorical approach enable us to understand the functions of genre from the perspective of the actor who must draw on genre knowledge to perform effectively.

Bakhtin argued that genres and other forms of verbal communication are sites of tension between unifying ("centripetal") forces and stratifying ("centrifugal") forces. According to Bakhtin (1981), "The authentic environment of an utterance, the environment in which it lives and takes shape, is dialogized heteroglossia, anonymous and social as language, but simultaneously concrete, filled with specific content and accented as an individual utterance" (p. 272). Genres are "typical forms of utterances" (Bakhtin, 1986, p. 63), and as such, they should be studied in their actual social contexts of use. In particular, analysts should pay attention to ways in which genre users manipulate genres for particular rhetorical purposes. Bakhtin (1981) argued that this "intentional dimension" can be fully understood and appreciated only by observing "insiders":

> For the speakers of the language themselves, these generic languages and professional jargons are directly intentional—they denote and express directly and fully, and are capable of expressing themselves without mediation; but outside, that is, for those not participating in the given purview, these languages may be treated as objects, as typifications, as local color. For such outsiders, the intentions permeating these languages become *things,* limited in their meaning and expression. (p. 289)

To date, very little work on genre in rhetorical studies has been informed by actual case research with *insiders*. Instead, there has long been a tendency among genre scholars to reify genres, to see them as linguistic abstractions, and to understate their "changeable, flexible and plastic" (Bakhtin, 1986, p. 80) nature.

In this essay we argue for an alternative way of looking at the genres of academic cultures, focusing on the ways in which writers use genre knowledge (or fail to use such knowledge) as they engage in such disciplinary activities as writing up laboratory experiments, judging conference proposals, negotiating with reviewers over the revisions of a research report, reading the drafts of a scientific article, or creating a new forum for scholarly publication. Our thinking is based on 8 years of rhetorical and linguistic analyses of case study data that foreground individual writers' language in use; this approach has led to our present view that writers acquire and strategically deploy genre knowledge as they participate in their field's or profession's knowledge-producing activities. . . .

From our research and from this literature we have developed [four] principles that constitute a theoretical framework:

1. Dynamism: Genres are dynamic rhetorical forms that develop from responses to recurrent situations and serve to stabilize experience and give it coherence and meaning. Genres change over time in response to their users' sociocognitive needs.
2. Situatedness: Our knowledge of genres is derived from and embedded in our participation in the communicative activities of daily and professional life. As such, genre knowledge is a form of "situated cognition," which continues to develop as we participate in the activities of the culture.
3. Form and content: Genre knowledge embraces both form and content, including a sense of what content is appropriate to a particular purpose in a particular situation at a particular point in time.
4. Community ownership: Genre conventions signal a discourse community's norms, epistemology, ideology, and social ontology.

In the sections that follow, we explicate each of these principles in detail, referring to a number of constructs in the literature mentioned above. We are not so much articulating a fully developed sociocognitive theory of genre as we are working toward one by integrating concepts from a number of fields. Thus we present a synthesis of perspectives and constructs from which a sociocognitive theory of genre can be developed.

DYNAMISM

Genres are dynamic rhetorical forms that develop from responses to recurrent situations and serve to stabilize experience and give it coherence and meaning. Genres change over time in response to their users' sociocognitive needs.

This principle is derived from contemporary rhetorical examinations of genre (as reviewed by Campbell & Jamieson, 1978; and Miller, 1984) and is perhaps best exemplified by Bitzer's (1968) discussion of recurrent rhetorical situations:

> From day to year to year, comparable situations occur, prompting comparable responses; hence rhetorical forms are born, and a special vocabulary, grammar, and style are established. . . . The situations recur and, because we experience situations and the rhetorical responses to them, a form of discourse is not only established but comes to have a power of its own—the tradition itself tends to function as a constraint upon any new response in the form. (p. 13)

Although Bitzer did not use the term *genre,* his notion of rhetorical forms emerging in response to recurrent situations sparked several scholarly discussions of rhetorical genres. A number of scholars invoked Bitzer's notion of recurring rhetorical responses to situational exigencies to characterize genre (Campbell & Jamieson, 1978; Harrell & Linkugel, 1978; Miller, 1984; Simons, 1978).

In a widely cited essay that reconceptualized rhetorical views of genre from a sociological perspective, Miller (1984) proposed that "recurrence" does not refer to external conditions (a realist view) but rather is socially constructed . . .

Miller's social constructionist view of genre, which incorporates Schutz's notion of typification, has been significant to rhetorical studies of genre for a number of reasons. First, it has influenced scholarship in the rhetoric of science (e.g., Bazerman, 1988; Swales, 1990). Second, it has provided scholars with an interpretive framework for dealing with the thorny issue of the relationship between socially determined human communicative activity and agency. Finally, Miller's treatment of typification extricates the concept of genre from its moorings in Aristotelian and literary classification systems and relocates it in a more microlevel understanding of everyday communicative behaviors. According to Miller,

> To consider as potential genres such homely discourse as the letter of recommendation, the user manual, the progress report, the ransom note, the lecture, and the white paper, as well as the eulogy, the apologia, the inaugural, the public proceeding, and the sermon, is not to trivialize the study of genres; it is to take seriously the rhetoric in which we are immersed and the situations in which we find ourselves. (p. 155)

Miller's insistence that considerations of genre encompass the discourse of the agora as well as that of the senate has been important to studies in technical and organizational communication (see e.g., Devitt, 1991; Herndl, Fennell & Miller, 1991; Miller & Selzer, 1985; Yates & Orlikowski, 1992). And in locating genre in the social actions and practices of everyday life (in the professions and other social institutions such as the school), Miller's essay anticipated the interest in Bakhtin's construct of "speech genres," which will figure importantly later in this discussion.

But just as language itself must accommodate both stability and change, genres must do more than encapsulate intersubjective perceptions of recurring situations. They must also try to deal with the fact that recurring situations resemble each other only in certain ways and only to a certain degree. As the world changes, both in material conditions and in collective and individual perceptions of it, the types produced by typification must themselves undergo constant incremental change. Furthermore, individuals have their own uniquely formed knowledge of the world; and socially induced perceptions of commonality do not eradicate subjective perceptions of difference. Genres, therefore, are always sites of contention between stability and change. They are inherently dynamic, constantly (if gradually) changing over time in response to the sociocognitive needs of individual users. This dynamism resembles that found in other aspects of language acquisition, including for example the negotiated learning and use of individual words (see Huckin, Hayes, & Coady, 1993; Pinker, 1984) and, to a lesser extent, the construction of sentences via "emergent" grammar (Goodwin, 1979; Hopper, 1988).

An example of this internal dynamism can be found in Huckin's (1987) study of 350 scientific journal articles published between 1944 and the late 1980s. Huckin analyzed formal patterns and interviewed a number of working scientists who regularly read and contribute to the literature. The scientific journal article has long been thought of as a conservative, relatively static genre, especially on the formal level, yet Huckin found that it had actually undergone significant changes over this 45-year period. For example, they found experimental results increasingly being foregrounded in titles, abstracts, introductions, and section headings but methods and procedures sections increasingly being relegated to secondary status. The interviews with scientists revealed perhaps the main reason for these changes, namely, that in this age of information explosion, readers of scientific journals cannot keep up with the literature and are forced to skim journal articles the way many newspaper readers skim newspapers. These scientist readers are also writers, and their individual reading behavior affects their writing strategies. Inasmuch as they also belong to a scientific community, they find themselves responding in similar ways to similar communicative pressures. Thus, on both a communal and individual (i.e., sociocognitive) level, scientists shape the genre to better serve their needs. The result is a continually evolving, not static, genre.

SITUATEDNESS

Our knowledge of genres is derived from and embedded in our participation in the communicative activities of daily life and professional life. As such, genre knowledge is a form of "situated cognition" (Brown, Collins, & Duguid, 1989) that continues to develop as we participate in the activities of the culture.

From a sociocognitive perspective, genre knowledge of academic discourse entails an understanding of both oral and written forms of appropriate communicative behaviors. This knowledge, rather than being explicitly taught, is transmitted through enculturation as apprentices become socialized to the ways of speaking in particular disciplinary communities. Because it is impossible for us to dwell in the social world without repertories of typified social responses in recurrent situations—from greetings and thank-yous to acceptance speeches and full-blown, written expositions of scientific or scholarly investigations—we use genres to package our speech and make of it a recognizable response to the exigencies of the situation. . . .

From a Bakhtinian dialogical perspective, academic—or any other institutional discourse—can be seen to take place on a "conversational continuum" that for the language user inevitably involves a transition from "naturalistic" conversational turns to turns that are extended and monological. Along similar lines, Bergvall (1992) has argued that

> academic discourse takes place on a variety of levels: casual hallway chats, lectures, conversations between teachers and students in and out of class, e-mail, memos, scholarly papers, books. Each of these is a form of academic "conversation," with a variety of levels of formality, personal involvement, number of participants, etc. The length of turns ranges from the quick exchanges of informal, intense conversation to the extended monologues of writing. Usually conversation is a natural pattern learned in childhood, but the appropriate use of the voice in academic conversation, particularly the monologic style, requires extensive training, and enculturation into the modes of conversation sanctioned by academic discourse communities. New members must learn style, vocabulary, citation format, organization and length of texts or talk, etc. (p. 1)

This view that knowledge of academic discourse in its various permutations grows out of enculturation to the oral and written "forms of talk" of the academy brings us to our next point—that genre knowledge is a form of *situated cognition,* that is, knowledge that is indexical, "inextricably a product of the activity and situations in which it [is] produced" (Brown et al., 1989, p. 33). Learning the genres of academic discourse, like other forms of concept learning, evolves "with each new occasion of use because new situations, negotiations, and activities inevitably recast it in a new, more densely textured form" (Brown et al., 1989, p. 33). As we have seen in our own research and that of others dealing with "cognitive apprenticeship" (Collins, Brown, & Newman, 1989), generally the enculturation into the practices of disciplinary communities is "picked up" in the local milieu of the culture rather than being explicitly taught. As Brown et al. (1989) suggested

> Given the chance to observe and practice *in situ* the behavior of members of a culture, people pick up the relevant jargon, imitate behavior, and gradually start to act in accordance with its norms. These cultural practices are often recondite and extremely complex. Nevertheless, given the opportunity to observe and practice them, people adopt them with great success. Students, for instance, can quickly get an implicit sense of what is suitable diction, what makes a relevant question, what is legitimate or illegitimate behavior in a particular activity. (p. 34) . . .

These views undergird much of what has recently been written about the situated nature of individual concept development. For example, Brown et al. (1989) argue that acquiring conceptual knowledge, like learning the use of tools, is

> both situated and progressively developed through activity. . . . People who use tools actively rather than just acquire them . . . build an increasingly rich, implicit understanding of the world in which they use the tools and of the tools themselves. The understanding, both of the world and of the tool, continually changes as a result of their interaction. . . . The culture and the use of the tool act together to determine the way that practitioners see the world; and the way the world appears to them determines the culture's understanding of the world and of the tools. Unfortunately, students are too often asked to use the tools of a discipline without being able to adapt to its culture. To learn to use tools as practitioners use them, a student like an apprentice must enter the community and its culture. (p. 33)

An activity-based theory of genre knowledge would therefore locate our learning of academic genres in the processes that Vygotsky described as "socially distributed cognition," occurring in the situated activities of a practitioner in training. Genre knowledge, as we have seen in our own research, is very much a part of the conceptual tool kit of professional academic writers, linked to their knowledge of how to use the other tools of their trade: the biologist's lab assay, the literary historian's knowledge of how to synthesize information from an archival microfiche, the psychologist's use of statistical procedures to determine degrees of freedom, the metallurgist's knowledge of the workings of the electron microscope. This is what we mean when we claim that genre knowledge is a form of situated cognition, inextricable from professional writers' procedural and social knowledge. *Social knowledge,* as we are using the term here, refers to writers' familiarity with the research networks in their field (Kaufer & Geisler, 1989). It is the knowledge they draw on to create an appropriate rhetorical and conceptual context in which to position their own research and knowledge claims. Genre knowledge, procedural knowledge (which includes a knowledge of tools and their uses as well as of a discipline's methods and interpretive framework), and social knowledge are acquired incrementally as students progress through a period of apprenticeship—generally at the graduate level.

Learning of the genres of disciplinary or professional discourse would therefore be similar to second language acquisition, requiring immersion into the culture, and a lengthy period of apprenticeship and enculturation. In contrast, undergraduate university students, like secondary school students, learn many institutional, or curriculum, genres. Following Brown et al.'s line of reasoning, we would contend that many of these pedagogical genres contain *some* of the textual features and *some* of the conventions of disciplinary genres but that they are also linked to and instantiate classroom-based activities such as reading, writing, solving decontextualized math problems, or conducting simple experiments of the kind found in lab manuals. This view has a number of important implications for current notions of the teaching of disciplinary discourse. It may be the case, for example, that writing-across-the-curriculum programs should try to sensitize faculty in the disciplines to the fact that, in contrast to the specialized rhetorics they routinely use in their professional writing, the genres of the undergraduate curricula are characterized by quite different textual features and conventions, given their classroom-based contexts and rhetorical functions.

FORM AND CONTENT

Genre knowledge embraces both form and content, including a sense of what content is appropriate to a particular purpose in a particular situation at a particular point in time.

If genres are dynamic rhetorical structures and genre knowledge a form of situated cognition, it follows that both genres and genre knowledge are more sharply and richly defined to the extent that they are *localized* (in both time and place). Traditional generic classifications are pitched at such a broad level of generality that they can describe only superficial parameters of form or content. For example, "the business letter," as discussed in traditional writing textbooks, is depicted in largely formal terms with only vague comments like "a letter from a Utah bank promoting a new savings program" can be more fully described, with reference made to specific aspects of content (e.g., subtopics such as interest rates, security, tax benefits, etc., discussed in ways that are relevant to Utahans). In the dynamic, grounded view of genre that we are advocating here, what constitutes true genre knowledge is not just a knowledge of formal conventions but a knowledge of appropriate topics and relevant details as well.

Recent studies of academic discourse contain numerous examples of how deeply content is implicated in genre knowledge. For instance, Marshall and Barritt (1990), in their study of *American Educational Research Journal (AERJ)* articles, explained how this particular genre is strongly affected by philosophical considerations. They noted that "the forms of argument, in other words the rhetoric, used by scholars who publish in *AERJ* continue to be influenced by the objectivist tradition of research that owes so much to the analogy between natural and social events" (p. 605). They showed how this positivist stance manifests itself in particular textual features, such as the way teachers, students, and parents are referred to. . . .

Another aspect of content that should be considered in defining a genre is background knowledge, that is, knowledge (of the world, of a particular community, of a discipline, etc.) that readers of that genre are assumed to have. . . .

Closely related to background knowledge is the concept of surprise value or novelty, which can also play a role in definitions of genre and genre knowledge. In writing up news reports, for example, a journalist is expected to have a keen sense of what aspects of a story are most "newsworthy." Indeed, newsworthiness is the primary factor in the use of the so-called inverted-pyramid text schema (Van Dijk, 1986) . . .

Another aspect of content that should be taken into account in much academic writing (as well as journalism and other fields) is that of *kairos,* or rhetorical timing. A good illustration of this strategy can be seen in the history of the discovery of DNA, as discussed in Miller (1992). DNA was first theorized by Oswald Avery and two colleagues in 1944. Nine years later, its structural properties were described by James Watson and Francis Crick, who received much greater acclaim than did Avery, as well as the Nobel prize. . . . Miller observed that the rhetorical conditions for the two reports were vastly different. Avery was far ahead of his time, breaking new ground at a pace that the scientific community was unprepared for. Watson and Crick, by contrast, were riding the crest of a wave long in the making and well-known to many observers. According to Miller (1992), "Avery was working at one end of a nine-year 'revolution' in the understanding of genetic mechanisms, Watson and Crick at the other. The *kairos* in each case was quite different" (p. 311). In Giltrow's terms, the background knowledge that each writer could assume of his audience was very different. Thus Avery was compelled to painstakingly lay out his methodology and findings and carefully situate his work in the larger body of scientific knowledge, whereas Watson and Crick could rush into print with only the sketchiest of details. Indeed, as Miller notes, "We might suspect that the two papers belong to quite different genres, which are defined in part by the rhetorical action achievable within the differing scientific situations" (p. 318).

In these examples, we can see how matters of content— epistemology, background knowledge, surprise value, kairos—influenced the selection and use of formal features in the instantiation of particular genres. Considerations of audience and situation are fundamental to these determinations, underscoring the rhetorical nature of genre knowledge and genre use. This is especially apparent in more "localized" cases where the characteristics of the audience and the situation are more sharply delineated. . . .

We feel that genericness is not an all-or-nothing proposition and that there is not a threshold as such. Instead, communicators engage in (and their texts reveal) various degrees of *generic activity.* No act of communication springs out of nothing. In one way or another, all acts of communication build on prior texts and text elements, elements that exist on different levels including words, phrases, discourse patterns, illustrations, and so on. If texts arise out of discursive differences, as Bakhtin, Kress, and many others have argued, such texts can be expected to embody different kinds of "recurring rhetorical responses" in different ways. Thus, rather than taking a holistic, normative approach to genre, as is done in traditional studies, we feel it makes more sense to take a more articulated approach in which individual texts are seen to contain heterogenous mixtures of elements, some of which are recognizably more generic than others. . . .

COMMUNITY OWNERSHIP

Genre conventions signal a discourse community's norms, epistemology, ideology, and social ontology.

Asserting a relationship between the concept of genre and that of *discourse community* is a slippery proposition, because neither concept refers to a static entity. Nevertheless, recent research in composition studies and discourse analysis supports our view that studying the genres of professional and disciplinary communication provides important information about the textual dynamics of discourse communities. For example, Swales's work on the conventions of the experimental article (Swales & Najjar, 1987) and more recently on the genres of academic writing (Swales, 1990) made a strong case for understanding the functions of genre in terms of the discourse communities that "own" them (Swales, 1990, pp. 25–27).

Similarly, Bazerman's (1988) study of the development of the experimental article in the natural sciences established an important connection between the formation of a scientific discourse community and the development of appropriate discursive strategies for making claims about experiments that, in turn, reveal the inner workings of the natural world. In examining the evolution of the experimental article in the natural sciences (in the first scientific journal, the *Philosophical Transactions of the Royal Society of London*), Bazerman demonstrated a fruitful historical methodology for understanding the emergence of a genre's textual features and rhetorical conventions in relation to disciplinary community formation. His study of the development of the features and conventions of scientific writing between 1665 and 1800 revealed how the increasingly complex interactions of an emergent argumentative community of natural scientists is tied to the appearance of genre conventions. . . .

A study by Berkenkotter (1990) of the formation of a disciplinary subspecialty in literary studies, as seen through the evolution of a scholarly journal, revealed how disciplinary norms and values are codified as the forum becomes professionalized. In this case study, an emergent community of literary specialists interested in reader-response theory, criticism, and pedagogy organized a newsletter as a forum for exchanging ideas. The early issues of the newsletter contained a number of informal personal statements that express the discontent of young professors with the norms of scholarly writing. These writers specifically inveighed against the elaborate style of "professional" discourse with its jargon, convoluted syntax, and pedantic authorial persona. A number of the contributors to the newsletter declared themselves to be members of a vanguard interested in transforming conventional academic writing with its underlying elitist, hegemonic value system. Despite this concern, as the newsletter evolved into a scholarly journal, it incorporated the formal textual features and conventions of literary scholarship and thereby demonstrated its movement into the disciplinary mainstream. The contributors' increasing use of the standard conventions of formal scholarly discourse with its overt intertextual mechanisms suggests that, despite a short period of rebellion, the textual instantiation of the values of the academy was an inevitable outcome of the institutionalization of the journal. What counted as knowledge had to be couched in the formal discourse of the literary scholar. . . .

CONCLUSION

. . . As social actors, we are constantly aware of the available patterns through which we might act at any given moment, yet we are also capable of modifying those patterns to accommodate our reading of the rhetorical moment. We determine, for example, when a colleague offers a "Good morning, how are you," those occasions when "what is called for" is a short, conventional reply, and those occasions (given our relation to that colleague) when it is appropriate for us to unburden ourselves of the rage we felt when we could not start the car because it was −10° outside. We have the linguistic and rhetorical repertoires to choose our comments *artfully* in light of our reading of the occasion and of our relation to our interlocutor as we conceive it through both retrospective and prospective structuring of other occasions. It is through our constitution of many such encounters as they are enacted across time and space that we construct our social worlds.

Full participation in disciplinary and professional cultures demands a similarly informed knowledge of written genres. Genres are the intellectual scaffolds on which community-based knowledge is constructed. To be fully effective in this role, genres must be flexible and dynamic, capable of modification according to the rhetorical exigencies of the situation. At the same time, though, they must be stable enough to capture those aspects of situations that tend to recur. This tension between stability and change lies at the heart of genre use and genre knowledge and is perhaps best seen in the work of those who are most deeply engaged in disciplinary activity. The fully invested disciplinary actor is typically well aware of the textual patterns and epistemological norms of his or her discourse community but is also aware of the need to be at the cutting edge, to push for novelty and originality. As the intellectual content of a field changes over time, so must the forms used to discuss it; this is why genre knowledge involves both form *and* content. In using the genres customarily employed by other members of their discourse community, members of a discipline help to constitute the community and simultaneously reproduce it (though, as we noted earlier, not in a simple replicative way). Thus genres themselves, when examined closely from the perspective of those who use them, reveal much about a discourse community's norms, epistemology, ideology, and social ontology.

References

Bakhtin, M. (1981). *The dialogic imagination* (C. Emerson and M. Holquist, Trans.; M. Holquist, Ed.). Austin: University of Texas Press.

Bakhtin, M. (1986). *Speech genres and other late essays* (V. W. McGee, Trans.; C. Emerson & M. Holquist, Eds.). Austin: University of Texas Press.

Bazerman, C. (1988). *Shaping written knowledge: The genre and activity of the experimental article in science.* Madison: University of Wisconsin Press.

Bergvall, V. (1992, April). *Different or dominant? The role of gender in the academic conversation.* Paper presented at the annual meeting of the American Educational Research Association, San Francisco, CA.

Berkenkotter, C. (1990). Evolution of a scholarly forum: Reader 1977–1988. In G. Kirsch & D. Roen (Eds.), *A sense of audience in written communication* (pp. 191–215). Newbury Park, CA: Sage.

Bitzer, L. (1968). The rhetorical situation. *Philosophy and Rhetoric, 1,* 1–14.

Brown, J. S., Collins, A., & Duguid, P. (1989). Situated cognition and the culture of learning. *Educational Researcher, 18,* 32–42.

Campbell, K. K., & Jamieson, K. H. (1978). Form and genre in rhetorical criticism: An introduction. In K. K. Campbell & K. H. Jamieson (Eds.), *Form and genre: Shaping rhetorical action* (pp. 9–32). Falls Church, VA: Speech Communication Association.

Collins, A., Brown, J. S., & Newman, S. E. (1989). Cognitive apprenticeship: Teaching the craft of reading, writing, and mathematics. In L. B. Resnik (Ed.), *Knowing, learning and instructions: Essays in honor of Robert Glaser* (pp. 453–494). Hillsdale, NJ: Lawrence Erlbaum.

Devitt, A. (1991). Intertextuality in tax accounting: Generic, referential, and functional. In C. Bazerman & J. Paradis (Eds.), *Textual dynamics of the professions: Historical and contemporary studies of writing in professional communities* (pp. 336–357). Madison: University of Wisconsin Press.

Geertz, C. (1983). *Local knowledge: Further essays in interpretive anthropology.* New York: Basic Books.

Giltrow, J. (1992, April). *Genre and the pragmatic concept of background knowledge.* First presented at the International "Rethinking Genre" Conference, Carleton University, Ottawa, Canada.

Goodwin, C. (1979). The interactive construction of a sentence in everyday conversation. In G. Psalthas (Ed.), *Everyday language: Studies in ethnomethodology* (pp. 97–122). New York: Irvington.

Harrell, J., & Linkugel, W. A. (1978). On rhetorical genre: An organizing perspective. *Philosophy & Rhetoric, 11,* 262–281.

Herndl, C. G., Fennell, B. A., & Miller, C. R. (1991). Understanding failures in organizational discourse: The accident at Three Mile Island and the shuttle Challenger disaster. In C. Bazerman & J. Paradis (Eds.), *Textual dynamics of the professions: Historical and contemporary studies of writing in professional communities* (pp. 279–305). Madison: University of Wisconsin Press.

Hopper, P. (1988). Emergent grammar and the *a priori* postulate. In D. Tannen (Ed.), *Linguistics in context connecting observation and understanding* (pp. 117–134). Norwood, NJ: Ablex.

Huckin, T. (1987, March). *Surprise value in scientific discourse.* Paper presented at the March Conference on College Composition and Communication, Atlanta, GA.

Huckin, T., Hayes, M., & Coady, J. (1993). *Second language reading and vocabulary learning.* Norwood, NJ: Ablex.

Kaufer, D. S., & Geisler, C. (1989). Novelty in academic writing. *Written Communication, 6,* 286–311.

Kress, G. (1982). *Learning to write.* London: Routledge & Kegan Paul.

Kress, G. (1988). Genre in a social theory of language. In I. Reid (Ed.), *The place of genre in learning: Current debates* (pp. 35–45). Geelong, Australia: Deakin University Press, the Centre for Studies in Literary Education.

Kress, G. (1989). *Linguistic processes in sociocultural practice.* Oxford: Oxford University Press.

Marshall, M. J., & Barritt, L. S. (1990). Choices made, worlds created: The rhetoric of *AERJ, American Educational Research Journal, 27,* 589–609.

Miller, C. R. (1984). Genre as social action. *Quarterly Journal of Speech, 70,* 151–167.

Miller, C. R. (1992). Kairos in the rhetoric of science. In S. White, N. Nakadake, & R. Cherry, *A rhetoric of doing: Essays honoring James L. Kinneavy* (pp. 310–327). New York: Guilford.

Pinker, S. (1984). *Language learnability and language development.* Cambridge, MA: Harvard University Press.

Ryan, M. L. (1981). Introduction: On the why, what and how of generic taxonomies. *Poetics, 10,* 109–126.

Schutz, A., & Luckmann, T. (1973). *The structures of the life-world* (R. M. Zaner & H. T. Englehardt, Jr., Trans.). Evanston, IL: Northwestern University Press.

Simons, H. W. (1978). "Genre-alizing" about rhetoric: A scientific approach. In K. K. Campbell & K. H. Jamieson (Eds.), *Form and genre: Shaping rhetorical action* (pp. 33–50). Falls Church, VA: Speech Communication Association.

Swales, J. M. (1990). *Genre analysis: English in academic and research settings.* Cambridge: Cambridge University Press.

Swales, J. M., & Najjar, H. (1987). The writing of research articles: Where to put the bottom line? *Written Communication, 4,* 175–191.

Van Dijk, T. (1986). News schemata. In C. Cooper & S. Greenbaum (Eds.), *Studying writing: Linguistic approaches* (pp. 155–185). Beverly Hills, CA: Sage.

Vygotsky, L. S. (1978). *Mind and society: The development of higher psychological processes.* (M. Cole, V. J. Steiner, S. Scribner, & E. Souberman, Eds.). Cambridge, MA: Harvard University Press.

Vygotsky, L. S. (1986). *Thought and language* (A. Kozulin, Trans. and Ed.). Cambridge, MA: MIT Press.

Yates, J. A., & Orlikowski, W. J. (1992). Genres of organizational communication: A structurational approach. *Academy of Management Review, 17,* 299–326.

Taking Thought: The Role of Conscious Processing in the Making of Meaning

Linda Flower

Linda Flower is professor of rhetoric at Carnegie-Mellon University. "Taking Thought: The Role of Conscious Processing in the Making of Meaning" was originally published in Thinking, Reasoning, and Writing, *edited by Elaine P. Maimon, Barbara F. Nodine, and Finbarr W. O'Connor (Longman, 1989). This very brief excerpt can contribute to our understanding of metacognition by showing how writers function at various levels of conscious awareness as they write.*

In understanding the role of consciousness in writing it is important first to acknowledge the advantage of nonconscious processes (if they can do the job) and the importance of mental activity of which we aren't aware. Conscious processes are only a part of the performance, yet they appear to play a very important role in the process of experts, for whom we might suppose they would be less necessary. We can see this role more clearly if we look at conscious thought as a level of processing in which writers can choose, at certain times, to engage, and if we ask the question, Why do they make this choice?

One approach to understand thought, which we have already seen, is to categorize the knowledge itself as tacit or explicit, learned or acquired, conscious or unconscious, and then—in some cases—to argue for the value of one kind of knowledge over the other. Mandel for instance, locates creativity in unconscious knowing: "Writing is occurring, there is no one at home thinking about it—at least not during the process itself" (372). Krashen argues for the virtues of naturally "acquired" language skills and the limited utility of "learned" rules. And yet can knowledge be so easily pigeonholed as one kind or another? Experience shows us that the conscious knowledge novices struggle to learn and labor to use (e.g., how to spell hard words or write a newspaper lead) can later become so well learned that its use is automated. They are able to use this automated knowledge without conscious attention to it. How they acquired the knowledge becomes immaterial in comparison to how they use it. Research has also shown that the efficient, tacit knowledge of experienced business writers can be brought back to awareness and made explicit if they are asked to make choices or decisions about features of their text (Odell and Goswami). Even the profession of psychotherapy is based, finally, on the premise that unconscious motivations can with effort be made conscious.

In understanding writers, we think it will be more fruitful to concentrate not on knowledge as an artifact packaged in one form or another but on the act of thinking. From this perspective, consciousness becomes an optional action, rather than a kind of knowledge. Conscious awareness is a feature of a thinker's processing system, not of the knowledge itself. It is a mode of thought or a level of awareness at which information can be considered, worked over, altered, and/or applied to the task at hand. . . . Thinkers, it follows, can work at various levels of awareness—each of which has unique advantages and limitations. Let us consider some of these.

Tacit Processes. Some processes, including memory search, perception, complexly coordinated motor processes such as a tennis swing, and even some value judgments appear to be largely or completely tacit: The process of judgment, search, and so on is unavailable to introspection (Nisbett and Wilson) and resistant to conscious control. Much of the writer's language production process—Krashen's "acquired" knowledge of grammar, vocabulary, and acceptable locution—operates in this blessedly tacit manner. Native speakers, like the lilies of the field, can do many things for which they are required to take no thought.

Automated Processes. Some processes start life as conscious, attention-grabbing processes, but with experience they slowly drop out of awareness, and we say they have become automated. "Practice makes perfect" because it gradually transfers much of the task over to highly efficient, automated procedures. As the writer learns to "sound like Samuel Johnson," the process of writing long parallel constructions or maintaining a formal style consumes less and less of the limited space available in short-term memory (or conscious attention). However, if a sentence becomes too long, this automated "parallelism producer" may hit its limits and force this task to be shifted up to conscious attention or to be ignored. We would expect to see this sort of fluent production and limited conscious attention in the performance of anyone doing an easy or well-learned task. Ironically it may also characterize the level of awareness some inexperienced writers maintain even when the task is beyond their current well-learned skills. . . .

In general, automated processes are the rewards of learning—they let the writer learn to do more with less effort and less attention. However, most complex writing tasks cannot be managed at this level of attention, except by the easy but inefficient process of generate and test.

Active Awareness/Rhetorical Problem Solving. When a writer is engaged in fast, fluent production, her active awareness is occupied with content information and the language of her discourse. The act of composing is guided by automated processes. But if a problem arises or automated processes are unavailable, the work of writing is shifted to conscious attention. As the writer enters into active rhetorical problem solving her attention is no longer devoted solely to the generation of content, but becomes engaged in the process of drawing inferences, setting goals, making plans, analyzing the reader, simulating a reader's response, evaluating not only the text produced so far, but also the plans and goals that are in place, and diagnosing problems. And to complete the circle, the writer may go from the detection and diagnosis of a problem back to fresh planning. . . .

This shift to active awareness is itself a decision. For example, when the automated attempt to produce a complex parallel structure runs amok, the writer can either ignore the problem and accept whatever comes, initiate a series of generate and test efforts, or rise to active awareness. At this level she might notice that the text isn't working, maybe diagnose the problem as parallelism and isolate the offending words, or perhaps step back even further and wonder if the ideas themselves were logically parallel. If this were a major introductory sentence, this diagnosis might lead to a whole new episode of text-level planning.

Reflective Awareness.   This fleeting awareness is, of course, not always the case. Writers can also choose to rise to what we might call a reflective awareness or meta-knowledge of their own process. Even greater conscious attention is demanded as the writer tries to consider not only the task but herself performing the task.

Although active problem solving and reflective awareness of that problem solving are often discussed within the general notion of metacognition (Brown), I am drawing a distinction here in order to highlight the *thinker's own level of active awareness,* since highlighted awareness appears to be the fast lane of learning from experience. When writers take a reflective, "rise above it strategy" (Scardamalia and Bereiter, 1985), they may choose to categorize and evaluate the approach they are taking, or to evaluate and reflect upon their own behavior.

This level of knowing has an interesting status. Researchers such as Brown and Scardamalia and Bereiter (1986) have made a strong case for meta-knowledge as a skilled processing strategy, one that offers writers far more control and more options. Composition theorists associated with the "new rhetoric" and textbooks that reflect this perspective (Young; Young, Becker, and Pike; Hairston; Lauer, Montague, Lunsford, and Emig; Flower 1985) emphasize teaching not only heuristics for managing the writing process but a new degree of self-consciousness about using those methods. . . .

The limitations of working at the higher levels of active awareness are obvious: the writer's limited attention is momentarily diverted from the ultimate goal of generating content and is channeled into the less immediately "productive" process of thinking *about* the task and about the process of doing the task. On the other hand, taking thought may in the long run be the best or even the only way to solve some problems. Writers, we would argue, work at all of these levels of awareness, from fully tacit to highly reflective thought, and they do so because each level serves special purposes. Working at the lower levels of awareness is more efficient (when it is possible) and more productive in terms of generating topical content and language. Shifting to active awareness is a problem-solving procedure in which the difficulty of the problem seems to justify the use of this more expensive level of operation.

Works Cited

Brown, Ann L. "Metacognitive Development and Reading." *Theoretical Issues in Reading Comprehension.* Ed. Bertram Bruce, Rand Spiro and William Brewer. Hillsdale, NJ: Erlbaum, 1980.

Flower, Linda. *Problem-Solving Strategies in Writing.* 2nd ed. San Diego: Harcourt Brace Jovanovich, 1985.

Hairston, Maxine. *A Contemporary Rhetoric.* Boston: Houghton Mifflin, 1978.

Krashen, Stephen. "The Monitor Model for Second-Language Acquisition." *Second Language Acquisition and Foreign Language Learning.* Ed. Rosario Gingram. Washington, DC: Center for Applied Linguistics, 1981. 1–26.

Lauer, Janice, Gene Montague, Andrea Lunsford, and Janet Emig. *Four Worlds of Writing*. New York: Harper & Row, 1985.

Mandel, Barrett. "The Writer Is Not at Home." *College Composition and Communication* 31 (1980): 370–377.

Nisbett, Richard, and Timothy Wilson. "Telling More Than We Can Know: Verbal Reports on Mental Processes." *Psychological Review* 84 (1977): 231–259.

Odell, Lee, and Dixi Goswami. "Writing in a Non-Academic Setting." *New Directions in Composition Research*. Ed. Richard Beach and Lillian Bridwell. New York: Guilford, 1984. 233–258.

Scardamalia, Marlene, and Carl Bereiter. "Development of Dialectical Processes in Composition." *Literacy, Language, and Learning: The Nature and Consequences of Reading and Writing*. Ed. David Olson, Nancy Torrance, and Angela Hildyard. Cambridge: Cambridge University Press, 1985. 307–329.

———. "Composition." *Handbook of Research on Teaching*. Ed. M. Wittrock. New York: Macmillan, 1986.

Young, Richard, Alton Becker, and Kenneth Pike. *Rhetoric: Discovery and Change*. New York: Harcourt Brace Jovanovich, 1970.

Young, Richard E. "Arts, Crafts, Gifts, and Knacks: Some Disharmonies in the New Rhetoric." *Reinventing the Rhetorical Tradition*. Ed. Aviva Freedman and Ian Pringle. Conway, AR: L & S Books, 1980. 53–60.

Consensus Groups: A Basic Model of Classroom Collaboration

Kenneth A. Bruffee

One model of collaborative learning, although by no means the only one, is classroom consensus groups. In consensus groups people work collaboratively on a limited but open-ended task, negotiating among themselves what they think and know in order to arrive at some kind of consensus or agreement, including, sometimes, agreement to disagree. In organizing these groups, teachers typically do four things:

- They divide a large group—the class—into small groups.
- They provide a task, usually designed (and, preferably, tested) ahead of time, for the small groups to work on.
- They reconvene the larger group into plenary session to hear reports from the small groups and negotiate agreement among the group as a whole.
- They evaluate the quality of student work, first as referee, then as judge.

Organizing small consensus groups is not hard to do. But satisfactory results require college and university teachers to behave in their classrooms in ways that strike many who are used to traditional teaching as at best unusual. The nitty-gritty of this process of social organization can look trivial on the page. But it adds up to fairly sophisticated expertise that includes some familiarity with the research on "group dynamics," some forethought, some sensitivity to social situations and relationships, a somewhat better-than-average understanding of what is being taught, and self-control.

This chapter describes what happens in a typical consensus-group class and outlines some of the relevant research. It explains what goes into designing a good collaborative learning task. It explains how teachers draw a collaborative class back together to develop a consensus of the whole. And it explains how they evaluate students' individual contributions to the class's conversation through the students' writing.

A collaborative class using consensus groups goes something like this:

After explaining what's going to happen, the teacher divides students into groups of five or six. This usually means that the teacher acts a bit like a social director at a vacation resort or summer camp, counting students off, wading in to help them rearrange chairs, separating groups to minimize noise from other conversations, and encouraging group members to draw close enough together to hear one another over the din and to make the group more likely to cohere.

Then the teacher gives students a sheet with a task and instructions on it. An alternative is to pick out a passage of text as it appears in a book that all the students have at hand and write questions and instructions on the blackboard. (Later in this chapter I will explain what is distinctive about collaborative learning tasks and offer suggestions for designing them.)

Once students are settled in their groups, teachers ask them to introduce themselves (if necessary) and decide on a recorder, a member of the group who will take notes on the group's discussion and report on the consensus the group has reached when the work is over. As the small-group work starts, the teacher backs off. Emphatically, the teacher does not "sit in" on consensus groups, hover over them, or otherwise monitor them. Doing that inevitably destroys peer relations among students and encourages the tendency of well-schooled students to focus on the teacher's authority and interests.

If a teacher's goal is productive collaboration among peers, closely monitoring student small-group discussion is self-defeating. That is because the message that teachers deliver when they monitor student small-group discussion is a foundational message: that students should first and foremost be striving to use the language of the teacher's discipline, the teacher's own community of knowledgeable peers. This is a foundational message because it reinforces dependence on the teacher's authority and unquestioning reliance on the authority of what the teacher knows. Students fear that they will "get it wrong." Teachers fear that discussion will "get out of hand"—that is, go in some direction that the teacher has not anticipated and thereby cast doubt on the teacher's classroom authority and the authority of the teacher's knowledge.

While students are at work, the teacher's main responsibility is keeping time. Time is a nonrenewable natural resource. The teacher's job is to conserve it. The length of time that students spend on a task depends on the complexity of the task and on how accustomed students are to working together. Depending on how much time is available, the teacher sets a time limit for the work or simply asks each group at some point how much more time they think they will need. When most groups have completed the task, the teacher asks the recorder in each group to report and, acting as recorder for the class as a whole, writes out the results on the blackboard or asks the recorders to write their results on the board themselves. If most groups have been able to complete only part of the task, the task the teacher has assigned was too long or complex for the time available. Recorders report on the part the group has been able to complete and leave the rest for another time.

When the small-group work is finished, the teacher referees a plenary discussion in which the class as a whole analyzes, compares, and synthesizes the groups' decisions, negotiating toward an acceptable consensus. Here, the teacher serves as recorder for the class as a whole, not only writing out and revising the consensus as the discussion proceeds, but also pointing out gaps, inconsistencies, and incoherence. Finally (as we shall see later in this chapter), the teacher compares the class's consensus with the current consensus in the knowledge community that the teacher represents.

Throughout this process—group work toward local consensus plus reports, followed by plenary discussion toward plenary consensus—alert teachers will expect some awkwardness at first. During the small-group work, teachers and students alike may have to adjust to the noise produced by several excited conversations going on at once in the same room. Classroom noise is partly a matter of room size and sound-absorbing materials. Sensitivity to classroom noise is largely a matter of expectation. Teachers who normally think that students should sit quietly and take notes or speak only after they have raised their hands find that the din of conversation in a smoothly running collaborative classroom takes a lot of getting used to. Most college and university teachers and students have not experienced classes where active, articulate students are the norm. They decidedly are the norm within the protective security of collaborative consensus groups. With experience, some teachers even become so acutely sensitive to the register of sounds generated by consensus group conversation that they can tell by the tone of the din whether or not things are going well.

Teachers and students alike may also be disturbed at first by what they feel as the chaos of collaborative classes. This feeling of chaos is also a matter of expectation. . . . Classroom social interaction of the sort that goes on in collaborative learning is rare in the classrooms that most college and university teachers are used to. Traditional teaching places teachers at the center of the action and makes teachers the center of attention. Conversation goes on between the teacher and each individual student in the room. Traditional lecturers seem to be speaking to a socially coherent group of people. Actually they are speaking one to one, to an aggregate set of isolated individuals among whom there are no necessary social relations at all. Even when discussion among students in the class does occur, it tends to be a performance for the teacher's benefit, just as the teacher is performing for the students' benefit.

In place of this traditional pattern of one-to-one social relations, collaborative learning substitutes a pattern in which the primary focus of students' action and attention is each other. Teachers teach for the most part indirectly, through reorganizing students socially and designing appropriate tasks. Students converse among themselves with the teacher standing by on the sidelines, for the time being mostly ignored. Once consensus-group collaborative learning finally "takes" in a class, even when teachers lecture and conduct drills and recitations (as they almost inevitably must do once in a while), the negotiated understanding among the students changes the lecturer's position relative to the class. Teachers no longer lecture to a set of aggregated individuals. The fact that the students have become a transition community of people who know one another well means that whatever the teacher says takes its place in the context of an ongoing conversation among the students to which the teacher is not entirely privy. Empowered by their conversation, students are less likely to be wowed into passivity by whizbang lectures. They are more likely to question actively and synthesize what the teacher has to say.

So, both in organizing consensus groups and in lecturing to classes in which students have worked together collaboratively, teachers used to traditional classroom organization may at first feel that a collaborative learning class is desperately out of control—that is, out of the teacher's control. It may well be out of control if the collaboration is successful, but from the point of view of nonfoundational teaching it is comfortably and productively so. And the teacher's initial feeling of lost control tends to dissipate as students and teachers alike understand and accept the unaccustomed social structure of collaborative learning.

Much of the research on the negotiations that go on in collaborative learning consensus groups was done in the 1950s and 1960s, although in recent years there has been some resurgence in this research. Because to date most research has studied "decision-making groups" in businesses, government, and the military, some of it is only marginally related to college and university teaching. The relevant work is nevertheless important to collaborative learning, and awareness of it can be useful to teachers organizing consensus groups. It has mainly to do with group composition (effective group size relative to the type of task and the effects of heterogeneity and homogeneity), the quality of decisions made (number of options considered or variables accounted for), the phases of work through which groups pass in negotiating decisions (openings, transitions, endings; resistance to authority, internalization of authority), barriers to effective group decision making (authority-dependency problems, effects of reticent and dominating personalities), the nature of consensus, and the effects and fate of dissent.[1]

Studies suggest that the optimum size for decision-making groups (such as classroom consensus groups) is five. More than five will not change the social dynamics much but will dilute the experience, negligibly in groups of six but significantly in groups of seven and eight, and almost totally in groups of nine, ten, and more. Fewer than five in a group will change the dynamics in fairly obvious ways. Groups of four tend to subdivide into two pairs; groups of three tend to subdivide into a pair and an "other"; and groups of two (called "dyads") tend to sustain levels of stress sharply higher than those of any other group size. In contrast to consensus or decision-making groups, however, working groups (students doing research projects together for several days, weeks, or months, for example) seem to be most successful with three members. Long-term working groups larger than three often become logistically cumbersome.

Degree of heterogeneity or homogeneity is another issue in group composition. In general, heterogeneous decision-making groups work best because . . . differences tend to encourage the mutual challenging and cancellation of unshared biases and presuppositions that Abercrombie observed. Groups that are socially or ethnically too homogeneous (everyone from the same home town, neighborhood, family, or fraternity; close friends, teammates, clique members) tend to agree too soon, since they have an investment in maintaining the belief that their differences on basic issues are minimal. There is not enough articulated dissent or resistance to consensus to invigorate the conversation. Worse, homogeneous groups tend to find the differences that do arise difficult to endure and are quick to paper them over. On the other hand, members of decision-making groups that are too heterogeneous may have no basis for arriving at a consensus—or no means for doing so: they find that they cannot "come to terms" because they "don't speak the same language."

This inability to come to terms can be literally the case in some highly diverse student populations in which many people are struggling with English as a second language. Too much heterogeneity can also occur when the different languages in question are community dialects of standard English (ethnic, regional, or neighborhood) that students bring with them to class. But difficulty in coming to terms does not of course afflict only students. Lawyers, physicians, accountants, and members of the academic disciplines have "community dialects," too. For example, ask a group composed of otherwise cooperative, well-disposed faculty members from a half-dozen different disciplines (say, biology, art, mathematics, English literature, cultural anthropology, and history) to arrive at a consensus on the definition and proper use of the word "natural," and the only resulting agreement is likely to be an agreement to disagree.

Some of the most troublesome differences that teachers organizing consensus groups may encounter are ethnic differences, often masked by stereotyping (including self-stereotyping) or by superficial conformity. Difficulties arise because collaborative learning requires students to do things that their ethnic background may not have taught them to do or that it actively disposes them not to do.

Some ethnic groups (indeed, some families) accustom people to negotiating decisions that affect all members of the group. Students with this kind of background tend to be comfortable with collaborative learning and know how to go about it. In other ethnic groups (and families), decisions are made autocratically by one person or by a small in-group. Negotiation is unknown. Dissent is forbidden and punished. Students with this kind of background tend to feel uncomfortable in collaborative learning, don't know how to do it, and resist it.

In still other cases—typically among adolescents—the pressure to maintain the coherence of cliques or gangs can curtail participation in other relationships, such as working collaboratively in classroom consensus groups. Classroom collaboration on tasks that excite interest can threaten clique values and, by cutting across clique loyalties, weaken them.

On the average, most students take well to collaborative learning, but many still have something to learn about it. Many students working together in small groups go through a fairly predictable process of adaptation in which they relate to each other differently at different times during their collaboration. Studies of people working together tend to identify two such "phases of work," dependence and interdependence, and two "major events" that challenge people's preconceptions, one at the beginning of each phase.[2]

Each phase of work displays a characteristic source of disruptive stress. In the first phase, the source of stress is stereotyped attitudes toward authority that people bring with them into a group. *Authority* here refers to feelings about the way power is distributed in the group: who makes the decisions and how those decisions are enforced. The major event that precipitates an authority crisis in consensus groups is withdrawal of the acknowledged external authority. It may happen in collaborative learning, for example, if the teacher leaves the room.

The second source of stress comes into play in the second phase, as the group develops interdependence. It is the stereotyped attitudes toward intimacy that people bring with them into a group. *Intimacy* here means how people normally get along with their peers. The event that precipitates an intimacy crisis is being asked as peers to exercise authority with regard to one another. In collaborative learning, typically, it happens when the teacher asks students to evaluate one another's work.

Teachers organizing consensus groups have to keep all these variables in mind—degree of heterogeneity, group size, ethnic background, phases of work, and so on. When collaborative learning "just doesn't work," any number of forces may be in play. The first few times students work together at the beginning of a term the principal agenda may have to be, for some students, learning how to negotiate effectively. For others, it may be feeling comfortable negotiating at all. Sometimes, when teachers find that some students need to learn how to work together productively, they may have to teach them what they need to know through role playing or modeling. Very occasionally, teachers may have to suggest some basic rules for respecting others in conversation. Some students may have to be told explicitly not to interrupt when others are talking, to maintain dissent firmly but not obstreperously if they continue to believe in it, and to expect that negotiation and consensus building may involve compromise—giving up something you want in order to get something else you need or want more.

Students may also resist consensus group work or other kinds of collaborative learning simply because social engagement can be hard work. It calls upon a range of abilities that many college and university students may not yet have developed fully or refined: tact, responsive listening, willingness to compromise, and skill in negotiation. But it is usually a lot better for teachers to assume until they find out otherwise that their students have learned at least some rudimentary skills of the craft of interdependence and are socially mature enough to work together productively. Most college and university students, whatever their age and background, have had a lot more informal experience working collaboratively than most teachers give them credit for. Only when ethnic background, personal incompatibility, or social immaturity gets in the way of working on the task will it help for teachers to call attention to the process as opposed to the task. Even then, usually, the best way to do it is to turn the way the group is working together— the way people are helping or not helping get the task done—into a task like any other task for the group to work on collaboratively.

Partly because of the many variables involved in successful collaboration, many teachers find that, over time, changing the makeup of consensus groups from class hour to class hour tends to ease classroom tensions. Change in group makeup helps students enlarge their acquaintance, escape aversions and entrenched enmities, dissolve entrapment in cliques, and acquire new interests and abilities by working with a variety of student peers. In any case, the teacher's goal is to create a collaborative class as a whole, not an aggregate of loosely federated mini-classes coherent in themselves but unrelated to all the others.

On this issue of regularly changing the composition of consensus groups, as in the other practical matters, there is room for disagreement among teachers who have had experience with collaborative learning. Peter Hawkes argues, for example, that social coherence among students working in small groups may be time-consuming to achieve, and achieving it may be demanding and complex for the students involved. In that case, keeping students in the same small groups all term may be more efficient than mixing them up from class to class. A teacher's decision on this score may be in part a function of institutional conditions such as size, composition of the student body, whether students are in residence or commute, and so on. . . .

There is no foolproof method for devising consensus tasks. I have written plenty of tasks that I believed would work perfectly and wound up revising every one of them again and again. I have nevertheless found that the following set of principles, devised by Peter Hawkes, covers the basic issues in collaborative learning task design.[3]

1. **Head every worksheet with the same general instructions.** This eliminates the time groups may spend interpreting new directions. One heading that works well is this:

   Instructions.

   Once the groups have been formed, please introduce yourselves to each other. Then agree on one person to record the views expressed in the group, including both the decisions the group makes collaboratively and significant dissent. The recorder will speak for the group. For each question, decide on one answer that represents a consensus among the members of the group.

2. If the task asks students to discuss a written passage (a primary, secondary, or student-written text), in the first instruction following the general instructions **ask one member in each group to read the whole task aloud.** To encourage participation, the person reading the task aloud should not be the recorder.

3. Because arriving at a consensus can be time consuming, **make the material to be analyzed short.** A single short paragraph or even just a sentence or two is plenty—often more than enough—for a thirty- or forty-minute discussion.

4. For the same reason, **limit the number of questions that the task asks students to address.** In most cases one question is enough. More than two or three can be overwhelming.

5. **Make the questions short and simple.** Conversation leads students in most cases into as much profundity and complexity as they can handle and in some cases more than the teacher bargained for.

6. **Make the questions concrete and clearly expressed.** Otherwise, students are stymied and throw the questions back. That is, the task becomes figuring out the terms of the question and the teacher's intent, not dealing with the substantive issue.

7. **Sequence the questions within each task, and sequence tasks from class to class and week to week.** The general direction should be from low-involvement, nonthreatening questions and tasks to high-demand questions and tasks.

   For example, a task might begin by asking students to explain to one another their first impressions of a topic, problem, or text, or to survey how each student in the group would define key terms (that is, do some "polling"). Then it might ask an analytical question. Finally, the task might ask a broad question that requires students to synthesize the material and their answers in order to climb a few rungs on the abstraction ladder. A whole semester of tasks could be developed on this general sequence.

8. **Ask questions that have more than one answer.** Different responses ensure that recorders' reports do not become repetitive and will provide issues for debate. In a composition course, for example, "What's wrong with sentence five?" is less effective than "How would you improve the weakest sentence in this essay?" If the task is to analyze material drawn from a subject matter textbook, the questions should go beyond "What does it say?" to "What does it assume?"

9. In some tasks **ask controversial questions.** Some of these can be based on issues raised by prominent authorities in the field but not yet satisfactorily resolved. After the groups have made their decisions and the class has discussed them, the teacher can read aloud some of the published controversy for comparison and further discussion.

10. In some tasks **ask students to analyze short passages concretely.** These passages can be typed out or reproduced from the printed page, or the task can refer to a page in a book that everyone brings to class. Make the questions directing students' analysis pointed: ask about specific words and phrases, what they mean, their relation to other specific words and phrases, their significance in the whole passage, and so on.

11. **Whenever the task asks students to generalize, ask them to support their generalizations with particulars.** For example, if the task is to evaluate a student essay, also ask the groups to specify, say, three examples from the essay that support their opinion. If the

task is to discuss a substantive issue, don't just ask "What are the implications of the passage?" Ask "Where exactly—with which words—does the passage imply what you think it implies?"

Teachers have to be prepared for the fact that faulty tasks often provide an occasion for students to draw the teacher into the small-group discussion. Even under the best conditions and with the best-designed tasks, traditional dependence on a teacher's authority exerts a powerful undertow on students and teachers alike. It sometimes leads to "performance" questions—requests for information or clarification made in the belief that the student role demands it. These apparently innocent requests take the form of "What does X mean?" or "How are we supposed to do Y?" Teachers handle questions like these best by turning them back to the students to decide in group discussion what they think X means or how they think they should do Y, and then go on with the task.

For example, sometimes a task turns out to be ambiguous in a way that the teacher hadn't noticed or fails to supply a basic item of information. When that happens, in addition to apologizing, teachers can redirect students' appeal for help or information in several ways. One way is to ask if any group has found the necessary information, in the textbook or elsewhere, or has discovered a way to clarify the ambiguity or work around it. Another is to provide the whole class with the necessary information or clarification. A third is to ask the groups to stop discussing the question asked in the task and begin discussing instead how they would go about getting the information they need in order to answer the question, or how they would debug the task.

The payoff for teachers who turn questions back to consensus groups in this way is that the teacher is likely to get an unusually precise (and sometimes dismaying) estimate of just how much students really understand so far about the course material, in contrast to an estimate of the native student ability to parrot answers. This new awareness has been known to undermine college or university teachers' previously unquestioned belief in the imperative of "coverage," because it tends to explore the tacit but widely held notion that (as Elaine Mamion has aphoristically put it) "I know I've taught it, because I've heard myself say it." Asking students to question the task can sometimes also sow healthy, unanticipated doubts in the minds of the most self-confident college and university teachers about their own grasp of the subject matter and the universality of some of their discipline's least questioned, most authoritative truths.

The third responsibility taken on by teachers who organize consensus groups, or any other kind of collaborative learning, for that matter, is to evaluate the quality of students' work, both individual and collaborative. Teachers fulfill this responsibility in two ways, or rather, during two phases of the process: as referees while the work is going on and as judges after the work is over.

Every social relation that involves differences of opinion requires a referee. Someone has to represent, not the interests of one party or another, but the values and mores of the larger community that has a stake in the peaceable, profitable outcome of negotiations that go on in the subcommunities it encompasses. Even in sandlot baseball games, kids know the importance of nominating someone in the group to call strikes, balls, and outs. In jury trials, defense and prosecution lawyers represent the defendant and the state, respectively. The jury represents the local community of the defendant's peers. The judge referees, representing the legal system as a whole: the larger community that includes all of us who agree to live by the rule of law.

Consensus-group collaborative learning also needs a referee. Whenever small groups of students negotiate toward consensus, there are, within groups and among them, both resolvable differences of opinion and unresolvable dissent. When students disagree on the main point of a paragraph because they understand a key word differently, for example, they may be able to resolve their difference by resorting to a dictionary. But if two factions in the discussion disagree because they are making different assumptions, based, say, on ethnic, gender, or class differences, the disagreement may not be so easy to resolve. One faction may dissent from the consensus being forged by the other members of the group and refuse to be budged. In this case, the group agrees to disagree. That is its consensus. That agreement (and an account of what led to it) is what its recorder reports in the plenary session.

Throughout this stage of the process, teachers typically remain uninvolved in any direct way. Once the small-group work is over, however, teachers become more actively and directly involved, not by taking sides but as referees who organize and moderate a plenary discussion based on the reports delivered to the class as a whole by the groups' reporters. Whether or not they understand every aspect of their agreements and differences, most student consensus groups will be prepared, and usually eager, to maintain their position against different positions arrived at by other groups. The teacher's role in plenary discussion is to help the class synthesize reports of the groups' work and draft a synthesis that draws together major points in those reports, if possible helping to construct a consensus that represents the views of the whole class.

Here dissent becomes especially important. In collaborative learning, teachers should make it clear that dissent is welcome and actively encourage recorders to mention in their reports dissenting views that were expressed during the group's discussion. By a "dissenting view" I do not mean only a hard-line, entrenched position. I mean any opinion or view expressed by anyone in any group, anytime during the discussion, perhaps only in passing, perhaps incompletely formulated, that could not be completely assimilated into the group consensus.

Dissent is important in collaborative learning for at least two reasons. First, it may frequently happen that dissent in one group turns out to be the essence of another group's consensus. A split opinion within or between groups may be just what is needed to disrupt complacent or trivial decisions arrived at by the rest of the class. It can also happen, even more strikingly, that one lonely voice of dissent in a class can eventually, in the course of plenary discussion, turn the whole class around, leading it out of a quandary and toward a more satisfactory consensus of the whole or toward a more correct or acceptable view—that is, toward the view that is currently regarded as correct or acceptable by the teacher's disciplinary community.

Another reason for ferreting out dissent is that part of the point of collaborative learning is to teach the craft of interdependence to students who face a world in which diversity is increasingly evident, tenacious, and threatening. Plenary discussions may therefore explore the sources of dissent in ethnic, gender, class, and other "background" differences. Part of the lesson in that case, as John Trimbur has argued, is that understanding why people dissent can be as important to reaching accord as understanding the dissenting opinion itself.

In order to achieve a larger consensus of the class as a whole when the issue is divided, teachers direct student energies in the plenary discussion toward debating two (or more) sides of the issue. The debate ends when the differing parties arrive at a position that satisfies the whole class, or when they agree to disagree and understand the reasons for their disagreement. Occasionally, of course, a lone dissenter or small faction of dissenters will hold out against the class as a whole, taking a position that would not be regarded as correct or acceptable by the teacher's discipline. In that case, wise teachers trust the negotiating process over time either to bring the dissenters within the boundaries of what is currently regarded as acceptable, or (rarely, but also possible) to move the teacher's own and the discipline's current view of what is acceptable in the direction of the dissenters' position.

The teacher's role changes once again once the class reaches a plenary consensus—some sort of agreement that most members of the class as a whole can "live with," including perhaps, for some members, an agreement to disagree. At this stage in the process teachers act for the first time directly and overtly as representatives of the larger community they are members of and that their students hope to join. That community may be a disciplinary one, a community of mathematicians, historians, chemists, sociologists, or whatever, depending on the course and teacher's field of expertise. Or it may be the larger community of those who write, and who expect to read, standard written English organized in certain conventional ways. In speaking for the community at large at this stage of collaborative work, teachers are in the educationally fortunate position of not having to label the consensus formed by the class as merely right or wrong. Rather, the teacher's role is to tell the class whether or not its consensus corresponds to or differs from the prevailing consensus of the larger community.

If the class consensus is more or less the same as the consensus of the larger community, in most cases that's that. Next task. But if the consensus reached by the class differs from the consensus of the larger community in a significant way, then the issue becomes "Why?" To answer that question, teachers usually send the class back to small-group discussion. The task is to examine the process of consensus making itself. How did the class arrive at its consensus? How do the students suppose that the larger community arrived at a consensus so different from their own? In what ways do those two processes differ?

Here the teacher's job, although quite a bit different from the job of a baseball umpire, still looks a lot like the job of a judge in a court of law. Umpires do not explain their decisions to players. But judges often explain their decisions in terms of precedents: the existence of similar decisions in other cases, arrived at by other members of the judge's community of knowledgeable peers. That is, they show that their views are consistent with the views of the community they represent. When they do that, judges are acting a lot like college and university teachers who organize collaborative learning.

Teachers do not tell students what the "right" answer is in consensus-group collaborative learning, because the assumption is that no answer may be absolutely right. Every "right" answer represents a consensus for the time being of a certain community of knowledgeable peers: mathematicians, historians, chemists, sociologists, or whatever—or perhaps only some mathematicians, historians, chemists, sociologists, or whatever. The nature of the answer depends on the nature of the reasoning conversation that goes on in differently constituted communities. And the authority of the answer depends upon the size of the community that has constructed it and the community's credibility among other, related knowledge communities. Once the teacher has shown the class the relation between its own process of negotiation and the negotiations that go on in larger, professional communities, it is poised to take an important step beyond reliance upon external authority toward learning more about the process by which ideas, values, and standards are constructed, established, and maintained by communities of knowledgeable peers.

Comparing the class consensus with that of the larger community is one way to evaluate students' work. The other way is by judging the work that students do individually, based on their collaborative work. That is, teachers evaluate the degree to which students have internalized the language of the conversation that has gone on both in small-group discussion and in the plenary discussions. In this capacity, college and university teachers do not usually judge the quality of students' social behavior in class or how effectively they work with each other in collaborative groups, although (rarely) they may find it appropriate to do that. They evaluate the quality of students' contributions to the class's conversation in its displaced form, writing.

Writing enters the collaborative process at several points. In the first place, conversation in consensus groups prepares students to write better on the topic at hand by giving them an opportunity to rehearse and internalize appropriate language. Recorders write reports, and the groups they represent help edit them. Teachers can ask students to write their own essays or reports on the basis of consensus group conversation, or to revise what they have already written based on it. And . . . teachers can ask consensus groups to undertake tasks that increase students' ability to talk effectively with one another about writing itself and to help one another revise. As a result, after students have begun to acquire language appropriate to peer evaluation—that is, as they begin to learn how to talk effectively with one another about writing— teachers can ask students to begin writing peer reviews of one another's writing and then evaluate the helpfulness, incisiveness, and tact of their remarks.

But in the end, it is the writing that students produce individually as a result of this process that counts in evaluating them. It is with their writing, after all, that students apply for official membership in the communities—of chemists, lawyers, sociologists, classicists, whatever—that are larger, more inclusive and authoritative than any plenary classroom group, reaching well beyond the confines of any one college or university campus.

One reason for judging the quality of students' written contributions to the working conversation among peers is that, as agents of the institution, teachers must satisfy the college or university's grading requirements in order to maintain institutional records. A more important reason is that judging the quality of students' output helps students understand the responsibility they accept when they join a community of knowledgeable peers. The process fosters in students the responsibility to contribute to that community, to respect the community's values and standards, to help meet the needs of other members of the community, and to produce on time the work they have contracted to produce. When students join the community of those who write standard English organized in conventional ways, for example, they accept responsibility on terms agreed to by that community for the writing and reading that they do. They write so that others in the community can understand what they have written. And they read one another's work carefully enough so that if they were to report on what they have read, the writer would agree that that indeed was what was intended. . . .

Notes

1. For a more thorough survey of this research see "Developing a New Group Service: Strategies and Skills" in Gitterman and Shulman.
2. This and the next two paragraphs are loosely based on Bennis and Shepard.
3. Edited version republished by permission of Peter Hawkes.

Works Cited

Abercrombie, M. L. J. *The Anatomy of Judgment*. New York: Hutchinson, 1960.

Arons, Arnold B. *Guide to Introductory Physics Teaching*. New York: Wiley, 1990.

Bennis, Warren G., and Herbert A. Shepard. "A Theory of Group Development." *Human Relations* 9 (1956): 415–37.

Gitterman, Alex, and Lawrence Shulman, eds. *Mutual Aid Groups, Vulnerable Populations, and the Life Cycle*. New York: Columbia UP, 1993.

Hawkes, Peter. "Collaborative Learning and American Literature." *College Teaching* 39 (1991): 140–44.

Rorty, Richard. *Contingency, Irony, and Solidarity*. Cambridge: Cambridge UP, 1989.

Thomas, Lewis. *The Lives of a Cell: Notes of a Biology Watcher*. New York: Bantam, 1975.

Vygotsky, L. S. *Mind in Society: The Development of Higher Psychological Processes*. Ed. Michael Cole, et al. Cambridge: Harvard UP, 1978.

From Simple to Complex: Ideas of Order in Assignment Sequences

Elizabeth Rankin

Elizabeth Rankin directs the composition program at the University of North Dakota and edited the first edition of The Great American Bologna Festival and Other Student Essays *(St. Martin's, 1991). "From Simple to Complex: Ideas of Order in Assignment Sequences," which initially appeared in the* Journal of Advanced Composition *in 1990, suggests ways of designing a writing course.*

The professional literature on composition course design often stresses the importance of sequencing assignments. Some discussions directly address the subject, usually in the context of a general assemblage of advice for writing teachers. In others, it occurs as part of a rationale for a particular approach to teaching writing.

An example of the former is Richard Larson's advice in "Teaching Before We Judge: Planning Assignments in Composition":

> Think of a sequential program not merely as a chronological arrangement of assignments but as a structure in which assignments are closely related to each other in service of the goals of the program. . . . The goal of each assignment in a true sequence should be to enlarge the student's powers of thinking, organizing and expressing ideas so that he can cope with a more complex, more challenging problem in the next assignment. (212)

Although written nearly twenty years ago, Larson's advice is not dated. In fact, it is fairly consonant with the advice offered in these two recent texts for writing teachers:

> Effective writing assignments encourage students to define progressively more complex rhetorical problems. Since students learn to write by writing, our responsibility is to control and vary the rhetorical demands of writing tasks to give students practice in adjusting relationships among writer, reader, and subject, manipulating more and more complex variables. (Lindemann 205)

> The backbone of an effective writing course . . . must be a carefully planned sequence of tasks set in gradually broader and more complex contexts. (Foster 124)

In all three passages, the explicit expectation is that sequenced assignments will be arranged in order of increasing *complexity.*

Numerous assignment sequences described by teachers and course designers reiterate this notion. Roger Garrison includes in the final chapter of *How a Writer Works* a list of "writing tasks," and although he insists that these tasks do not constitute a particular sequence, Garrison nevertheless entitles his chapter, "Writing Tasks: From Simple to Complex." In a recent article in *College Composition and Communication,* Malcolm Kiniry and Elaine Strenski describe the academic writing course initiated by Mike Rose at UCLA. The course attempts

> to structure writing tasks recursively, so that even as students move on to more *complex* tasks, they find themselves increasingly capable of turning back profitably to those expository strategies they already have begun to master. (192; emphasis added)

And in his introduction to a collection of courses designed at the 1979–80 NEH/Iowa Institute, Carl Klaus explains,

> These courses typically move through progressively more *complex* perceptual, conceptual, or rhetorical re-engagements with a topic, problem, or activity implicit in the initial assignment. (xviii; emphasis added)

I could offer many more examples: David Bartholomae's reading and writing course, which moves toward "that *complex* negotiation where a writer or reader uses the work of others . . . to enable work that he can present as his own" (37); Marilyn Katz's expository writing sequence, which works toward "the *complex* academic paper, our final goal" (291; emphasis added); James Kinneavy's text on *Writing in the Liberal Arts Tradition,* in which "all the major sections of the book . . . develop from the simplest to the most *complex* and difficult" (xv; emphasis added). These are only a few.

What is interesting about these examples is their great variety. All of these compositionists agree that a structured sequence of writing assignments is preferable to a random arrangement. All agree that the sequence should move in the direction of greater complexity. The problem, however, is in defining *complexity.* In the examples just cited, the implicit definitions of *complexity,* while perhaps not wholly contradictory, are different enough to raise questions about what we really mean when we order writing tasks "from simple to complex."

Although much has been written on the subject of assignment design, few attempts have been made to compare or classify kinds of assignment sequences. Lynn Diane Beene surveys a few sequence designs in her bibliographical essay on assignment making, and Kenneth Dowst attempts a rough classification in his discussion of the epistemic approach to teaching writing, but only David Foster addresses the issue directly. In his review of the ways teachers might organize an effective writing course, Foster argues that the basis of such a course "is a series of purposeful writing tasks. This series can be organized in several ways: for example by means of the writer's logical processes or in terms of a sequence of topics or as a sequence of different rhetorical situations" (124). Foster's classification, informal and incomplete as it is, helps us see some broad distinctions between kinds of sequences and notions of complexity. But these distinctions are *too* broad, creating odd, eclectic groupings that confuse as much as clarify. For instance, Foster places in the "logical processes" category sequences as diverse as Kinneavy's traditional modal arrangement; Ann Berthoff's "assisted invitations" in forming, thinking, and writing; and Katz's personal-academic analysis sequence. In the "topics" category, he includes not only variations on the typical writing-about-literature course but also William Coles' inventive "epistemic" theme courses. If we are to truly understand the various meanings of *complexity,* we must make some finer distinctions than these casual categories allow.

In the pages that follow, I will outline a set of terms we might use to make such distinctions. As I do so, I will show how those terms allow us to understand the logic of various sequences, to compare and contrast related sequences, and ultimately to evaluate the concept of assignment sequence itself.

TYPES OF ASSIGNMENT SEQUENCES

The first major distinction is between hierarchical and non-hierarchical assignment sequences. A non-hierarchical sequence is one in which the first assignments are not regarded as *prior to* but simply *other than* those that follow. Although most assignment sequences (including those that presume to move "from simple to complex") are hierarchical, a significant proportion qualify as non-hierarchical, and examples of these can be found in all three of Foster's categories. For instance, certain writing-across-the-curriculum sequences in which the order of writing assignments follows the thematic content of the course may be said to be non-hierarchical. Likewise, case approaches whose aim is to provide the writer with a variety of rhetorical situations may be non-hierarchical. Even logical process sequences may fall into this category on occasion: "patterns of exposition" sequences, for example, in which the range and variety of patterns tend to be more important than their order.

Most assignment sequences, however, are explicitly hierarchical, based on various principles of subordination. We might call one such principle *formal primacy,* in which certain forms of writing are regarded as basic or fundamental to others. An example of such a sequence would be the traditional sentence-paragraph-theme approach that formed the basis of so many "current traditional" texts in the 1950s and early 1960s. Although largely discredited by process practices in composition instruction, this atomistic sequence, as it is called by its detractors, has a powerful small-to-large, part-to-whole logic that reflects two of Aristotle's topoi. Perhaps for that reason, it is still in evidence today, most notably in some basic writing courses and in research paper sequences that progress from one-paragraph summaries to short "synthesis" assignments and then to a long "research paper."

Other hierarchical sequences are based not on notions of formal primacy but on theories of mind or cognitive development. The traditional modal sequence is a case in point. As Robert Connors and others have shown, the original modes—narration, description, exposition, and argument—were connected to outdated theories of faculty psychology adhered to by their inventor, Alexander Bain, and his contemporaries. Modern rhetorical theorists, notably Frank D'Angelo and Kinneavy, have offered more sophisticated rationales for similar sequences. This theoretical backing, combined with the considerable weight of tradition, helps account for the great popularity of the modes and other patterns of exposition sequences, even today.

Closely related to the various modal sequences, and almost as widely employed, are the developmental sequences. Based on the theories of Jean Piaget, Jerome Bruner, and other cognitive psychologists, developmental sequences purport to follow a natural learning order, usually beginning in egocentric, subjective experience and moving outward toward integration with "other," the world outside the self. Although existent in some forms long before they acquired any sophisticated psychological rationale (Connors, "Personal"), developmental writing sequences came into their own in the 1960s, in direct response to the theories of James Britton and James Moffett. Though Britton and Moffett themselves were careful not to suggest that assignment sequences be based on their theories (Britton 198; Moffett 54), curriculum planners and textbook writers have in fact cited their work as the rationale for sequences moving from "expressive" to "transactional" writing, from familiar to more abstract writer/audience/subject relationships.

Consider, for example, Stephen Judy's "experiential approach," described in *Eight Approaches to Teaching Composition*. Judy says his course follows "the inner worlds to outer worlds pattern that one finds described in the works of Piaget, Creber, Moffett, and others." He describes this pattern and argues, "The inner worlds/outer worlds pattern, valid as it is for human growth in a broad sense, works nicely for individual writing courses as well" (49–50). Ken Macrorie's research sequence in *Searching Writing* is another that is clearly based on developmental assumptions. And well-known "theory based" texts like Axelrod and Cooper's *St. Martin's Guide to Writing* frankly acknowledge a developmental bias in their organization of writing tasks (*Instructor's Manual* 3).

PRINCIPLES OF ORDER

Just as hierarchical assignment sequences have different principles of subordination, they can also have different principles of order. The major difference here is between assignments that follow in serial order and those that are cumulative. The serial arrangement, probably the more common, involves a number of separate, discrete assignments, each of which is regarded as an independent writing occasion. The typical modal or pattern sequence falls into this category, as do thematic sequences in which writers respond to a succession of different readings or groups of readings. Casebook approaches in which each new assignment is a response to a new, "more complex" rhetorical situation are also ordered serially.

In contrast, a cumulative sequence is one in which the later assignments "grow out of" or subsume earlier ones. One example is the research sequence in which students begin by writing summaries and syntheses of source materials which are eventually incorporated into a larger research paper at the end of a course. Unlike a serial research sequence, in which early assignments are viewed as practice for later ones, this cumulative sequence has a kind of organic structure. In a formalist course, it grows into a traditional research paper; in a developmental sequence, it might produce Macrorie's "I-Search" report.

Another example of a cumulative sequence may be seen in the expository writing program designed by Rose and his colleagues at UCLA. This program, "drawing on research in educational and cognitive psychology," involves a "master sequence" of eight kinds of writing activities frequently found in academic writing assignments. Each kind of writing (listing, definition, seriation, and so on) involves a subsequence of "discrete problem-solving exercises of gradually increasing difficulty" which "recapitulate and anticipate" the order of the whole. The sequence is designed to be "recursive" in the sense that it moves "not only forwards but circularly backwards, reinforcing and recouping . . . previous gains as [students] call upon the earlier writing strategies in service of the later ones" (Kiniry and Strenski 195). Perhaps the most well-known cumulative courses are those organized around particular topics or themes. Coles' courses, as described in *The Plural I, What Makes Writing Good,* and elsewhere, are cumulative, as are Dowst's "epistemic" approach, Klaus's "courses for change in writing," and Bartholomae's college reading and writing courses, outlined in *Facts, Artifacts and Counterfacts*. Like the UCLA course described by Kiniry and Strenski, these thematic sequences have a recursive, organic structure:

> In an initial assignment, the students address a certain issue related to the general theme of the sequence. . . . A subsequent assignment provides enough data and questions to complicate the issue in various ways, so that the students must reformulate their positions. Later assignments introduce new data, new questions, new perspectives. (Dowst 78)

While the UCLA sequence is based on "generalized cognitive models," the courses of Coles, Dowst, Klaus, and Bartholomae share a different set of theoretical assumptions—assumptions having to do with the nature of language and reality. Dowst explains some of these assumptions in "The Epistemic Approach: Writing, Knowing, and Learning." Citing the philosophy of John Dewey and Bruner as fundamental to this approach, Dowst says,

> Education . . . involves more than increasing the number of data that direct or vicarious experience leads one to know. No less importantly, education involves composing language to connect one datum with another, one experience with another. This establishes patterns by which one can make sense of known data and in terms of which one can discover new data as well. A typical epistemic writing assignment assumes with Dewey that all "teaching and learning [is] a continuous process of reconstruction of experience" . . . It directs students to follow the experience of composing with some "reflective review and summarizing" of what they have been doing. (75)

Because the relationship between assignments in an epistemic sequence is so crucial and sometimes hard to articulate, course designers often rely on metaphor to explain the connection. Here is Dowst describing his own assignment sequence in terms of a spiral: "In an epistemic course, an assignment is part of a sequence of assignments that spiral around a central idea, progressing from relative simplicity to relative complexity of thought and expression" (78). Claus offers a musical analogy: "Thus each of these courses proceeds according to an organizational strategy somewhat like the musical form of theme and variation" (xviii). Coles speaks of his sequence as creating "dialogues" or "conversations" between students and teacher (Coles and Vopat 2; *Plural I* 4, 13). And Bartholomae, quoting Steiner and Said, says his allows students to "translate" themselves in the act of "inventing a discipline" (7–9).

The difference between a simple cumulative sequence and an epistemic one, then, is this: in the former, the writer uses language to synthesize knowledge—often the knowledge of others, which he comes to "make his own"; in the latter, the writer uses language to *construct* knowledge and, in the process, a way of knowing. Although usually associated with thematic sequences such as those mentioned here, the term *epistemic* can also be applied to logical process sequences, such as Berthoff's "assisted invitations" in *Forming/Thinking/Writing*.

Thus, there are several ways to categorize and differentiate writing assignment sequences. They may be non-hierarchical or hierarchical; based on formal, cognitive/developmental, or epistemic principles. They may center on themes, logical processes, or rhetorical situations, and they may be ordered serially or cumulatively. No doubt there are other useful distinctions we could make as well, but my aim is not to exhaust the possibilities. Rather, I'm interested in exploring what is meant when different sequences are described as moving "from simple to complex," and for that purpose, these terms will suffice.

DETECTING CONFLICTING ASSUMPTIONS

Not only do these terms clarify what different people mean when they use the ambiguous phrase "from simple to complex," but they enable us to see the conflicting theoretical assumptions between (and sometimes within) related sequence designs. For instance, consider the sequences Foster lists in his "thematic" category. At one end of the thematic spectrum are those traditional sequences based on readings in literature or essay anthologies. In purest form, these sequences are non-hierarchical, following no particular logic of their own but simply reflecting the arrangement of the readings themselves. In the middle of the spectrum are conventional "topic" courses which might be overlaid with formalist or logical process sequences—or possibly with both. (Philip Snyder's "Working 1-002: A Theme Course for Freshman Composition" is a good example of the latter.) At the far end of the spectrum are the epistemic sequences of Coles, Dowst, Klaus, and Bartholomae. Based on developmental principles and rooted in dialectic, these courses could not be less like the conventional thematic sequence.

To see how the terms I've proposed help detect conflicting assumptions *within* sequences, examine a course described by Katz in "From Self-Analysis to Academic Analysis: An Approach to Expository Writing." As the title suggests, the primary order of Katz's sequence seems to be developmental. "Since college students, in particular," she says, "are interested in understanding their own experience, self-analysis seems a logical place to begin to teach them about the process of abstract thinking and its relationship to writing" (289). Katz then "overlays" the primary sequence with a second hierarchy of formal skills that includes constructing a thesis and writing topic sentences. So far, no inconsistency. The conflict comes when Katz introduces a third organizing principle, the epistemic concept of "discovery":

> In this course, students move from close analysis of aspects of their personal experience to analysis of academic material. They discover for themselves those thought processes which underlie the rules of paper organization we teach in expository writing courses. (288)

Now it's true that Katz herself never uses the term "epistemic," nor explicitly attempts to align herself with that theoretical approach. Nevertheless, it is the claim to "discovery" that sets her approach apart from numerous other sequences that integrate developmental and formalist principles. Implicitly, she is promoting a dialectic in which students "discover for themselves" the knowledge they need as writers. But something rings false in this declaration. To see what it is, we need only read what Coles says on the subject of discovery. The object of a true epistemic sequence, says Coles, is

> to keep things open, to pursue an idea in such a way as to allow a student to have ideas of his own, to find himself in the act of expression, to become conscious of himself as becoming through the use of language or languages. No set of assignments which fails to pursue an idea can allow for these possibilities. No set of assignments which closes an idea, which has a "point" to get, or moves to a predetermined conclusion, can allow for them either. ("Teaching of Writing" 32)

When Katz asks students to "discover for themselves" a set of "rules" that the teacher knows in advance, she is violating the principles of the epistemic approach.

It is important to note that there is no *necessary* contradiction between the formalist sequence and the epistemic approach. Conceived broadly, as in Bartholomae's or Berthoff's courses, formal skills are perfectly compatible with an epistemic sequence. Students discover not formal "rules," like use of "the topic sentence," but the concept of form itself. The problem in Katz's scheme is that she defines formal skills too narrowly. The whole course is based on a hidden agenda incompatible with the notion of true "discovery" and thus undercuts its own credibility.

SOME CAUTIONS

The terms I've proposed here also enable us to evaluate certain trends or developments in assignment sequence design. The post-Dartmouth Conference interest in personal, expressive writing resulted in more developmental approaches. The "back-to-basics" movements of the early 1970s spawned a new generation of formalist sequences. And now, the epistemic rhetoric of the 1980s, along with the writing-across-the-curriculum movement and a heightened awareness of the social contexts of discourse, has sparked interest in new and (dare I say?) more complex kinds of assignment sequences.

As usual, these sequences have been slow to make their way into textbooks—except in such idiosyncratic texts as Coles', Berthoff's and Bartholomae's. But rationales for such sequences are becoming more and more prominent in the professional literature. Rich in intellectual content and based on post-structuralist theory that has elucidated our understanding of how language works, such rationales are emerging in journal articles, in professional publications, and on conference programs. Before long, I suspect, they will be evident in "mainstream" texts as well. But before they do, I would like to offer a caution.

In our eagerness to implement the principles of this newest "new rhetoric," let us remember what those principles are. An assignment sequence that "works" (whatever that means) works not because of some inherent logic. To believe in a "true" and "natural" sequence is to contradict the very principles of dialectic and social construction on which these new courses are built. It is also to ignore a long history of *successes* in the writing classroom—a history too often obscured by our young profession's need to repudiate its beknighted elders.

At the same time, to imagine that we can be free of sequence is equally illusory. Those who lay claim to such freedom, by making no assignments at all, are only buying into the notion that student-generated writing occasions are somehow more "natural" than teacher-initiated ones—as if one could ignore all the social constraints imposed by the classroom environment.

Ultimately, we cannot allow our rage for order—in our classrooms, in our profession, in our lives—to seduce us into thinking that any order is sacrosanct. The notion of sequence, like our various notions of simple and complex, is itself a social construct. It is a way of asserting order in the midst of chaos, a means by which we assure ourselves and our students that we are making "progress." To put it simply, an assignment sequence is a necessary fiction.

Works Cited

Axelrod, Rise B., and Charles R. Cooper. *Instructor's Resource Manual for The St. Martin's Guide to Writing*. New York: St. Martin's P, 1985.

Bartholomae, David, and Anthony R. Petrosky. *Facts, Artifacts, and Counterfacts: Theory and Method for a Reading and Writing Course*. Upper Montclair, NJ: Boynton, 1986.

Beene, Lynn Diane. "Assignment Making." *Research in Composition and Rhetoric: A Bibliographical Sourcebook*. Ed. Michael G. Moran and Ronald F. Lunsford. Westport, CT: Greenwood P, 1984, 239–62.

Berthoff, Ann E. *Forming/Thinking/Writing: The Composing Imagination*. Portsmouth, NH: Boynton, 1982.

Britton, James, et al. *The Development of Writing Abilities (11–18)*. London: Macmillan Education, 1975.

Coles, William E., Jr. *The Plural I—and After*. Portsmouth, NH: Boynton, 1988.

———. "The Teaching of Writing as Writing." *College English* 29 (1967): 111–16.

Coles, William E., Jr., and James Vopat. *What Makes Writing Good: A Perspective*. Lexington, MA: D.C. Heath, 1985.

Connors, Robert J. "Personal Writing Assignments." *College Composition and Communication* 38 (1987): 166–83.

———. "The Rise and Fall of the Modes of Discourse." *College Composition and Communication* 32 (1981): 444–55.

D'Angelo, Frank J. *A Conceptual Theory of Rhetoric*. Cambridge, MA: Winthrop, 1975.

Dowst, Kenneth. "The Epistemic Approach: Writing, Knowing, and Learning." *Eight Approaches to Teaching Composition*. Ed. Timothy R. Donovan, and Ben W. McClelland. Urbana: NCTE, 1980. 65–85.

Foster, David. *A Primer for Writing Teachers: Theorists, Issues, Problems*. Upper Montclair, NJ: Boynton, 1983.

Garrison, Roger. *How a Writer Works*. Rev. ed. New York: Harper, 1985.

Judy, Stephen. "The Experimental Approach: Inner Worlds to Outer Worlds." *Eight Approaches to Teaching Composition*. Ed. Timothy R. Donovan and Ben W. McClelland. Urbana: NCTE, 1980. 37–51.

Katz, Marilyn. "From Self-Analysis to Academic Analysis: An Approach to Expository Writing." *College English* 40 (1978): 288–92.

Kiniry, Malcolm, and Ellen Strenski. "Sequencing Expository Writing: A Recursive Approach." *College Composition and Communication* 36 (1985): 191–202.

Kinneavy, James L. *A Theory of Discourse*. 1971. New York: Norton, 1980.

Kinneavy, James L., William McCleary, and Neil Nakadate. *Writing in the Liberal Arts Tradition*. New York: Harper, 1985.

Klaus, Carl H., and Nancy Jones, eds. *Courses for Change in Writing: A Selection from the NEH/Iowa Institute*. Upper Montclair, NJ: Boynton, 1984.

Larson, Richard L. "Teaching Before We Judge: Planning Assignments in Composition." *The Writing Teacher's Sourcebook*. Ed. Gary Tate and Edward P. J. Corbett. New York: Oxford UP, 1981. 208–19.

Lindemann, Erika. *A Rhetoric for Writing Teachers*. New York: Oxford UP, 1982.

Macrorie, Ken. *Searching Writing*. Rochelle Park, NJ: Hayden, 1980.

Moffett, James. *Teaching the Universe of Discourse*. Boston: Houghton, 1968.

Snyder, Philip. "Working 1-002: A Theme Course for Freshman Composition." *College Composition and Communication* 33 (1982): 315–17.

Responding to Student Writing

Nancy Sommers

Nancy Sommers is associate director of the expository writing program at Harvard University. In "Responding to Student Writing," which was originally published in College Composition and Communication *(May 1982), she reports what she learned studying composition instructors' comments on students' papers. Her findings have special import for those of us who teach writing as a process.*

More than any other enterprise in the teaching of writing, responding to and commenting on student writing consumes the largest proportion of our time. Most teachers estimate that it takes them at least 20 to 40 minutes to comment on an individual student paper, and those 20 to 40 minutes times 20 students per class, times 8 papers, more or less, during the course of a semester add up to an enormous amount of time. With so much time and energy directed to a single activity, it is important for us to understand the nature of the enterprise. For it seems, paradoxically enough, that although commenting on student writing is the most widely used method for responding to student writing, it is the least understood. We do not know in any definitive way what constitutes thoughtful commentary or what effect, if any, our comments have on helping our students become more effective writers.

Theoretically, at least, we know that we comment on our students' writing for the same reasons professional editors comment on the work of professional writers or for the same reasons we ask our colleagues to read and respond to our own writing. As writers we need and want thoughtful commentary to show us when we have communicated our ideas and when not, raising questions from a reader's point of view that may not have occurred to us as writers. We want to know if our writing has communicated our intended meaning and, if not, what questions or discrepancies our reader sees that we, as writers, are blind to.

In commenting on our students' writing, however, we have an additional pedagogical purpose. As teachers, we know that most students find it difficult to imagine a reader's response in advance, and to use such responses as a guide in composing. Thus, we comment on student writing to dramatize the presence of a reader, to help our students to become that questioning reader themselves, because, ultimately, we believe that becoming such a reader will help them to evaluate what they have written and develop control over their writing.[1]

Even more specifically, however, we comment on student writing because we believe that it is necessary for us to offer assistance to student writers when they are in the process of composing a text, rather than after the text has been completed. Comments create the motive for doing something different in the next draft; thoughtful comments create the motive for revising. Without comments from their teachers or from their peers, student writers will revise in a consistently narrow and predictable way. Without comments from readers, students assume that their writing has communicated their meaning and perceive no need for revising the substance of their text.[2]

Yet as much as we as informed professionals believe in the soundness of this approach to responding to student writing, we also realize that we don't know how our theory squares with teachers' actual practice—do teachers comment and students revise as the theory predicts they should? For the past year my colleagues, Lil Brannon, Cyril Knoblauch, and I have been researching this problem, attempting to discover not only what messages teachers give their students through their comments, but also what determines which of these comments the students choose to use or to ignore when revising. Our research has been entirely focused on comments teachers write to motivate revisions. We have studied the commenting styles of thirty-five teachers at New York University and the University of Oklahoma, studying the comments these teachers wrote on first and second drafts, and interviewing a representative number of these teachers and their students. All teachers also commented on the same set of three student essays. As an additional reference point, one of the student essays was typed into the computer that had been programmed with the "Writer's Workbench," a package of twenty-three programs developed by Bell Laboratories to help computers and writers work together to improve a text rapidly. Within a few minutes, the computer delivered editorial comments on the student's text, identifying all spelling and punctuation errors, isolating problems with wordy or misused phrases, and suggesting alternatives, offering a stylistic analysis of sentence types, sentence beginnings, and sentence lengths, and finally, giving our freshman essay a Kincaid readability score of 8th grade which, as the computer program informed us, "is a low score for this type of document." The sharp contrast between the teachers' comments and those of the computer highlighted how arbitrary and idiosyncratic most of our teachers' comments are. Besides, the calm, reasonable language of the computer provided quite a contrast to the hostility and mean-spiritedness of most of the teachers' comments.

The first finding from our research on styles of commenting is that *teachers' comments can take students' attention away from their own purposes in writing a particular text and focus that attention on the teachers' purpose in commenting.* The teacher appropriates the text from the student by confusing the student's purpose in writing the text with her own purpose in commenting. Students make the changes the teacher wants rather than those that the student perceives are necessary, since the teachers' concerns imposed on the text create the reasons for the subsequent changes. We have all heard our perplexed students say to us when confused by our comments: "I don't understand how you want me to change this" or "Tell me what you want me to do." In the beginning of the process there was the writer, her words, and her desire to communicate her ideas. But after the comments of the teacher are imposed on the first or second draft, the student's attention dramatically shifts from "This is what I want to say," to "This is what you the teacher are asking me to do."

This appropriation of the text by the teacher happens particularly when teachers identify errors in usage, diction, and style in a first draft and ask students to correct these errors when they revise; such comments give the student an impression of the importance of these errors that is all out of proportion to how they should view these errors at this point in the process. The comments create the concern that these "accidents of discourse" need to be attended to before the meaning of the text is attended to.

It would not be so bad if students were only commanded to correct errors, but, more often than not, students are given contradictory messages; they are commanded to edit a sentence to avoid an error or to condense a sentence to achieve greater brevity of style, and then told in the margins that the particular paragraph needs to be more specific or to be developed more. An example of this problem can be seen in the . . . student paragraph [on page 319].

In commenting on this draft, the teacher has shown the student how to edit the sentences, but then commands the student to expand the paragraph in order to make it more interesting to a reader. The interlinear comments and the marginal comments represent two separate tasks for this student; the interlinear comments encourage the student to see the text as a fixed piece, frozen in time, that just needs some editing. The marginal comments, however, suggest that the meaning of the text is not fixed, but rather that the student still needs to develop the meaning by doing some more research. Students are commanded to edit and develop at the same time; the remarkable contradiction of developing a paragraph after editing the sentences in it represents the

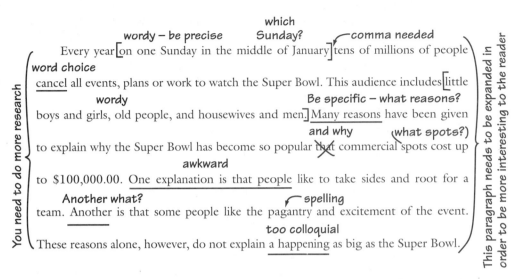

confusion we encountered in our teachers' commenting styles. These different signals given to students, to edit and develop, to condense and elaborate, represent also the failure of teachers' comments to direct genuine revision of the text as a whole.

Moreover, the comments are worded in such a way that it is difficult for students to know what is the most important problem in the text and what problems are of lesser importance. No scale of concerns is offered to a student, with the result that a comment about spelling or a comment about an awkward sentence is given weight equal to a comment about organization or logic. The comment that seemed to represent this problem best was one teacher's command to his student: "Check your commas and semi-colons and think more about what you are thinking about." The language of the comments makes it difficult for a student to sort out and decide what is most important and what is least important.

When the teacher appropriates the text for the student in this way, students are encouraged to see their writing as a series of parts—words, sentences, paragraphs—and not as a whole discourse. The comments encourage students to believe that their first drafts are finished drafts, not invention drafts, and that all they need to do is patch and polish their writing. That is, teachers' comments do not provide their students with an inherent reason for revising the structure and meaning of their texts, since the comments suggest to students that the meaning of their text is already there, finished, produced, and all that is necessary is a better word or phrase. The processes of revising, editing, and proofreading are collapsed and reduced to a single trivial activity, and the students' misunderstanding of the revision process as a rewording activity is reinforced by their teachers' comments.

It is possible, and it quite often happens, that students follow every comment and fix their texts appropriately as requested, but their texts are not improved substantially, or, even worse, their revised drafts are inferior to their previous drafts. Since the teachers' comments take the students' attention away from their own original purposes, students concentrate more, as I have noted, on what the teachers commanded them to do than on what they are trying to say. Sometimes students do not understand the purpose behind their teachers' comments and take these comments very literally. At other times students understand the comments, but the teacher has misread the text and the comments, unfortunately, are not applicable. For instance, we repeatedly saw comments in which teachers commanded students to reduce and condense what was written, when in fact what the text really needed at this stage was to be expanded in conception and scope.

The process of revising always involves a risk. But, too often revision becomes a balancing act for students in which they make the changes that are requested but do not take the risk of changing anything that was not commented on, even if the students sense that other changes are needed. A more effective text does not often evolve from such changes alone, yet the student does not want to take the chance of reducing a finished, albeit inadequate, paragraph to chaos— to fragments—in order to rebuild it, if such changes have not been requested by the teacher.

The second finding from our study is that *most teachers' comments are not text-specific and could be interchanged, rubber-stamped, from text to text*. The comments are not anchored in the particulars of the students' texts, but rather are a series of vague directives that are not text-specific. Students are commanded to "Think more about [their] audience, avoid colloquial language, avoid the passive, avoid prepositions at the end of sentences or conjunctions at the beginning of sentences, be clear, be specific, be precise, but above all, think more about what [they] are thinking about." The comments on the following student paragraph illustrate this problem:

Begin by telling your reader what you are going to write about.

In the sixties it was drugs, in the seventies it was rock and roll. Now in the

avoid "one of the"

eighties, one of the most controversial subjects is nuclear power. The United States

elaborate

is in great need of its own source of power. Because of environmentalists, coal is not

be specific

an acceptable source of energy. [Solar and wind power have not yet received the

Avoid "it seems"

technology necessary to use them.] It seems that nuclear power is the only feasible

means right now for obtaining self-sufficient power. However, too large a

be precise

percentage of the population are against nuclear power claiming it is unsafe. With as

be precise

many problems as the United States is having concerning energy, it seems a shame

that the public is so quick to "can" a very feasible means of power. Nuclear energy

should not be given up on, but rather, more nuclear plants should be built.

Thesis sentence needed

Think more about your reader.

One could easily remove all the comments from this paragraph and rubber-stamp them on another student text, and they would make as much or as little sense on the second text as they do here.

We have observed an overwhelming similarity in the generalities and abstract commands given to students. There seems to be among teachers an accepted, albeit unwritten canon for commenting on student texts. This uniform code of commands, requests, and pleadings demonstrates that the teacher holds a license for vagueness while the student is commanded to be specific. The students we interviewed admitted to having great difficulty with these vague directives. The students stated that when a teacher writes in the margins or as an end comment, "choose precise language" or "think more about your audience," revising becomes a guessing game. In effect, the teacher is saying to the student, "Somewhere in this paper is imprecise language or lack of awareness of an audience and you must find it." The problem presented by these vague commands is compounded for the students when they are not offered any strategies for carrying out these commands. Students are told that they have done something wrong and that there is something in their text that needs to be fixed before the text is acceptable. But to tell students that they have done something wrong is not to tell them what to do about it. In order to offer a useful revision strategy to a student, the teacher must anchor that strategy in the specifics of the student's text. For instance, to tell our student, the author of the above paragraph, "to be specific," or "to elaborate," does not show our student what questions the reader has about the meaning of the text, or what breaks in logic exist, that could be resolved if the writer supplied specific information; nor is the student shown how to achieve the desired specificity.

Instead of offering strategies, the teachers offer what is interpreted by students as rules for composing; the comments suggest to students that writing is just a matter of following the rules. Indeed, the teachers seem to impose a series of abstract rules about written products even when some of them are not appropriate for the specific text the student is creating.[3] For instance, the student author of our sample paragraph presented above is commanded to follow the conventional rules for writing a five-paragraph essay—to begin the introductory paragraph by telling his reader what he is going to say and to end the paragraph with a thesis sentence. Somehow these abstract rules about what five-paragraph products should look like do not seem applicable to the problems this student must confront when revising, nor are the rules specific strategies he could use when revising. There are many inchoate ideas ready to be exploited in this paragraph, but the rules do not help the student to take stock of his (or her) ideas and use the opportunity he has, during revision, to develop those ideas.

The problem here is a confusion of process and product; what one has to say about the process is different from what one has to say about the product. Teachers who use this method of commenting are formulating their comments as if these drafts were finished drafts and were not going to be revised. Their commenting vocabularies have not been adapted to revision and they comment on first drafts as if they were justifying a grade or as if the first draft were the final draft.

Our summary finding, therefore, from this research on styles of commenting is that the news from the classroom is not good. For the most part, teachers do not respond to student writing with the kind of thoughtful commentary which will help students to engage with the issues they are writing about or which will help them think about their purposes and goals in writing a specific text. In defense of our teachers, however, they told us that responding to student writing was rarely stressed in their teacher-training or in writing workshops; they had been trained in various prewriting techniques, in constructing assignments, and in evaluating papers for grades, but rarely in the process of reading a student text for meaning or in offering commentary to motivate revision. The problem is that most of us as teachers of writing have been trained to read and interpret literary texts for meaning, but, unfortunately, we have not been trained to act upon the same set of assumptions in reading student texts as we follow in reading literary texts.[4] Thus, we read student texts with biases about what the writer should have said or about what he or she should have written, and our biases determine how we will comprehend the text. We read without preconceptions and preoccupations, expecting to find errors, and the result is that we find errors and misread our students' texts.[5] We find what we look for; instead of reading and responding to the meaning of a text, we correct our students' writing. We need to reverse this approach. Instead of finding errors or showing students how to patch up parts of their texts, we need to sabotage our students' conviction that the drafts they have written are complete and coherent. Our comments need to offer students revision tasks of a different order of complexity and sophistication from the ones that they themselves identify, by forcing students back into the chaos, back to the point where they are shaping and restructuring their meaning.[6]

For if the content of a student text is lacking in substance and meaning, if the order of the parts must be rearranged significantly in the next draft, if paragraphs must be restructured for logic and clarity, then many sentences are likely to be changed or deleted anyway. There seems to be no point in having students correct usage errors or condense sentences that are likely to disappear before the next draft is completed. In fact, to identify such problems in a text at this early first draft stage, when such problems are likely to abound, can give a student a disproportionate sense of their importance at this stage in the writing process.[7] In responding to our students' writing, we should be guided by the recognition that it is not spelling or usage problems that we as writers first worry about when drafting and revising our texts.

We need to develop an appropriate level of response for commenting on a first draft, and to differentiate that from the level suitable to a second or third draft. Our comments need to be suited to the draft we are reading. In a first or second draft, we need to respond as any reader would, registering questions, reflecting befuddlement, and noting places where we are puzzled about the meaning of the text. Comments should point to breaks in logic, disruptions in meaning, or missing information. Our goal in commenting on early drafts should be to engage students with the issues they are considering and help them clarify their purposes and reasons in writing their specific text.

For instance, the major rhetorical problem of the essay written by the student who wrote the second paragraph (the paragraph on nuclear power) quoted above was that the student had two principal arguments running through his text, each of which brought the other into question. On the one hand, he argued that we must use nuclear power, unpleasant as it is, because we have nothing else to use; though nuclear energy is a problematic source of energy, it is the best of a bad lot. On the other hand, he also argued that nuclear energy is really quite safe, and therefore should be our primary resource. Comments on this student's first draft need to point out this break in logic and show the student that if we accept his first argument, then his second argument sounds fishy. But if we accept his second argument, his first argument sounds contradictory. The teacher's comments need to engage this student writer with this basic rhetorical and conceptual problem in his first draft rather than impose a series of abstract commands and rules upon his text.

Written comments need to be viewed not as an end in themselves—a way for teachers to satisfy themselves that they have done their jobs—but rather as a means for helping students to become more effective writers. As a means for helping students, they have limitations; they are, in fact, disembodied remarks—one absent writer responding to another absent writer. The key to successful commenting is to have what is said in the comments and what is done in the classroom mutually reinforce and enrich each other. Commenting on papers assists the writing course in achieving its purpose; classroom activities and the comments we write to our students need to be connected. Written comments need to be an extension of the teacher's voice—an extension of the teacher as reader. Exercises in such activities as revising a whole text or individual paragraphs together in class, noting how the sense of the whole dictates the smaller changes, looking at options, evaluating actual choices, and then discussing the effect of these changes on revised drafts—such exercises need to be designed to take students through the cycles of revising and to help them overcome their anxiety about revising: that anxiety we all feel at reducing what looks like a finished draft into fragments and chaos.

The challenge we face as teachers is to develop comments which will provide an inherent reason for students to revise; it is a sense of revision as discovery, as a repeated process of beginning again, as starting out new, that our students have not learned. We need to show our students how to seek, in the possibility of revision, the dissonances of discovery—to show them through our comments why new choices would positively change their texts, and thus to show them the potential for development implicit in their own writing.

Notes

1. C. H. Knoblauch and Lil Brannon, "Teacher Commentary on Student Writing: The State of the Art," *Freshman English News,* 10 (Fall, 1981), 1–3.
2. For an extended discussion of revision strategies of student writers see Nancy Sommers, "Revision Strategies of Student Writers and Experienced Adult Writers," *College Composition and Communication,* 31 (December, 1980), 378–388.
3. Nancy Sommers and Ronald Schleifer, "Means and Ends: Some Assumptions of Student Writers," *Composition and Teaching,* 2 (December, 1980), 69–76.
4. Janet Emig and Robert P. Parker, Jr. "Responding to Student Writing: Building a Theory of the Evaluating Process," unpublished papers, Rutgers University.
5. For an extended discussion of this problem see Joseph Williams, "The Phenomenology of Error," *College Composition and Communication,* 32 (May, 1981), 152–168.

6. Ann Berthoff, *The Making of Meaning* (Montclair, NJ: Boynton/Cook Publishers, 1981).
7. W. U. McDonald, "The Revising Process and the Marking of Student Papers," *College Composition and Communication*, 24 (May, 1978), 167–170.

Minimal Marking

Richard H. Haswell

Richard H. Haswell teaches at Washington State University. In "Minimal Marking," originally published in College English *(October 1983), he offers a scheme for helping students identify and edit sentence-level problems.*

It is a disturbing fact of the profession that many teachers still look toward the marking of a set of compositions with distaste and discouragement. Reasons are obvious, not the least being the intuition that hours must be put in with little return in terms of effect on the students or on their writing. C. H. Knoblauch and Lil Brannon's recent survey of the research on the effect of marking unfortunately supports this intuition. Positive results of teacher intervention through written commentary simply have not yet been found ("Teacher Commentary on Student Writing, *Freshman English News,* 10 [1981], 1–4). The problem is analogous to that of the teaching of grammar in composition courses—hundreds of thousands of hours spent, and being spent right now, on a task of little proven benefit. Fortunately, however, Knoblauch and Brannon balance their description of unfruitful paths with a model of paths still promising. Otherwise, an essentially useful method that is easily discredited because easily disliked might seem finally unprofitable.

Whether Knoblauch and Brannon's model of beneficial written commentary can be verified by research remains to be seen, but I would like to provide evidence here that suggests it will be. In essence they propose commentary that 1) facilitates rather than judges, 2) emphasizes performance rather than finished product, 3) provides double feedback, before and after revision, and 4) helps bridge successive drafts by requiring immediate revision. All these requirements are met by a method of marking surface errors in writing that I have been using for several years and recommending for use by teaching assistants. Admittedly errors of this sort—misspelling, mispunctuation, etc.—constitute a nonessential element of writing, or at least one I do not wish to spend much time on at any level of instruction. But the method by which I comment on these errors, besides conforming to Knoblauch and Brannon's criteria, brings measurable improvements and serves as a paradigm for a scheme of written commentary that may be transferable to more central aspects of writing, especially aspects not amenable to peer evaluation.

The method itself is by no means solely my own, no doubt having undergone autogenesis time and again. I developed it for my own use six or seven years ago; a retired colleague of mine said he knew of a teacher at Vassar who used it in the early 1940s; recently Sheila Ann Lisman has described it as her "X system" ("The Best of All Possible Worlds: Where X Replaces AWK," in Gene Stanford, et al., eds. *Classroom Practices in Teaching English 1979–1980: How to Handle the Paper Load* [Urbana, Ill.: National Council of Teachers of English, 1979], pp. 103–105). My own application is as follows. All surface mistakes in a student's paper are left totally unmarked within the text. These are unquestionable errors in spelling, punctuation, capitalization, and grammar (including pronoun antecedence). Each of these mistakes is indicated only with a check in the margin by the line in which it occurs. A line with two checks by it, for instance, means the presence of two errors, no more, within the boundary of that line. The sum of checks is recorded at the end of the paper and in the gradebook. Papers, with checks and other commentary, are then returned fifteen minutes before the end of class. Students have time to search for, circle, and correct the errors. As papers are returned to me I review the corrections, mending those errors left undiscovered, miscorrected, or newly generated. Where I feel it is useful, mistakes are explained or handbooks cited. Within those fifteen minutes I can return about one third of the papers in a class of twenty-five, and the rest I return the next session. Until a student attempts to correct checked errors, the grade on the essay remains unrecorded.

The simplicity of this method belies its benefit. First, it shortens, gladdens, and improves the act of marking papers. Because the teacher responds to a surface mistake only with a check in the margin, attention can be maintained on more substantial problems. The method perhaps goes a long way toward dimming the halo effect of surface mistakes on evaluation, since much of this negative influence may arise from the irritation that comes from correcting and explaining common errors (*its* and *it's!*) over and over. On the second reading the teacher does not lose the time gained initially, for according to my count students will correct on their own sixty to seventy percent of their errors. (Lisman reports her "least capable students" are able to find sixty percent of their errors.) Conservatively, I would say the method saves me about four minutes a paper. That is nearly two hours saved with a set of twenty-five essays.

Second, the method forces students to act in a number of ways that have current pedagogic sanction. In reducing the amount of teacher comment on the page, it helps to avoid the mental dazzle of information overload. It shows the student that the teacher initially assumed that carelessness and not stupidity was the source of error. It forces the student, not the teacher, to answer the question. It challenges students with a puzzle (where is the mistake in this line?) and reinforces learning with a high rate of successful solutions. It engages students in an activity that comes much nearer to the very activity they need to learn, namely editing—not the abstract understanding of a mistake someone else has discovered, but the detection and correction of errors on one's own. Finally, improvement is self-motivated. The fewer mistakes students submit originally, the sooner they leave other students still struggling in the classroom with checks by every third line. Progress during the semester is also easily seen, if not by checks on individual papers at least by totals in the gradebook shared with a student during conference.

Third, this method will help teachers analyze the nature and sources of error in ways that lately have proved so insightful among composition specialists.[1] Consider the following breakdown of the corrections that twenty-four freshmen in one of my recent classes made on their first inclass essay (without recourse to a dictionary).

Category of Error	Number of Errors Checked in Margin by Teacher	Number of Errors Correctly Emended by Students	Percent Corrected by Students
Semantic Signalling (capitalization, underlining, quotation marks, apostrophes)	97	74	76.3%
Syntactic Punctuation	142	81	57.0%
Spelling (including hyphenation)	132	74	56.1%
Grammar (including tense change, omission of word, pronoun-disagreement)	30	16	53.3%
All Errors	401	245	61.1%

Crude as this breakdown is, a useful fact immediately emerges. Students are able to find and correct different kinds of errors at about the same rate. In short, more than half of the surface errors students make, *regardless of type,* occupy a kind of halfway house between purely conceptual and purely performance-based (only a few seem truly slips of the pen). They are threshold errors, standing on the edge of competence in an unstable posture of disjunction ("I know it is either *conceive* or *convieve*") or of half-discarded fossilization ("I don't know why I capitalized 'Fraternities.' I *know* that's wrong."). It is good for the teacher to be reminded that, after all, the majority of errors—all kinds of errors, and differently for different students—"mark stages," in David Bartholomae's words, "on route to mastery" ("The Study of Error," p. 257). Further, the method isolates, for each individual student, those errors of deeper etiology. It is remarkable how often the method winnows away a heterogeneous clutter of threshold errors to leave just a few conceptual errors—errors, though again idiosyncratic and multiplied by repetition, now accessible for focused treatment. So the method is an ideal first step in the pedagogical attack on error recommended by Paul B. Diederich, Beth Newman, Ellen W. Nold, and others: keep records, isolate a few serious errors, individualize instruction.[2]

Even for teachers who have less time than they would like for individual instruction, there will be progress if this method of marginal checking is maintained during the entire course. At least there has been in my classes. Using inclass, fifty-minute, impromptu essays written the first and last week of the semester, with two switched topics to eliminate influence of topic, I have calculated change in error rate in three regular freshman composition sections. Overall, the drop was from 4.6 errors per 100 words to 2.2 (.52). This rate of decline was consistent despite different semesters and different topics and considerably different course plans (52%, 53%, 50%). Further, nearly all students participated in the improvement; only four of the sixty-nine did not register a decline in rate. This improvement in error rate, it should be noted, was not acquired at the expense of fluency, for final essays were 23% longer than first essays. Pearson product-moment correlation between initial and final error rates is high (.79), suggesting little connection between initial verbal skill and subsequent gain. Even though, given the above figures, it was nearly superfluous, I calculated a correlated t-test for significance of pre/post change in rate, largely to relish (at least once in my life) a truly giant t-value ($t = 25$–43, $p < .001$). Of course what other factors influenced this gain must remain conjectural. I devoted a small amount of class time to three or four common errors of punctuation, worked occasionally in conference with individual problems, and reminded students to save five minutes at the end of an inclass essay to proofread. I have not had the heart to set up a control group to isolate this marking technique; it has been valuable enough for me that I prefer to sell it rather than to deprive any students of it deliberately.

The ultimate value of this method for me is that it relegates what I consider a minor aspect of the course to a minor role in time spent on marking and in class, while at least maintaining and probably increasing the rate of improvement in that aspect. Crudely put, less work for the teacher, more gain for the student. But the gain may be compounded in ways more complex than this suggests. Knoblauch and Brannon rightly point out that commenting must be evaluated in terms of the "full teacher-student dialogue." Now too much commenting can harm this dialogue in at least two ways. It will embitter the teacher with the knowledge that the time and energy spent on it is incommensurate with the subject and the results. And it will frustrate both teacher and student because judgmental commentary unbalances the teacher-student equilibrium in an authentic learning situation, that is, where the student is doing most of the work. Long ago Comenius put it best: the more the teacher teaches, the less the student learns. (The more you teach, one of our older teaching assistants said to me mournfully, the more you quote that maxim.) In terms of Elaine O. Lee's useful scale ("Evaluating Student Writing," *CCC* 30 [1979], 370–374), this marking technique postpones correcting, emoting, and describing—where the teacher does all of the work—and instead suggests, questions, reminds, and assigns. Because students do most of the work, the discouragement of which I first spoke subsides, and a certain freshness and candor return to the dialogue. (Lisman's article describes this renewed energy well.)

Can this method be transferred to other aspects of writing? I think so, although right now I must speculate. Certainly problems of writing that lend themselves to spot improvement could well be marked with marginal checks: injudicious diction, needed transitions, unsupported generalities. Larger, structural problems such as stumbling introductions and disordered paragraphs might be signalled with marginal lines. More interestingly, so might fallacies and other lapses in thinking. In each case the effort would be to find the minimal functional mark. The best mark is that which allows students to correct the most on their own with the least help. An obvious pedagogical truth—but one that runs counter to the still established tradition of full correction.

Notes

1. See especially Mina P. Shaughnessy, *Errors and Expectations: A Guide for the Teachers of Writing* (New York: Oxford, 1977); Barry M. Kroll and John C. Schafer, "Error-Analysis and the Teaching of Composition," *College Composition and Communication,* 29 (1978), 242–248; and David Bartholomae, "The Study of Error," *CCC,* 31 (1980), 253–269.
2. Diederich, *Measuring Growth in English* (Urbana, Ill.: National Council of Teachers of English, 1974), pp. 21–22; Newman, *Teaching Students to Write* (Columbus, Ohio: Merrill, 1980), pp. 292–297, 398; Nold, "Alternatives to Mad-Hatterism" in Donald McQuade, ed., *Linguistics, Stylistics, and the Teaching of Composition* (Conway, AK: L&S Books, 1980), pp. 103–117. See also Shaughnessy, Kroll and Schafer, and Bartholomae above. Marginal checking isolates deep errors in a way parallel, but not identical, to Bartholomae's method of "oral reconstruction" ("Study of Error," pp. 259–268). The two methods may prove to have different, though overlapping, diagnostic values.

Bringing Practice in Line with Theory: Using Portfolio Grading in the Composition Classroom

Jeffrey Sommers

Jeffrey Sommers teaches at Miami University–Middletown. "Bringing Practice in Line with Theory: Using Portfolio Grading in the Composition Classroom" first appeared in Portfolios: Process and Product, *edited by Pat Belanoff and Marcia Dickson (Boynton/Cook Heinemann, 1991). If you are thinking of using portfolio grading or already do so, you will find this discussion of different models of portfolio evaluation interesting and helpful.*

Portfolio assessment in the composition classroom offers not a methodology but a framework for response. Rather than provide definitive answers to questions about grading criteria and standards, the relationship between teacher and student, and increased paper loads, the portfolio approach presents an opportunity for instructors to bring their practice in responding to student writing in line with their theories of composing and pedagogy. My essay proposes to take an exploratory look at how portfolio evaluation compels instructors to address a number of important, and long-lived, issues underlying response to student writing. When an instructor chooses to use a portfolio system, certain other decisions must inevitably follow, and it is the implications of these decisions that I propose to examine most closely.

As the writing process has become the focus of composition classes over the past three decades, it seems an almost natural evolution for portfolio evaluation to have entered the classroom. Emphasizing the importance of revision to the composing process—regardless of which theoretical view of composing one takes—ought to lead to a classroom practice that permits, even encourages, students to revise. While such revision can, of course, occur in a classroom in which the writing portfolio is not in use, the portfolio itself tends to encourage students to revise because it suggests that writing occurs over time, not in a single sitting, just as the portfolio itself grows over time and cannot be created in a single sitting. Elbow and Belanoff argue that a portfolio system evaluates student writing "in ways that better reflect the complexities of the writing process: with time for freewriting, planning, discussion with instructors and peers, revising, and copyediting. It lets students put these activities together in a way most productive for them" (this volume 14).

Additionally, the portfolio approach can help students discover that writing is indeed a form of learning. Janet Emig has argued that writing "provides [a] record of evolution of thought since writing is epigenetic as process-and-product" (128). Portfolios provide a record of that record. Emig also describes writing as "active, engaged, personal—notably, self-rhythmed" (128). The notion that writing occurs over time in response to the rhythms created by the individual writer—a notion that makes eminent sense when one considers that no two writers seem to work at precisely the same pace and that no two pieces of writing seem to take form at the same pace even for the same writer—is another excellent argument for using portfolios. The portfolio approach allows writers to assemble an *oeuvre* at their own pace, within the structure of the writing course and its assignments, of course. Nevertheless, the portfolio by its very nature suggests self-rhythm because some pieces will require more drafts than others, even if explicit deadlines are prompting their composition.

For good cause then have portfolio systems of evaluation become commonplace in composition classrooms. But with these portfolios also come serious issues about grading standards and criteria, about how teachers and students relate to one another, about how teachers handle increased paper loads. Before examining how these issues might be resolved, perhaps it is time to acknowledge that this essay has yet to define *portfolio*. I have deliberately avoided doing so for two reasons: first, *portfolio* is a familiar-enough term and not really all that mysterious, and thus what I have written so far should be comprehensible to my readers; second, no consensus exists about just what a portfolio is or should be, however familiar the concept may seem. In fact, two distinctly different models of portfolios exist, each compelling its adherents to address the central issues of response in very different theoretical ways.

The first model is described well by James E. Ford and Gregory Larkin, who use as an analogy an artist's portfolio. Each student's work is "collected, like the best representative work of an artist, into a 'portfolio' " (951). We are to see students in the role of free-lance commercial artists approaching an art director at an advertising agency with a large portfolio case containing their "best representative work." Such a model is easily transformed into the writing classroom. Students in the writing course produce a certain number of written documents during the term, agreeing in advance that only a specified number of those documents will be graded by the instructor. Commercial artists would never compile a portfolio that consisted of every piece of work they had done and neither do the students; the idea is to select a representative sampling that shows the creators at their best.

This portfolio model most likely grows out of instructors' concern with grading criteria and standards. Ford and Larkin, as the title of their article suggests, came to the portfolio as a means of guaranteeing grading standards. Instructors are justified in upholding rigorous standards of excellence because their students have been able to revise their work and select their best writing for evaluation. As Ford and Larkin comment, "A student can 'blow' an occasional assignment without disastrous effect" (952), suggesting that the instructor is being eminently fair. Elbow and Belanoff, in the context of a programmatic portfolio-assessment project, make a similar argument, one equally applicable to the individual composition classroom. "By giving students a chance to be examined on their best writing—by giving them an opportunity for more help—we are also able to demand their best writing" (this volume 13). This portfolio system "encourages high standard from the start, thereby encouraging maximum development" (Burnham 137).

To Ford and Larkin, Burnham, and Elbow and Belanoff, a portfolio is a sampling of finished products selected by the student for evaluation. Although the instructor using this model may very well be concerned with the students' development as writers, as Burnham's remark indicates, essentially this portfolio model is grade driven and could be accurately labeled a *portfolio grading system*. It is grade driven because the rationale for using the portfolio framework grows out of an understanding that the student's written work will ultimately be evaluated.

However, portfolio grading, paradoxically, not only grows out of a concern for eroding standards, but also out of a concern for the overemphasis upon grades in writing courses. Christopher Burnham calls the students' "obsession" with grades a "major stumbling block" (125) to effective learning in the composition classroom and turns to portfolio grading as a means of mitigating the students' obsession with grades. Burnham concludes that the portfolio system "establishes a writing environment rather than a grading environment in the classroom" (137).

Thus, by addressing the issue of responding to the student's writing, Burnham wants to change the relationship between the student and the instructor. He wants to create a more facilitative role for the instructor, in accordance with suggestions about response from Donald

Murray, Nancy Sommers, and Lil Brannon and C. H. Knoblauch. He not only wants to allow students to retain the rights to their own writing, he wants them to assume responsibility for their writing, asserting that portfolio grading "creates independent writers and learners" (136).

The question then of when and what to grade becomes quite significant. Although grading criteria must be established by the instructors who employ portfolio grading, new criteria for grading the final drafts do not generally need to be developed. Presumably, instructors will bring to bear an already developed set of criteria for grading, applying these criteria rigorously to designated papers, thus protecting the integrity of their standards.[1] Nonetheless, a crucial question arises: when will student work receive a grade: at midterm, only at the end of the term, with each submission? Some instructors grade every draft and revision as students submit them, some grade only the revisions, some grade only papers designated as final drafts. In some portfolio-grading systems, the students select a specified number of final drafts at midterm and a second set at the end of the term.

Instructors using portfolio grading must decide when to offer grades. Grading every draft keeps the students informed, but, because even a temporary grade has an air of finality to many students simply because it is a grade, this policy may undercut the idea that each draft may potentially develop into a finished product. Grading revisions only may encourage the grade-obsessed student to revise if only to obtain a grade, thus introducing revision to some students who may otherwise lack the motivation to revise, but also reinforcing the primacy of grades.

By deferring grades until the end of the term, instructors can extend the duration of the "writing environment" that Burnham hopes to substitute for the "grading environment" in the course. However, if students are indeed obsessed with grades, as he argues, then it seems likely that for a substantial number of students, or perhaps for all of the students to varying extents, there will always be a grading environment lurking beneath the writing environment of the course. If instructors respond effectively and frequently and confer with students individually, they can keep students informed of their approximate standing in the course, possibly deflecting their grade anxiety, but it is disingenuous to claim that portfolio grading removes grade obsession. If the portfolio ultimately produces an accumulation of individual grades, grade obsession cannot really be eliminated although it certainly can be reduced.

Yet a larger issue arises, an issue related to one's pedagogical assumptions about the significance of grades. Burnham discusses the portfolio system as a means of leading to student development, a development inevitably measured by the final grades earned by the student's portfolio. Inherent in this model is the idea that students can improve the writing, and thus the grade, by revising and selecting their best work. Inevitably, then, instructors using portfolio grading must address the issue of grade inflation. Although one of the motivating forces behind portfolio grading, as we have seen, is protecting grading standards, the system itself is designed to promote better writing by the students, and it stands to reason that many students are going to be submitting portfolios that consist of writing better than they might be able to produce in a classroom employing a traditional grading system. Will instructors raise the standards so high that even the improved writing in the portfolios falls into the usual grading curve? Or, and this seems much more likely, will the grades themselves on the whole be somewhat higher because of the portfolio approach despite the higher standards? Should higher grades be of significant concern to instructors? Do higher grades mean "grade inflation"? What is the role of grades in writing courses? Portfolio grading compels instructors to consider these important questions.

Finally, portfolio grading presents problems to instructors in handling the paper load. Since most programs suggest or stipulate a certain number of assignments per term, instructors using the portfolio system must determine how they will count assignments. Will newly revised papers count as new assignments? By doing so, the instructor can keep the paper load from mushrooming. Let's focus on a course that requires seven papers in a semester (the situation at my institution), with the understanding that the portfolio will consist of four final drafts selected by the student. If instructors count revisions of papers 1 and 2 as papers 3 and 4, their paper load will be less because students will still only produce seven drafts for them to read. On the other hand, the students' options at the end of the term will be reduced by this method of counting; they will have to select four final drafts from only five different pieces in progress. To ensure students the full choice of seven, however, instructors commit themselves to more responding. In our hypothetical case, they will read at least nine drafts, seven first drafts and revisions of the first two papers. Thus a routine decision actually has important pedagogical implications.

Several methods of controlling the paper load do exist. One is to divide the term in half, asking students to produce two miniportfolios. At midterm, for instance, in the situation already described, students are required to submit two final drafts for grading out of the first four assigned papers. At the end of the term, students must select two of the final three assigned papers for grading. Thus the paper load is under greater control because the students cannot continue work on the first four papers after midterm. On the other hand, Burnham's desire to create a writing environment rather than a grading environment will be affected because grades will become of primary concern not once but twice during the term.

Another method for controlling the paper load is to limit the number of drafts students may write of individual papers. Without such a limit, some students will rewrite and resubmit papers almost weekly, adding greatly to the paper load; of course, one can argue that such students are developing as writers in an important way. Deadlines for revisions of papers can also be used to control the paper load since "real" writers always work under deadlines. They may revise and revise and revise, but ultimately they must conclude. Instructors may allow students to revise a given assignment as often as they wish but within a designated period of time. Another method of controlling the paper load is to limit the number of revisions students may submit at one time or to designate specific times when revisions may be submitted. Late in the term, industrious students may have revisions of three or four different assignments ready to be submitted; some limit on the number they may hand in at one time can help instructors manage the course more effectively. Stipulating that revisions can be handed in only on certain days can allow instructors to plan their time for responding more efficiently.

Eventually, the end of the term arrives, and for many instructors using portfolio grading, the paper load explodes. Portfolios of four papers or more per student come in at the end of the term and must be graded quickly in order to submit final grades on time. Holistic grading can make the paper load manageable as instructors offer no comments but just a letter grade on each final draft. Grading portfolios at the end of the term undeniably requires more time than grading a single final exam or final paper would. However mundane these questions of handling the paper load may seem, the answers one supplies affect the entire portfolio grading system because many of these decisions may influence the relationship between students and their instructors, and some may influence, or be influenced by, instructors' grading criteria and standards.

To sum up then, a portfolio grading system defines a portfolio as a sampling of students' finished writing selected by the students for evaluation. Portfolio grading offers instructors a means of keeping their grading standards high while employing their usual grading criteria, it presents one potential method for reducing students' obsession with grades and transforming the classroom environment into one more engaged with writing than grading, and it increases instructors' paper loads. Instructors' decisions about when to grade and how to manage the paper load raise complications because they affect the relationship between instructors and their students. Thus, teachers planning on implementing portfolio grading need to consider carefully how they will do so in a way that will keep their practice in line with their own theoretical assumptions about writing and about composition pedagogy.

The second, newer, portfolio system I will call the "holistic portfolio." The holistic portfolio is a response to continued theorizing about the nature of the composing process. Louise Wetherbee Phelps argues that theories underlying teaching practices evolve toward greater depth, and she sketches a hierarchy of response models to student writing beginning with one she labels "evaluative attitude, closed text" (49). In this model, the instructor treats the student text as "self-contained, complete in itself . . . a discrete discourse episode to be experienced more or less decontextually" (50). This concept of response to a text views reading as evaluation; instructors responding in this model may speak of "grading a stack of papers." The next response model described by Phelps is one she calls "formative attitude, evolving text" (51). Instructors read students' drafts as part of a process of evolution, thus entering into and influencing the students' composing process. In this model of response, instructors locate "learning largely in the actual composing process" (53).

Phelps describes a third model of response as "developmental attitude, portfolio of work": "Whereas the first group of teachers reads a 'stack' of papers and the second reads collected bits, scraps, and drafts of the composing process, the third reads a 'portfolio' of work by one student" (53). Phelps elaborates on two ways to work with portfolios, describing first the portfolio grading model we have already examined, which she dubs "the weak form." In this approach, she writes, "teachers continue to read and grade individual papers, attempting to help students perfect each one" (53). As Phelps has described the models of response, we can see that she has first described portfolio assessment used in a programmatic approach to large-scale decision making about student proficiency and placement. Her second model fairly accurately describes the portfolio-grading approach of Ford and Larkin and Burnham, elaborated upon somewhat in her description of "the weak form" of her third response model.

In the second method of using portfolios, Phelps also describes a different portfolio system. Some instructors employ portfolios because they wish to respond from a *developmental* perspective." From this perspective, the student writing "blurs as an individual entity" and is treated as a sample "excerpted from a stream of writing stimulated by the writing class, part of the 'life text' each literate person continually produces" (53). Phelps concludes:

> The reader's function is [to read] through the text to the writer's developing cognitive, linguistic, and social capacities as they bear on writing activities. The set of a single writer's texts to which the reader has access, either literally or through memory, is the corpus from which the reader tries to construct a speculative profile of the writer's developmental history and current maturity. (53)

This definition of portfolio no longer serves as an analogy to the commercial artist's carefully assembled portfolio of a representative sampling of her best work. Instead it more closely resembles an archivist's collection of a writer's entire *oeuvre*. Instructors do not deal with selected writings but evaluate the entire output of the student writer. The implications of such a definition are quite different from those of the portfolio grading model defined by Ford and Larkin, Burnham and Elbow and Belanoff.

While portfolio grading systems are driven by pedagogical concerns with fair grading as well as with composing process theory, the holistic portfolio system is primarily driven by a pedagogical concern with composing process theory. Although Knoblauch and Brannon's polemic *Rhetorical Traditions and the Teaching of Writing* does not discuss portfolio evaluation, its view of the composing process might very readily lead to it. Knoblauch and Brannon describe the "myth of improvement" that has stifled writing instruction by focusing on the kind of evaluation Phelps details in her first model of response (evaluative attitude, closed text). Knoblauch and Brannon suggest that "the most debilitating illusion associated with writing instruction is the belief that teachers can, or at least ought to be able to, control writers' maturation, causing it to occur as the explicit consequence of something they do or ought to do" (165). This illusion is reductionist, leading to a view of the writing course "in minimal functionalist terms" (165). This "myth of improvement" has produced a definition of teaching and curricular success that stresses "trivial but readily demonstrable short-term 'skill' acquisitions" and has led some teachers "to imagine it is fair to 'grade on improvement,' mistaking a willingness to follow orders for real development" (165).

While Knoblauch and Brannon's book remains controversial, their critique of "the myth of improvement" cogently articulates many instructors' reservations about grading practices based on the artificial academic calendar, a system that demands students learn at a given pace, defined by a ten-week quarter, a fourteen-week trimester, or a sixteen-week semester. Knoblauch and Brannon conclude by arguing that "symptoms of growth—the willingness to take risks, to profit from advice, to revise, to make recommendations to others—may appear quickly, even if improved *performance* takes longer" (169).

For instructors whose conception of the composing process is compatible with the developmental schemes underlying Knoblauch and Brannon's book and Phelps's third model of response, the holistic portfolio should have great appeal. It presents these instructors with difficult decisions, however, in the same areas that the portfolio grading system presented its practitioners: grading criteria and standards, the teacher–student relationship, and handling the paper load.

While upholding grading standards was the catalyst for portfolio grading, holistic portfolio systems appear to be less concerned with the notion of grading standards, at least in traditional terms. Because the holistic portfolio system does not focus instructors' attention on specific final drafts, it does present instructors with some major decisions about criteria for the final evaluation.

Several possibilities exist. Instructors may create a grading system that weights final drafts but also grades draft materials, notes, peer commentary, and so on. Counting the number of drafts or the variety of included materials is a way to "grade" preliminary materials. However, any counting method might distort the course's emphasis on development by encouraging students to create "phony" drafts, drafts written after the fact simply to pad the portfolio (just as many of us used to compose outlines *after* completing high school term papers as a way of meeting a course requirement).

Another way to grade the final portfolio is more holistic, and thus probably "purer" in the sense that it avoids treating individual drafts as "collected bits, scraps, and drafts" and treats portfolios as part of "the life text" (Phelps 53). The instructor looks for "symptoms of growth," to borrow Knoblauch and Brannon's phrase—"the willingness to take risks, to profit from advice, to revise, to make recommendations to others." Those students who demonstrate the greatest growth receive the highest grades, assuming that the instructor has developed a scale that measures growth—no small assumption.

While the holistic portfolio can fit very nicely into a developmental view of the composing process, it presents great difficulties in fitting at all into a traditional academic grading system and poses serious questions for instructors about how they see their writing courses fitting into the academy. This method of evaluation works most readily in a pass/no pass grading situation, indeed is an argument for such a grading system. But pass/no pass writing courses are the exception rather than the rule. Unfortunately, neither Knoblauch and Brannon nor Phelps really addresses the issue of how to grade in a writing course that emphasizes a developmental perspective on writing. It is conceivable that an instructor holistically evaluating a set of portfolios could assign an entire class of industrious students grades of A, having developed grading criteria that emphasize "symptoms of growth"; such an instructor can have rigorous standards in that only those students who have made the effort and demonstrated the growth receive the As. However, one suspects this instructor would face a one-to-one meeting with a concerned writing program administrator or department chair sometime after submitting the final grades.

Some compromise or accommodation must undoubtedly be made by instructors, perhaps along the lines discussed earlier of weighting final drafts. The important point to make here is that instructors should be aware of how the grading criteria they develop correlate with the theory underlying their use of portfolio evaluation.

Given the problematic nature of grading holistic portfolios, why would instructors adopt this model of the portfolio system? The holistic portfolio system offers distinct advantages in defining a healthy teacher–student relationship. Burnham's hopes of creating a writing environment rather than a grading environment are more readily realized in the holistic portfolio system. Because the final portfolio will not be graded in any traditional sense, because individual grades on drafts do not occur, in theory the classroom using the holistic portfolio can indeed become a writing environment, since there is no reason for it to become a grading environment, and the instructor can truly doff the evaluator's role and don instead the facilitator's role.

Burnham praises portfolio grading for encouraging students to assume responsibility for their learning; portfolio grading "creates independent writers and learners," he concludes (137). His point is that when students know that they can control their grades through extra effort in revising and through the selection process available to them prior to final evaluation, they become "empowered." However, the motivation comes from a concern with grades.

In the holistic portfolio system, the students are also afforded the opportunity to become more responsible, not for their grades so much as for their development. They can indeed become independent learners, independent of traditional grading obsessions as well. The teacher and student can become "co-writers," in Phelps's phrase. The emphasis in the course falls not on improving texts as a means of improving a grade but instead falls on developing as a writer, understanding that this development is more important than grades on individual texts.

Both models of portfolios, then, hope to free students of the tyranny of the grade. The portfolio grading system does so temporarily, but also readily accommodates the traditional institutional need for grades. The holistic portfolio system can indeed free students to become learners and writers for the duration of a writing course but only if instructors have resolved the essential conflict between their course and the institution's demand for traditionally meaningful grades.

In the final area of paper load, it seems most likely that the holistic portfolio system will produce a heavier paper load than the portfolio grading system will. Any schemes to limit students' output would likely conflict with the theoretical assumptions that lead to using the holistic portfolio system. Thus students' portfolios are likely to grow in length as well as in the hoped-for depth of development. At the end of the term, instructors must read not merely a specific number of selected final drafts, but entire portfolios, certainly a slower process. Periodic reading of the growing portfolios—which instructors taking such a developmental perspective will probably wish to do—may reduce the paper load at the end of the course since instructors can scan the familiar materials in the portfolio, but it will not significantly reduce the paper load so much as spread it out over the course of the term.

Instructors contemplating a portfolio system of either sort, or a hybrid version of the two models described, are faced with the need to answer some important questions for themselves before incorporating the system into their writing classes. Louise Wetherbee Phelps concludes her discussion by commenting that her depiction of response models represents an increasing growth on the part of instructors. She argues that "experience itself presses teachers toward incrementally generous and flexible conceptions of the text and the reading task" (59). If she is correct, as I think she is, then the movement in composition classrooms toward portfolio systems of one sort or another will accelerate as the emphasis on the composing process as central to writing courses continues.

As the profession continues to refine its thinking about composition pedagogy, portfolio systems seem destined to proliferate in use and to grow in significance. The portfolio system of evaluation has tremendous advantages, . . . but it also requires great thought on the part of instructors because a portfolio system implemented in a scattershot manner may well undercut the goals of a writing course. The portfolio offers instructors wonderful opportunities to bring their teaching practice in line with their theoretical assumptions about writing and about teaching, but that convergence can only occur if instructors ask themselves the right—and the tough—questions and work out the answers that best provide what both instructors and students need in the writing course.

Note

1. I am assuming that instructors themselves will grade the papers. Ford and Larkin describe a programmatic use of portfolio grading wherein the portfolios are graded by a team of graders not including the students' instructor. My interest in this essay, however, is in the issues faced by individual instructors who do not have the power to implement such grading practice but must conduct their own evaluations.

Works Cited

Burnham, Christopher. "Portfolio Evaluation: Room to Breathe and Grow." *Training the New Teacher of College Composition.* Ed. Charles Bridges. Urbana, Ill.: NCTE, 1986.

Emig, Janet. "Writing as a Mode of Learning." *College Composition and Communication* 28 (1977): 122–28.

Ford, James E., and Gregory Larkin. "The Portfolio System: An End to Backsliding Writing Standards." *College English* 39 (1978): 950–55.

Knoblauch, C. H., and Lil Brannon. *Rhetorical Traditions and the Teaching of Writing.* Portsmouth, N. H.: Boynton/Cook, 1984.

Phelps, Louise Wetherbee. "Images of Student Writing: The Deep Structure of Teacher Response." *Writing and Response: Theory, Practice, and Research.* Ed. Chris M. Anson. Urbana Ill.: NCTE, 1989.

Local and Global Networking: Implications for the Future

Michael Spitzer

When the computer was introduced into the classroom, it was viewed as a panacea that, through drill-and-practice software, would transform education. Gradually, the computer has come to be seen as a tool that can support sound pedagogical practices. In composition classes, grammar drills have given way to an emphasis on word processing as a means of improving writing. Countless writers have learned to appreciate the ease with which they can compose and revise with a word processor, and creative teachers have begun to develop effective techniques for encouraging sound composing and revising strategies.

Advances in computer technology now make it possible for computer networks to be used in instruction. . . .

COLLABORATION AND SOCIAL CONSTRUCTION

The major benefit of a computer network is that it permits computers to talk to each other, allowing users to communicate easily with one another. Computers, which were once thought to promote isolation, may in fact prove to be of greatest help in creating cooperative learning environments. Many teachers who have used computers in a process-based writing classroom have discovered, sometimes serendipitously, that computers promote collaboration. Usually, one student asks a question about how to perform a particular function, and another suggests an answer. Before long, if this sort of cooperation is encouraged rather than stifled, students begin to talk about their writing as well. In an environment in which students write collaboratively, their writing becomes more meaningful to them and their efforts are more productive.

Imaginative teachers have devised numerous assignments to promote collaboration in writing classes with stand-alone computers. As we shall see, networks can foster more systematic collaboration. Students using networks can pool their insights and ideas, engaging in collaborative brainstorming, in writing, with results available to all participants. On a network, students can write to one another; the interaction conveys, with more force than was ever before possible, the idea that writing is a means of communicating.

Written discussion on a computer network, as Trent Batson has noted, changes the social and pedagogical dynamics of a classroom. In a traditional class, the teacher is clearly in command. The students are arrayed in rows, facing the teacher, who controls discussion, directing comments to the class or receiving and redirecting comments from students. On a network, teachers must yield power; their comments have no more prominence than those of the students, and the reduction in authority translates into increased empowerment for students. Group discussion on a network encourages the creation of what Batson calls an "on-line discourse community" that makes it possible for students to move naturally from writing as conversation to more formal modes of writing (32). If knowledge is socially constructed, then an "on-line discourse community" can be a powerful tool in the process of creating a community of knowledgeable and skilled writers. Whether the students all work in the same classroom or send messages across the country, the social context of the network provides them with an immediate audience, one concerned not simply with "correcting" their papers, and their writing can assume a purpose that is recognizable to them. Because they can change the social dynamic of a classroom and also provide student writers with a genuine and uncontrived audience, networks have the potential to transform student writing from listless academic drudgery into writing that is purposeful and reader-based. . . .

COLLABORATIVE ACTIVITIES FOR STUDENTS

While we can wax eloquent about the virtues and wonders of the technology, it is important to remember that our purpose in using networked computers is to improve writing. Fortunately, the changes in writing habits and practices that the technology makes possible are precisely those changes we want to encourage in our students. Collaborative writing on the computer makes writing more enjoyable, extends students' willingness to spend time writing, enlarges their awareness of audience, makes it easier for them to face the blank screen, clarifies the need for revision, and facilitates revising. Students can learn that their peers have experiences similar to their own and that these experiences can be discussed with, and illuminated by, others. Collaboration thus can help produce a self-reflective attitude (whose absence is often a major weakness among student writers), and encourage students to attend to the needs of a real audience (see Batson; Peyton and Michaelson; Sirc; Skubikowski and Elder; Thompson).

Teacher Intervention and Modeling

A major advantage of having students work on a network is that the teacher has the opportunity to intervene directly during the writing process. In most writing classes, students write papers, then submit them to the teacher for comments and grades. By the time the papers are returned, the students have lost interest or must turn their attention to the next assignment. If the students are writing in a networked environment, the teacher can intervene while the text is being created, when students are most receptive to advice and when that advice can do the most good because it can be adopted and applied instantly. This approach to instruction—used by teachers of swimming, tennis, music performance, and . . . studio art—makes much more sense than does the prevailing writing-instruction approach of collecting drafts and returning them later.

While intervention during the writing process is possible in any computer writing class, the network permits the instructor to intervene on the student's individual screen, and makes the process easier and more direct. In a networked classroom, the instructor can model global revision strategies so that they appear directly on each student's screen. Research has shown that students tend to avoid such global revision when left to their own devices (see, e.g., Collier; Harris; Hawisher, "Effects"), probably because they don't understand what teachers mean when they speak of "developing ideas." The students may know the commands needed to move or insert blocks of text but do not understand the reasons for using these commands. The use of a network to show revision as it occurs may prove to be the most effective method of explaining and demonstrating the process. For example, a teacher using a network can take a paragraph from a student's text in progress and present it on every screen in the class. Then, working with the entire class, the teacher can show how a statement can be expanded into an argument. Working together, the class can decide what supporting details are needed to buttress the argument and where they can best be added.

When teachers show students where and when to use the features of the word processor that expert writers take for granted but that novice writers ignore or misapply, students learn how to use the computer to improve their writing. Diane Thompson reports:

> Very few of my students have ever spent much time doing extensive revision, although all of them, when pressed, can explain what revision ought to be. [The network] allows me to walk students through the revision process, discussing the hows and whys of each change as they watch it being made. After

students have participated in two or three of these dynamic revision sessions, they become comfortable using the power of the computer to make significant revisions in their writing, not just surface corrections. (96)

The Teacher as Coach

A significant change in the relationship between teacher and students occurs when the teacher comments on texts as they are being composed instead of after they have been written. Instead of being a judge, the teacher functions more like a coach or an editor, someone who makes suggestions, asks for clarification, and gives encouragement. In addition, the teacher serves, again, as a model whose own writing is visible to the students. The effect of these changes is to turn the writing classroom into a virtual electronic workshop.

In such a workshop, teachers can orchestrate a variety of simultaneous activities that put students in control of their own learning and create collaborative environments advocated by writers such as Bruffee ("Collaborative Learning") and Elbow. The value of these activities was endorsed by George Hillocks, who argues that by far the most successful mode of writing instruction incorporates a high degree of peer interaction among students (*Research* 122). In a networked classroom, some students can work individually on their composing or revising, while others work in network-supported electronic peer groups for review of a given text or the texts of groups of students. Yet another group of students can engage in cooperative prewriting activities.

Networked computers may, in fact, prove most valuable for students during prewriting, when they can collaborate in brainstorming or other creative strategies. It is possible, of course, for students to brainstorm together in a conventional classroom, and hardly a writing teacher exists who has not written, on a chalkboard, lists of ideas that students generate collaboratively. While this classroom exercise shows students what they can accomplish when they work together, it is teacher directed and requires students to take notes in order to benefit fully. If, however, the brainstorming takes place through a network, students can manipulate text and rearrange ideas together. In a traditional classroom, students have to shift gears to move from verbal discussion to written discourse; on a network, they do all the preliminary work in writing and thus no shift is needed. When the brainstorming session is over, each student has access to a printed record of the shared experience; some networks allow each student to save the session on a word-processing file and then use the file as the basis for writing a draft, either collaboratively or individually.

Student Creativity and Responsiveness

Distant networks and computer conferencing also offer opportunities to enrich the writing of students by affording them audiences of their peers and an authentic sense of purpose. Teachers have often encouraged students to develop pen pals as a means of corresponding, say, with people their own age and of exploring other cultures. But the exchange of letters is slow and student enthusiasm for the activity often wilts as the time lag between letters grows. Betsy Bowen and Jeffrey Schwartz, in a project connected to the Bread Loaf School of English, report on an experiment in which high school students in a suburb of Pittsburgh communicate regularly with one group of students on an Indian reservation in South Dakota and another group of students living in a small farming community in Montana. Using conferencing, the students write to one another regularly and receive responses within a day or two. The students' enthusiasm has not waned, according to their teachers. . . . At Middlebury College, Kathleen Skubikowski and John Elder used a conferencing technique to have students respond electronically to the journal entries of classmates. The experience generated excitement and commitment among the students that delighted their teachers (199). Perhaps the success of these experiments is the result, in part, of their novelty, but it appears that the immediacy of response and feedback is equally important.

Student writing in these computer conference projects should be markedly different from the writing produced by students for their teachers. In 1975, James Britton and his colleagues studied two thousand pieces of writing by high school students and concluded that up to eighty-four percent was "transactional"—that is, intended to inform or persuade—rather than expressive, a mode more congenial and helpful to students learning to write (Martin 26–27). This statistical breakdown is misleading, I think, because when students write assignments for school, generally, their chief purpose is to demonstrate mastery of a subject to their teachers. The primary exception to this practice occurs in writing classes, in which rhetorical modes such as persuasive essays are assigned.

Even in writing classes, the situation is artificial: the only purpose students have for writing is that they are required to do so, and they write for a captive audience, the teacher. Students do not have to determine who their readers will be, how much or how little their readers will know about their subject, or how to provide information and organize it so that it is useful to their readers. But when these same students write to other students in their class, or to students in another town or in another part of the country, they must consider such questions as: What are my readers like? What do they know about my subject? What do I have to tell them so they will understand my point? In other words, participating in networks provides students with a focus and sense of purpose that are absent in most academic writing. Instead of writing for their teachers, they write *to one another.*

An Electronic Library

A network can provide students with other resources that are helpful to writers. The file server might contain a database of information relevant to a particular topic or to several topics. Students in need of information about the topic can summon up files from the database—either commercially available or prepared specifically by the teacher for a given assignment—then transfer that information into their own word-processing files. This activity can take place whenever needed, allowing students to obtain help as they are writing, without having to leave their texts to go to the library. When reference material is accessible in this way, research becomes an integral part of the writing process rather than an arbitrarily assigned task. Just as a teacher's comment is most helpful during composing, resource material is most beneficial if it is available when needed.

Mainframe computers and distant networks provide students with the same research resources as local area networks. In fact, these networks offer the additional advantage of being available at all times and of being accessible via modem from any location. Generally speaking, local area networks function best when all participants use the network simultaneously. For distance networks, the same is not the case, since the host computer stores all data until it is called for, and the data are available to users so long as the host computer is operational. Distance networks, therefore, are not restricted to users who must be present in the same place at the same time, and have particular appeal for asynchronous use. . . .

Today, when the majority of writing teachers still do not use computers in their classrooms, an essay that anticipates a time when students will work in writing classrooms equipped with networked computers linked to large databases and classes in other schools, and writing teachers will collaborate electronically with colleagues throughout the country, may seem esoteric, far-fetched, and foolhardy. The development of networks for teachers and students just since 1984, however, suggests that those people who have been introduced to networking and its advantages have recognized its potential and the benefits it offers. . . .

Works Cited

Batson, Trent. "The ENFI Project: A Networked Classroom Approach to Writing Instruction." *Academic Computing* (Feb. 1988): 32–33, 55–56.

Bowen, Betsy, and Jeffrey Schwartz. "What's Next for Computers: Electronic Networks in the Writing Classroom." NCTE convention. San Antonio, Nov. 1986

Bruffee, Kenneth A. "Collaborative Learning and the 'Conversation of Mankind.' " *College English* 46 (1984): 635–52.

Collier, Richard. "The Word Processor and Revision Strategies." *College Composition and Communication* 34 (1983): 149–55.

Elbow, Peter. *Writing Without Teachers.* New York: Oxford UP, 1973.

Harris, Jeanette. "Student Writers and Word Processing: A Preliminary Evaluation." *College Composition and Communication* 36 (1985): 323–30.

Hawisher, Gail E. "The Effects of Word Processing on the Revision Strategies of College Freshmen." *Research in the Teaching of English* 21 (1987): 145–59.

Hillocks, George, Jr. *Research on Written Composition: New Directions for Teaching.* Urbana: ERIC and NCTE, 1986.

Kidder, Stephen. Write On: The Statewide Telecommunications and Writing Conference. Ongoing computer conference on the New York Institute of Technology conferencing system.

Martin, Nancy, et al. *Writing and Learning Across the Curriculum* 11–16. London: Ward Lock Educational, 1976.

Peyton, Joy K., and Sarah Michaelson. "The ENFI Project at Gallaudet University: Focus on Teacher Approaches and Reactions, 1986–87 School Year." Unpublished report, 1987.

Sirc, Geoffrey M. "Learning to Write on a LAN." *T.H.E. Journal* 15.8 (1988): 99–104.

Skubikowski, Kathleen, and John Elder. "Word Processing in a Community of Writers." *College Composition and Communication* 38 (1987): 198–201.

Tamplin, John. "Penn State Enjoys Success with On-Line Editor." *Electronic Education* (Jan. 1986): 10–16.

Thompson, Diane P. "Teaching Writing on a Local Area Network." *T.H.E. Journal* 15.2 (1987): 92–97.